From the COALFIELDS to the HUDSON

From the
COALFIELDS
to the
HUDSON

A History of the
Delaware & Hudson Canal

Larry Lowenthal

PURPLE MOUNTAIN PRESS
Fleischmanns, New York

From the Coalfields to the Hudson:
A History of the Delaware and Hudson Canal

First Edition: 1997
Second Edition with a supplement beginning on page 299: 2009

Published by Purple Mountain Press, Ltd.
P.O. Box 309, Fleischmanns, New York 12430-0309
845-254-4062, 845-254-4476 (fax)
purple@catskill.net
http://www.catskill.net/purple

Library of Congress Control Number: 2009926206

ISBN-13: 978-1-930098-98-5
ISBN: 1-930098-98-7

5 4 3 2
Manufactured in the United States of America on acid-free paper.

Frontispiece:
Lumber being loaded at Rose's Basin, Phillipsport, NY, courtesy of the Minisink Valley Historical Society.

Cover design:
Peter Osborne III

Table of Contents

Introduction

NEARLY A CENTURY HAS PASSED since the last boatload of anthracite floated down the Delaware & Hudson Canal from the coalfields to the Hudson. The canal and the gravity railway that fed it, with all their picturesque vitality, have receded beyond living memory. Year by year nature and human activity erase the deep mark they left on the land and on the human landscape.

Meanwhile, as some remnants of the canal and railway fade and echoes of the regional economy they created grow faint in a highway and electronic-oriented age, interest in the D&H seems to increase. With the perspective and detachment of a hundred years, it is time to take a new look at this transportation system and the company that managed it.

Accustomed as we are to the rapid—if not intolerable—speed of movement and communication, the pace of the canal era seems placid. Whether we like to admit it or not, our impressions are influenced indelibly by the charming paintings of E. L. Henry and by photographs taken with slow shutter speeds in the quiet declining years of the canal. Through these lenses the D&H appears either unimaginably bucolic or indescribably swarming with activity in a labor-intensive economy.

Because of this calm and slow-moving outward appearance, it is deceptively easy to be lulled into thinking that the history of the canal was equally serene. This impression, though understandable, is especially inaccurate on the D&H. In truth, the history of the company was one of almost continual insecurity and controversy. Except in its final years, the history of the canal was marked by a series of crises or conflicts, each of which threatened the survival of the company or at least offered the possibility of taking a drastically different course.

The system that had become hopelessly obsolete by the 1890s—a muddy ditch and an antiquated railway—was the work of one of America's great pioneer enterprises. The D&H not only had to operate a challenging business in a remorselessly competitive environment but, with few examples to guide it, had to invent itself in the process. Out of necessity corporations like the D&H shaped a model for large private enterprises. This was true of all early companies, but especially those in transportation. Railroads are often described as the first entities to apply uniform management over territorial expanse, but the canals were there first. While the complexity of their bureaucracy did not equal the major railroad companies, canals pioneered techniques that railroads and others employed on a larger and more systematic scale. Even before that they had demonstrated how to plan and build great engineering works. Yes, much is hidden in the murky, seemingly motionless waterway. It is time for a new and fuller appreciation of this remarkable enterprise.

On a personal note, I initially approached the writing of this book with some reluctance. The D&H may already have had more pages per mile written about it than any other canal. Any historian should enter cautiously into a field that seems to have been picked so heavily. Closer analysis shows, however, that these earlier works, while valuable, have limitations. Each has a specialized emphasis (engineering, geography, folklore) and each tends to treat the canal in isolation, as if, because it did not connect with other canals, it was not part of some larger economic universe. Little effort is given to placing the D&H on the spectrum of canals in terms of purpose, timing, traffic, profitability, or competition with other canals or railroads.

Insofar as this is a corporate history it has a predecessor in *Century of Progress*. Published in 1925, it is one of the more thorough corporate histories in existence, but it suffers from some of the flaws one often finds in this genre. It is based almost entirely on company sources and inevitably glosses over unpleasant situations. Furthermore, it is by now effectively unobtainable. Thus, while it is not advisable to begin a book in a defensive posture, it is obvious that a new entry into a crowded field has to make a strong case to justify itself. I hope that by taking a different perspective and using original sources which, while not strictly new, have not been exploited previously, the result will prove worthwhile.

Nevertheless, without the predecessors my own task would have been vastly more difficult. The basic facts would have had to be discovered and all the operations described. The earlier works make it possible for me to direct readers whose main interest is technical operations, geography or local history to them while leaving me free to explore larger themes. In this sense I am standing on the shoulders of the earlier writers, and this indeed is how it should be in historical research. No one owns a chapter of history, and no one ever says the last word on a historical topic. We can never truly find the past, yet we should never stop seeking it.

Acknowledgements

THE ROUTE OF THE D&H CANAL AND GRAVITY RAILWAY is lined with individuals and institutions which care a great deal about this part of their past. In working on this book I had the great good fortune to benefit from their generosity and dedication. These individuals, who already had enough work to occupy two or three people, agreed that a new look at the D&H was needed and gave freely of their support to help make it possible. In addition to completing the book, another positive outcome for me was the chance to assist in bringing these groups together.

I am grateful for the constant assistance of Lance Metz of the National Canal Museum, Easton, PA. His unrivaled grasp of the period and its historical resources helped shape this effort. Vicki Doyle of the D&H Canal Museum, High Falls, NY, and Peter J. Osborne, III, of the Minisink Valley Historical Society, Port Jervis, NY, repeatedly found time they did not have to help me. Craig Williams of the New York State Museum and Patricia and DeWitt Clinton likewise responded generously to urgent requests.

Gayle Grunwald and Dietrich Werner of the Century House Historical Society, Rosendale, NY; Deerpark, NY, town historian Norma Schadt; Sandra S. Schultz of the National Park Service; Donna Steffens of the Neversink Valley Area Museum, Cuddebackville, NY; Bill McKelvey; Ken Shuker; and Jim Ransom also contributed greatly to this book.

Thanks also to Christopher Baer of the Hagley Museum and Library; Barbara Holmes of the Waymart, PA, Area Historical Society; Allynne Lange of the Hudson River Maritime Museum, Kingston, NY; Phil Ruth; Tom Grasso; Steven Lang and Bob Thayer for their kind assistance.

No acknowledgement would be complete without giving credit to my publishers, Wray and Loni Rominger. Beyond my personal gratitude for their efforts in publishing this book, I think everyone who is interested in the field owes them a debt for keeping regional history alive and accessible. After watching them I came away impressed with the hard work and sacrifice it takes to succeed in a challenging and often frustrating business.

Since work on this book has extended over several years, I may have unintentionally neglected to thank some who helped. If this has happened, I hope they will accept my apology. As always, any faults this book may have are not the fault of the numerous people who wished me well in its preparation. I hope they are pleased with the result.

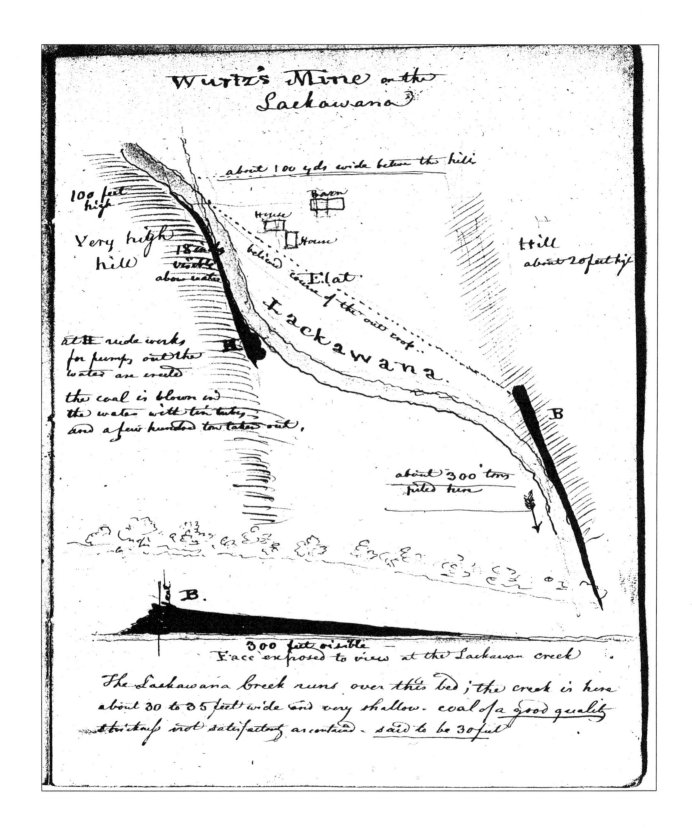

Wurtz's Mine on the Laekawana

about 100 yds wide between the hills

Barn

House

House

100 feet high

Very high hill

18 ... visible above water

believe

Flat

line of the out crop

Hill about 20 feet high

Laekawana

at E rude works for pumps, out the water are erected

the coal is blown in the water with tin tubs, and a few hundred ton taken out.

about 300 tons piled here

B

B.

300 feet visible — Face exposed to view at the Laekawan creek

The Laekawana breek runs over this bed; the creek is here about 30 to 35 feet wide and very shallow. coal of a good quality thickness not satisfactorily ascertained - said to be 30 feet

WHEREAS it is desirable that a channel should be opened through which the city of New-York and other parts of this state, may receive a supply of stone coal . . .

Wurtses Wandering in the Anthracite Wilderness

THE STORY OF THE D&H in its early stages is part of the story of anthracite, and even now it is a story that could benefit from more research and analysis. It is a chronicle in which figures of mythological dimensions stride through the hazy borderland between history and legend, an epic that might have been sung by Homeric bards and recited through the generations.

A few solid, generally accepted names and events stand out like headlands to guide the explorer along the misty shore. The abundance of anthracite that had been deposited by a weird geological caprice in a restricted zone of northeastern Pennsylvania was well known. What remained to be demonstrated was whether the glossy black stuff had any commercial value. It was only around 1770 that the brothers Obadiah and Daniel Gore conducted the first successful burning of anthracite in their blacksmith shop in Wilkes-Barre. Like many pioneers of the American Industrial Revolution, the Gore brothers originated in New England. And this breakthrough of Obadiah begat the advance of Jesse Fell of Wilkes-Barre, who employed anthracite in his nailery in 1788, generally considered to be the first industrial use of the substance.

The Gores and Fell had demonstrated that anthracite was a fuel. Gradually its use expanded in blacksmithing and certain related manufacturing in its local area. It had not yet been demonstrated that the black stuff had any prospects for home heating. Its common name, "stone coal" tells the story: in the popular mind there was no more likelihood of burning it in a fireplace than ordinary fieldstone. Again Jesse Fell, an inventor underappreciated outside his native region, persisted and in 1808 devised a grate that made domestic consumption of anthracite feasible.

Thus, it was only in the nineteenth century that the technical obstacles to the widespread use of anthracite were cleared away. Even these developments did not necessarily create a market for it. Extraordinary as it may seem, the country found it more efficient to import British coal than to develop and transport its native supply, though the consumption of coal from any source was inconsequential compared to the use of wood.[1] The War of 1812 and the dislocations of trade that preceded it, while perhaps not of great military consequence, had lasting effects in disrupting commercial patterns. While New England whaling and Southern agriculture were harmed, New England textile manufacture was encouraged, and interest suddenly intensified in Pennsylvania's anthracite reserves.

One does not have to subscribe to doctrines of determinism to accept the proposition that anthracite would have come into general use in the early nineteenth century regardless of whether one experimenter or another achieved some particu-

FACING PAGE
Drawing from Jacob Cist's "Sketch Book of Coal Mines, Luzerne."
CREDIT
Ewell Sale Stewart Library, The Academy of Natural Sciences of Philadelphia.

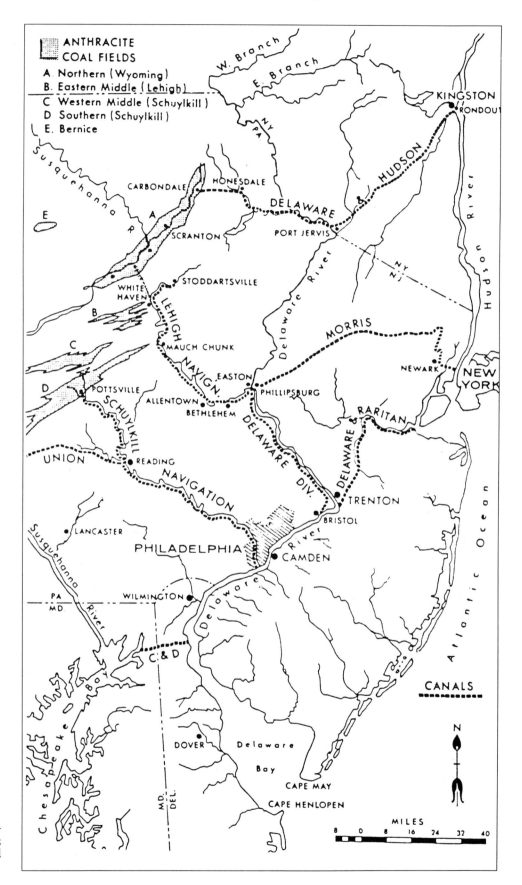

CREDIT
US Army Corps of Engineers, Philadelphia District; courtesy National Canal Museum, Easton, PA.

lar refinement. However, the inevitability that applies to the anthracite region as a whole is less binding in each of the distinct and separate fields that make up the region. What are called the Southern and Western Middle fields lie on the upper reaches of the Schuylkill River, which offers such an obvious outlet that there was no incentive to look for another. There was little doubt that coal from these districts would be controlled and marketed by Philadelphia. The Eastern Middle field lay along the Lehigh River, and there was less certainty about its destination. Finally, the Northern, or Wyoming, field was open to the greatest range of choices as to how it would be developed. A glance at a regional map will show that while some of the fields had an indisputable advantage in Philadelphia, all were about the same distance from New York City. Straight lines on a map, however, usually conceal the actual costs and difficulties of moving goods from mine to market.

The fact that anthracite from the northernmost district was exploited at a particular time and place and that it moved northward to reach New York City by an indirect route was not the result of impersonal historical forces, but was due to the efforts and limitations of one family. If Jesse Fell and Obadiah Gore had never existed, someone else undoubtedly would have lit a fire in the anthracite region, but without the Wurts family the course of development in the Lackawanna Valley would have been quite different.

There are several traditional accounts of how four Wurts brothers (Maurice, William, Charles Stewart, and John, three of whom were active at one time or another in a dry-goods business) became involved in the seemingly unrelated anthracite trade. One student of the D&H cites at least five different explanations.[2] It is easy to sympathize with the historian of Honesdale, who writes that "As one attempts to reconstruct the early efforts of the Wurts brothers to market their coal, he is plagued by inconsistencies in accounts and by statements which seem dubious at best."[3] However often repeated, most or all of the accounts seem to derive from D&H company sources. While colorful and romantic, they also tend to be uncritical.

No independent history of the Wurts family has been written. The closest approximation is a privately printed genealogical record by a family member, who traced the line back to Switzerland in the thirteenth century.[4] While it is the best available source, it suffers from the usual defects of the genre. According to this account, the D&H Wurtses are descended from Johannes Conrad Wirz, who was born in Zurich in 1706 and came to America in 1734 as part of the German pietist emigration to the Middle Colonies. For a name containing only four letters, it has been rendered into English in a surprising number of variations. Johannes was a pastor in German churches in Pennsylvania and New Jersey. His son John was born in 1744 and settled in Flanders, Morris County, New Jersey, where he became an iron manufacturer. It is said that at the age of 16 he could speak no English. He died in 1793, before his fiftieth birthday, but by then in 20 years of marriage with Sarah Grandin had fathered nine children.

It is the four youngest brothers who became involved with the D&H. All were born in Flanders: Maurice June 16, 1783; William May 6, 1788; Charles Stewart August 8, 1790; and John August 13, 1792. Neither this part of the family nor their ironworks is mentioned in the standard nineteenth century history of Morris County.[5] After the premature death of the father the family seems to have dispersed, and although some members later resided in New Jersey, it was not at the Flanders homestead. The D&H Wurtses were all young children when their father died and probably went to live with older brothers. According to family tradition, Maurice, at the age of about 18, tied up his belongings in a pocket handkerchief and walked to Philadelphia. This would have been around the turn of the nineteenth century. He immediately secured a job in a dry goods store, became a partner in about three years, and succeeded to the business when the senior partner died soon after. He then took his brother William into partnership; this must have been around 1810, for William married a Philadelphia woman in that year. Again according to the family account, this business was liquidated before 1819, despite having prospered with a government contract during the War of 1812.

Maurice (who probably pronounced his name "Morris" judging by the frequency with which it was spelled that way) was responsible for the family's presence in Philadelphia. Prior to 1800 they had no known involvement with the Quaker City. It is the next stage of the family saga, which brought them into the Lackawanna Valley, that is problematical. During the War of 1812 a fuel shortage arose when the British blockade cut off the city's supply of bituminous coal from places such as Virginia and Nova Scotia. Interest turned to local anthracite and some hesitant efforts to develop the resource were made. Here, however, lack of adequate transportation was a critical deterrent, and the use of anthracite did not become commercially practical until several years after the war. As active residents of the city the Wurts brothers surely would have been aware of the situation, but why, as dry goods merchants, they felt compelled to do anything about it is a mystery. At first one might surmise that their father's participation in the iron industry had turned their thoughts in that direction, but at that time the smelting of iron with anthracite had not been perfected, although many believed it would be achieved. Maurice was for one term (1817-18) a director of the Philadelphia National Bank, which later invested heavily in the Chesapeake & Delaware Canal, but it is a tenuous link between that and Lackawanna coal mines.[6] Except for a tantalizing reference to the brothers receiving a 70,000-acre tract in Pennsylvania known as the "Holland Purchase" as partial payment from the government, the family genealogy, perhaps wisely, avoids the question altogether. (It does not say where the land was located, but implies that it had no connection with the anthracite region.) The traditional accounts tell a romantic story of how William and Maurice, especially the former, took to wandering about northeastern Pennsylvania, a territory then virtually uninhabited, looking for outcrops of coal which then had no recognized value. The practice of wilderness vacations was not yet in vogue; indeed, the idea of vacations among those who had to work at all was not highly developed.

In *Philadelphia's First Fuel Crisis* H. Benjamin Powell describes a network of Pennsylvania men, with Jacob Cist at the center, who were active in promoting anthracite, particularly in the Lehigh Valley.[7] The Wurtses were moving in the same direction, but there is no solid evidence they had contacts with any of the individuals mentioned by Powell. At one point between 1813 and 1816 Cist surveyed the anthracite district and actually visited the Wurts mining site, but there is no indication he was acquainted with them. The Wurtses were part of a visible and vigorous trend, but the details of how and why they jumped in remain elusive. It is as though they joined one of the parades that have always been popular with Philadelphians without knowing any of the marchers or leaders.

A related question is how the Wurtses, who if prosperous were by no means wealthy, managed their business while one or two of the brothers were off on extended expeditions to the anthracite country; in other words, who was minding the store? They were not, as has sometimes been implied, members of the Philadelphia aristocracy of the sort who dwelled along the Main Line when that stellar thoroughfare came into being. Indeed, in the various histories of Philadelphia the Wurts family makes scarcely an appearance. The D&H company history, *Century of Progress*, implicitly acknowledges the problem. After cautiously observing that the Wurts business "seems to have been prosperous," it explains further that a partner, John Rodman, was taken into the firm in 1819 or 1820.[8] The genealogy, however, presents a fuller and more complicated picture: the former firm of Maurice and William had gone into liquidation before 1819. In that year William and Charles Stewart began a dry goods business on Market Street, below 5th Street; Maurice seems not to have been active in it. Only three months later Rodman joined the firm, but his input of capital was $3000, an inconsiderable sum even at that time.[9] (While this source makes it obvious that the family business was altogether incapable of financing the D&H, its claim that, conversely, two years later it was involvement with the D&H that put the commercial business on a firm basis is equally improbable.)

The fundamental uncertainty about why the Wurtses were active in the Lackawanna Valley in the first place extends to the details of their activity. Horace Hollister, in his history of the region, says that William Wurts "explored the various gaps in the mountain bordering the Lackawanna Valley upon the east, with a view of discovering a possible outlet to the coal which he had found beneath the high bluff in the western part of the present town, [Carbondale] and a vein or two he had opened in Providence, twelve miles farther down the valley."[10] Although Powell seems certain that the work observed by Cist in his report completed by 1816 was the later primary D&H mine in Carbondale, *Century of Progress* states that the Wurtses did not reach that point until around 1822, while Hollister implies that their first mines—in Providence—were not opened until 1816.[11] He is vague about when the brothers became active at Carbondale, but his convoluted wording seems to place this event about 1817. To compound the confusion, Hollister, who seems to have compiled his history over a period of years, elsewhere asserts that William Wurts's first mine, from which he made his first coal shipment, was located in Berkely and opened in 1814.[12] Cist included in his notebook a sketch headed "Wurtz's Mine on the Lackawana," which indicates an outcrop of coal on the east side of a gentle bend in the Lackawanna River and "rude works for pumping out the water" on the opposite bank. Also on the west bank about 300 tons of coal were piled. Cist, however, does not name the place because at the time it was no place. With the river channel having been altered repeatedly, it is nearly impossible to relate the sketch to any present location with certainty.[13]

When we reach the account of the Wurts's first efforts to transport their coal, the shadows that make their exploration of the Lackawanna Valley almost as obscure as the Northmen's voyages to Vinland in the eleventh century seem to dissipate a little. In 1815, according to Hollister, William attempted to transport two sled loads of coal down Jones's Creek, an erratic tributary of the Wallenpaupack, which in turn flowed into the Lackawaxen and then the Delaware. (This raises again the question of whether the coal had been extracted at present Carbondale.) Within a mile of its launch the raft struck a rock and capsized—a long way from Philadelphia.[14] After a delay lasting one year or several, the Wurtses next hauled some coal overland directly to the Wallenpaupack, then portaged to the Lackawaxen, and by this laborious method brought it to their home city. There, however, they found that Lehigh coal, delivered at a lower price, had satisfied the limited demand. Again there is a quiet period of indeterminate length, after which the brothers appear definitely at Carbondale in 1822, the year that unimaginative but appropriate name was first used. They built a log house for their miners, the first dwelling place in the vicinity, which remained standing for many years.[15] Hollister says that "The mine was kept free from water by a rude pumping apparatus moved by the current of the river." Another mystery; for even this crude mining operation required mechanical knowledge and financial investment. Where did the Wurtses acquire either? For nearly ten years the brothers' involvement in the anthracite region had yielded no discernible income. Land speculation could not have been a source of significant gain, since the land had little value until the coal could be marketed. How were the brothers able to sustain their prolonged and costly adventure in the wilderness? A related question is what became of the mining properties William owned in Providence and Berkely; Hollister provides only a partial answer by stating that some land in present Archbald reverted to its previous owner.[16]

Now, as we come at last to the end of myth and the dawn of history, we arrive immediately at a point of decision in the story of the D&H. The natural impulse of the Wurts brothers was to reach the familiar Philadelphia market. Given sufficient time they probably could have succeeded in bringing quantities of coal to that city, but it was also apparent that they would not be able to compete against better-situated rivals in the Lehigh and Schuylkill basins. Conceivably, the Wurtses could have employed a southern outlet to Philadelphia over the Lehigh system, but the additional distance and tolls would have still left them unable to compete—and restricted their independence besides. Geographical determinism is no longer as fashionable among historians as it once was, but it seems to retain an inescapable validity in explaining a feature bound as intimately to the land as a canal. Lacking ancestral ties to a city in which such things mattered a great deal, they may have felt little reluctance to shift their focus from Philadelphia to New York City. This decision, taken entirely for rational market considerations, determined the identity and character of the D&H Canal.

Within a short span of time William and Maurice Wurts had experienced two revelations that determined the character of their enterprise: first, that they would have to abandon the Philadelphia market in favor of New York; second, that they could not rely on natural waterways. These insights arrived at an important period of transition in American transportation. Any major improvement in transportation meant water transportation; railroads did not yet exist and conveyance of heavy or bulky freight by road remained inconceivable until the twentieth century. It was only in the 1790s that it had become at all feasible to consider man-made waterways in the United States, either by improving rivers or creating artificial channels. Only in the following decade was the first entirely man-made waterway of substantial length (the Middlesex Canal) completed, and another decade passed before the first really long canal through largely unsettled country (the Erie Canal) was attempted. Experience on the Erie confirmed the general assumption that canals moved freight at only 10 percent the cost of land transport.[17] There was, in sum, no doubt that the Wurtses would have to turn their attention to artificial waterways, but the exact form remained to be determined.

In the Legislative Wilderness

LIKE SHADOWS grudgingly yielding to daylight, the legends of the Lackawanna Valley's early settlement give way to historical documentation. The point of intersection between the hazy, private and somewhat secretive activities of the Wurts brothers comes, of necessity, in 1823. At that point, if their plans were to advance to the next stage, they had to go before the Pennsylvania Legislature and gain approval to convert a public asset, the Lackawaxen River, for their private use. The Wurtses could hardly imagine how frequently they would make the trek to the state capitol in the next few years, each journey more trying than the last. John Wurts was then in the state senate, where he was in a position to manage his brother's bill. In that period state legislatures normally conducted only one session a year, meeting in the late winter and early spring period of agricultural inactivity. A bill would be prepared, introduced and debated over a period of several weeks or months before the date of passage. Correspondence among the brothers traces its course; for example, the bill passed a committee of the House of Representatives on February 24.[18]

In brief, the charter, passed March 13, 1823, granted to Maurice Wurts the privilege of improving the Lackawaxen River and any of its tributaries "to make a good and safe descending navigation" from Wagner's or Rix's Gap to its mouth. It further granted the right to create a complete "slackwater" navigation in the river and to use it for water power.[19] One restriction was that the navigational improvements could not interfere with lumber rafting. This was the only amendment made to the bill and, given the strongly expressed sentiments of the raftsmen, John "found it necessary to consent."[20] Additional detailed clauses established minimum dimensions for locks and required that when the master of a vessel "shall arrive within one quarter of a mile from any lock so erected, under the penalty of two dollars, to blow a trumpet or horn, whereupon the keeper of such lock shall attend for the purpose of opening the gate or sluice to let the said boat, ark or other vessel pass without unnecessary delay and in safety." Of greater consequence, the eighteenth clause in effect gave the state the option of taking over the works after 30 years. The wording is convoluted, but since it is of potential importance, the full provision is presented as follows:

> That at the expiration of thirty years from the passage of this act, the said Maurice Wurts . . . shall render under oath or affirmation to the legislature, an exact account of the amount of money expended by them in making said navigation and in keeping the same in repair, and also of the amount of tolls received by them during that time. And if it shall thereupon appear that the tolls during that time have amounted to so much above six percentum per annum on the amount so expended in making and in keeping in repair said navigation, as will be equal to the capital sum so expended, then the legislature may resume all the rights, liberties and franchises hereby granted; but if it shall appear that the tolls during that time have not amounted to so much above six per centum per annum on the amount of money so expended in making and in keeping in repair said navigation, as will be equal to the capital sum so expended, then it shall be lawful for the legislature, on payment to the said Maurice Wurts . . . of the difference or deficiency, to resume all the rights, liberties and franchises hereby granted.[21]

It is noteworthy that this charter was granted to Maurice and his associates, although earlier William seemed to be more prominent in the Lackawanna adventure. The reasons for this are not clear, except that William was still involved with the family store, whereas the development of coal might have become nearly a full-time occupation for Maurice. In practice it would have made little difference, for one of the most striking characteristics of the brothers was their exceptional and enduring closeness----perhaps a result of the traumatic disruption following their father's early death. No matter what strains they were under, their correspondence, which becomes voluminous after 1823, is a remarkable testimony to mutual concern and support without any hint of discord. Business matters were discussed with complete candor, and usually took precedence. A letter from William to Maurice in 1828 opens with a paragraph of mourning over the death of William's wife, "which has placed my family in mourning and filled my heart with sorrow," then fills the remainder of two pages with the customary business matters.[22] They often passed along each other's letters with appropriate comments, creating a sort of round robin. Moreover, the abilities and personalities of the brothers were complementary, so that they functioned as a strong and cohesive team. In this process the youngest brother, John, who had pursued a different course, was gradually drawn into company affairs. He was the first member of the family to obtain a college education (Princeton), and he entered the legal profession. He served in both houses of the Pennsylvania Legislature and in 1824 was elected to the U.S. Congress. Charles Stewart Wurts was never an active participant in the D&H or its antecedents, but remained on the periphery, offering advice and perhaps financial support. A brother-in-law, Thomas Young, who married Anna Wurts, sometimes assisted the brothers in investigating and acquiring land.

The grant to Maurice Wurts resembled closely the rights given in 1818 to Josiah White, Erskine Hazard and George Hauto in the Lehigh Valley, except for the key difference that the Lehigh act did not include the right to create a slackwater navigation.[23] After conceding extensive rights to a river that was much larger and closer to Philadelphia, the legislature presumably would have felt less concern about the remote Lackawaxen. Nevertheless, John, already displaying the caution that characterized his later dealings, feared that opposition might arise, either locally or in Harrisburg. States were jealous of their prerogatives and shared their sovereignty only reluctantly. On a less elevated level, the issue of which persons, groups or regions would benefit from state concessions was a matter of concern to the legislators. John Wurts's strategy consisted in slipping the bill through almost surreptitiously. Using appropriate imagery, he wrote "If I can make as smooth water for it in the Senate, we shall sail quietly down the stream without the public noticing it, for hitherto there has been no debate on it." He added "It cost me some trouble to keep the Western members silent."[24] William later seconded this attitude, noting in a letter of March 19 that "Our law or bill scarcely known or spoken of" in Philadelphia.[25] Events proved that John's policy was correct; the more the company became known, the less it was able to conceal its intentions, and the more opposition it encountered. Unlike jungle warfare, better illumination led to a harder struggle.

After the bill had passed two readings in the Senate, John Wurts breathed a sigh of relief. "I have managed to get it through without noise or opposition," he said, "but it has nevertheless cost me a good deal of trouble, and in fact been a charm upon my tongue, and a shackle upon my ankle during the whole session."[26] The young senator, then only 30, did not realize that he was caught in the early stages of a process by which the D&H became all absorbing, until his previous career pretensions shriveled to nothing. He chose to ignore the verbose provision by which the state seemingly reserved a right to acquire the Lackawaxen improvements and told Maurice that the act "does in effect give you a monopoly of the river; and that forever."[27] This tendency to overlook unfavorable features would recur in later legislative bouts. As to the monopoly, John Wurts felt that he had won that by securing a rate of toll that made it difficult for other mining ventures to compete.

This concept lay at the core of the Wurts's strategy for many years: they did not need to own all the coal lands; as long as they controlled the only transportation outlet, they had an effective monopoly.

The charter the Wurtses had obtained, hard fought though it was, in a sense was worthless. It gave them the possibility of sending coal on a risky voyage down the Delaware, so that it might reach Philadelphia, where it would be unable to compete in price. In this period an odd episode occurred, seemingly running against the flow of events, which indicates that Maurice had not completely abandoned the Philadelphia market. He had corresponded with William about sending down a raft load of coal, and William had arranged for wharf space on the Delaware at Kensington.[28] This seems to have been an experiment, as John called it, as in the phrase, "I fear your experiment this winter will not be a profitable one."[29] Again in 1825 the arrival of a small amount of Maurice's Lackawaxen coal (ten tons) was announced in the Philadelphia gazettes. As in 1823 the outcome was not recorded, but by then the emphasis was shifting to New York. William Wurts observed that perhaps "a few ton could be spared to any of your friends in N. York."[30]

There is no doubt that the Wurtses were looking toward New York even while their legislation was grinding through the mills of Harrisburg. In his earliest extant letter on the subject, February 24, 1823, John noted "it will be too late to do anything in N.Y. during the present session."[31] He repeated this advice a few days later, but at that time he believed that the New York Legislature would adjourn the same time as Pennsylvania, which he expected to be April 1. It was brother William who added urgency to the New York effort; without his intervention the Wurtses might not have approached the neighboring legislature until 1824. A letter from him to Maurice on March 19 made his reasons clear. After reporting that his latest information indicated that New York would remain in session until at least April 20, he wrote:

> I should be greatly in favor of proceeding in N.Y. at once as Dr. Hosack of N.Y. & others own lands adjoining us, & as soon as they understand our object---will of course oppose a high toll & it is of great importance that we get such privilege as to rates of toll there as will amount in its effect to a complete monopoly of the coal---the sooner it is pushed through the less danger of opposition besides our situation & other reasons that could be urged against delay . . . .[32]

William pressed Maurice to leave his activities in Pennsylvania, and it may that this kept Maurice from pursuing his plans in Philadelphia and extinguished the last glimmer of hope of entering that market.

Eager as he was to plunge into the New York Legislature, as late as March 26, 1823, William had no real plan of attack. "If the Coal Compy in N.Y. will join us on the right terms & have the capital it may do to associate with them, if not, we must either form a company & said company proceed to get the charter, or we backed by our N.Y. friends make the application at Albany for the necessary law not in our individual right, but for a Comp'y & form the Comp'y & get the stock subscribed afterwards . . . ."[33] Yet less than a month later, on April 23, an act creating the D&H company was passed. The sequence of events makes it clear that the Wurtses already had influential "friends" in New York City who could push through complex legislation with exceptional speed. Details of the initial contacts between the Wurtses and their eventual New York allies are another of the disturbing gaps in the early history of the D&H. The extant family papers begin later; D&H company records, which are formal reports in any case, begin only with the formation of the company in March 1825; Philip Hone, the most prominent of the New York associates, did not begin his famous diary until January 1826. Neither he nor any of the other New York investors seem to have left an account that has survived. Powell reports that Jacob Cist had established contacts with several New York merchants in March 1815; but peace intervened before any coal shipments could be made, and it is unlikely that a tentative interest in anthracite could have survived a chill of eight years.[34]

Hollister's unpublished history of the D&H implies that William and Maurice Wurts had prepared a map, and possibly a pamphlet, that could have been used to generate interest in New York. Unfortunately, Hollister's chronology is so garbled and contradictory that one cannot be sure how many maps there were, or their date. He also refers to a map which made a favorable impression on New York capitalists and "led to the consideration and advancement of this great project,"[35] but it is impossible to determine whether he is referring to a map prepared by the Wurtses in 1823 or earlier, or to the one resulting from preliminary surveys conducted during the summer of 1823 and published as part of the Wright/Sullivan report of 1824. Furthermore, in a turn of plot that would delight a romantic novelist, one map he describes is now lost. Two copies of it were known to Hollister: one, given to him by William Wurts in 1856, was later "carried away" by someone who intruded into his office; the other had been in the D&H archives but had been taken by officers of the Pennsylvania Coal Co. and not returned.[36] If such a map existed and was circulated in the first weeks of 1823, it could account for the willingness of New York investors to incorporate the D&H. Hollister's inconsistencies make it impossible to be certain; indeed, most of his statements suggest that the map he cites did not exist at the time the D&H was incorporated. If he had returned to the D&H project---and presumably made it more coherent---or if the sources he used survived, we might be able to form a better judgment. Lacking that, we must assume the existence of an active but unrecorded network of personal contacts to explain how New Yorkers were enlisted in the support of the new D&H enterprise.

One individual who may have played a role behind the scenes is the Dr. Hosack who William Wurts noted as a threat. David Hosack (1769-1835) was a noted physician and one of the most influential New Yorkers of the age. According to Powell, he had purchased 8000 acres in Luzerne County in 1807.[37] Any involvement in coal lands was presumably a speculation, since his main interests lay in his medical profession and his hobby of botany.[38] Hosack knew everyone of consequence in New York and was closely acquainted with Philip Hone. He was also a friend and admirer of Governor DeWitt Clinton, inseparably associated with the Erie Canal, and he wrote a biographical essay after Clinton's death.[39] At a time when decisions were made by a small congenial circle of cultured men, a few casual remarks by Hosack would have been sufficient to turn attention to anthracite even though he is not known to have taken any part in the affairs of the D&H.

William's letter of March 26, as well as other evidence, suggests that the Wurtses at first had another partner than the D&H in mind, or at least were open to other possibilities. John informed Maurice on March 10 "there is a Coal Company already incorporated in N.Y. with a capital of $500,000; and I dont see why you might not drive a good bargain with them." He went on to describe the charter and advised that Henry Eckford, "ship builder of N.Y. and one of the directors of the U.S. Bank," was president of the company.[40] William may have been referring to the same coal company in his March 26 letter to Maurice. Again, in the rush of events there was no time to open new negotiations, and the brothers had to stick with people they already knew—by whatever means they had made the contact. Eckford's interest in coal and transportation investment was authentic, for he appeared as one of the first directors of the Morris Canal & Banking Co. in 1824. He was a renowned naval architect and ship builder, who had performed vital services during the War of 1812.[41] Later he built the steamboat *Robert Fulton*, and by combining clues it is possible to speculate that he had in mind the use of coal as a fuel in steamboats, which became a compelling quest of the next decade. Possibly the Wurts brothers were fortunate to have avoided closer contact with Eckford, who was later indicted for conspiracy to defraud as a result of a hasty transaction in Morris Canal stock, although this was a damaging and inconsistent episode of an otherwise distinguished career.[42]

It is likely that DeWitt Clinton, then between terms as governor of New York, was instrumental in promoting the D&H application. John Wurts was conducting his surreptitious maneuvers in Harrisburg against a backdrop of momentous events in the history of canals. In New York State long portions of the Erie Canal had already been opened, and the Champlain Canal had been completed, though it was not officially opened until September 1823. Already, as Ronald E. Shaw has written, the Erie's "burgeoning commerce foretold its phenomenal success once the entire waterway was completed in 1825."[43] More than any other individual Clinton was responsible for this success. He had become a veritable canal god, whose benediction was essential before any new canal venture could be properly launched. The Wurts papers contain a letter from Charles H. Ruggles of Kingston soliciting Clinton's opinion (and preferably endorsement) of the first survey of the D&H in 1824.[44] The Governor had earlier supported the D&H, predicting that it would be essential to meet New York City's rapidly growing demand for coal. This led the writers of *Century of Progress* to conclude that "his approval of the Delaware and Hudson canal project was, without question, gratifying and during 1823 and 1824 very helpful to the new company."[45]

Trouble is, Clinton was one of those deities who spread his blessings too freely. Sometimes compared to Apollo, he shed his rays on all canals equally. With his imposing appearance and enormous prestige, he was the first choice to dignify canal ceremonies; on July 4, 1825 he journeyed to Ohio to turn the first shovelful for that state's canal even while the Erie was racing to meet its deadline for completion. In late 1824 he angered John Wurts by conspicuously endorsing the Morris Canal in New Jersey, potentially a severe rival to the D&H. "The man who advocates all projects cannot be useful to any," he fumed.[46] Wurts tried to get some of the newly-reelected governor's friends to "point out the injury he is doing to his own State."

No one was more keenly aware than Clinton of the need to balance sectional interests within the state. That this was not merely a theoretical consideration was borne out by a resolution adopted at a meeting in Marbletown, Ulster County, on October 16, 1824 which noted pointedly

> That while the people of the county have cheerfully and willingly borne their proportion of the great and heavy expenses incurred by the erection of the Western and Northern Canals, their immediate and local interests have been but remotely, if at all, benefited thereby; and that they consider the pending application for Legislative aid by the Hudson and Delaware Canal Company as a proper occasion for the government to manifest that its favors and benificience will be impartially

dispensed to every part of the country, and be felt by every portion of community.[47]

Earlier a state senate committee had endorsed this notion of entitlement, reporting that it was "disposed to think very favourably of any project that would extend canal navigation to a section of the state, which although it has borne part of the burthen, has not hitherto participated in any of its advantage."[48]

The charter that had breezed through Albany mingled archaic language with advanced concepts. It created an entity with the cumbersome name of "The President, Managers and Company of the Delaware and Hudson Canal Company," a title that was retained as long as the canal remained in operation. The most charitable explanation is that there were few precedents to guide the legislators. Since the days of the Inland Lock Navigation companies of the 1790s, few private canals were chartered in the state; all were more limited in scope, and only the Seneca Lock Navigation Co. seems to have conducted any serious work.[49] Conversely, the preamble displayed visionary phrasing that bordered on grandeur:

> WHEREAS it is desirable that a channel should be opened, through which the city of New York, and other parts of this state, may receive a supply of stone coal, which is found in the interior of the state of Pennsylvania: *And Whereas* there is a large body of this valuable article, belonging to Maurice Wurts . . . and the legislature of that state has recently passed an act authorising the above named individual to improve the navigation of the said river: *And whereas* it is represented that a water communication can be formed between the rivers Delaware and Hudson . . . so that a supply of this coal may be had from the source aforesaid . . .[50]

The active clause empowered the new company "to make, construct, and forever maintain a canal or slack water navigation, of suitable width, depth and dimensions . . . from such point on or near the river Delaware, through any one or more of the counties of Orange, Sullivan and Ulster, to such point on the river Hudson as the said corporation shall judge best." There is a feeling of majesty in these phrases, although perhaps they seem dramatic only because we know what the D&H became. Elsewhere the charter contained miscellaneous provisions relating to damages and the blowing of trumpets to warn lock tenders. These articles had become routine as one new company imitated another, especially since John Wurts had a hand in drafting the New York act.

Eleven commissioners were named in the act, seven from New York City and two each from Orange and Ulster Counties. Subsequently most of them participated at least in the early stages of organizing the D&H. A group of such substantial men, sufficiently aware of the Wurts mine and committed to the concept of introducing anthracite in New York, could not have been mobilized on short notice. Considerable and detailed preparation would have been necessary, though we do not know how it was accomplished. In a New York so small that Greenwich Village was still a suburb, personal contact remained the most effective means of communication. This is where the best known of the commissioners, Philip Hone, may have been pivotal. That he had acquired one of New York's large fortunes was undoubtedly useful, but perhaps more valuable was his network of contacts with virtually anyone of importance in business and politics, on up to DeWitt Clinton. He was also an exceptionally cultured gentlemen, who was not only interested in the arts but became a virtual arts commissioner of the expanding city. Philip Hone

surely deserves considerable credit for the fact that New York City developed into the cultural center of the nation, which was not a foregone conclusion in 1825.

Explorations in New York

PRIOR TO 1822 the Wurts Brothers, no matter how much they wandered around northeastern Pennsylvania, would have had little reason to cross into New York. The 1823 charter changed all that and compelled them to examine the area more seriously. A letter from John Wurts to Maurice dated February 24, 1823 includes a marginal note apparently in Maurice's writing "Distance from Delaware to Hudson between 55 & 60 miles."[51] The fact that he felt it necessary to record such a basic piece of information seems to confirm how little he then knew about the area. According to one account Abraham Cuddeback, a prominent member of a family that was prolific in Orange County suggested the route up the long valley to Kingston. This tradition may be gratifying to local sensitivities, but is hardly necessary; Maurice Wurts could not have overlooked a transportation corridor that had been in use for over a hundred years (and probably for much longer by the Indians).

Whatever exploration either of the brothers had conducted earlier, probably the first serious examination took place in July 1823. On this occasion William Wurts was accompanied by Josiah White, one of the principals of the Lehigh Coal and Navigation Co. This expedition was intended to seek a practical route for a canal, and White was one of only a handful of Pennsylvanians with the necessary experience. The two men began at Kingston, investigating several approaches to the Hudson. For a total of 20 days they explored a vast stretch of country, extending into the Lackawaxen and Lackawanna Valleys and down the Delaware to the Water Gap. Although it was the height of summer, when dense vegetation would have obscured long perspectives, the travelers must have come away with a good understanding of the region's geographical imperatives.

Almost more interesting than the expedition and its findings is the identity of the explorers; for White's journal, which has only recently come to light, shows that he and the Wurtses were acquainted.[53] This is remarkable, considering the later hostility between the two enterprises. At the outset of the trip, White notes that he traveled "in company with William Wurts," without feeling it necessary to identify him; implying that they were already acquainted. It is tempting to speculate that on their tedious journeys through rough and primitive country they reached some informal understanding about dividing the market, foreshadowing the arrangements made by the anthracite cartel later in the century. In reality, however, whatever harmony was established by sharing rough roads, bad food and thick mosquitoes did not endure, and in later years the Wurtses regarded the Lehigh company with unremitting enmity.

This expedition was conducted mainly for William Wurts's enlightenment. It could not substitute for a serious survey and was hardly detailed enough to lure potential investors. Even before William set off on his journey the Wurtses had arranged for a competent survey. At that time Benjamin Wright, who had educated himself on the Erie Canal, and to some extent on its predecessor, was the foremost canal engineer in the nation, something of a one-man consulting firm. In 1824-25, while still chief engineer for the Erie, which was racing to meet its deadline for completion, he was also engaged on the Blackstone, Farmington, Chesapeake &

Delaware and Kanawha Canals. One more project must have seen inconsequential, so in May 1823 he agreed to survey a route for the Wurtses.

Reinforcing the parallel to a modern architecture-and-engineering firm, Wright, the principal, delegated the D&H contract to a junior member, John B. Mills. Young Mills had assisted Wright on the Erie Canal; the process by which the "Erie School" became the main academy for training public works engineers in the early republic was already functioning. Mills measured the route during the summer of 1823. In December a more experienced canal engineer, John Langdon Sullivan, went over the route with Mills at Wright's request. Sullivan, the son of the founder of the Middlesex Canal in Massachusetts, had studied English canals and had spent 12 years managing, improving and extending the Middlesex—while consulting on other projects.

Wright then reviewed Sullivan's findings, and their conclusions were presented as a joint report, published in January 1824.[54] Their plans called for a canal 117 miles long, 32 feet wide on the surface and four feet deep. It would not actually be an artificial canal over the entire distance; nine dams would create a slackwater navigation on the Delaware, and portions of the Lackawaxen and Rondout Valleys would also rely on slackwater. The total cost was calculated at $1,208,632, or $10,330 a mile—comparable to the Erie. Similar care was taken in estimating that coal could be delivered in New York City for $3.84 per ton. This was a sophisticated estimate, in which the importance of depreciation and interest were recognized by allowing $1.20 per ton. A supplement to the report compared the project to the Lehigh and Schuylkill regions, with favorable results.

Sullivan also included sections explaining composite (wood and stone) locks and advocating a "perpendicular lift" designed by Benjamin Dearborn of Boston, an educator and sometime inventor. Dearborn (1755-1838) was distantly related to the famous Revolutionary War officer and political figure Henry Dearborn. He was part of that great outburst of Yankee amateur ingenuity that showered sparks over the United States in the first half of the nineteenth century. The only one of Benjamin's sparks that seems to have caught was a patent balance, said to be "extensively known." He also made plans for erecting tide mills, formerly a common form of capturing power on the New England coast, and this suggests an interest in hydraulics that expressed itself in his perpendicular lift.[55] This device, described more fully by LeRoy and in Hollister's manuscript, was essentially an elevator capable of raising or lowering boats by a system of counterweights. It is unlikely to have been tried in anything larger than a model (if that) and would have been of dubious practicality for a variety of reasons.

Sullivan's willingness to advocate the hydraulic lift, beyond his personal stake in it, was a recognition of a fundamental geographic problem facing the Wurts enterprise. Their mines lay in the Lackawanna Valley, while their proposed outlet to the Delaware and beyond was down the Lackawaxen. Between the two rivers loomed a long ridge known as Moosic Mountain, not boasting notable height, but steep. Several passes through this range existed, but all presented an ascent that would be severe for a canal. This is where Dearborn's lift, which might have replaced three or four locks became attractive to those willing to believe in it. In their report Sullivan and Wright noted various alternative routes, relying on ponds that had been found in the vicinity. Sullivan also raised the possibility of a railway from the mines. By this he meant an animal-powered "tramway" such as had long been in use in England, since steam locomotives had not quite come into being. A map of what was called the "Hudson and Delaware Canal" accompanied the Wright/Sullivan report, but it described a specific route reaching only as far as the Delaware.[56] The engineers had noted a range of methods to overcome the Moosic obstruction, but did not carry out a detailed examination; the problem was left to vex future engineers and managers.

The report must have come as a shock to the Wurtses, since the estimated cost exceeded by two and a half times the $500,000 capitalization authorized by the D&H act of incorporation. The figure of half a million dollars, which would have instantly made the D&H one of the nation's largest private enterprises, must have seemed immense to the Wurtses; yet it proved altogether inadequate to accomplish the purpose. Furthermore, the tendency for costs to exceed estimates, however carefully formulated, was already well established. There was no reasonable prospect of challenging a report signed by the nation's most highly respected civil engineers; so the Wurtses responded in a more constructive manner. At its next session the New York Legislature approved a tripling of the D&H capital stock to $1,500,000.[57] This amendment was approved on April 7, 1824, only three months after the presentation of the Sullivan-Wright report and, allowing for the time required to move through committee, shows that the Wurtses and the D&H had lined up effective allies in New York.

At this point came an odd and often-overlooked lull in the affairs of the D&H. There was no legal or physical reason why the company could not organize or even begin construction. The New Yorkers who had chartered the D&H could not very well proceed without the leadership of the Wurtses, but the brothers seemed almost disoriented by the rapidity with which things had moved and perhaps the magnitude of their undertaking. More immediately, everyone probably realized that the necessary financial backing, especially after the enormous increase in capitalization, was not assured.

Some writers on the D&H have asserted that the Sullivan-Wright report was used to enlist backing in New York. This is not entirely true, since New Yorkers had chartered the D&H a month before Wright was even commissioned to conduct the investigation. It is likely, however, that much of 1824 was used to drum up additional financial support, although the period is not well documented. The strongest indication that financial concerns prevailed in this blank period is a piece of legislation approved in New York on November 19, 1824, which allowed the company to use $500,000 of its capital for banking purposes. The authors of *Century of Progress* seem puzzled by the diversion into banking, writing "It is not known just what were the reasons which led the incorporators . . . to desire this banking power . . . . At this time, other industrial concerns operated in part as banks, and it can be conjectured that the incorporators may have concluded . . . that the possession of banking privileges, carrying the power of issuing bank bills, might provide currency facilities that would be convenient in making payments to contractors and others."[58] All this was true, but a more compelling motivation was that the banking operation could yield a quicker profit. If they depended on the canal alone the first investors would tie up large amounts of money for several years before they received any return. This was acknowledged in December 1825, when the board considered requesting a $500,000 increase in the banking capital. At that time the committee that looked into the matter reported that "the risks and uncertainty attending an investment of money in the main objects of the company have deterred many Capitalists from adventuring permanently in the stock, and the scarcity of money has consequently reduced its value, and produced serious losses."[59]

John L. Sullivan must have been impressed by what he had seen when going over the D&H route, for he sought a more lasting involvement with the enterprise. In one sense his willingness to back up his technical findings with a personal, financial commitment might indicate exceptional integrity, but there was more to it. He was probably the most conspicuous and wide-ranging example of what Daniel Hovey Calhoun has characterized as the proprietor-engineer.[60] In his perceptive study Calhoun described engineers of this stamp as seeking a participatory, financial involvement with their projects, as opposed to the disinterested organization man whose first loyalty was to the canons of his profession and whose responsibility to his employer was limited to the competent performance of specified duties. Wright had started as something of a proprietor-engineer, but evolved into the corporate engineer, a type represented more fully by his pupil John B. Jervis. Within his own lifetime Sullivan saw the individualistic model he represented become obsolete, bypassed by the rapid maturation of the engineering field. In 1824, however, he still seemed to be ascendant, having recently been named by President Monroe as the only civilian member of the Board of Engineers for Internal Improvements. His effort to promote the Dearborn hydraulic lift, in which he held an interest, was characteristic of his approach. Later, his methods led him into greater controversy. As the Wurtses and others found, Sullivan was not an easy man from whom to detach, especially where money was at stake.

At a point when the outlook for their venture probably seemed gloomy, the Wurtses may have succumbed to Sullivan's promotional tendencies. The record is incomplete and one-sided, consisting only of indirect references in the Wurts correspondence, but it seems that Sullivan persuaded William Wurts to sign an agreement under which the engineer would serve the company by "using his efforts among monied men, and being on the spot to make answers if questions should be asked in regard to the proposed work."[61] (The letters do not specify what Sullivan would receive in return.) Earlier, there had been another agreement between Sullivan and the Wurtses in which the engineer received stock, apparently in return for his services. Sullivan apparently believed, and convinced the Wurtses, that his reputation would be sufficient to open New York purse-strings. If so, both parties were disappointed; for New York was a hard sell even in those days, and Sullivan was an outsider. Sullivan's proposition probably accounts for an otherwise puzzling exchange in the Wurts papers. On December 28, 1824 Benjamin Wright, then in Philadelphia, responded to an inquiry in which John Wurts had asked about Sullivan. Wright testified favorably to Sullivan's reputation, although it is interesting that he seemed to have little or no personal acquaintance with him.[62]

Although, as John Wurts later summarized, "the New York public had no confidence" in Sullivan,[63] the hope that he would prove useful may have encouraged the Wurtses to press ahead at a difficult time. We should never lose sight of the fact that, in trying to develop an unproven resource by constructing a public improvement in two states and which required a huge infusion of outside capital, the Wurtses had few examples to guide them. Not only the steps they took, but their timing and pace were important. Each had to be carefully considered and executed. Sometimes, as in the entanglement with Sullivan, they miscalculated; perhaps they proceeded more slowly than was necessary; but their caution was understandable, and their overall campaign was managed successfully.

In their next move the Wurtses showed impeccable timing, as they arranged to have their first load of coal delivered to New York on December 10, 1824.[64] Next they demonstrated its heating capabilities at the Tontine Coffee House, where the

ABOVE
Tontine Coffee House by
Manville B. Wakefield. Construction of the Tontine was
begun in 1792 by an association of merchants organized
in 1790. William L. Stone in
his 1872 history of New
York City described the
Tontine in the years immediately after the D&H or-
ganizational meeting:
"About the room were nu-
merous small tables, and after supper, in fair weather,
around the tables could be
seen many of the wealthy
city men diminishing the
contents of their pewter
mugs, or planning, amid the
curling smoke in the room,
their operations the next
day." It was demolished and
replaced in 1855.
CREDIT
D&H Canal Museum and
Barbara Purcell

FACING PAGE
CREDIT
National Canal Museum.

city's handful of active capitalists met and matched wits. At the Tontine, which was probably drafty and uninsulated, the clean, intense heat provided by the previously ridiculed "stone coal" must have seemed a marvel, especially appreciated when chill winds from the harbor sliced through the forest of masts and rattled the windows of this embryonic stock exchange. Meanwhile, the promoters had set up an office at a nearby hotel; there and at the Tontine the Wright/Sullivan report and other promotional materials were displayed.[65]

All this was in preparation for January 7, 1825, when the stock subscription books of the D&H would open at last. In addition to the Tontine, the commissioners opened books at banks in Goshen and Kingston, New York, a shrewd tactic to win up-country support. No effort was made to sell shares in Pennsylvania. This was not as surprising as it might seem, since Philadelphians presumably would not be supportive, and the Lackawanna region had so few people and so little surplus capital that it was pointless to make an effort there. On January 7 the careful advance work paid off handsomely, as the stock was fully subscribed in a day. There could be no better testimony to how fast the country was growing: five years earlier anthracite was an unknown, suspect commodity, and a $1,500,000 capitalization would have seemed breathtaking.

After another lull, part of which would have been occupied preparing the necessary public announcements, the next definitive step was taken on March 8, 1825, when the D&H company was formally organized. Gathering again in the congenial confines of the Tontine, seven of the eleven commissioners named in the act of incorporation met and elected 13 managers, as provided in the same act. Two of the commissioners from New York City, G. B. Vroom and George Janeway, did not attend; presumably they had lost whatever interest they had in the venture. Six of the seven commissioners who met on March 8 were named managers. They were joined by other New Yorkers, as well as Maurice Wurts and John Bolton. Wurts obviously represented the Lackawaxen interest, and his knowledge was indispensable. The others were probably affluent men who had been persuaded to invest in the new enterprise by the effective promotion it had conducted. On the following day the Board of Managers held its first meeting. Probably the entire business could have been conducted on March 8, but that would have meant sacrificing another mellow session at the Tontine. Philip Hone, who had been chairman of the commissioners' meeting, was elected president, with Bolton chosen as treasurer.[66] Bolton was considered capable; Hone had prestige; Wurts had the coal and a mental map; the others had money; everything seemed in order. If one accepts the traditional saga, ten years had passed since William Wurts began roaming the coal district. By March 9, 1825 the legal and financial path seemed clear, but the coal still had a long way to travel before it reached market---assuming there was a market.

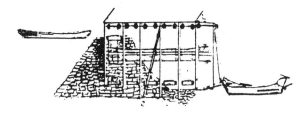

AN OUTLINE of the Lift, shewing the situation of an ascending Boat; the relative distance and elevation of two levels of a Canal. The Transit; the Weights of one side; the Pullies, Axis and Chains also of one side only, that the sketch on this small scale might not appear confused.

To suspend a boat of 25 tons with the water, in which she floats, which together with the counterpoise is about 60 tons, four chain cables of one inch iron would be sufficient; or 16 chains of half inch iron. But in practice, the additional expense of ¼ inch iron, would give 125 per cent more strength to the chains than is theoretically requisite.

The load, whatever it be, necessarily distributes itself over the whole foundation, upon every pillar, to every chain, and with a steady pressure.

The controul or management of the Transit, is principally by levers, which are established in the roof with other apparatus, not necessary now to describe; nor the manner of *compensation* for the transfer of the chains over the pullies.

This improvement will be applicable to elevated districts of country, and to Canals conducted along vallies, where there are mills; when, instead of taking the whole water from them, it borrows only enough for the operation of the Lifts, so small a quantity as scarcely to be a damage. For example, the upper mill pond of a stream, would in the spring, by its redundant water fill the Canal; which would then leave almost the usual quantity to follow its natural course; thus saving the proprietors a heavy expense, and the neighbourhood of the Canal from the inconvenience of an interruption of a productive branch of business.

J. L. SULLIVAN,
Agent for Mr. Dearborn.

TABLE OF DISTANCES
ON THE
DELAWARE & HUDSON CANAL,
SHOWING ITS
Divisions and Sections, Counties, Telegraph Calls, Numbers of Locks, &c., and the Location of Aqueducts, Feeders, Stop-Gates, Waste-Weirs, &c.

ARRANGED FOR THE INFORMATION OF THE TELEGRAPH DEPARTMENT,   BY CHARLES PETERSEN, SUPERINTENDENT.

Division / Section	NAMES OF PLACES	Telegraph Office Calls	Miles from Honesdale	Miles from Eddyville	No. of Locks	Remarks	County
PENNSYLVANIA SECTION. LACKAWAXEN DIVISION.	*HONESDALE	H		108	37	RR. Main Battery. Feeder.	Wayne.
	LEONARDSVILLE		1	107	36		
	HOLBERT'S BASIN		2	106	35		
	BEARDSLEE'S BASIN		3	105		Aqueduct	
	BEACH FLAT		4	104	34		
	WHITE MILLS	CD	5	103	33	RR	
	BRINK'S DAM		6	102	32	Feeder	
	DANIELS'		7	101	31		
	NEWCASTLE		8	100			
	HAWLEY	HY	9	99	29 30	RR	
	TUMBLEDAM ROCK		10	98	27 28	Feeder	
	POOLPIT		11	97	25 26		
	PUNCH CAMP		12	96	24		
	NARROWS		13	95	21 22 23	RR	
	SNYDER'S EDDY		14	94	19 20	Feeder	
	SHIMER'S EDDY		15	93	18		
	BLUE EDDY		16	92	17		
	MOUTH OF BLOOMING GROVE.		17	91	16	RR.	Pike.
	BLOOMING GROVE ISLAND		18	90	15		
	CRISWOLD	GD	19	89	13 14		
	WESTFALL'S		20	88	11 12	RR. Aqueduct.	
	ROWLANDS		21	87	10	RR.	
	PORT HOWARD		21	87	9		
	LITTLE NARROWS		22	86	7 8		
	RIDGWAY		23	85	4 5 6		
	LACKAWAXEN	XN	24	84		RR. Aqueduct.	
NEW-YORK SECTION. SECOND DIVISION.	DELAWARE AQUEDUCT		25	83	70 72	Delaware Feeder.	
	STOP LOCK		26	82		Four Mile Level.	
	BEAVER BROOK		27	81			
	PANTHER BROOK		28	80		Aqueduct	
	BARRYVILLE	B	29	79	68 69	Stop Gate. Hanging Rock.	
	MITCHIC		30	78			
	HANDSOME EDDY		31	77	67	Waste Weir	
	BUTTERMILK FALLS		32	76			Sullivan.
	CRAIGSVILLE		33	75	65 66		
	VAN TUYLE'S BASIN		34	74			
	VAN TUYLE'S BROOK		35	73	64		
	POND EDDY	RM	36	72	63		
	DECKER'S DOCK		37	71			
	FISH CABIN		38	70	62	Shad Fishing.	
	VAN AUKEN'S BRIDGE		39	69	61		
	STAIRWAY BROOK		40	68	60		
	DICKERSON'S EDDY		41	67			
	MONGAUP	MP	42	66	58 59	Feeder. Aqueduct.	
	BUTLER'S FALLS		43	65	57		
	BOLTON BASIN		44	64			
	HONESVILLE		45	63			
	SPARROWBUSH		46	62			
	WESTFALL'S BASIN		47	61		Stop Gate.	
	*PORT JERVIS	SB	48	60		Twelve Mile Level.	Orange.
	BEN CUDDEBACK'S		49	59			
	PINE WOODS		50	58		Stop Gate.	
	BIRD-NEST ROCK		51	57			
	HORNBECK'S CULVERT		52	56			
	HUGUENOT		53	55		Waste Weirs	
	VAN ETTEN'S BRIDGE		54	54			
	PORT CLINTON		55	53	56		
	NEVERSINK AQ.	Q	56	52	54 55	Neversink Feeder	
	CUDDEBACKVILLE		57	51		Stop Gate.	
	VAN INWEGEN'S BASIN		58	50			
	STAUNTON'S BASIN		59	49		Stop Gate.	
	WESTBROOKVILLE	WB	60	48		Aq't. Yankee P'd Feeder.	
	TUNNEL HILL		61	47		Stop Gate.	
	INDIAN SPRING		62	46			
	OAK BROOK		63	45		Aqueduct	
	BROWN HAVEN		64	44		Summit Level	
	MANERZA SMITH'S		65	43			
	GRAHAM'S DOCK		66	42		Stop Gate	Sullivan.
	SNEED'S BASIN		67	41			
	*WURTSBORO	WS	68	40		Aqueduct, Stop Gate.	
	GUMAER'S BROOK		69	39		Waste Weir. Stop Gate.	
	SWAMP BRIDGE		70	38			
	LOG HOUSE		71	37			
	BEATYSBURG		72	36			
	DAVIS		73	35	49 50	Summit. Waste Weir.	
NEW-YORK SECTION. FIRST DIVISION.	PHILLIPSPORT	SO	74	34	41 48	Topping's Res. Feeder.	
	COUNTY LINE		75	33	38 40	Aqueduct. Change Bridge.	
	PENNY'S BASIN		76	32	36 37	Feeder	
	JARED RITCHIE'S		77	31	34 35		
	BRODHEAD'S BRICK-KILN		78	30	33		
	CUTLER'S BASIN		79	29	32		
	*ELLENVILLE	RF	80	28	30 31	Mountain Brook Aqueduct.	
	TERWILLIGER'S		81	27	28 29	Feeder	
	DECKER'S		82	26	27		
	NAPANOCH		83	25		Enderly's Basin.	
	PORT BENJAMIN		84	24	26	Aqueduct.	
	PORT HYXSON		85	23	25	Rondout Creek Feeder.	
	BRUYAN'S BASIN		86	22		Two Mile Level.	
	MIDDLEPORT, (Kerhonkson,)	MI	87	21	24	Dumond's Aq. Stony Kill.	
	MOUNTAIN BROOK		88	20		Mountain Brook Aq.	
	C. P. HORNBECK'S		89	19			
	DAVID VERNOOY'S		90	18		Four Mile Level.	
	PORT JACKSON		91	17			
	STONY KILL		92	16	23	Aqueduct	Ulster.
	FREELAND'S		93	15			
	JOHN S. DEPUY'S		94	14	22	Basin.	
	ALLIGERVILLE	VI	95	13	21	Peterskill Feeder & Aq't.	
	SNYDERVILLE		96	12			
	CLOVE CHURCH		97	11		Four Mile Level.	
	HASBROUCK'S		98	10			
	HIGH FALLS	HF	99	9	12 20	† Main Battery. Feeder.	
	COLE'S BASIN		100	8	10 11		
	LAWRENCEVILLE		101	7	8 9		
	ROSENDALE	RA	102	6	7		
	LE FEVER'S FALLS		103	5	6	Basin	
	HARDENBURG'S		104	4	5	‡ Basin.	
	CREEK LOCKS	CK	105	3	2 4	§	
	HORNBECK'S BRIDGE		106	2			
	GREENKILL		107	1			
	*EDDYVILLE	DE	108		1	Guard & Weigh Lock.	
	RONDOUT;	D. & H. C. Co... RN					
	RONDOUT	Private Office... RD					

* Collector's Office.   † Suspension Aqueduct. Double Tow-path from Lock 12 to Lock 20.   ‡ Junction of Wallkill and Rondout Creeks.   § Boats pass three miles through Rondout Creek.

THOUGH there were rather serious obstacles on the route between the Hudson and Delaware Rivers . . .
the country generally had a reasonably fair look for a canal. —John B. Jervis

Plotting a Course

ONCE THE FORMALITIES of organizing the company had been completed, the managers rapidly began to take on the attributes of a going concern. One essential step was to set up a corporate headquarters. On March 21, 1825 they purchased a house and lot at 13 Wall Street from Garret Storm for $29,000. Wall Street was already recognized as the financial center of the city, but what a difference in appearance! The streetscape compared to the modern scene as the easy chairs and long clay pipes of the Tontine compare to the trading floor of the present commodities exchange, and the D&H office was essentially a residence of three stories with a dormer attic.

In its first two weeks of operation the company decided to use $500,000 of its capital for banking purposes, as had been authorized in November 1824. In those days of strict constructionism, every expansion of the company's power required an amendment to the charter, which translated into more business for Albany innkeepers. Eventually this process became unacceptably cumbersome, but it was only in the last quarter of the nineteenth century that states began drafting general railroad laws that made the granting of charters and supplements routine.

The expectation that an increase in the banking capital would "present an inducement to Capitalists to become permanent holders of the Stock" was justified by experience. According to the company's first annual report, it was not until June 27, 1825 that the treasury had enough money to open the bank. Thereafter the banking stock earned at an 8% rate and as early as May 1826 began paying semiannual dividends of 3%. Investors thus benefited during the long startup period while the canal was under construction, but it is possible that the Wurtses owned little if any of this stock.[1]

The legislators had inserted several provisions intended to keep the banking operation from becoming overly attractive. First, they limited interest the bank could charge on loans to 6% per annum. To ensure that the company did not lose sight of its purpose, the amendment provided that if it did not commence "making the navigation" within six months after electing officers and complete it within seven years, the banking privileges would lapse. Finally, the banking rights were limited to 20 years.[2] The managers were able to resist the temptation presented by the bank better than their counterparts on the Morris Canal, whose unwise loans bankrupted the company. In April 1826 a proposal for the D&H to loan money to the Ohio Canal Fund was defeated by a vote of five to four.[3] By this narrow margin financial ruin may have been averted. To the D&H managers the glitter of quick profits was not as bright as the steady gleam of anthracite, and at the end of the 20-year term they made no effort to renew the banking privilege.

FACING PAGE
Table of Distances on the
Delaware & Hudson Canal
CREDIT
National Canal Museum.

Preparations to Build

CONSIDERING THE MAGNITUDE OF THEIR TASK, the D&H managers moved with admirable rapidity and assurance. The company had been formally organized on March 8, 1825, and on June 1 the order was given to begin construction. In that interval several essential preliminaries had to be dealt with: the final selection of a route; obtaining legislation in Pennsylvania to permit the D&H to acquire the Lackawaxen/Wurts property; and, once this had been accomplished, negotiating the merger of the two interests.

Without necessarily reflecting unfavorably on John L. Sullivan's competence, it was possible to consider his report as being only preliminary, so that a more detailed study was required. This assignment was given to a serious, hardworking young engineer, John Bloomfield Jervis. Typical of the way personal links connected the small, select group of American civil engineers, Jervis had learned his skills under Benjamin Wright on the Erie Canal. He and his colleagues were not trained as civil engineers; indeed, there was no place in the country where they could have obtained such training. Civil engineering as it was then practiced was an expansion of surveying. As Jervis has described in his autobiography, capable men entered the field by a regular, if informal progression, beginning as rodman on a survey party. The experience of hacking brush for survey parties imbued these men with a bone-bred practicality. Several of these self-taught but gifted men who learned on the Erie and honed their skills on the D&H went on to become the revered leaders of the profession.

With work on the Erie nearing completion, Jervis ended his assignment there in early March 1825. Almost immediately Wright, by then Chief Engineer for the D&H, recruited him for that project and arranged for him to meet with the D&H managers. Jervis, though not yet 30, must have made a favorable impression, for he was promptly hired as Wright's chief assistant.[4] Scarcely a week passed between the time Jervis left the Erie and joined the D&H. Shortly afterward he was in Kingston to begin his examination of the canal route, accompanied by John B. Mills, who still knew the ground better than anyone else as a result of his work in 1823. Wright, with commitments all over the country, entrusted most of the work on the ground to Jervis. As he described it in his later reminiscences, and with the advantageous Erie fresh in his mind, Jervis

found a more rough country for a canal along the lower ten miles of the Rondout Valley than I had been accustomed to see. Though there were rather serious obstacles on the route between the Hudson and Delaware Rivers . . . the country generally had a reasonably fair look for a canal.[5]

Water was high in the Delaware, forcing the engineers to trudge over the adjacent hills, an experience that etched itself in Jervis's memory: "The bold rocks rising nearly perpendicular from fifty to two hundred feet above the river, the turbulent action of the water at its base, with the general gloom as heightened by the snow and the wild surroundings . . . made an impression on my mind that fifty years have not eradicated." The country was still so wild that at one point Jervis's foot was caught in a bear trap, fortunately without injuring him. Indeed, looking back after reaching the future site of Honesdale, Jervis observed that "there was but a very small portion of the land settled after we left the Neversink Valley."[6]

Jervis studied the approach to the mines at Carbondale with great care, and his conclusions differed radically from those of Sullivan. In his survey Sullivan had supposed the canal could be brought directly to the mines, although a railway might be needed at first to cover part of the distance. Jervis, however, "saw nothing to warrant this suggestion, and supposed it had its origin in the views of that day on the superior economy of canal transportation."[7] Whereas Sullivan had proposed to

---

NEW-YORK,   182

BANK *of the* DELAWARE *and* HUDSON CANAL COMPANY,

PAY to   *or Bearer,*

.   *Dollars.*

_____

Dlls.
_____

The weight of responsibility at a young age added to John B. Jervis's naturally serious disposition.
CREDIT
National Canal Museum.

FACING PAGE TOP
Along the Delaware at Pond Eddy; as on the Rondout the canal followed the river in a separate channel.
CREDIT
D&H Canal Museum.

FACING PAGE BOTTOM
"The country generally had a reasonably fair look for a canal."
CREDIT
D&H Canal Museum.

use slackwater navigation over much of his system, even some of the portion between the Delaware and Hudson, Jervis concluded that "an independent canal would be at least as cheap, and at the same time afford a better navigation."[8]

Jervis's findings must have shocked the managers. Although the D&H records do not explain the exact sequence of events, the board apparently decided that Wright should check up personally on Jervis's rather startling conclusions. For Jervis this was a turning point of his long career. Entrusted with great responsibility at an early age, he had displayed courage in making recommendations at odds with those of Sullivan, an experienced canal man. Now it was up to "the chief"—Wright—to determine if these ideas were valid. A few weeks after Jervis had submitted his report, he and Wright journeyed over the line of the proposed canal. In his subsequent report, Wright confirmed Jervis's conclusions almost entirely, and the young man's career in engineering was thereafter secure.

Wright's report, presented on May 21, followed Jervis's findings that the canal should be independent throughout its length, except for a small section of slack water at the crossing of the Delaware. He also agreed that it was not feasible to extend the canal beyond the forks of the Dyberry (present Honesdale) leaving a railroad as the likely alternative to reach the mines, although he did not commit himself fully to this concept until later. In addition, Wright opined that the locks should be constructed of stone instead of wood backed by stone (composite locks).[9] These recommendations, while sound, were invariably more costly. The company stock issuance had been based on earlier cost assumptions and could not be increased without new legislation. The managers had no choice but to accept Wright's advice, but as they went ahead with contracting they must have felt some qualms about the effect on the company's financial resources.

Jervis's survey came close to settling the vexing question of the final route to the mines, although many details remained to be decided. The Wurts brothers, as has been noted, were aware of several possible approaches and had tried some of them in their unsuccessful attempts to float coal to the Delaware. In 1824 the Wright/Sullivan report was careful to note the three main gaps through Moosic Mountain and mentioned Middle Creek and the Wallenpaupack River as offering still other options, although they were not investigated at that time. A letter in the Wurts papers instructs John B. Mills to conduct a careful examination of Rix's Gap and Cobb's Gap so that the D&H might "decide upon a final termination of their canal." This document, unfortunately, is undated, but is not earlier than 1825, since the D&H name is used.[10]

In July 1825 Thomas Young, a Wurts brother-in-law who apparently possessed surveying skills, made a careful examination of Cobb's Gap. This route aimed eastward, toward the Wallenpaupack drainage, by which the Lackawaxen could have been reached downstream; although it was a roundabout way from Carbondale and would have seemed more suited to the earlier Wurts diggings in Providence

Township. At this time, Henry Drinker, a prominent Pennsylvanian, was seeking to develop his vast landholdings east of present Scranton and in 1819 had opened a turnpike connecting them with the Delaware Water Gap. Naturally Drinker tried to promote this route for a canal, but Young saw enough of it "to satisfy me of its total impractability." At the same time, Drinker was important enough not to risk offending; Young suggested allowing Mills or Jervis to spend a few days surveying the route (at Drinker's expense).[11] In this way the Wurts's options were gradually narrowed. It had become virtually certain that the canal would end at the Forks of the Dyberry. Meanwhile Jervis had discarded some of Sullivan's more fanciful notions of extending the canal to Keen's pond, or even further by means of tapping nearby ponds or using Dearborn's boat elevator. The only remaining unresolved issue—and it was a big one—was the method of bringing the coal over the mountain to the canal terminus.

Orange-Ulster Controversy

IN A TIME OF SLOW TRAVEL people could not help acquiring an intimate acquaintance with the land they passed over. Maurice Wurts had examined the proposed canal route between the Delaware and Hudson Rivers and by all indications seemed satisfied. Under ordinary circumstances there would have been no further debate over the issue, and it would have been left to the engineers to work out the details of mastering the terrain. But in the history of the D&H few matters were ever decided without discord. Maurice might be content with the route he had viewed, and his decision might be wise on its merits, but other factors intruded. In early 1825 the D&H leaders became aware of agitation in Orange County to have the canal terminate there instead of Kingston, and Maurice Wurts attended a meeting at Goshen, NY, probably in January.[12]

Formal announcement of the controversy was delivered on March 10, 1825, when a delegation of Orange County men appeared before the newly-organized D&H Board of Managers to propose a route through their county. Any presentation by Orange County had to be taken seriously because their backing was essential. The D&H could not expect support from the counties along the Erie Canal or in northern New York. If it did not earn the wholehearted endorsement of the people directly along its route, its cause would be dubious. Furthermore, General George D. Wickham, a resident of Goshen and perhaps Orange County's most prominent citizen, had signed on as a conspicuous promoter of the D&H. If he became alienated, the damage could be catastrophic. Thus Jervis was instructed to explore the Orange route and, as the result of another intervention, extended his investigations into Sussex County, New Jersey.[13] In this way the dispute between what became known as the Orange and Ulster routes emerged to disturb what little serenity the D&H managers might have enjoyed in the middle of 1825.

In practice the issue boiled down to a contest between Kingston and Newburgh, the leading Hudson River ports of their respective counties. Geography seemed to favor Newburgh, and a superficial glance at a map made its claims hard to ignore, for the town lay more than 30 miles closer to New York City than its rival. Unfortunately for its aspirations, the Shawangunk ridge, equally hard to ignore, imposed itself between Newburgh and its dreams. No canal could have operated successfully with the number of locks it would have taken to climb that mountain; nor could a water supply have been maintained for it.

Even in their most fanciful moments the Orange men conceded the massive reality of the Shawangunks. As early as their first presentation before the D&H board they proposed to resolve the problem by building a tunnel under the ridge. Probably this idea seemed as preposterous to the Wurtses and the New York City directors as it does to us. A full generation later it took 25 years to complete the Hoosac Tunnel in neighboring Massachusetts, and then only with massive state intervention. It is likely that if they had set out to dig the Shawangunk tunnel with the methods available in 1825, they would still be at it. However, since it was General Wickham who introduced the motion to explore alternate routes, no one on the board could afford to laugh. The good members nodded approval and on April 30, 1825 instructed Benjamin Wright to examine "such of the different routes for the proposed canal as he shall deem necessary."[14]

In private correspondence (though to a Kingston supporter) Maurice Wurts made his own views unmistakably clear. He referred to the "old proposition of tunnelling the mountain," which he said "was first thrown out by Col. Cuddeback in derision." Wurts left no doubt that he shared this derision, and added that he had attended the meeting in Goshen only to prevent the company's enemies in Pennsylvania from exerting an undue influence. Another consideration was to keep Wickham on the correct path: "What course Gen'l Wickham might have taken under other circumstances, I know not."[15]

A puzzling entry in the managers' minutes of May 19, 1825 authorizes the acquisition of land for the Kingston route. This would make it appear that the issue had been settled, yet references to the controversy continue for some months longer. Wright may have expressed his opinion in favor of Kingston, but the Orange faction was not ready to give up. In a letter of May 27, 1825, John Wurts quoted Wright as saying "he never saw so much division and discord as to route."[16] In this letter John refers to "two or three members of the Board [who] travel over the route in order to ascertain whether the opinion of Judge Wright is to be depended upon rather than the crude notions of interested and ignorant persons." This category may include Wickham, which would be understandable, but also Bolton; for an earlier letter to Maurice from a Kingston supporter raised doubts about how solidly Bolton favored the Ulster route.[17]

Naturally, the Kingston group had reason to be concerned about the rumblings from Orange County. Lucius, or Lucas, Elmendorf, a Kingston ally of the Wurtses, warned of a "formidable attempt by the New Burgh People to make a diversion of the canal route." He also regretted that Abraham Hasbrouck was the only member of the newly-elected D&H board who came from Ulster County and feared that "He is not a match for Wickham."[18] Hasbrouck himself had expressed concern about the Shawangunk tunnel more than a month earlier, although, in his mild way, conceding that "if you prefer the tunnel it will be only because the interests of the Company will be thereby better subserved."[19] Yet for Maurice Wurts the risk of alienating Kingston was at least as great as it was for Orange; even the accommodating Hasbrouck warned of "disappointments" his neighbors would feel. It was in reply to Hasbrouck's letter that Wurts spoke derisively of the Shawangunk tunnel. The Wurtses felt some obligation toward their Kingston supporters, an attitude revealed in an offhand comment by John Wurts. In March 1825, while he was battling to secure favorable legislation in Harrisburg, in which the issue of tolls was paramount, John wrote that if they were going to charge by the mile, it would be better to go to Kingston than Newburgh. Then he added, "It would at any rate be ungrateful to desert the Kingston people, for those who have opposed us."[20] Ulster County stock ownership, while not massive, was too substantial to ignore. Figures for the first year are not available, but in 1826 citizens of that county had subscribed for 285 shares of D&H (nearly 2%) and in 1827 owned 220 shares (about 1.5%).[21]

Ever resourceful, the Orange crowd reserved an alternate tactic in case their tunnel proved unattainable. It is possible that they tied into a movement that had arisen independently in New Jersey. Under this concept, the canal would be continued down the Delaware beyond Carpenter's Point (present Port Jervis) to some point where it could climb over the Kittatinny Ridge (the continuation of the Shawangunks) in New Jersey. From there it could gain the valley of the Wallkill, which would carry it northeastward into Orange County to some outlet on the Hudson. Another variation, known as the "Orange and Sussex," considered flanking Kittatinny Mountain by following the Delaware through the Water Gap, then turning north in the valley of the Paulinskill. The Orange and Sussex Canal Co. was granted a New York charter on April 9, 1824. Due to some of the same political considerations, such proposals also had to be considered, and the managers duly directed the peripatetic Jervis to investigate Sussex County.[22] Indeed, Wickham, from the point of view of the Wurtses, seemed all too supportive of the Orange & Sussex and apparently had persuaded Jervis to look over its route without the approval of the D&H board. With reason, John Wurts wondered how Wickham "had been able to prevail upon Jervis to explore at the expense of his present employers, the route of a rival company."[23]

It is difficult to determine the precise date at which the board determined to stick with the Ulster route. In the mind of Maurice Wurts, who had considerable influence on the decision, there had probably never been much doubt, and the other surveys were largely a formality. Wright's report, completed on May 21, 1825, left no doubt of the superiority of the Ulster route. The Board of Managers minutes do not record a formal decision on the subject, but *Century of Progress* cites a notice in a commercial newspaper of June 20 to confirm that the Kingston route had been selected by then.[24] In his speech at the commencement of construction on July 13, 1825 Philip Hone added that a committee of managers had investigated the two routes before making a choice.

Even after the decision was final, the managers had to be careful to avoid offending the losers. Perhaps that is why Hone, always a masterful diplomat, spent considerable time explaining the reasons during his address on July 13.[25] In doing so he quoted at length from Wright's report, and the fact that he felt obliged to spend so much time in a tedious recitation during what was otherwise a joyful ceremonial occasion testifies to the importance he placed on the matter. Hone concluded with the unequivocal statement that "Upon a full, and to me satisfactory, examination of the several proposed plans . . . I am fully convinced, that the best route and the one most for the interest of the Company to pursue, is what I have called the Ulster Route;" nevertheless he felt it necessary to defend the decision.

As related by Hone, Wright found it would be relatively easy to pass from the vicinity of Newburgh into the Wallkill Valley by way of what was then called Moerderar's (Murderer's, now Moodna) Creek.[26] Then the Shawangunks intervened. Wright calculated that at an elevation of 618 feet the shortest possible tunnel would be over two miles long (3740 yards). In addition, an embankment to get over the Neversink Valley would require three to four million cubic yards of fill. The total cost would be $1,380,000 and, as Hone affirms, "the report very properly concludes by saying 'this plan ought therefore to be abandoned.' "

Investigating the Sussex route, Wright's report presented the results of the examination by Jervis and Mills. The proposal envisioned crossing over Culver's Gap, depending on Long Pond and Culver Pond for a water supply. After measuring the true elevations of these bodies of water, Wright concluded: "Comparing this with the Ulster route, the differences of expense was found to be so great as to leave no doubt of the propriety of rejecting it." The Orange & Sussex line, despite considerable local backing, was similarly dismissed. By following the Delaware to its junction with the Paulinskill, Wright calculated, the length of the canal would be increased by 50 miles, and 375 feet of lockage would be added. When Hone noted that as a result of remaining in the Delaware Valley so long, the canal would come within 20 miles of Easton, he was reminding his audience that Easton was the outlet of the competing, better situated, Lehigh system.

Rejecting the rivals to the Ulster route still did not bring peace, for a division of opinion arose within that route itself. Fortunately, it did not produce as much acrimony as the debate between Ulster and Orange. Even the very preliminary investigation conducted by William Wurts and Josiah White in 1823 had examined more than one approach to Kingston. The Wright/Sullivan report identified and depicted two main alternatives, described as the "Kingston" and "Rondout" routes. They diverged at Hardenburgh Bridge, near present Port Jackson, 15 or 16 miles from Kingston. From there one route essentially followed the old road, roughly equivalent to Rt.209, into Kingston, in part through the valley of the Esopus. The other, which might be called the low road, went down into the valley of the Rondout and terminated at what was then called Eddy's factory (now Eddyville,) with boats reaching Kingston on the Rondout itself. Actually, the terminus of canal

LeFever Falls looking south, showing why the canal needed to be separated from Rondout Creek. At Creek Locks, a short distance to the north, slackwater navigation began where the canal entered the river.
CREDIT
D&H Canal Museum.

operations and the transfer point to river boats for both routes would be at what was called the Strand along the Kingston waterfront.

Hasbrouck, the only Ulster representative on the D&H board, professed to be neutral on the subject though "much amused with sage remarks from those who two years ago knew not what a canal was."[27] Elmendorf, a Kingston man whose advice Maurice Wurts respected, favored the route direct to his village. Under his plan the canal would descend from the valley of the Esopus to the Kingston waterfront, using the Esopus in part as a water supply. He recognized that the steep descent into Kingston would pose difficulties and, far-sighted and perhaps influenced by developments at the Pennsylvania end, sought to resolve the problem with what he called a railway. As he described this concept, it seemed to resemble the inclined planes later used on the Morris Canal.[28]

Once again Benjamin Wright was ordered to examine the alternatives, and he presented his findings to the board on October 25, 1825. Wright conceded that, all else being equal, the Kingston route would be preferable: "It would be desirable in all cases to accommodate and benefit old established villages where business is done and considerable active capital located, and unite the interest and feelings of the inhabitants of the Village of Kingston, who have from the beginning taken a warm and active interest in favour of this work, and many of whom are stockholders."[29] Hasbrouck had earlier written "The Villages . . . with a few exceptions wish the Canal to pass by their own doors."[30] Nevertheless, geographical reality dictated the opposite choice. The route to Kingston would be more than four miles longer and cost $103,586 extra. Wright's report settled the question, for even though the engineering profession scarcely existed at that time, awe for its technical expertise was already widespread.

What were the consequences of this long and ofttimes nasty debate, in which the protagonists were seldom charitable about the motivation of their opponents? The route chosen by the D&H was surely, from an objective standpoint, the best of the alternatives. From a political and economic perspective, the company probably preferred the Kingston version of the Ulster route, but here too deferred to engineering and cost considerations. On the negative side, the controversy could not help drawing attention to the inherent flaw of the D&H Canal, which is that at Kingston its coal was only slightly closer to New York City than when it came to the surface at Carbondale. Thus there was a persistent temptation to look for a more direct route, and these efforts provided a rallying point for the enemies the company accumulated over the years. Some of these proposals developed astonishing durability, and became chronically troublesome to the D&H.

Disputes over routing were common during the canal era and carried over with no loss of intensity into the railroad age. Few canals escaped these controversies. There was probably never any doubt that the Blackstone Canal would run between Worcester and Providence. On the Middlesex the end points seem to have been agreed, but a serious difference of opinion arose about the intermediate portion. Although the distance between the two places was small, there was a nasty rivalry between Black Rock and Buffalo to become the western terminal of the Erie Canal.[31] Perhaps the closest parallel to the D&H situation occurred on the Chenango Canal where a concerted effort by Utica citizens forced a change in the initial plan to terminate in Whitesboro.[32]

Another crucial step during this busy period in the company's history included naming Maurice Wurts agent to supervise construction. Wurts, unmarried and familiar with the area and its people, was a logical choice, and his selection helped bind the Wurts interests to those of the New York investors.

Pennsylvania Legislation

THIS PERIOD OF AMERICAN HISTORY was characterized by intense rivalry among the states, and one of the bitterest struggles was between New York and Pennsylvania for access to the expanding West. New York had surpassed Philadelphia in population around 1810, and the Pennsylvania city was fearful of being left farther behind. In that climate it would be suicidal for New York investors to apply at Harrisburg to take control of valuable properties in the Keystone State. It was inevitable that the Wurtses would have to lead this campaign, in particular John as a former member of both houses of the Pennsylvania Legislature. He had been elected to the U.S. Congress in 1824, but Congress must not have been in session often during the first part of 1825, as John spent most of that period guiding the D&H legislation through Harrisburg.

Even for John Wurts any venture into the legislative forest was an uncertain business. With self-interest providing a pointed incentive, the 33-year old lawyer pulled down his visor, tilted his lance and rode off to the State Capitol. At first he approached his crusade with trepidation: "A single remonstrance in these ticklish times would blow us up,"[33] he wrote. And there was sure to be opposition: all public improvement bills were controversial, especially one featuring what could be portrayed as a land grab by Yorkers. Though it cannot be demonstrated with certainty, it is likely that when Pennsylvania legislators granted the right to improve the Lackawaxen they assumed that the ultimate destination of the coal would be Philadelphia; they had no reason to expect that the coal would move to New York over a route controlled by New Yorkers.

It was essential to demonstrate strong popular support in the affected region, and the Wurtses had prepared well. Numerous petitions were presented, so that John Wurts could conclude "nearly the whole population of Wayne and Pike [Counties] must have signed."[34] Nathaniel B. Eldred, a prominent Wayne resident, performed great services at Harrisburg, as did Nathan Smith, a Philadelphian who had an active interest in the Lackawaxen venture. William Wurts later said of Eldred "the bill could not have been got without him."[35]

The D&H/Lackawaxen bill passed the senate with little difficulty, but a tougher fight was expected in the lower house. There a young representative named Read led a vigorous opposition. Read was a nephew of Thomas Meredith, a resident of the Lackawanna Valley who had already emerged as a venomous foe of the Wurtses. Not long before, Meredith had expressed the opinion that Wurts's activities were "contrary to republican principles."[36] Another influential opponent was Judge David Scott, who feared that the D&H represented a New York takeover of Pennsylvania resources and markets.[37] Indeed, the Wurts holdings were sometimes described as the "New York Colony."[38]

The Wurts's opponents shrewdly placed the issue of tolls at the center of the conflict: If a high rate was approved, the Wurtses would have an effective monopoly of the coal traffic; a lower rate might make the canal something of a public highway in which other mine owners could ship coal in competition with the Wurtses. Only a small difference seemed crucial in this regard—the company was seeking a rate of 1½ cents per ton per mile, while Read was demanding a reduction to 1¼ cents. The contest came to a head on March 27, 1825, when John Wurts asked Maurice to "Write me two letters—one stating what you really believe would be the decision of the company in relation to 1¼ cents per ton, and one stating that the company would not undertake the work at less than 1½ cents."[39]

The Wurtses and their backers apparently approved the quarter-cent reduction, since they seemed satisfied when the final act set a rate of 1¼ cents. John Wurts returned from Harrisburg on April 3 with a bill signed by the governor. He gloated that Read found the act "as objectionable as the Bill which originally passed the Senate."[40] While the toll had been reduced slightly on the Lackawaxen and on the Delaware, it remained unchanged in New York State, allowing John Wurts, with his capacity to overlook unfavorable provisions, to argue that "the monopoly is complete even if a boat attempts to find a market by going down the Delaware."[41] Although the act provided free navigation of the Delaware, he noted it had been 13 years since a boat had ascended the river as far as Milford. Despite his confident front, John Wurts must have felt some doubts about how the board would receive the act he had won. In his letter to Maurice he went to great lengths to explain that, compared to other charters, the D&H was "the most powerful in this country" and boasted that "it was a matter of astonishment to every one that such a Bill should have passed."[42]

John's apprehensions proved justified. Although *Century of Progress* makes it seem that approval of the Pennsylvania act by the D&H board was a "technical requirement," in fact the topic caused heated debate. The board members were conservative by nature, and their counsel John Duer was even more cautious. The minutes of June 15, 1825 record the board's detailed and sometimes agonizing examination of the act and John Wurts's defense of it. A clause that gave the Pennsylvania Legislature the right to repeal the law was particularly offensive, as it seemed to show hostile intent. Only after it was ascertained that other Pennsylvania laws contained this phrase did the board acquiesce in the provision, on the basis that "If a state sinks so low as to forget justice and lose sight of Honor all having relations with said state must suffer."[43] When John Wurts was trying to put a good face on the newly-passed act, he opined that "when the provisions of the bill are fairly read and fully understood, I think that it will be found to be one that will fully carry into effect the views of the D. & H. canal Company."[44] His prediction was accurate, but a long and painful process was required before the board came around to accept his reasoning.

Merger

ONE OF THE MOST VITAL but least appreciated factors in the early history of the D&H is that it was in reality a combination of two companies, which shared a common goal but were different in ownership and sometimes divergent in interests. Although the two factions were based in different states, the fundamental issues did not stem from the separate jurisdictions; some of the same problems would undoubtedly have arisen if the Wurtses had confined their efforts to Pennsylvania by seeking to compete in Philadelphia.

At some time in 1823 the Wurtses and their Philadelphia financial backers had organized themselves as the Lackawaxen Company. This probably occurred after the granting of the Pennsylvania charter, which was given to Maurice Wurts and his associates. Virtually nothing is known about the Lackawaxen company as a separate entity, even the amount of its capitalization. It may have been a partnership, rather than a corporation. The negotiations between it and the D&H proprietors in New York have some parallels to the merger activity of the 1980s, but with a more constructive purpose than many recent examples. As with other aspects of the formation of the D&H, there were few useful precedents in American business history, and the company had to invent itself as it went along. Perhaps this was a good thing, since there were few limits placed on the creativity of the negotiators, and they were able to craft an agreement that, like custom-made clothing, was uniquely suited to the situation.

It is unclear when actual negotiations began, although the eventual combination must have always been on the minds of the participants as they worked together sufficiently to secure legislation in both states. Partly because the D&H company was not organized and did not begin keeping minutes until March 1825, the documentation of this episode depends almost entirely on Wurts family papers. Inevitably, this creates a one-dimensional portrait, which is especially regrettable because the Wurts correspondence implies a good deal of distrust. (If the Lackawaxen organization kept records separate from those of the Wurts family, they seem not to have survived.)

The concept of paying for the Wurts properties with deferred stock in the D&H seems to have originated quite early and persisted as a central principle of the negotiations. This was an imaginative approach to the situation; it tied the Wurtses to the success of the overall company while allowing the New York investors to apply their capital to building the canal for the benefit of both parties. A document in the Wurts papers, unfortunately undated, but apparently quite early, proposes a sale of the Lackawaxen company to the D&H for $100,000 initial stock and up to $400,000 additional stock in the D&H. The latter amounts would be issued in increments when the profit of the D&H reached 6, 9, 12 and 20%. The innate suspicion toward the New Yorkers is evident, for the proposal provides safeguards "to protect the interest of the Lackawaxen company."[45]

For the Wurts Brothers the negotiations represented the culmination of years of unrewarded effort. In trying to reach this fulfillment they were like canoeists navigating dangerous rapids. On one side was the D&H, largely unknown and with its own interests to protect. To the Wurtses in early 1825 the D&H board in New York, with whom they were nominally allied, was composed of distant strangers. When John Wurts wrote from Harrisburg on March 17, 1825 that "I am informed that an election for managers has taken place in the Delaware and Hudson Canal Company," he reveals the lack of close contact with the supposed partner, although by then Maurice had been elected one of the original managers.[46]

On the other shore, which should have been secure, there was ample cause for worry. The other owners of Lackawaxen stock, a group of obscure Philadelphia businessmen with names like Sheepshanks and Ellmaker, were not above speculating in the stock and pursuing other actions that put them at odds with the Wurtses. At one point of accumulated frustration John Wurts referred to "much meanness and knavery exhibited by these fellows."[47] On another occasion William Wurts described Levi Ellmaker as "obstinate" and added that it was "a degradation to open my mouth to him again."[48] Such were the relations of the Wurtses with their associates in the Lackawaxen Company—or more accurately, the men with whom they were forced to associate because of their lack of capital.[49] Apparently the discord was caused by the propensity of some of the Lackawaxen investors to sell their stock for a quick profit. This irritated the Wurtses, first, because "of the bad effect it may have upon our negotiations with the board," presumably meaning the

THE locks on the D & H were numbered in order westward from Rondout to Lackawaxen and from Lackawaxen to Honesdale. For the most part the boatmen referred to the lock by some name which was derived from the proprietor or from some peculiar feature nearby. The most common names were: 1—Eddyville, 2 to 4—Creek Locks, 5—Milban's, 6—Websters, 7—Rosendale, 8-9—Lawrenceville, 10—Humphreys, 11—Cole's Basin, 12-14—Nigger Locks, 15-20—High Falls, 21—Alligerville, 22—Foleys, 23—Stony Kill, 24—Middleport, 25—Port Hickson 26—Port Benjamin, 27—Bob Decker's, 28—Chris Ginniel's, 29—Shirley's, 30-31—Ellenville, 32—Sam Taylor's, 33—Youppy's, 34—Ostrander's, 35—Callahan's, 36—Penny's, 37—Mose Charles', 38—Louie Beardsley, 39—Joe McKane, 40—Hank Woods, 41—Jack McCarthy, 42—Bill Foster, 43—Bill Robinson, 44—Dan Hanion, 45—Enoch Rogers, 46—Huck Rogers, 47—Will Donnelly's, 48—Will Halstead's, 49—Wm. E. Rose's, 59—P. O. Callahan's, 51-55—Neversink, 56—Mineral Springs, 57—Butler's, 58-59—Mongaup, 60—Woolsley's, 61—Pa Gene Smith's, 62—Widow Kelly's, 63—Pond Eddy, 64—Squire Van Tuyler's, 65—Decker's, 66—Lambert's, 67—Handsome Eddy, 68—Barryville, Lower 69—Barryville, Upper, 70-71-72—Gilson's Locks.

Here the canal crossed the Delaware and Lackawaxen Rivers. The first three locks on the Lackawaxen were abandoned after the completion of the aqueducts. 4-5-6—Ridgeway's, 7—Joe Tague or Tinsmiths, 8—O'Donnell's, 9—Bishop's, 10—George Rowland's, 11—Saxon's or Larson's, 12—Westfall's, 13-14—Griswold's, 15—Jim Avery's, 16—Corkonian's or Chidesters, 17—Rodgers, 18—Jim Hanner's, 19—Abe Rowland's, 20—Pat Gannons, 21—Field Bend, 22—Mike Harrison's, 23—Him Harrison's, 24—Frank Danniel's (Pat Harrison), 25—Poolpit, 26—Baisdens, 27—Carroll's (Billy O'Brien), 28—Rock Lock (Mike Connors), 29—Lower Hawley (Conklin's), 30—Upper Hawley (Hennessey's), 31—Wier's (O'Han's), 32—McKahill's, 33—White Mills, 34—Lonsome Lock (Dan Carroll), 35—Tom Whitaker's, 36—Chris Lane's (Miles Bishop), 37—Honesdale-Twin Locks.

It should be born in mind that no two such lists of names would be the same, but those given seem to have been the most common in the last years of the canal.

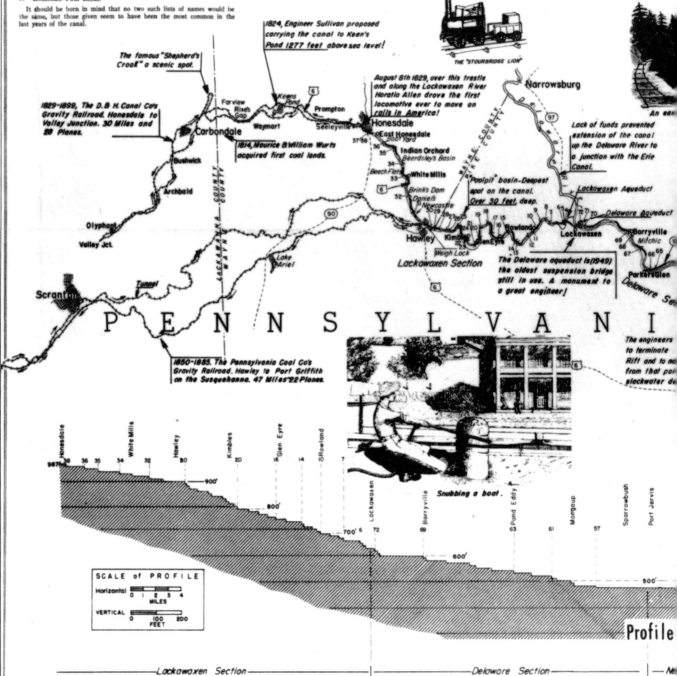

1828-1898
The Delaware & Hudson C
and the
Gravity Railroads connecting with the

This great engineering work was the first private enterprise in the United States to cost more than a million dollars. It was constructed to bring the anthracite coal of Pennsylvania to the eastern markets and until well after the civil war, carried most of New York City's coal.

The project was first visualized by Maurice & William Wurts and financed through the influence of Philip Hone, then mayor of New York.

The canal was originally only 3' deep bottom and 32' at the top. It was f a depth of 6', a bottom width of 3 width was little changed. The origi 76' X 9' but were enlarged in 1850

As the canal was enlarged the t boats increased:- 1828-10 tons, 1840-30 1850-140 tons. There were 22 aqueducts bridges, 22 reservoirs, 16 dams, 14 feed

THE "STOURBRIDGE LION"

1824, Engineer Sullivan proposed carrying the canal to Keen's Pond 1277 feet above sea level!

The famous "Shepherd's Crook" a scenic spot.

1829-1899, The D. & H. Canal Co's Gravity Railroad. Honesdale to Valley Junction. 30 Miles and 29 Planes.

August 8th 1829, over this trestle and along the Lockawaxen River Horatio Allen drove the first locomotive ever to move on rails in America!

1814, Maurice & William Wurts acquired first coal lands.

Lack of funds prevented extension of the canal up the Delaware River to a junction with the Erie Canal.

Poolpit basin—Deepest spot on the canal. Over 30 feet deep.

The Delaware aqueduct is (1949) the oldest suspension bridge still in use. A monument to a great engineer!

1850-1885. The Pennsylvania Coal Co's Gravity Railroad. Hawley to Port Griffith on the Susquehanna. 47 Miles 22 Planes.

Snubbing a boat.

The engineers to terminate Rift and to from that po slackwater d

PENNSYLVANIA

Carbondale · Bushwick · Archbald · Olyphant · Valley Jct. · Scranton · Tunnel · Lake Ariel · Farview · Rixe's Gap · Waymart · Keens Pond · Prompton · Seeleyville · Honesdale · East Honesdale · Indian Orchard · Beerdsley's Basin · Beech Flats · White Mills · Brink's Dam · Daniels · Newcastle · Hawley · Kimble · Glen Eyre · Weigh Lock · Rowland · Lackawaxen · Barryville · Mitchic · ParkersGlen · Narrowsburg

WAYNE COUNTY · LACKAWANNA COUNTY

Lackawaxen Section · Delaware Section

SCALE of PROFILE
Horizontal 0 1 2 3 4 MILES
Vertical 0 100 200 FEET

900' · 800' · 700' · 600' · 500'

Profile

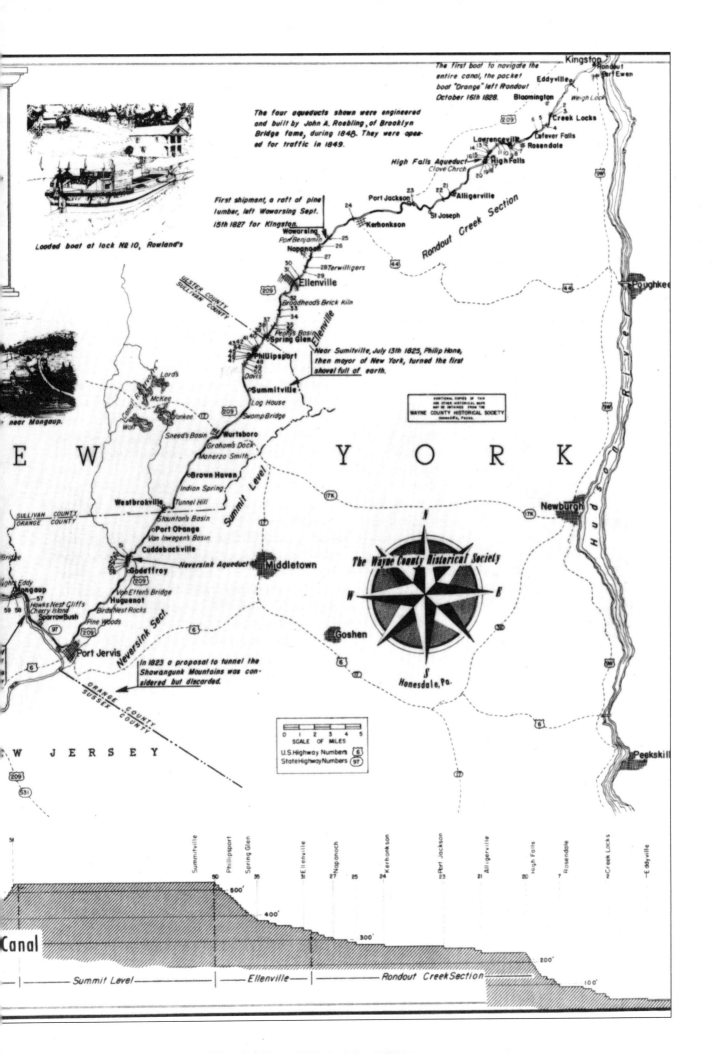

D&H.[50] Charles S. Wurts himself was not above advocating the sale of Lackawaxen shares, but at least wanted to wait until the engineers had finished their survey.[51]

Many of the inside references in the Wurts correspondence are problematical. The letters can be interpreted to show that, as the negotiations continued, with the idea of deferred stock taking hold, ownership of the Lackawaxen stock became critical. Apparently, as they realized that by selling prematurely they were sacrificing their chance for future participation, the Philadelphia investors had to perform some unseemly scrambling to preserve their interest. Meanwhile, suspicion of the D&H flared again when the board instructed Jervis to explore alternate routes. "It is altogether unreasonable that we should be held fast to our contract, while the D & H Co. are not bound and are sending engineers from Dan to Bersheba [sic] to find some other route for a canal than the one we have designated."[52]

Negotiations entered a critical phase in June 1825. Two months earlier the Lackawaxen board, though it begrudged any expenditures, had agreed to pay Maurice Wurts $150 per month while he stayed in New York to represent the company's interests.[53] In June John found it necessary to join him in order to influence the D&H board—to "draw their minds into the right track," as he put it.[54] At that time the board was wrestling with the interrelated issues of the new Pennsylvania legislation and the agreement with the Wurts interests, and there were signs that its determination was wavering. There were times when the Wurtses themselves seemed to weary of the long struggle: on one occasion John sighed "it is vexatious to find so many ebbs and flows in this business"—and his involvement in it was much more recent than that of his brothers! But in the end, girding his loins, he acknowledged "we have a stake so deep in the business that we ought to look after it," and sailed for New York.[55]

The sequence of events makes it reasonably clear that the D&H board concluded the agreement with the Lackawaxen company only after it had considered and approved the Pennsylvania amendment. If the legislation had been found unsatisfactory, it might have decided to rethink the entire venture. On June 15, 1825, the same day it accepted the legislation which allowed it to assume the Wurts privileges, the board appointed a committee to purchase the Wurts rights and property. Thereafter, negotiations must have proceeded rapidly, for the terms of the agreement were presented and approved on July 2.[56]

The arrangement provided for the Lackawaxen interests to receive $40,000 in cash immediately and $200,000 in deferred stock, payable when the net profits of the company reached 6%.[57] Other stipulations providing "for the better assuring to the Lackawaxen Company the full benefits intended to be secured to them by such deferred stock," were designed to protect the deferred stock from dilution, along the lines of the earlier proposal.[58] Another important but often overlooked provision bonded the D&H in the amount of $400,000 to guarantee payment of the deferred stock.[59] This clause must have served, as intended, as a red-hot iron in the rear of the D&H board; for if they failed to complete and make a success of the canal, the large obligation would remain.

For its part the board inserted another clause to protect it against an unwelcome contingency. This provision stated that the deferred stock could not be transferred until the D&H's right "to make an independent canal in Pennsylvania fed by the waters of the Lackawaxen river or some one or more of its branches . . . shall be secured"—either by an act of the legislature, a court decision, or a license from the governor.[60] (The Pennsylvania act of April 1825 allowed the D&H to acquire the Wurts rights, but these rights were limited to improving the navigation of the

Lackawaxen and did not specifically cover the building of an independent water-way.) Since the Wurtses would have the primary responsibility for securing this approval by means of another ordeal in Pennsylvania politics, this provision was the practical equivalent of the bond imposed on the D&H.

The deferred stock, as has been noted, had been a staple of the negotiations, but the final amount was much less than had been mentioned earlier, an indication of the increasingly acute financial distress the Wurtses were feeling. Payment of the initial $40,000 was authorized on August 9, following the formal transfer of the Wurts holdings. While this payment relieved some of the Wurts's financial uncertainty, it probably did not lessen their suspicion about the motives of the D&H board. A few weeks earlier, but after the terms of the agreement had been settled, John Wurts had written "I incline to the opinion that there are in the N. York board, those who would shake us off if they could."[61]

The Wurtses were both vital and marginal to the D&H. *Century of Progress* is careful to note that Maurice was elected one of the original managers in March 1825, but ignores the fact that his tenure lasted only a year. He was asked to resign on February 25, 1826, in order that his seat might be filled by "a member residing in the City."[62] At the annual election a few days later, changes in the makeup of the board were attributed to the need to have members located in the city in order to perform as bank directors. Possibly this explanation represents the full story, since it is recorded that even notables such as Philip Hone spent many evenings destroying defaced D&H bank notes.[63] Another possibility is that we are observing an elaborate maneuver to pry Wurts off the board. One of the other ousted members, banker Lynde Catlin, may have felt some resentment, since he later seems to have supported a rival company. The same broom swept out two other stalwarts, George D. Wickham and Abraham Hasbrouck, who had been influential in winning regional support for the enterprise.

While the conclusion in *Century of Progress* that in the merger the two parties "joined forces on fair terms, and with mutual satisfaction and esteem," may be true in a broad sense, the actual wording of the agreement and the associated correspondence shows that it was a cautious embrace with both sides protecting their interests as carefully as possible. John Wurts's remark about the New York board testifies to the underlying attitude. The agreement allowed work to begin, but it would go forward in an atmosphere of mutual distrust that could only be relieved by time and experience.

The solidest and most startling evidence of the alienation the Wurtses felt toward the D&H is provided by a bold stock manipulation they considered in June 1827. It is the sort of episode that will not be found in the pages of *Century of Progress*. Based on the proposition that "our stock must be sold so soon as we could reap on it all the benefit of the opening of the canal," John and Charles Wurts and Nathan Smith had come up with a purse of $25,000. Their scheme was simply to purchase stock at $90 to $92 which, coincident with opening the canal, would create a rush that would boost its value to at least $95, perhaps even to par. Smith had an arrangement with Ellmaker in which he would receive a fee if the plan could run the value of Ellmaker's stock back to par.[64] It was, as John Wurts conceded, an exercise in "stock jobbing," in which he professed to be unskilled; nonetheless, he had thought it through and found little risk. It was apparently a prosperous time in Philadelphia, and John wrote that "People here do not know what to do with their money."[65]

It is noteworthy to find some of the maneuvers that later characterized the stock market appearing at such an early stage of its development. Since the Wurtses owned some D&H stock, they were compelled to be buyers and sellers simultaneously. "The selling and buying must be distinct operations," wrote John, adding that Maurice should immediately put his stock in another's name. The impression of John's complete detachment from the affairs of the D&H is strengthened by his inquiring of Maurice "What is the character of the stockholders generally?—is much of it held by speculators? Or is the mass of it in the hands of permanent holders?"[66] Subsequent correspondence does not establish whether the stock jobbing scheme was actually put into practice. Further delays in completing the canal may have deferred it until it became impractical. If successful, the plan might not have ended the Wurts involvement with the D&H, since they still had their deferred stock, but it would surely have changed the character of the relationship.

Further evidence that the merger of the New York and Pennsylvania interests was an imperfect weld is seen in proposals to separate soon after the marriage. On February 25, 1826 Bolton, by then president, wrote to Nathan Smith, who was representing the company in Harrisburg, instructing him to offer to sell the Pennsylvania portion of the canal to that state. Another option presented was for the state to complete the canal and then lease it to the D&H to operate. Under both propositions, the D&H would transfer all its property and rights in Pennsylvania except its coal lands (and even they might be sold separately). Clearly the harshness of the debate in the Pennsylvania legislature over expanding the company's rights had made a deep impression on Bolton. He seemed to be sensitive to allusions that the D&H was made up of "speculators," which made him fearful of "these collisions and suspicions, which might possibly ensue from the operations of a company foreign to that State." Specifically he feared that, since there had been so much agony in expanding the canal privileges, Pennsylvania might give the company even more of a hard time over acquiring rights to build a railway, without which "it will be in vain that we make a canal."[67]

It is not known whether Smith presented these proposals, or how they were received. Smith was a shrewd individual, and the letter made him aware that the board, Bolton in particular, was willing to sell their Pennsylvania assets. Although he had made no progress, the idea continued to prey on Bolton's mind, and early in the following year he raised it again in a conversation with Smith. This time Smith followed with a letter to Maurice Wurts proposing the "bold project of an offer for a lease of the whole line." He was convinced that a market already existed at New York for 50,000 tons of coal annually, so that, as he concluded, the lease would be "the most valuable contract ever obtained in the United States." Adding a powerful endorsement, William Wurts declared that "the board are entirely incompetent to take up that department of their business and totally ignorant of the value of the thing just within their grasp."[68]

Smith must have obtained the approval of the Wurtses, for on February 2, 1827 he proposed the terms of a lease to Bolton. He did not disclose the identity of those he was representing, except to say they were "members of the Lackawaxen Co. who approach the lease as an affair of business which they feel themselves competent to manage." Smith also stressed the urgency of completing the system before the Lehigh company could gain access to the New York market.[69] The records do not establish whether Bolton actually presented the offer to his board; obviously, the lease was never put into effect. The consequences were of a more subtle nature. Bolton was now identified as emphasizing the D&H as a transportation or financial enterprise, less interested in mining coal or ensuring a monopoly of coal traffic. This put him at odds with the Wurtses and their allies. Already, as Smith had noted, there had been some fear that Bolton's initial offer to Harrisburg might result in a lease "at a rate of interest which would forbid the expectation of recovering dividends on the deferred stock" (in which Smith himself may have had a stake).[70] The two interests, united by a pact that only formalized their mutual suspicions and with little direct contact except for the position of Maurice Wurts as company agent, watched each other warily. It was hardly an open, affectionate partnership.

The merger agreement, with its creation of the deferred stock, had the unanticipated effect for the Wurtses of renewing an unwelcome relationship with John Langdon Sullivan. Under an agreement made in the early stages of his relationship with the company, Sullivan seemed to be entitled to 2½% of the Lackawaxen stock; perhaps he had taken his fee in stock rather than cash. This was distinct from the contract under which Sullivan was supposed to help loosen New York purse strings, and which John Wurts later called "one of the most silly contracts ever made."[71] Obviously John had not been consulted on that agreement, but the earlier agreement could not so easily be dismissed, although he, characteristically, tried to ignore the unfavorable portions. Wurts exclaimed that "Sullivan is a natural fool," but he must have recognized that the engineer had a valid claim, since William Wurts had offered him $700 or $800 to surrender it.[72]

Obviously aware of the merger terms, Sullivan believed that whatever rights he held would be worth $5000 once the deferred stock was issued. He thought this could happen in the first year of operation, but then had the effrontery (from the Wurts perspective) to suggest that this could occur only if he were "introduced into the management."[73] Calhoun, in his study of the early engineering profession, was not aware of this incident; it surely would have reinforced his identification of Sullivan as the fullest expression of the "proprietor engineer." Sullivan also offered, in return for an advance on his stock, to investigate "the best means of improving the Delaware higher up, and of crossing by a rail way to the Susquehanna, &cccc." This provoked John Wurts to blurt again "I mean literally therefore that the fellow is a natural fool, or else he thinks we are," but then he added ruefully "and in truth our past contracts with him look very like it."[74] Another source of embarrassment for the Wurtses was that Bolton and other members of the D&H board were unaware of the obligation to Sullivan and presumably would not have been happy to learn of it, even though it would not seem to change their obligation.

It is apparent that the Wurtses did not concede anything to Sullivan in 1825, but the engineer was nothing if not persistent. Two years later, after John Wurts had written a letter "denying his right to sell what he holds and telling him that he gave no value for it," Sullivan served notice that he would file a bill in Chancery directing the D&H to give him 2½% of the deferred stock, and also that he would seek an injunction to stop the transfer of any deferred stock until this was done.[75] This also had the effect of bringing the matter to the attention of the D&H board, if it had not known of it already. John Wurts exclaimed again "Did you ever meet with so impudent a scoundrel!" Yet reading between the lines, one sees that despite his efforts at denial, Wurts perceived that Sullivan had a valid claim. His chagrin at having been outsmarted filters through his blustering references to the "scoundrel."[76] Unfortunately, the subject does not seem to reappear in the Wurts correspondence, so the final outcome is uncertain. Whatever satisfaction John L. Sullivan may have obtained in this case would scarcely mitigate the unsatisfactory conclusion of his career. Calhoun summarizes by saying that "From the middle 1820's, he worked increasingly at ideas that never came to fruition and that made him appear the crank"—and this probably without knowing of Dearborn's hydraulic lift! Sullivan's relatively fleeting contact with the D&H furnishes another example of what Calhoun terms "the special character of his failure, with its dogged commitment to unrealistic, unwanted projects."[77]

Wurts Financial Strains

THERE RUNS BENEATH THE NEGOTIATIONS, like a strong, persistent undercurrent, the financial distress of the Wurts brothers. Probably this dark stream was invisible to the New York investors, who had only a slight and distant acquaintance with the Wurtses, but it makes a mockery of the traditional idea that the brothers were wealthy independent businessmen who could bargain on terms of relative equality with the New Yorkers. Their sense of economic vulnerability compared to the affluent New Yorkers who controlled the D&H explains some of the distrust they felt.

By 1825 the financial position of the Wurtses was not substantially better than has been described in the previous chapter. In May of that year the brothers were apparently considering the purchase of stock in the Delaware & Raritan Canal. This shows a genuine commitment to internal improvements, but as Charles Stewart ruefully conceded, "our means would not reach far."[78] Another letter from Charles in the following month indicates that the brothers also owned stock in the other major transportation ventures in the region—the Schuylkill Navigation, and "Hauto" stock in the Lehigh Valley. These holdings were apparently neither large nor secure: $2700 in Schuylkill stock had to be sold to pay off a note, and there was fear the brothers would have difficulty meeting the call for an installment on D&H stock in June 1825.[79]

A month later John Wurts gave a starkly despairing appraisal of the family's financial situation: "William and Charles are doing no business and have not the means to change their system at present. Mine is totally gone, and I consider myself if possible poorer than I was a year ago." He added that "My present absence has broken up the connexion with the few clients I had."[80] John's law practice was still his main, if not only, source of income, and attending to the affairs of the D&H had eroded it severely. "I lost the last two trial terms in toto, by my absence at Albany and Harrisburg," he lamented.[81] By late July 1825 the agreement with the D&H had been concluded, but finalizing it depended on a transfer of property, and John wrote, "the sooner things come to an issue in this business the better." This rather desperate tone shows unmistakably that the Wurtses were not able to negotiate from a position of strength, and explains why they settled for less satisfactory terms than they had hoped to gain.

Matters did not improve during the summer of 1825. On August 26 John wrote "Business is dull; both in law and merchandize."[82] By the end of the year a true crisis had developed. On November 17 Charles wrote in an alarmed mood that William's partnership might soon be dissolved and he would be "thrown upon his own resources." In a state of near panic, Charles provided an extremely illuminating summary of the family resources. Their means at that time consisted of $1550 in Schuylkill stock, $5500 in Hauto stock, the D&H deferred stock and "Connecticut bonds" in unspecified amount. The Schuylkill and Hauto stocks represented par value, which could not be realized in the market, and the D&H was of uncertain value. Finally, Charles concluded that "we cannot carry more than $1000 out of our business."[83]

In this crisis atmosphere, drastic actions were considered. William contemplated dissolving with Rodman and moving to New York, and Charles conceded that "if we pursue the Dry goods business New York is the place for us." The Schuylkill and Hauto stock would not yield enough "to aid us in an arrangement for business in New York," although there was some discussion of using it as collateral for a $10,000 loan from the D&H. That would not be an immediate solution, so an even more shocking alternative was considered: selling the D&H stock. Unfortunately, Charles concluded "at the present price it would hardly furnish money enough for our purpose," and, in this pessimistic frame of mind, added that "I think the stock will be lower and do not see how we can continue to hold it and meet instalments."[84] It is an irony in the history of the D&H that only the poor prospects of the company may have preserved the Wurts family involvement with it, although it was not a step that would be taken lightly: Even in the depths of gloom Charles Stewart Wurts conceded "I do not feel quite willing to sell until I am forced to."

John Wurts was not the best person to boost his brother's morale. At that stage he may have lacked William and Maurice's lasting commitment to the Lackawaxen and regarded it as an unwelcome intrusion on his law practice. "It seems to me that we shall not very soon escape from the labours of this concern . . . which has thus far been a source of vexation and trouble rather than of profit."[85] "Wall Street" even then had the meaning it has earned today. John, throwing coal on his brother's despair, said, "I cannot help 'minding the price of the stock in Wall St.'—For I cannot resist the conviction that it will get worse and that we cannot hold it." At the end of the year a resolution to the financial crisis was largely achieved—"good feeling has been restored in Walnut St," as William Wurts put it.[86] William achieved a settlement with his partner and father-in-law Lentz and dissolved his partnership with Rodman, making it possible to "go on in the old business" with Charles. This outcome, although it cleared the air financially, was not truly satisfactory. William said flatly "the result of this business is a shame and disgrace to us all." In other respects matters had not improved: another D&H instalment of $15 had been called, and William opined "I fear it will plague you." Meanwhile, the Schuylkill stock, instead of improving, had fallen to 75.

Family issues added to the litany of troubles, and because of the customary closeness of the brothers were felt acutely. Charles had "imprudently engaged himself to Miss [Mary] Vanuxem & is desirous to get married in a hurry," as William put it.[87] Regrettably from the Wurts point of view, the young lady had "no resources to bring in aid of his slim means." As William phrased it, "she is an amiable fine girl . . . but he need not break his neck to secure her." William wisely recognized that no objections could be raised to the match, but sought to delay it for a year (advice that was not accepted). Writing on the last day of 1825, the year in which the D&H had been organized and begun construction and a year that should have brought great satisfaction to the Wurtses, William urged his brother to delay marriage because "we find our years work so unproductive."

NO WORK of equal magnitude has been constructed in Europe or America with such limited means in so short a period and with such persevering industry. ----Philip Hone, Oct. 10, 1828

Linking the Delaware and the Hudson

CONSIDERING THAT THE D&H was generally conceded to be the largest private undertaking of its time, we know distressingly little about its actual construction. The records deal mainly with formal matters such as contracting and expenditures. They tell us almost nothing about the people who built the canal----their lives, their hardships, even their names. Much of what we assume about the methods of construction derives from other canals. For example, a stump puller, a simple device but one that used mechanical advantage to great effect, had been invented on the Erie Canal.[1] Since many of the same engineers supervised the D&H, it is reasonable to assume that it and innovations such as improved plows were employed there as well, but there is no direct confirmation.

The tempestuous era of canal building is inextricably associated with the Irish, and with a vivid if tiresome folklore built around their reputation for six days of brutal toil rewarded by one day of riot. How much of this is true and how much the creation of local historians who felt that they needed such bombast to hold an unsophisticated audience is difficult to say. The heaviest influx of Irish, following the potato famine of the late 1840s, did not arrive until after the peak of canal building. However, there were already enough Irish in some parts of the country in the 1820s and 1830s to be conspicuous on canals and to add words like donnybrook and shillelagh to the language. Perhaps because they were living mainly in construction camps, the Irish of those decades were not as noticeable as their post-famine brethren, and one student has labelled them "Invisible Immigrants."[2] Another writer says simply, "They were among the ranks of those migrant laborers who have wandered from job to job throughout the ages, leaving very few records of their existence."[3]

Referring to the Erie Canal, Shaw notes that "The New York canal commissioners reported in 1819 that three-quarters of the laborers were 'born among us.' But after 1821 Irish and Welsh immigrants appeared in greater numbers."[4] On the Blackstone Canal, built at the same time as the D&H, it was reported that in 1826 fully 80% of the workers were Catholic Irish.[5] In the following decade Irish were conspicuous on the Chenango Canal.[6]

Information for the D&H is anecdotal. The D&H did not have the good fortune of being built during a census year, as was the Western RR of Massachusetts in 1840, so that a resolute enumerator could locate and count a colony of Irish workmen.[7] Irish names do not appear abundantly among the contractors on the D&H, but in the 1820s that is hardly surprising.[8] The strongest testimony to the presence of the Irish is provided by John W. Johnston, who as a boy witnessed the building of the

FACING PAGE
Old Fort Decker in Port Jervis served as a hotel and tavern, operated by Stephen St. John, during the time the D&H Canal was under construction. John B. Jervis stayed here while working in the vicinity. This folk art is probably the earliest surviving representation of the first boats that plied the canal. This is a facsimile of the original sign.
CREDIT
Minisink Valley Historical Soc., Port Jervis, NY.

◆ 47

Delaware & Hudson CANAL.

LABOURERS accustomed to the use of the Spade, or to working in Rock, will find employment on a line of forty miles of the above Canal. The Rock Work on the Delaware River is now going on, and the excavation of earth will proceed so soon as the season will permit. Persons wishing to reach the work from the North River, may land either at Kingston or Newburgh.
March 13, 1827.   JOHN BOLTON, President.

NOTICE.

THE Stockholders of the Morris Canal and Banking Company, are hereby required to pay an instalment of TWENTY Dollars on each share, at the Bank in Jersey City, on Wednesday the 28th inst. under penalty of forfeiture of all previous payments. By order of the Board of Directors.
J. T. TALMAN, Cashier.
Jersey City, June 13, 1828.   51,2w.

Newspaper notices.
CREDIT
Bill McKelvey.

D&H. Although he did not write his reminiscences until many decades later, his statement that "Every contractor employed, from necessity, a large number of laborers, mostly, and in many cases wholly, of Irish nationality" cannot be dismissed.[9] In the early stages of work the D&H advertised for laborers in New York, Connecticut and Pennsylvania newspapers.[10] This confirms that the local labor supply was not sufficient and creates an opening to which Irish could have responded.

One Irish worker is recorded by name in the D&H annals because he figured in an exceptional incident in the spring of 1826. This man, Patten, succeeded in blasting a rock about 40 feet high and 25 feet wide in Marbletown. Loading the hole with 70 pounds of powder, he not only dislodged the rock but "placed it so exactly on the bank of the canal, as to prove a substitute for the embankment."[11] Blasting was the most dramatic and dangerous feature of construction in the era before dynamite and electronic ignition. Johnston has provided a good description of how a charge was set off: After a suitable hole had been drilled by hand in the rock,

the requisite quantity of course [sic] grained powder was first deposited in the bottom of the drill hole, then the priming rod; a steel about 16 inches long, a ring at the top, about 3/8 in. at the ring and regularly and smoothly tapered to a point at the other end, was inserted to the extent of 1/2 in. or thereabout in the powder, held upright in the center of the hole and tamped around tightly as possible, usually with crushed stone and the priming rod carefully withdrawn by means of the ring.

Then the smaller opening left by the rod was filled with fine powder, forming a column supposed to connect with the charge at the bottom. In the top of this column was inserted a strip of match paper about one inch wide and a length sufficient to enable the blaster to escape to a place of safety, which being fired at the distant end continued to burn until its fire reached the powder and exploded the charge. The match paper was prepared by soaking brown paper in water impregnated with saltpeter, which when dried would burn more or less rapid according to the strength of the solution. Care was therefore required that too much saltpeter be not used, least [sic] the progress of the fire would prevent the escape of the blaster. Matches had not then been invented and the blaster was obliged to keep a small fire burning at a safe distance from his work as a means of lighting his match paper.[12]

Some of the Irish immigrants were skilled stonemasons, who employed their abilities in the precise fitting of the locks. Thanks to writers like Johnston, who had nothing good to say about the Irish, it is the more boisterous features of their reputation that have endured in folklore. "Sundays especially, with vengeance in their hearts, blood in their eyes, shelalales [sic] in their hands, probably whiskey in their stomaches [sic] and certain as a meeting took place a fight ensued." The most memorable Irish fracas on the Erie Canal was a clash between Orange and Green at Lockport in 1824, and even Johnston concedes that much of the discord he witnessed originated in the old country. He added, "To intensify the hostility and invigorate the action, the influence of whiskey was frequently invoked, a power at ready command . . . . Almost every Irish shanty holder . . . together with a number of the citizens maintained jug saloons."[13]

To Johnston's way of thinking, and those who have repeated similar accounts, the brawling had no higher purpose than recreation. One of the few serious studies of the issue was conducted by Peter Way, who investigated the chronic labor discord on the Chesapeake & Ohio between 1834 and 1840. He concludes that "Irish workers perpetuated the ritualized, internecine fighting common in Ireland, but, as in the old country, tribal clashes masked class conflict."[14] Irish workers, living on the edge of subsistence, resorted to violence to protect their paltry livelihood. Contractors, usually inadequately financed, were caught in the middle. On the D&H, as on the C&O, laborers were employed by contractors, not directly by the canal companies; but the D&H did not experience the money shortages that placed C&O contractors in a bind and thereby threatened the survival of the workers. Way's figures for wages on the C&O, beginning in 1828, are probably comparable to those on the D&H and are more fully documented. He found that laborers received $10-12 a month, plus board, while skilled workers were paid $2-2.50 a day.[15] One of the few figures that has been recorded for the D&H states that in 1825, at the outset of construction, men were paid $12 to $14 per month.[16]

At least one disturbance occurred on the D&H which superficially resembled the troubles on the C&O, but it was due to individual wrongdoing, rather than a company's financial weakness. Otis Button, a partner in a contracting firm, absconded with a $3000 payroll in July 1826. He was overtaken at Ithaca, and all but $400 was recovered. In the interim, however, the unpaid workers had rioted, and it reportedly became necessary to call out the militia. One correspondent editorialized that "People should be careful not to intercede unnecessarily in to an *Irish row*," indicating the nationality of at least some of the participants.[17]

The most fully documented episode of construction is the groundbreaking ceremony on July 13, 1825 that formally began it. A gathering of this sort on a high summer day in an isolated area that had made almost no previous impact on recorded history, among a population hungry for any diversion from its tedious routine, was sure to be memorable. There has been some difference of opinion as to the setting of this event, with Mamakating (present Wurtsboro, New York) and Summitville, or Beatysburg, about four miles away, being suggested. Strong evidence is provided by Philip Hone in the manuscript form of his diary, which states that the site was in "Rome, Mamakating Hollow." The best testimony as to the precise location of the event was provided by James S. McEntee, who although writing nearly 50 years later, had been a participant. McEntee states that ground was broken "in a field in the rear of Dr. Morrison's house."[18] Wherever the site, it had surely never witnessed a larger or more enthusiastic assembly.

The practice of turning the first earth at some point on the "summit" level, the stretch of high ground where no locks were necessary, had become customary. In these areas the work was less challenging, and rapid progress could be shown. The most familiar example occurred on the Erie Canal, where work was commenced on the long level at Rome, New York, on July 4, 1817. In an odd coincidence, Mamakating, before it became Wurtsboro, had been known as Rome. The Rome in the Mohawk Valley, on the site of historic Fort Stanwix, was a straggling village in 1817, but retained its name and went on to become a more important place. With the Declaration of Independence still within living memory, and in a time of spread-eagle patriotic fervor, it was becoming customary to begin grand public works on the Fourth of July. Possibly the D&H had planned to stage its event on that auspicious day but had run into some now-forgotten delay.

Articles of Agreement, *made and concluded*

the   day of   in the year eighteen hundred and twenty-

Between

of the one part, and the President, Managers and Company of the Delaware and Hudson Canal Company, of the other part, whereby it is covenanted and agreed as follows, to wit; The said

covenant and agree to construct in a good, substantial and workmanlike manner, all that part of the   Canal which is included in section

of the line of said Canal, and reference being herein had to the location of said line, and the maps thereof by the Engineer in the employment of said President, Managers and Company : The grubbing and clearing to be at least fifty feet wide, and laid out as shall be directed by the Engineer ; from which width all trees, saplings, bushes, stumps and roots shall be cut up, and together with logs, brush and wood of every description, shall be removed at least   feet from the centre of the Canal ; and a strip fifteen feet wide on

side, and adjoining the abovementioned grubbing, shall have all its trees, saplings, bushes and stumps, cut within one foot of the ground, and together with wood of every kind, shall be removed wholly without said strip ; and no part thereof, nor any other substance, shall be laid, felled or left on either of the sections adjoining this contract, unless permitted in writing by some Engineer on the Canal. All large trees, not embraced in the grubbing and clearing aforesaid, which stand within sixty feet of the centre of the Canal, and which by felling after the Canal is completed, might break the bank or obstruct the navigation, shall be cut down and removed as shall be directed : For a space of suitable width under each bank, all vegetable or perishable matter, and all porous earth, shall be excavated and wholly removed into the outside of the bank. The banks of the Canal shall be constructed of the most pure, solid and water-tight earth that can be obtained from the adjoining excavation ; and care shall be taken to place all coarse materials, or such as are perishable or permeable to water, entirely in the outer extremity of the banks ; and to form the inside of the banks of the most solid and water-tight earth that can be obtained as aforesaid. All earth necessarily excavated under or between the banks, shall be estimated as excavation ; and in all cases where the earth necessarily excavated is not to be removed more than   feet, to form the adjoining bank or banks, no estimate for embankment shall be made ; and wherever the prism of the Canal does not require any excavation, or falls short of being sufficient to form and complete the adjoining bank or banks, then the materials necessary to complete such embankment, shall be taken from the nearest surplus excavation, or such other place as the aforesaid Engineer shall direct ; The spoil banks, or surplus earth, shall be laid with as much evenness and regularity, and with as little injury to the adjoining lands as may be ; and all trees, logs, stumps, roots and bushes, shall be burned up or disposed of with a like precaution ; nor shall any unnecessary injury of any kind be done to the owner or owners of the adjoining land through which the Canal passes. No public or private road which crosses the Canal line, shall be obstructed by excavation or otherwise, until directions shall be given by one of the Engineers in the employment of the President, Managers and Company aforesaid, to complete the Canal across such road or highway ; nor shall any crops of grain, grass or vegetables, nor any dwelling houses or other building on said section be disturbed, unless by the direction of said Engineer, The Canal to be so constructed that the water shall be at least thirty-two feet wide at the top water line, twenty feet at the bottom, and four feet deep ; the banks shall be at least two feet perpendicular measurement above the top water line, and such a slope preserved, both above and below the top water line, as that one foot perpendicular rise shall give a horizontal base of eighteen inches. The surface of the towing path shall be at least ten feet wide, and the surface of the bank opposite the towing path shall be at least six feet wide. The landings for bridges across this section to be of such width, heighth and slopes as may be directed by said Engineer.

And the said

further agrees that

will perform this contract in every respect agreeable to the directions of the Engineer or Engineers employed by the Managers aforesaid, and that during the progress of said work,   will conform to such deviations from the present line of Canal, and such alterations in the form, slope and dimensions in the towing path, berm, or any of the other works, as said Engineer from time to time may direct : And it is mutually agreed that the said works during their progress, shall be carefully examined and inspected, and to prevent all disputes, litigation and misunderstanding, it is agreed that some competent Engineer in the employment, and to be selected by the said President, Managers and Company, shall be the inspectors of said works, and shall estimate the number of cubic yards of excavation, and the number of cubic yards of embankment, and the value of any extra work that may have been caused by an alteration of the line of Canal, and determine every other question necessary for the adjustment and final settlement of this contract, and his estimate and decision shall be final and conclusive, between said parties : And the said President, Managers and Company, covenant and agree to pay to the said

for completing this contract as aforesaid, the sum of
dollars for grubbing, and at the rate of   cents per cubic yard for excavation,
and

cents per cubic yard for embankment, including bridge embankments

And it is further agreed, that if in the opinion of said Engineer in the employment of said Company, the said

shall refuse or unreasonably neglect to prosecute this contract, as shall be required by said President and Managers, or their Engineer, such Engineer shall have the power of determining that he has abandoned it, and such determination shall exonerate the said President, Managers and Company from every obligation imposed on them by this contract, and they may immediately thereafter proceed to dispose of the said section in the same manner as if this contract had never existed.   And it is further agreed, that whenever this contract in the opinion of said Engineer, shall be completely performed on the part of the said

the said Engineer shall certify the same in writing under his hand,
together with his estimate as aforesaid; and the said President, Managers and Company shall, within ten days after notice of such certificate, pay to the said

the sum which according to this contract, and the said estimate shall be due   PROVIDED, HOWEVER, and it is
expressly covenanted and agreed, on the part of the said

that this contract shall be fully performed and completed on
part by the   day of   in the year eighteen hundred and
twenty-

SIGNED, SEALED AND DEDIVERED IN THE }
PRESENCE OF   }

On July 13, 1825 the main address was given by Philip Hone. It has been remarked, especially in *Century of Progress*, that his speech was generally devoid of those pompous rhetorical flourishes that were characteristic of the time. Hone may not have been a frequent or noteworthy orator; it is likely that his persuasive skills were more suited to smaller, convivial gatherings. More importantly, he was not merely a dignitary brought in to lend prestige to the occasion, but the president and a major investor in the company. He felt it was his task to win understanding and support for the D&H from a sometimes skeptical audience. That is why, as has been noted, he spent a significant portion of his speech explaining the choice of the Ulster route over the Orange and assuring that rival projects such as the Orange & Sussex Canal did not represent a serious threat.

In the one passage in which Hone indulged in the flowery style of his day it was with the practical purpose of reminding his listeners that they were under some obligation to assist the company, or at least not obstruct it:

> But from you, Citizens of Orange, Sullivan, and Ulster, we have a right to expect something more, and judging by the friendly co-operation and support which many of you have hitherto afforded us, we have no apprehension that our expectations will be disappointed. We are preparing to open for you the means of communication with a sister State, rich in the productions of the soil and possessing an inexhaustible supply of coal, which from its situation and the imperfect navigation of the Rivers, is of little more value than the rich Gems which the dark unfathomable Caves of Ocean bear. The products of your own farms and the Timber of your own Forests will also be increased in value to an incalculable

FACING PAGE AND ABOVE
D&H Canal contract.
CREDIT
Wurts Papers, Hagley Museum & Library, Wilmington, DE.

amount by the facilities which will be afforded to you of conveying them with little Labour and expence to a Market, always calling for supplies and never supplied.[19]

Jervis, sobersided even as a young man, remarked that he "could not see the value of all this parade for so small an amount of work." One of the directors present, Abraham Hasbrouck of Rondout, replied "What would this world be good for if there was no good eating." This expressed the more congenial tradition of the Hudson Valley Dutch, for which Jervis had little sympathy, but he was at least good humored enough to tell this story on himself.[20]

On the same day contracts were signed to build 34 sections of a half-mile each. It will be recalled that a final decision had not yet been made on the route into Kingston, but there was no reason to delay work on the portions that were agreed. Additional sections were gradually let, and on December 6, 1825 the last remaining portions between the Hudson and the Delaware were put under contract. By then, with frost penetrating the ground, the time for shallow digging was coming to an end, and only deep excavation could continue. Most of the contractors had not been able to begin before September, so the 1825 construction season was a short one. Jervis had written on November 25 that the ground was already freezing and added that "common cutting" would soon have to be discontinued.[21] Though abbreviated, the season had been busy—1000 men were employed in September, according to one report.[22] By the end of the year Wright certified that work totaling $68,000 had been accomplished, and although only a small section of less than a mile had been completed, several other sections were nearly finished. Wright reported on February 4, 1826 that 500 men were working on the canal, mostly engaged in stone work for the locks, blasting, and deep excavation.[23]

By then Philip Hone had been replaced as president by John Bolton. Hone submitted his resignation January 7, 1826 because he had been selected mayor of New York. At that time mayors were not popularly elected; otherwise the refined benefactor of the future metropolis probably would not have offered his services. Even then, the office proved too contentious for Hone's taste, and he held it less than a year. Nevertheless, many writers on the D&H make much of referring to him as Mayor. While never again holding company office, he remained a prominent member of the D&H board until his death in 1851. Hone's experience at the D&H ceremony came in handy a few months later when he represented his city in Albany at the festival marking the opening of the Erie Canal.

Little is known of Bolton beyond what is contained in *Century of Progress*. Orphaned at an early age, he grew up in the South, and in the New York business world made a name as a competent financial manager. His position on the D&H was apparently based on his ability as, with only 30 shares in his name, he was not a large stockholder.[24] Despite having been born in Philadelphia, he was certainly not the choice of the Wurts Brothers. Their correspondence reveals many indications that they distrusted him.

In his report Wright expressed the hope that the 64-mile "overland" section between the namesake rivers in New York state and extending around to Saw Mill Rift on the Delaware, would be completed in 1826. This proved to be overly optimistic, although not by much. One reason for delay, problems with contractors, had already occurred. The most conspicuous example concerned Rensselaer Schuyler, who despite owning two of the noblest names in New York had his contract for building locks annulled in November 1825.[25] This contract had been given verbally by Maurice Wurts in June—a month ahead of the official commencement.[26] Schuyler claimed he had misunderstood some of the terms, but Benjamin Wright, ordered by the board to investigate, found that Schuyler "has not obeyed the directions and specifications in his contract." Although describing it as "unpleasant and a duty I would willingly avoid," Wright concluded by saying that he felt "a loss of confidence in the good intentions of the contractor."[27] This was surely an embarrassment to the family, although not nearly as severe as the one that shocked the financial community in the 1850s when Robert Schuyler, president of the New York & New Haven RR and a grandson of Gen. Philip Schuyler, was found to have embezzled large amounts of the company's funds.[28] With sympathy for Rensselaer Schuyler, and perhaps unwilling to offend the influential family further, the D&H appeased him with a payment of $1500 for his services and another $1200 for labor and materials.[29]

In August 1826 there was a potentially devastating splurge of contract cancellations.[30] The January 24 contract of James Ledgerwood, John Ledgerwood and Andrew Lawrence to construct the aqueduct over the Rondout near "the great falls" was cancelled for "having unreasonably neglected to prosecute the said work." A contract with these individuals to build locks 40, 41, 46, 47 and 48 was cancelled on the same grounds, as was a contract to build locks 40, 42, 43, 44, 45 and 49. Assuming the numbering system at that time was the same used when the canal was in operation, these defaults affected the series of locks descending from the summit at Phillipsport and represented a shocking total of nearly 18% of the locks in the overland section.

Despite these setbacks, dramatic progress on the canal during the summer of 1826 brought Wright's prediction close to fruition. At the peak of activity there were about 2500 men and 200 teams working on the canal.[31] The stones that were being hauled and set in that corner of southern New York formed only a small part of an exciting national boom. It was a dynamic period in American history, when the adolescent nation, conscious of its awakening powers, was reaching beyond its childhood limits to break the strings that had confined it to the Atlantic seaboard—"a busy, bustling, industrious population, hacking and hewing their way" through a vast continent, in the words of the maligned English visitor Frances Trollope. Much of this youthful energy was devoted to "internal improvements." In studying the canal era, or, less grandly, "canal mania," Harvey Segal has identified three distinct cycles of activity: (1815-1834, with a peak in 1828; 1834-1844, peaking in 1840; and 1844-1860), related to broad trends in the national economy and fluctuations in the enthusiasm of canal promoters. Chris Baer has plotted this graphically, except that his chart places the peak, in terms of miles added, in 1829 and 1830—immediately after the completion of the D&H. Both agree that the D&H falls near the climax of the first cycle.[32]

The United States at that stage of its history, like most adolescents, was characterized by uneven social development. It combined in uncertain proportions the inherited European culture, with most of its class distinctions, and an unruly, barely domesticated frontier element. How these extremes would mix in any given situation was wildly unpredictable. One social skill at which the young nation already excelled was the staging of ceremonial events. The solemnities that had marked the beginning of work in July 1825 left everyone satisfied that the project had been launched under the proper auspices. Now, as the New York portion drew to a close, the occasion demanded formal confirmation. In addition to the natural propensities of the populace, the Masonic order was powerful, with members occupying high places, from Governor Clinton on down. Ritual was a central

𝔖𝔭𝔢𝔠𝔦𝔣𝔦𝔠𝔞𝔱𝔦𝔬𝔫𝔰 of the manner of building Locks on the
Delaware & Hudson Canal.

The LOCKS to be composed of dry wall masonry, to support the embankment, and to have a facing of timber and plank to make it water tight. The main wall to be ninety eight feet (exclusive of timber at the head) in length, with suitable buttresses at the head. The wing walls at the foot to be fifteen feet in length. The chamber to be nine feet and four inches wide in the clear; and seventy six feet between the upper and lower quoins, and for four feet draught of water.

SPECIFICATION 1st.—The LOCK PIT, to be excavated as shall be directed by the Engineer for said Canal, and the bottom made smooth and level, so as to give a firm and uniform bearing to the foundation timber.

2nd. FOUNDATION.—Timber to be ten inches thick, well counterlined on the upper side, and not less than nine inches wide. To be placed at uniform distances, according to its width, so as to occupy or cover at least three fifths of the area of the foundation. To be of sufficient length to extend, at least four inches past the back line of walls. The foundation to be extended five feet above the head of lock, and to be thirty five in width at this extremity. The spaces between the timbers to be well filled, and puddled with fine hard gravel.

SHEET PILING.—A course across the head of foundation not less than four feet deep, (and six if required,) and thirty five feet in length; Two other courses, one under the lower miter sill, and one at the foot of wing walls; each course to be six feet deep, and twenty five and a half feet long. The sheet piling to be of two inch plank and lined with inch boards. A ditch to be excavated to receive the sheet piling, which are to be placed edge to edge, and the top well spiked to the foundation timber. The space excavated to be filled up with fine hard gravel, well puddled in, so as to render the work impervious to water.

3rd. FLOORING—Of two and a half inch plank, to be laid over the whole foundation timber, well jointed and every plank well treenailed, with two treenails at every three feet in length, to enter the timber at least five inches. On this floor the superstructure to be erected.

4th. CROSS TIMBERS—To support upper miter sill, running across and extending six inches under each wall; to be of white oak timber, sixteen inches deep and two or three sticks as may be most convenient to form a solid platform thirty four inches wide, well jointed together and covered with a flooring of three inch plank, on which the miter sill is to be placed.

5th. MITER SILLS—To be made of best quality white oak timber; the form and dimensions, to be agreeable to the plan and directions of the aforesaid Engineer: to be well jointed and bolted to the foundation timbers, with bolts of iron eighteen inches long, and one inch square, well ragged and headed: there shall be four bolts in each miter sill.

6th. LONGITUDINAL SILLS—Of white oak timber, to be eight by fifteen inches, placed on the foundation plank and well treenailed to the foundation timber: to be morticed and boxed to receive the side posts: to extend along on each side from breast wall to foot of lock or to twelve feet below lower gates.

7th. SECOND FLOORING or LINING—Of two inch white pine plank, to be well jointed, and laid on the foundation of chamber above upper miter sill, and a course twelve feet long below lower miter sill; to be well and firmly jointed to longitudinal and miter sills, so as to make a water tight flooring; each plank to be well treenailed with two treenails at each end, and one at each intermediate foundation timber; the treenails to be nine inches long: the plank to butt, or the end joint come over the foundation timber, so as to give a firm hold to the treenails.

8th. CROSS SILLS—Of hemlock timber, extend across between the longitudinal sills, on the second floor of foundation: those below and near the gates are boxed one and a half inches in the longitudinal sills, and the remainder drove in firmly without framing; the whole to be well treenailed to the foundation.

9th. TIMBERS AND PLANKING FOR WING SHEETING—For head of lock and for breast wall; to be of hemlock, and lined with inch pine boards; (except the wing sheeting, which is not to be lined.) For dimensions and manner of construction, see plan and bill of timber and plank, furnished by the aforesaid Engineer.

10. POSTS—Quoin and recess posts, and also posts at foot of lock, of white oak timber: other side posts of white pine timber: to have a tenon on the lower end of three inches, and enter a boxing of an inch deep in the sill; and to have a tenon of six inches on the top to receive the plate or coping timber. The quoin posts to have two tenons on the top, one to receive the chamber plate, and the other to receive the recess plate. For the number and dimensions of posts, see plan and bill of timber and plank referred to in ninth specification.

11th. PLATE OR COPING—Of white pine timber, ten by twelve inches, framed to receive and surmount the side posts, and also to receive the land ties on the top by a dovetailed joint. To extend along the whole length of walls, from rear of head buttress to lower end of wing walls; the whole surmounted with two inch pine plank, as per plan above referred to.

12th. DRY STONE MASONRY—Main wall, to be six feet thick on the foundation, and carried up plumb eight feet high, and then offset on the back one foot, leaving the wall five feet thick, and carrying the same plumb to a level with the under side of coping timber. Recesses to be made in the face of the walls to receive the gates, and suitable projections in the back of the walls to give stability to the work opposite the recesses. Buttresses, at the head extend back to a point eight feet from the face of main walls. Wing walls at foot of lock at the end adjoining main walls, to be of the same dimensions as main walls; at their extremity to be of such form and dimensions, as may be directed by the aforesaid Engineer. Breast wall to extend across from side wall to side wall, three feet thick and nine feet and a half high.

13th. LAND TIES—Of chesnut timber, to be well dovetailed and treenailed to the plate coping, and framed on the top of an anchor timber, which is to be placed vertically against the back of wall. The dimensions and number of ties and anchors to be agreeable to the plan and directions of the aforesaid Engineer.

14th. SIDING OR FACING—A siding of one inch pine boards, to be put on the face of the whole work, and lined with a course of one and a half inch pine plank. The boards to be good square edges, and put on as tight as may be without jointing. The plank to be well jointed, and spiked on with spikes six inches long, and a quarter of an inch square ; every plank to have at least two spikes in each post it embraces. Proper rabbets to be formed in the post, and on the under side of the plates to receive the plank flush. The whole to be made as impervious to water as practicable.

15th. FENDER TIMBERS—At head of lock to protect the corners, to be thirty feet long and twelve inches square, of hemlock timber.

16th. GATES—To be made of best quality white oak timber, except the ballance beams and planking, which are to be of white pine timber. To be constructed on a plan similar to those heretofore constructed on said Canal ; which plan is to be furnished by the Engineer aforesaid.

PADDLE GATES—To be made of best quality white oak plank two and a half inches thick at center, and uniformly taper to one and a half inches at the edges : to be two feet high, and eighteen inches wide in the clear : a rabbet to be made in the paddle studs three fourths of an inch deep, and plated with an iron plate a quarter of an inch thick, for the gate to shut against. A cast iron box set in the lower bar, for the paddle rod to work in : also cast iron boxes and pivots for hanging the main lock gates. All the irons for the locks to be in number and dimensions, agreeably to the plan and directions of said Engineer.

BALLANCE BEAMS—To be painted with two coats of oil and Spanish brown.

17th. EMBANKMENTS—To be twenty feet wide on the tow path side, and sixteen feet wide on the berm side of the lock ; (measuring from the face of lock) to have a slope of one and a half horizontal to one perpendicular, and carried up to a level with the top of lock, extending from head of lock to foot of wing walls. When the excavation for foundation extends beyond the ends of lock, the same shall be filled (by the contractor for the lock) to a level with the natural surface of the ground.

18th. For a more full explanation of the form and manner of constructing the locks in all their parts and details, and of the character and quality of the materials to be used ; a plan with a bill of timber and plank, will be furnished by the aforesaid Engineer ; who will also give such directions from time to time, during the progress of the work, as may appear to him necessary and proper, in order to make the work complete and perfect on the plan contemplated by the above specifications. And the work shall be performed in every respect agreeably to the directions of said Engineer.

---

feature of Masonic practice, and the order's involvement assured that the proceedings produced the desired pomp.

To the gratitude of the multitude, there were actually two celebrations, spaced just far enough apart that each could be savored fully. Both followed scripts that had been rehearsed on the Erie Canal, completed a year before. The first occasion marked the completion of the aqueduct over Rondout Creek at High Falls on September 2; and the second, on November 25, 1826, dedicated the tidewater lock at Eddyville. Each was carefully staged so that every element contributed to making the occasion memorable. At High Falls the ceremony centered around the placing of the keystone in one arch of the aqueduct. A small recess had been cut in the keystone, into which was placed a copper box containing silver plates, coins and an inscribed medallion. The stone was also engraved with letters, Masonic symbols and the numerals 1826. A reporter described how "the High Priest, King, Scribe and Captain of the Host of Mount Horeb Chapter No.75 made their appearance, dressed in the gorgeous habiliments of their ancient Order, and placing themselves at the head of the Lodges two abreast, the whole moved off with a lively air from the Kingston Band, to the apex of the arch." After the completion of Masonic rituals and speeches, the crowd adjourned to "a triangular table embowered in an orchard upon the top of the precipice" for an appropriate conclusion to the day's events.[33] It is puzzling how the aqueduct could have been completed at that time, since the contract for it had been cancelled less than four weeks earlier, and the new contract was supposed to have a completion date of October 1.[34] The work could not have started before 1826, as Jervis on November 25, 1825 was only at the stage of asking Maurice Wurts to bring up plans for the aqueducts and bridges.[35]

Determined to outdo the September ceremony, the neighboring Kingston lodge staged an even grander event at Eddyville twelve weeks later. On this occasion the final stone, or "perfect ashlar," of the tidewater lock was consecrated with impressive Masonic ceremony. A canal boat, the *Morning Star*, brought a load of guests from Twaalfskill landing on the Kingston waterfront; others traveled overland.

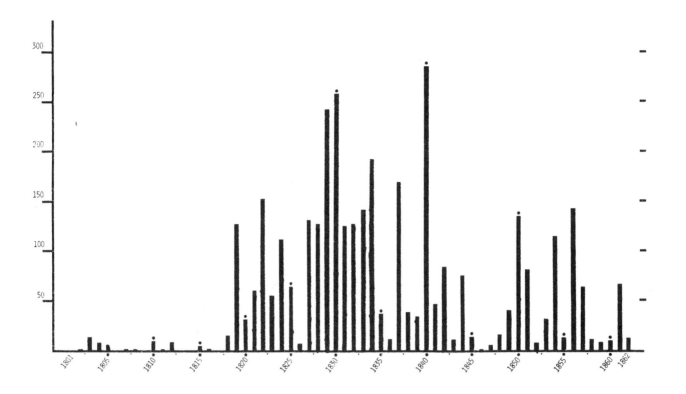

Cannon were discharged along the route and once again the Kingston Band accompanied the procession with rousing music. The boat rose in the lock beneath an arch of evergreens, after which President Bolton, Maurice Wurts, engineers Jervis and McEntee, and the builders came on board. In the words of a contemporary account, "At this juncture, a tow-line was attached to the boat, and two noble, well-trained horses, gorgeously caparisoned, drew her rapidly out of the lock, to the roar of an old *Thirteener* from the heights and *Yankee Doodle* from the band."

The boat apparently passed through the guard lock and upstream in the Rondout as far as Creek Locks, although that place was as yet unnamed. What might have seemed a disturbing portent occurred when the boat was grounded soon after entering the canal, due to the weight of spectators and the premature opening of a lower lock, but on this festive occasion no one was going to credit gloomy omens. After the boat returned to Eddyville the commemorative stone, accompanied by two inscribed marble slabs, was set with elaborate benedictions.

After speeches and blessings the crowd adjourned to what some undoubtedly considered the primary attraction—"an elegant cold collation" at the hostelry known as the Stone House. It was noted that some participants, inspired by the brisk Rondout air, "showed a disposition to attack the viands without further ceremony," but this impulse was detained by the realization that saying grace was required. At the close of the repast a total of 20 formal toasts were proclaimed to musical accompaniment. These declarations were intended for publication and are formal in tone; any thrusts of humor would have been extemporaneous. Jervis, ever serious, was in his element, hailing "The Internal Improvements of our country— They demonstrate the superior intelligence, and the moral energy, of a free People." Other salutes recognized Governor Clinton, the company, agent Maurice Wurts, the builders, the engineers, and generally the glories of the vigorous young republic.[36]

The festivities did not quite mark the completion of the overland section, but came close. At that point water was already being let in between the eastern end of the summit level and the Delaware. It was anticipated that the remainder would be finished in two weeks.[37] To their chagrin, the managers had to postpone the celebration of the completion to the following spring—attributing the decision to the uncomfortable weather and the possible interference with more urgent work on the canal.[38]

It was far too late in the season to consider using any part of the waterway that year, and even in 1827 a great deal of adjustment was needed. Nevertheless, it was a remarkable achievement to have built a canal more than 60 miles long in only about 18 months from the date of the first contract. By comparison, a generation earlier it had taken ten years (1793-1803) to construct the Middlesex Canal, only 27 miles long and built to smaller dimensions through a relatively highly developed part of Massachusetts.[39] In fairness, the Middlesex had been compelled to devise most of the construction techniques that were borrowed by all later canals. A more valid comparison is with the Farmington Canal, begun July 4, 1825 and built through generally similar country in neighboring New England. The Connecticut section of this waterway, 58 miles long and having roughly the same proportion of locks per mile as the D&H, took more than three years to complete.[40] Another contemporary New England canal, the Blackstone, required about four years to complete its 45 miles. Like the D&H, this canal averaged about a lock per mile. A later canal, the Chenango in central New York, one of the Erie laterals, built 97 miles in only three years, but benefited from the steady flow of state funding.[41]

FACING PAGE
GRAPH
Canals: Miles Added 1801-1862
CREDIT
From Christopher T. Baer, *Canals and Railroads of the Mid-Atlantic States, 1800-1860*, courtesy Hagley Museum & Library.

PHOTO
Arches of the original aqueduct at High Falls remained in place after replacement by the suspension aqueduct.
CREDIT
D&H Canal Museum.

A factor in the rapid completion of the canal was the early discovery of natural hydraulic cement along the route, in the vicinity of High Falls and Rosendale. A similar stroke of good fortune had facilitated the building of the Erie Canal, and until the discovery along the D&H it was expected that cement would have to be brought from Chittenango or other points on the Erie. Traditionally this find has been considered a lucky accident, but a D&H report speaks of "a geologist who was specially employed for that purpose."[42] If so, it is another example in which the D&H managers, cautious businessmen in many respects, displayed a surprisingly modern reliance on scientific opinion and technology. According to James S. McEntee, Simeon Depuy had a contract to grind all the cement used on the canal at his mill in High Falls.[43] The unexpected abundance of cement allowed the D&H to use it for "the whole mass of the mason work of our Locks," instead of only two feet of the interior.[44]

While their main energies were devoted to building the canal, the managers also had to prepare to operate it. Since there was some hope of using the canal in 1826, these plans took on considerable urgency. On March 1, 1826 the board directed the engineers "to inform them what particular situations on or near the line of the canal in their judgment will become objects of value . . . either as places of deposit [or] from their hydraulic privileges." It was stressed "that secrecy be enjoined on them."[45] The hope of profiting from sale of waterpower ("hydraulic privileges") as had been done on other canals was a persistent delusion in the early history of the D&H but seems never to have been realized to a significant extent. In this respect the experience of the D&H was similar to the Erie Canal.[46] Quite the opposite happened, and in 1838, when a long-bubbling dispute erupted, the board warned mill owners at Eddyville that it would take whatever measures were necessary to guarantee a water supply if they did not repair their dam.[47]

In April and May the company purchased substantial properties at Rondout. These consisted of the former Philip Swarts farm of about 50 acres, a six-acre lot with buildings and a dock, and a two-thirds interest in a 16-acre lot commonly called Caats Basin and formerly owned by Jacobus Van Gaasbeck.[48] Other sizable properties were acquired at the site that became Port Jervis and at the point where the Mongaup joined the Delaware.

There was still hope of partial operation in 1826 when the managers, on August 19, prepared a tariff listing tolls on the canal. This developed into an annual ritual, as each year the managers fixed a detailed list of rates for every commodity that could conceivably be transported on their waterway. Another obvious concern was boats. The minutes of August 30, 1826 record payment of C. Bergh & Company's bill for building a pattern boat, and on October 18 the board authorized building a boat designed to carry lumber and wood, which would cost less than the coal boats. A contract with the firm of Vedder & Barhydt to build 20 canal boats at $350 each had been ratified on July 12 (presumably Bergh's pattern boat had been finished by then).[49] Vedder & Barhydt were progressing rapidly at their yard in Mamakating (later Wurtsboro). One visitor in September found that "At this time there is one boat on the stocks, which in all probability will be launched in about a fortnight—a month since the timber was growing in our forests."[50] Haste that would have been risky in a seagoing vessel was evidently acceptable on the D&H Ocean. In December 1826, after hopes of using the canal that year had faded, the managers optimistically looked ahead and ordered Wright to prepare plans for locktenders' houses.

It was an remarkable achievement for the managers, busy with other activities and usually meeting no more than once a week, to supervise the construction of the canal while making arrangements to operate it. None of the managers had any known experience running a canal. Maurice Wurts, their agent, also lacked experience and, besides, was occupied negotiating with a multitude of contractors and landowners and was not able to attend board meetings regularly. Presumably they all relied for guidance on the small corps of engineers, most of whom were graduates of the Erie; yet the engineers themselves were absorbed in the unending pressure of building the canal and probably had little time for long-range planning.

Another Financial Crisis

ANYONE FAMILIAR WITH THE MANAGEMENT STYLE OF THE D&H would have reason to suspect that the festivity at Eddyville had deeper motivation than providing entertainment. If the intent was to portray the D&H as a dynamic enterprise on the verge of enormous success, there was a compelling reason; for at that moment the company had virtually exhausted its initial capital. Figures provided a short time later showed that the company had spent $772,000 on the canal between the Hudson and the Delaware, in addition to $37,000 up the Delaware, $20,500 for land, boats and equipment to operate the canal, and the $40,000 paid for the Wurts property. In addition to this total of $869,500 already spent, contracts brought the projected expenditure to $1,200,000—considerably beyond the $1 million capital stock dedicated to building the canal.[51]

This should have come as no surprise to the managers; in essence, it was merely time for them to face the consequences of accepting the revisions to Sullivan's plan that Jervis and Wright had recommended. In his speech at the groundbreaking Hone conceded that these changes would cost $400,000 extra. Subsequent improvements further increased the cost. In late 1825 the board had decided to build the Rondout aqueduct entirely of stone, instead of using wood in the trunk. This was partly compensated in January 1827 when it adopted the "composite" locks, with a

Boatbuilding at Creek Locks in a later era.
CREDIT
D&H RR Collection, New York State Library.

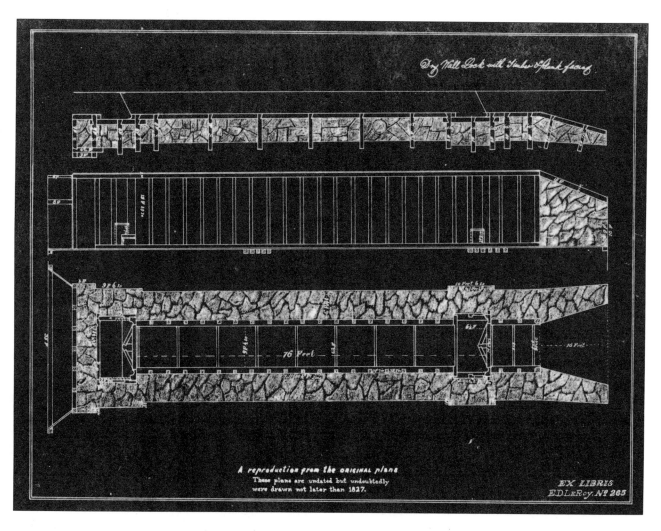

Dry Wall Lock with Timber Plank facing

A reproduction from the original plans
These plans are undated but undoubtedly
were drawn not later than 1827.

EX LIBRIS
E.D.LeRoy. Nº 265

replaceable wooden chamber supported by dry-laid stone walls, originally proposed by the discredited Sullivan, but now endorsed by Jervis.[52] Eventually 13 of these wood-lined locks were put in place on the Delaware section and 37 more on the Lackawaxen.[53] Revisions alone were not enough to account for the shortfall; the amount projected for the canal was simply inadequate—hardly the last time that happened.

Of three alternatives, the first—drawing on the $500,000 banking stock to build the canal—was dismissed as possibly illegal; unfair to holders of that stock, who may have not been identical with owners of the canal stock; and still inadequate to complete the work. The company was not authorized to issue more stock, and the amount required was far too great to remain unfunded. More critically, as was acknowledged subsequently, the D&H stock was then depressed and could not have been sold at anything near par.[54] The best course of action seemed to be to turn to the state for assistance. It was probably no accident that at the Eddyville gala the 20th and last toast was drunk to Governor DeWitt Clinton, "Father of our internal improvements." In his annual address on January 2, 1827 Governor Clinton responded by declaring that there was no private corporation "entitled to more commendation and public favor" than the D&H.[55]

Less than a month after the Eddyville bash the D&H board decided to ask the New York State Legislature for:

—a loan of $500,000,

—state subscription to $500,000 of stock,

—permission to use the entire existing stock to build the canal and to issue $1,000,000 of new banking stock,

—rights to operate a toll bridge over the Neversink,

—exemption from taxation until the company's profits reached 6%,

—authorization to extend the canal up the Delaware to Deposit, New York.

All the provisions but the first were eventually deleted, and the loan passed with only sniping opposition. The bill became law on March 10, 1827, and a few days later the D&H granted the state a mortgage of its property as surety.[56] The result was an odd hybrid security, called "New York State Stock" but which paid quarterly interest of 5%, had to be reimbursed after 20 years, at the state's discretion, and was treated as debt in the company's accounts.

Probably the financial uncertainty accounts for the otherwise puzzling reluctance of the D&H board to begin contracting the Delaware and Pennsylvania sections. Three times in late 1826 the board put off action on this vital matter. On December 9, when the subject was made the special order of the day, it was Philip Hone, characteristically cautious, who made the motion to postpone. The other members found it difficult to oppose a colleague with such prestige (and ownership of stock). Unless there was a prospect of someone else building the Pennsylvania section—and no such savior was visible—it is difficult to see how the company could be satisfied with only the New York canal. The hesitation is understandable

New-York State 5 per cent Stock.

STATE OF NEW-YORK,
Comptroller's Office.

Albany, March 16th, 1827.

Be it Known, That the People of the State of New-York are indebted to the President, Managers and Company of the Delaware and Hudson Canal Company, or their order, in the sum of one thousand Dollars, bearing interest at the rate of five per cent per annum from the day of the date hereof, payable quarterly, on the first day of the months of January, April, July, and October; being Stock created in pursuance of an Act of the Legislature of the State of New-York, passed 10th March, 1827: The principal of which Stock is reimbursable at the pleasure of this State, at any time after the year 1847; the interest to be paid at the office of the said Company, in the City of New-York, which debt is recorded in the office of the said Company in the city of New-York, and is transferable only by appearance in person, or by attorney, according to the provisions of the above recited act.

In Testimony whereof, I have hereunto set my hand, and affixed the seal of my office, the day and year above written.

Dep. Comp.   Comp.

NEW YORK STATE STOCK

1000 DOLLARS.

only as a consequence of financial anxiety. It was only on January 3, 1827, one day after Governor Clinton's endorsement, that the board gave the go-ahead to complete the canal. Several months later, on June 9, the board formally thanked President Bolton "for his successful exertions" in obtaining the critical loan and awarded him a $1000 bonus.[57] The last financial obstacles to completing the transportation system from the Hudson to the mines seemed to have been removed. To its credit, the D&H frankly conceded the importance of the state loan. In its 1828 annual report it acknowledged that "The loan of the credit of the state relieved your Board of Managers from the pecuniary difficulties with which they were threatened and assures the completion of the great work in which you are engaged."

When it applied for and accepted the state loan, the character of the D&H changed in a fundamental sense. Until then, as it frequently boasted, it was entirely a private enterprise, which placed it in the minority among canals. Goodrich estimates that $195 million was spent on canal construction in the period 1815 to 1860, of which 62% represented public works.[58] Harvey Segal comes up with a similar total of $188 million, of which an even larger proportion, 73%, was provided by state and municipal governments.[59]

The D&H was probably the largest of the private canals. It is claimed that it was the first million-dollar company in America. This is another way of saying that it was the largest private enterprise of its time. Thomas Dickson, a later president of the D&H, described the canal as "the largest undertaking that had ever been entered into upon the continent by any corporation," and although that assertion was made in 1875, it will stand until or unless a stronger claimant comes forward.[60] It has been claimed that the D&H was the only privately owned canal that operated in two states, but that assertion is simply erroneous. The Blackstone, the Farmington, the Susquehanna & Tidewater and perhaps others share this distinction. True, each required separate state charters, and the Farmington was composed of segments with different names, but these were only legal formalities. It is significant that although the D&H operated in two states it looked exclusively to New York for assistance. There was apparently no thought of turning to Harrisburg even though the main purpose of the additional funding was to complete the system in Pennsylvania and develop that state's resources.

Completing the Canal

IN 1827 THE AFFAIRS OF THE D&H increased in complexity, for the managers were simultaneously building one part of the canal while attempting to operate another portion. On April 4, 1827 the board instructed the chief engineer to survey and begin contracting the Pennsylvania section. By then Benjamin Wright, his expertise in demand all over the country, no longer held the position of chief engineer on the D&H. He had resigned on March 4 and been replaced by John B. Jervis, a protégé, but a man quite different in temperament.[61] Shortly after being assured of state aid, the managers began contracting the rest of the canal, a process which ended when James McEntee was instructed to let the remainder of the locks up the Lackawaxen on June 11. To demonstrate that it was a truly open bid, Maurice Wurts told the engineer "Please give all convenient publicity to this information."[62]

According to the 1828 annual report, bad weather in the fall of 1827 delayed the work, but an unexpectedly mild winter made up much of the loss. A report from agent Maurice Wurts on September 18, 1827 noted that 1700 men were working on excavation, with more than 300 others engaged in the skilled work on locks, aqueducts, bridges, lining and roads. A few contractors had abandoned their work but had been replaced.[63] Because of the favorable weather, some 600 men were able to go on working during the winter.

Perhaps the tradition of Irish involvement with building the D&H is more accurate on the Pennsylvania section. LeRoy, without citing a source, notes that a large barracks for housing Irish laborers was built at Hawley (then Paupack Eddy) and adds the obligatory comment that the workers "soon became the terror of the countryside."[64] There were so few people living in that part of Pennsylvania that it may well have been necessary to import outside laborers. The work was concentrated in a short distance, so that it would have been advantageous to gather the laborers in large camps, which made it easier to supply them.

One of the major difficulties of the work was damming the Delaware to create a section of water calm enough to permit canal boats to float from the Pennsylvania to the New York sides. A further complication was that the dam required a "sluice" 100 feet wide so that rafts could pass down the river. At one point the raftsmen complained about this construction, and Jervis provides an vivid account of how the engineers had to modify the dam. Water was overflowing the dam and, since it was March "the water from the melting snow was very cold."

Canal laborers.
CREDIT
National Canal Museum.

The carpenters considered the work impossible, leaving it to the three resident engineers, James Archbald, John T. Clark and Russel F. Lord.

> Such was the force of the current, they were only able to support themselves by reaching out and boring holes in the apron timbers, into which they drove a long pin and this pin was their foothold for that reach of their work. And so step by step they carried the work forward, the carpenters following. They began immediately after breakfast, and the flashing was completed at two o'clock in the afternoon. The engineers drank no liquor, but the carpenters thought whiskey indispensible; the latter gave out before the work was done, and left the engineers alone to complete it . . . . After their work they changed their wet clothes for dry, and reported they felt no harm from the severe exposure. Their minds supported their bodies.[65]

This story was full of the kind of moral lessons Jervis valued, but also illustrates the attitudes that drove the engineers. Beyond their salary, they were energized by the excitement of creating a great internal improvement that expressed the vigorous optimism of the era, a phenomenon that would be seen again and again as the profession matured.

This dynamic spirit was much in evidence at a jubilee in Bethany, Pennsylvania, on July 4, 1827. Local leaders, ever imaginative where an opportunity for festivities presented itself, combined the commemoration of national independence with a celebration of the D&H, even though the canal was still in the early stages of construction in that area. All the usual features were present: artillery and musket salutes, music, prayer, a dinner, and copious oratory. The D&H itself was well represented, with President Bolton in attendance, as well as Maurice and John Wurts. Twelve separate toasts were recorded, with several recognizing the exceptional exertions of Maurice Wurts. In the main speech of the day, L. C. Judson lauded Wurts in extravagant terms: "If we view him leaving the enjoyments of a refined city, alone and unknown, exploring the unfrequented valley, examining the various water courses, and climbing the rugged mountains which lie between the coal beds and the Hudson . . . and see him at length on Shawangunk's lofty summit, viewing with an eagle glance, a way by which to reduce his long nursed vision to a happy reality, we must admit his conceptions were great, his design was grand." Wurts responded with a graceful speech and toasted "The friends of internal improvement and domestic manufactures—May unqualified success crown their efforts, and advance the power and wealth of our country."[66]

Since work on the canal between the Hudson and the Delaware had been largely completed in 1826, it was expected that the section would be open for navigation during most of 1827. Unforeseen circumstances, however, interfered with this fond hope. Water was let into the canal during the Summer of 1827, but did not always stay there. The banks of the canal had been constructed, as the 1828 annual report explained, "during a season of unusual drought," and thus had to be saturated and allowed to settle slowly. Contrary to what might be expected, the canal bottom caused a more severe problem than the sides. Much of the waterway was constructed as a trough on the sides of hills. In other sections, especially at the summit, the bed rested on porous, stony soil, so that water escaped out the bottom, taking the canal lining with it. Correcting these problems by lining the canal with clay (puddling) and raising the banks in places was a laborious business.

As a result, during most of the 1827 boating season voyages were limited to the lower portions of the canal. Although the canal was reportedly navigable between the Hudson and the Delaware on July 14, the boat *Neversink*, which completed a passage from Wurtsboro to Eddyville on July 28, was apparently the first to do so.[67] "Thus do we see a new, and, let us add, a blessed era opening upon the good old county of Ulster and her daughter Sullivan," proclaimed a local editorialist.[68] By the end of the season it was possible for boats to travel from river to river, albeit cautiously. Boats navigated the canal to bring lock irons and a weighing machine to the unfinished Pennsylvania section. Even then, the period of adjustment was far from over. A time of heavy rains caused washouts and other troubles. The soil was not the only thing that needed time to settle, for some locktenders were found to be "inexperienced and, in some instances, neglectful," and even some overseers proved "deficient in the discharge of their duties."[69] By 1828 much of this roughness had been smoothed over by experience. Water was let in to the section between the rivers in April, as would become routine for the next 70 years, and the canal seemed to function with fair regularity for the rest of the season.[70] In an interesting comment, the 1828 annual report observed that the people of the region had spent so much of their effort working on the canal in 1826 that they had not been able to produce much, even lumber, that could be transported over it. This statement, although intended to lament the lack of business, implies that much of the labor that built the canal was local.

Maurice Wurts: "His conceptions were great, his design was grand."
CREDIT
D&H Canal Museum.

Meanwhile, the managers continued to prepare for full operation. During 1827 they purchased a dredging machine from George Buckmaster for $800 and authorized the building of 50 boats.[71] Canals, with the Erie again setting the pattern, were expected to provide passenger service, so on July 23 the managers authorized the building of two "passage boats."[72] Despite the delays, which may have defeated their stock manipulation scheme, the Wurtses found reason to be encouraged by the progress that had been made. Noting the recent failure of several Philadelphia business acquaintances, John Wurts observed that "Canalling after all is I believe better than merchandizing."[73]

At the Forks of the Dyberry

AS THE WORK IN PENNSYLVANIA ADVANCED, the selection of the end point of the canal became a more acute problem. Even after Jervis's recommendation that the waterway should go no further than the forks of the Dyberry had been accepted, it was necessary to determine the precise point at which the basin and transfer facilities would be located. In a distressingly familiar pattern, this seemingly routine matter became contentious, creating bad feelings at the time and uncertainty for the modern historian. For both eras the discussion centers around the redoubtable personality of Jason Torrey.

Torrey was born in 1772 in Williamstown, Massachusetts, near the western limit of influence of Bay Colony puritanism. As a young man he set out on purposeful roaming through the interior of New York and Pennsylvania—areas from which the Indian menace had only recently been removed. Torrey was seeking opportunity, as well as adventure, and found both—as well as severe toil that ruined his health in later years. A self-taught surveyor, he became a land agent and speculator; few if any men knew the wilds of northeastern Pennsylvania better than he.

Torrey had made his residence at Bethany, the earliest important settlement in the vicinity. He came into possession of land at the forks of the Dyberry fortuitously: for helping the occupant obtain clear title he was given half of the 400-acre property. The land appeared to have little value, and Torrey's first efforts to dispose of it were unsuccessful.[74] The approach of the D&H soon changed that. As discussion of the canal's terminus took firmer shape, Torrey perceived that his Dyberry property could become extremely valuable. He had already played an active part in helping the company secure the Pennsylvania legislation that was vital to its progress—"not only giving largely of his time, but contributing liberally to cover expenses." At the canal celebration in Bethany on July 4, 1827 Torrey hailed "The President & Directors of the Delaware and Hudson Canal Company—Wise in their plans, efficient and persevering in their movements."[75]

To help the D&H make the proper decision, Torrey offered to give the company half of his land, knowing that the village that would arise on his half would more than recover the value of his gift. The company seemed favorable to this proposal, and the 1828 report makes it appear that it was accepted.[76] Speaking of the canal terminus, the report states that a 100-acre tract belonging to the canal company "cost the proprietor four thousand dollars, who gives one half to the company, in consideration of the benefits that will accrue to the other half from the company's operations." Though the mistake is understandable since the offers appear similar, fuller examination shows that Torrey was not, in fact, the proprietor cited in the report.

In August 1827 President Bolton was at Dyberry Forks meeting with Jason Torrey. The two agreed on terms for a contract along the lines Torrey had proposed, although the actual wording was complex. As recounted later by Jason's son David, Bolton carried the contract back to New York and presented it to the board in September, whereupon the managers declined to approve it. The minutes do not confirm this, but show that correspondence with Torrey continued into June of the following year. Meanwhile, Torrey continued clearing his land and building a tavern.[77]

David Torrey is correct in stating that September 1827 is the month when the previous harmony between his father and the D&H fell apart. In a letter of September 18 summarizing the progress of construction to D&H treasurer Samuel Flewelling, Maurice Wurts reported that "difficulties with Major Torrey are causing serious delay . . . having already prevented the letting of the upper section, Basin, Feeder, 2 Locks, Dam &c."[78] At issue ostensibly was water: Torrey had already built a sawmill and probably had more factories in mind; the D&H feared that he would not guarantee an adequate supply of water for the canal.

Maurice Wurts's intervention may not have been entirely disinterested. Nearly two months earlier, on July 25, he had written the board offering the right to purchase lands belonging to Kimble across the Dyberry from Torrey's holdings.[79] The Kimble real estate had little value as long as the canal terminus was planned for Torrey land, but as Wurts noted, if the basin was placed on Kimble land it "will then come into immediate value." Wurts concluded that "if this plan is adopted, I will give up the purchase to the company, which cannot but turn out a profitable one."

Maurice had had his eye on the Kimble land for some time, for the subject is mentioned in a letter from John Wurts in 1825. At that time John warned "If I were to advise about it at all, it would merely be that you should not allow it to become the ground work of collision between yourself and the board."[80] In 1827 Maurice apparently operated shrewdly to keep the owner from perceiving its true value. On September 19, 1827 (one day after his letter criticizing Torrey and two months after he had received extravagant praise at the Bethany Independence Day celebration) he purchased 100 acres from Samuel Kimble—all his land west of the Lackawaxen—for $1000.[81] In January 1828 Wurts and the company reached an understanding in which the company took the land it needed for its facilities and allowed Wurts to retain the profits from the increased value of the remaining land.[82] No wonder, when Kimble learned the full story "he bitterly repented the transaction."[83] Paradoxically, the wording used in the negotiations between Maurice and the company suggests considerable distrust, and it is possible that Wurts's financial gains left him with a sour aftertaste—his brother's advice two years earlier had proved prophetic. The agreement clinched the choice of a site for the basin, and the board gave formal approval to the location on April 30, 1828.

Jason Torrey, despite his sustained support for the company and his supposedly close relations with Bolton, was kept largely in the dark about these developments. His sources were local gossip, casual comments dropped by engineers such as Mills while laying out the railway, and unsatisfactory conversations with Maurice Wurts. On February 4, 1828 Torrey wrote to Bolton to express his disappointment that a location for the basin had not yet been fixed and to probe into rumors that it would be located on the Wurts land. In retaliation, Torrey withheld his signature on a deed, leading to angry words with Maurice Wurts in which the D&H agent threatened a battle in the state legislature. Despite his irritation, Torrey ended on a conciliatory note, hoping "the difficulty can be removed without a public conflict of so unnatural a character, and fraught with consequent evils which can neither be measured or scarcely imagined."[84]

Leslie's conclusion that "The brothers Wurts were not known for their generosity or integrity in regard to land deals," is harsh but probably justified, and not only due to the Kimble episode. In 1825 John Wurts was informed that the members of the Lackawaxen Co. had passed a resolution "prohibiting any member from purchasing property on or near the line of the Canal, except for the joint benefit of all the members of the Company." He had not been present when the resolution was passed, declared it "unjust" and stated flatly that "I do not hold myself bound by it."[85]

Jason Torrey came to share Samuel Kimble's resentment. His son wrote, in restrained ministerial style, that what he termed the "quiet repudiation" of Jason's contract meant that "the co-operation between him and the company's agents should be less intimate and active than before."[86] Relations did not break down entirely, for Jason Torrey was a member of the delegation that celebrated the opening of the canal. Adjoining land ownership meant that communication had to be preserved. In June 1829 the D&H and Torrey negotiated a treaty under which

TO ADVENTURERS.

The completion of the

DELAWARE & HUDSON CANAL,

has opened a wide and promising field for enterprise, to the Farmer, the Merchant, and the Mechanic.

This Canal forms an inland navigation for Boats of twenty-five tons burthen, from tide on the Hudson River, at the village of Bolton, near Kingston, (Esopus) in Ulster County, New York, to the village of Honesdale, in Wayne County, Pennsylvania, a distance of 108 miles.

The Canal now is in successful operation through the whole line, sustaining a respectable and an increasing amount of transportation, which at this time rates at from 250 to 300 tons per day.

HONESDALE.

is located at the termination of the Canal.

The village plot, which was a heavy and unbroken forest about three years ago, now contains sixty families, and upwards of 400 souls. It is situated in the margin of an extensive region of valuable country, lying northward and westward, over which a multitude of settlements are planted in every direction, although the amount of the present population is small compared with the capacity of the country.

Honesdale is already becoming the depot for an extent of country of more than fifty miles westward and northward.—The Merchant there meets his Goods from New York; and there the Farmer finds a ready market for the products of Husbandry;—and those engaged in subduing the forest, now find an improved value for their timber, acquired by the facilities for transportation.

The face of the country is undulating and hilly, but not mountainous.—The timber, Beech, Sugartree, Hemlock, Ash, &c.—The soil, deep and strong;—much of it produces good crops of Grain, but it excels in the growth of the usual kinds of Grass, for Meadow and for Grazing.

Like most hilly countries, it is well watered and healthy,—and the country is intersected in all directions by Turnpikes and common roads.

BETHANY,

the County Town of Wayne County, is situated three miles northward from Honesdale, and contains fifty families and upwards of 300 souls.

From the termination of the Canal at Honesdale, a **RAIL ROAD** is constructed in a western direction, sixteen miles, to the exhaustless Coal beds at Carbondale, on which there is a daily transportation of more than 250 tons.

The Moral and Religious social privileges are good. In Honesdale is an organized Presbyterian Church, and settled Ministry; and a Methodist Society, the residence of a Circuit Preacher.——In Bethany, is a Presbyterian, a Methodist, and a Baptist organized Church. In each is a Bible Society, and in each, and in most of the considerable adjacent settlements, is a Sabbath School and Tract Society.

The facility afforded by the Canal, for a cheap, safe, and expeditious communication with the City of New York, presents to the Farmer, to the Merchant, and to proficients in the various Mechanic Arts, encouragement, which is greatly increased by the consideration that Honesdale, will perpetually be the principal depot and market place, for an extensive region of country, which is now in the commencement of a rapid increase in population and improvement.

The Subscriber offers for Sale, on moderate terms, to actual settlers, a large number of Village Lots, in the Villages of Honesdale and Bethany.—Also, several valuable scites for establishments, for Mechanics and Manufacturers, requiring water power, within a convenient distance from those villages.

And also, a number of Farms with small and large improvements, and upwards of 10,000 Acres of unimproved farm land, among which settlements are interspersed.—The titles are indisputable.

Maps of the Villages, and of the County, may be seen at the office of the subscriber in Bethany, and of John Torrey in Honesdale, where particular information to applicants will be cheerfully communicated.

JASON TORREY.

Bethany, June 17, 1830.   W. EARSHAW, PRINT, BETHANY, PA.

each gave half the ground needed for a public square.[87] A similar example of joint action occurred in July 1832, when the D&H agreed to donate two lots fronting the public square to the Episcopal congregation if Torrey made an equivalent grant to the Presbyterians. At that time the company also accepted Torrey's offer to run and record a "right line" between their properties.[88] Both parties shared an interest in the growth and prosperity of Honesdale. The issue of water arose again in 1840 when Torrey proposed to use the D&H dam for another mill. At that time John Wurts, by then president of the company, replied firmly that "no saving of money and no feeling of friendship or kindness would induce us to run any risk on the score of water . . . . We must act not for a day or a year, but for all future time," he concluded loftily.[89]

If the suppositions about the D&H land transactions at Honesdale are correct, they represent another of the shabby, troubled deals that seem to recur in the early history of the company. Jason Torrey—largely out of necessity—may have become reconciled with the D&H, but his former wholehearted support could not be regained. While saving the company money—or making money for the Wurtses—in the short run, such maneuvers ultimately proved damaging. They contributed to a distrust that was ready to ripen into hostility at any provocation—and the opportunities for troublemaking were all too abundant.

Torrey may have been responsible for naming the town. Prior to the coming of the D&H there was not enough of a settlement to require or deserve a name. Gradually "Forks of Dyberry" changed from a geographical designation to the name of a community. Historian Vernon Leslie offers three explanations of how the Forks became Honesdale. One, that the name was bestowed during the visit of Washington Irving in 1841, is obviously incorrect because the name was in use more than a decade earlier. Leslie, with ample reason, believes that the name originated on the books of Jason Torrey in October 1827.[90] It appears for the first time in the D&H minute book on July 23, 1828.

Naming new settlements in honor of prominent D&H personalities was a common practice—sort of an untaxable bonus. As early as November 1825 William Wurts proposed naming "Rome," by which he meant the place where the inaugural ceremony had taken place, Honesburg.[91] This was just after Hone acknowledged he owned 800 shares of D&H, while his nephew had bought 200 more. This suggestion was not pursued, and the hamlet was later named Wurtsboro[ugh] or in some early documents, Wurtsburg, perhaps recognizing the family's Swiss origin. The name seems to appear in the D&H minute book for the first time on September 12, 1827.

The Wurtses and Philip Hone were apparently not present when they were honored by having settlements named for them. John B. Jervis had the advantage in that regard, being on hand when the tiny settlement known loosely as Carpenter's Point was renamed Port Jervis. Another example occurred in the summer of 1828 when, as *Century of Progress* puts it, "the Managers had some leisure for comparatively minor matters" and named the company's property at the mouth of the Rondout Bolton.[92] This name did not stick, perhaps because Bolton's tenure as president was short and ultimately unsatisfactory. Later in the century the practice was continued, giving us Archbald, Olyphant, Hawley and Port Ewen. After the 1850s the custom passed out of use: the land was filling up; the innocent freshness of the early days had faded; and there was no longer much hope that a new settlement would grow into a teeming metropolis.

By the late summer of 1828 the managers at last could feel confident that construction was nearing an end, the exhausting struggle approaching fulfillment. A committee composed of Philip Hone and Rufus L. Lord was appointed on September 27 to celebrate the passage of the first boat.[93] It was in this capacity, since he was no longer a company officer, that Hone wrote a letter inviting members of the state legislature to join the excursion over the canal. Puffed with understandable pride, he declared "that no work of equal magnitude has been constructed in Europe or America with such limited means in so short a period and with such persevering industry."[94]

Honesdale: a town dominated by mountains of D&H coal.
CREDIT
National Canal Museum.

Despite Hone's prestige and the fact that, as his letter freely acknowledged, state aid had been essential in the successful outcome, the legislators declined to participate. Nevertheless, the celebration went forward as planned. According to *Century of Progress*, the managers left Rondout on October 16 in the *Orange Packet*, which became the first boat to navigate the length of the canal.[95] Hone's diary records that he left New York on the evening of October 22, landed at Newburgh, and worked his way cross country to Carbondale and Honesdale. Although he had made at least two previous trips to view work on the canal, this may have been his first visit to Honesdale. "The settlers of this town have done me the honour to give it my name and I have reason to be proud of it," he observed.[96] It was not an unqualified approval, for two years later he noted that Carbondale "is not equal in extent to Honesdale, but better taste has been observed in the style of building."[97]

Hone's journey down the canal with the return party began on October 26, 1828, although the first portion of the trip was made in a coach on the towpath, since water had not been let in to the proper depth. From at least Port Jervis to the easterly end of the summit level they used the boat *Superior* with, Hone noted, "a good stock of provisions and liquors which had been sent up to meet us." The party reached Twaalfskill after dark on the 29th. "All we saw confirmed our satisfaction and confidence in our great work," concluded Hone.[98]

The completed canal was 108 miles long, essentially the same as the Schuylkill Navigation. Only six canals ever built in America were longer than these two, but some were greatly longer—over 300 miles.[99] Eventually well over 4000 miles of towpath canal were constructed in the United States, so that the D&H comprised less than 2½% of the nation's canal mileage. In 1830, however, only 1317 miles of canal were in operation, and the D&H formed about 8% of that total.[100] With 110 locks the D&H considerably exceeded the number on the much longer Erie and was in turn exceeded by only three other American canals.[101] In its 108 miles the D&H overcame a total rise and fall of 1073 feet, exceeded by only four others; fortunately, one of these was the rival Morris Canal.[102]

It is a truism that American railroads were at first built to minimal standards, in the expectation they would be improved once the country they passed through generated sufficient business. This contrasted with British practice, in which from their inception railways were built through developed country, as if prepared to endure for centuries. What seemed initially to be a regrettable compromise later gave the Americans flexibility to adapt to new technology and evolving markets.

The same philosophy of expediency prevailed in canal building, as was evident on the D&H. Composite locks were one example of these shortcuts. The emphasis was on opening the canal so that some coal could move to market, and it is unlikely that it actually attained its supposed width and slope of its banks throughout its length. In particular, while earth settled, the depth of water in the canal was less than the advertised four feet. It took several years before this level was consistently maintained, which meant that even the capacity of 30 tons per boat could not be achieved. In the early years D&H boats routinely carried 10-15 tons, but the long-deprived managers were happy that coal was moving and bringing a return on their investment.

The Gravity to the Mines

ON THEIR VISIT IN OCTOBER 1828 the managers had viewed the coal beds at Carbondale and must have seen coal piled at Honesdale. This reminder presumably tempered their sense of triumph; for although Hone described the coal supply as "inexhaustible and of superior quality," the means of bringing it to market remained incomplete. This was the famed "gravity railroad," the critical link in the D&H system and the reason for much of the company's place in history books. This most vital segment of the D&H transportation route—the portion that actually reached the mines—had always been the most problematical. Sullivan, in his 1824 report, had projected the canal to run to Keen's pond, seven miles beyond the forks of the Dyberry.[103] From there he noted the possibility "of a rail way from the mine to Keen's, at 1500 to 2000 dollars a mile," although he did not prepare a detailed estimate.

Whatever one may think of John Langdon Sullivan and the disappointing course of his later career, he showed astonishing foresight in even contemplating a

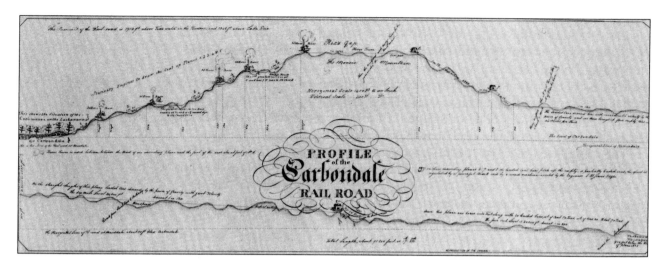

railway. At that time there were virtually no railways in the United States, certainly nothing of the magnitude that would have been necessary at Carbondale. Thomas Leiper, a Scottish immigrant, had built a small private railway in 1810 near Marcus Hook in the southeastern corner of Pennsylvania. It was described as the first permanent tramway in America (as with the development of anthracite, many of these claims to priority depend on carefully formulated definitions).[104]

Leiper's little railway was still carrying stone from his quarry when Sullivan was making his explorations in another part of the state, but it is uncertain whether he knew of its existence. There is a somewhat greater possibility that the Wurtses were aware of Leiper's work. Although Leiper (1745-1825) was a full generation older than the brothers, he had been active in Philadelphia banks and was president of the city's Common Council for several years between 1801 and 1814.[105] More significantly, he may have come to their attention because of a demonstration of a 65-foot railway he gave in a Philadelphia tavern yard in 1809. Leiper had also been one of the founders of the Pennsylvania Improvement Company, devoted to improving inland communication, in 1802.[106] Another founder was James Vanuxem, and this may provide a further link to the Wurtses. Charles Stewart Wurts married Vanuxem's daughter Mary, although this took place much later, in 1826.

Sullivan, like others in the engineering field, was aware of railway developments in England, the leader in the emerging technology of the Industrial Revolution. Even in England railways were few and mostly special-purpose. However, the commonest of these special purposes was to bring coal and stone down from quarries, an obvious inspiration in the Carbondale situation. With his connections in Massachusetts, Sullivan may also have known of a temporary tramway used to carry spoil from the reduction of Beacon Hill around 1807.

Jervis and Wright gave a strong impetus to Sullivan's tentative suggestion of a railway. During his examination of the route in March 1825 Jervis had found that although it would be possible to extend the canal seven miles from Dyberry forks to Keen's pond, it would require about 30 locks. This could add so much to the cost of construction and operation that the whole venture might become impractical.[107] Jervis thus advocated ending the canal at the forks and bringing the railway down to that point. Wright, in his report based on Jervis's findings, supported the idea of a railway, though leaving its end point purposely vague.[108] These men, especially

Wright who had built his career in canals, demonstrated exceptional vision in relying on the nearly untried expedient of a railway.

Whatever their flaws, the Wurtses display a remarkable ability to combine mundane concerns and flashes of dazzling prophecy. In December 1825, in the depths of financial distress, William Wurts wrote that "I have read some of the accounts on railways in England."[109] At that time the route from Dyberry forks to the mines had not been determined, and William suggested giving greater consideration to the "Paupack route"—one of the possibilities mentioned by Sullivan. William then added, in a letter otherwise filled with despair, that the railway should ultimately go to Pittston!

The managers accepted Wright's report, but did not act on it immediately. Their annual report presented March 1826 noted that "an inclined plane and rail way will probably be substituted for locks," but avoided a final decision. There was probably little doubt in their minds, but in their usual cagey style they would not reveal their plans "until it be absolutely necessary to avoid delay in the prosecution of the work," so as to keep landowners from inflating the price of the right-of-way. In fact, the board noted, as long as there was uncertainty about the route, landowners were more likely to make "gratuitous cessions."[110]

Another consideration was that nothing in the company's legislation gave it the right to build a railway, making another appeal to Harrisburg necessary. Each of these expeditions to the capitol became riskier. The time when the company could wangle privileges almost surreptitiously was past. With the previous amendment— granting the right to build a separate canal down the Lackawaxen—the support of the raftsmen had been valuable; but having (to their way of thinking) freed the river, those stalwarts found little reason to support a railway.

There is evidence that the board had tried to resolve the issue at an earlier date. In November 1825 Hone, then still president, wrote to John Wurts about acquiring new powers in Pennsylvania. At that time Wurts was seeking a supplement that would allow the company to reduce the size of its locks, and he balked at the suggestion that he should add a request to build railways and planes to the pending proposal. "We risk all by grasping at too much,"[111] he declared. This careful approach prevailed, for the legislature passed two separate supplements in early 1826. Nathan Smith, indefatigable lobbyist, was again effective in promoting the company's interests. The supplement approved April 5 allowed the D&H "to construct and maintain such railways or other devices as may be found necessary to provide for and facilitate the transportation of coal to the canal by them to be constructed." On the other hand the state limited the route of the railway to the mines and the forks of the Dyberry, assuring that the New Yorkers would not "cheat the folks out of the canal altogether," as William Wurts had earlier expressed it, or use the legislation to infiltrate railroads into other parts of Pennsylvania.[112]

It is possible that the managers and their engineers were stretched to the limit building the canal and had no resources left to tackle the railway even after securing authorization. Nearly a year passed, until April 4, 1827, before the board authorized a survey for the rail line to Carbondale.[113] In the interim, on September 30, 1826, Wright had elaborated on his earlier report and cautiously endorsed a railway extending the full distance from the mines to the forks of the Dyberry.[114] By the time the survey was authorized Jervis was chief engineer and was responsible for planning an effective mechanical system to move the coal, as well as the more usual task of laying out a route. As one of his first acts Jervis visited the recently-completed railway in Quincy, Massachusetts. Initially conceived to haul granite blocks for the

Bunker Hill monument, it is generally conceded to be the first commercial railway in the United States. To illustrate the rudimentary state of the nation's transportation, the Quincy line, at about three and a half miles, was the longest railway in the country. Jervis's interest would have been drawn not only by the solid construction of the relatively level portions, but by an inclined plane 315 feet long which overcame an 84-foot difference in elevation by means of a continuous chain, with empty cars serving as a partial counterweight to the descending ones.[115]

Jervis presented his findings and plans for the railway in a report to the managers in October 1827.[116] Ever cautious, the board submitted Jervis's proposal to James Renwick, an English-born professor of science at Columbia College. Respect for technical expertise was firmly established even then, and Professor Renwick was an acknowledged authority. The professor visited Jervis at Carbondale, pointed out an error in calculation, but otherwise reported to the board in terms of "unqualified approbation."[117] While the mechanics of Jervis's system were being reviewed, clearing for the railway line was placed under contract.[118]

There is general agreement about the layout of the railway, nearly seventeen miles long, as designed and constructed by Jervis. From the mines five inclined planes overcame a rise of about 950 feet to the summit of the Moosic range. Stationary steam engines provided the power to haul the cars, with descending empties acting as a partial counterbalance. The planes were separated by stretches of fairly level track on which the cars were to be pulled by horses. After a summit level of about a mile and a half, three long descending planes brought the track down to the canal basin in Honesdale. These planes relied entirely on gravity, in which the main problem was applying sufficient braking to avoid runaways. In addition to the summit level there were two other long levels: the "Six Mile Level" from Waymart to Prompton, and the "Four Mile Level" from Prompton to Honesdale. These were not true canal levels, but, with a grade of less than one percent, were level by comparison to the planes.[119]

Jervis had created a railway operation that was long and complex by the standards of the time. This was an exceptional achievement, but it was dwarfed by the even more extraordinary recommendation that steam locomotives be used instead of horses on the long levels. In the early stages of discussing the railway what had been meant was what we would now call a tramway or tram road—a rail on which wagons could move by gravity or animal power. In his December 1825 reference to railways—ahead of its time though it was—William Wurts was thinking only of horse power. Less than two years later, in his report to the managers, Jervis broached the subject of locomotives with an air of unassuming confidence. This was both a tribute to his foresight and a recognition of how rapidly technology was advancing. Except for an experimental model demonstrated by John Stevens at his home in Hoboken, New Jersey, no steam locomotive had operated in the United States; yet developments in England gave reason for assurance. Renwick himself had "received very recent information on the subject of Rail Roads in England by an Engineer sent out for that purpose."[120] The proliferation of steamboats had made Americans familiar with steam propulsion, and they were ready to hitch their future to the engine of new technology. Veterans of the War for Independence were then living out their final years, yet the hoofbeat-paced world of their youth already seemed to be a lost age of heroic simplicity.

Professor Renwick deserves credit for risking his considerable reputation on a new technology. His opinion was by no means universally held. For example, John

Wurts consulted with a reputedly knowledgeable friend named Lukens who "expressed himself in as strong language as he can use against locomotive engines as compared with horse power."[121] The managers did not know or care about this, and once Renwick had relieved their anxiety with his professorial endorsement, they began to act on Jervis's plan. Immediately after consulting with Renwick they instructed Maurice Wurts to begin contracting for the timber needed on the railway.

Horatio Allen, a young engineer who had assisted Jervis, was traveling to England. On December 29, 1827 the managers authorized him to procure "iron plates" for the railroad.[122] This was so close to the dawn of railroading that the names for the component parts had not been settled. The word "plates," following English usage, did not refer to means of fastening the track superstructure as it does in America today, but actually meant the rails. Long, rectangular strips of iron known later as strap rails, they rested on and protected the wooden strips that were called rails. Subsequently, the managers gave Allen more detailed specifications, requesting "the ends to be cut and fitted into each other." Always concerned about cost, they added that "the rounding of the edges of the plates will be advantageous, but is not so indispensible" as to justify excess expense.[123]

Most or all of the plates must have arrived from England by November 1828. At that time the Baltimore & Ohio RR, then building west from its home city, sought to obtain five tons of plates from the D&H, offering to pay directly or to buy replacements in England. The D&H managers ordered this quantity to be shipped from "the Delaware Turn," where they were being stored.[124] The actual shipment is not recorded, but if it occurred the D&H played an unacknowledged part in helping another pioneer railroad.

A more momentous order was given on January 16, 1828, when the managers instructed Allen "to procure one locomotive Engine complete, as a pattern." So little was known about locomotives in America that it would have been foolish for the managers to offer fuller instructions. Around this time, however, Jervis transmitted further specifications, which later developments proved critical. Allen was in England not only to buy locomotives and railroad iron, but to learn all he could about the new technology so that his purchases would be made wisely. At that time the ideal of an international scientific fraternity still largely prevailed, and the pioneer railroad builders, carried along by their own enthusiasm, gave Allen information freely. Ultimately he purchased four locomotives—three from Foster, Rastrick and one from Stephenson.

Some coal was transported to the canal even before it was completed; indeed, even before work had started on the railway. On June 30, 1827 the managers authorized Maurice Wurts to transport coal over the Milford & Owego Turnpike, chartered in 1804—another of those early transportation ventures that is astonishing for the reach of its ambition in a country so recently settled.[125] Within a month Wurts had arranged terms with the turnpike company.[126] The road did not actually extend from Carbondale to Honesdale, so the D&H used it largely to surmount Rix's Gap and built extensions at both ends. The D&H agreed to keep the portion it used in good repair and not to charge tolls on the extensions it built. By September 18, 1827 Wurts reported that all the new sections of turnpike had been put under contract.[127] Simultaneously the contracts for clearing the railroad route had been signed and Jason Torrey was building his tavern; so that the forks of the Dyberry, an undisturbed wilderness not long before, turned into a bustling construction site.

Carbondale: the "mother lode" of the D&H. In this view from the final years of the gravity railway, a train of coal cars is moving from the mines to the foot of Plane No. 1. The long trestle and station in the background belong to the NYO&W RR, a latecomer to the anthracite region, which arrived around 1890.
CREDIT
National Canal Museum.

Jervis, who apparently expected that his railway might be operational in 1828, was reluctant to move much coal by the costly expedient of hauling over the turnpike. In trying to save money he found an appreciative audience among the managers, and on November 5, 1827 Bolton advised Maurice to limit contracts for carting to 4000 tons.[128] This coincided with the decision to rely on locomotive power on the railway. It is unlikely the new roads were completed at that time, so that any hauling of coal over them must have occurred in 1828. This did not last long, for on July 26, 1828 the managers instructed Maurice Wurts to cancel the contracts for carting coal, "the benefit to be derived from transporting by Waggons so considerable a distance, any further quantity of coal being questionable."[129] Relations between the D&H and the Milford & Owego continued: in the following year the turnpike company offered to purchase the road the D&H had built into Carbondale in exchange for Milford & Owego stock, if the D&H improved its road to turnpike standards.[130] As Maurice pointed out, the prospect of the turnpike passing through Carbondale offered many advantages, and the managers accepted the offer.[131]

Coal was finally moving up from Carbondale, the village that owed its name and its existence to the substance, even if it was by the defective temporary method of horse and wagon. Canal boats loaded with coal arrived at Rondout on December 5, 1828, welcomed by a cannon and a large crowd. A colorful story, suspect because it had several decades to marinate in the juices of romance, has come down about this episode. According to this account the D&H had sent six boats to Honesdale, and after an absence of six weeks all sorts of dire rumors abounded. In this rustic version of the Columbus story "some said the boats had gone over the dam in the Delaware . . . and some said they had found some pieces of the boats at Philadelphia."[132] In February of that year the managers had contracted to build a steamboat "to ply between Eddy's and the Strand on the Rondout," the name Bolton having not yet been bestowed.[133] Perhaps this boat was already in service in December. Philip Hone recorded in his diary that the "first fruits of the Delaware & Hudson Canal" arrived at New York City on December 10, aboard the sloop *Toleration*. This vessel was owned by Charles McEntee, apparently a brother of young D&H engineer James S. McEntee.[134] Hone's elation was obvious, but it is well to recall that nearly six years had passed since the company was chartered and perhaps 15 years since the Wurtses began to prowl around the site of Carbondale.

Later in December the company "opened up shop," so to speak, with the following advertisement:

Lackawannock Coal
The Managers of the Delaware & Hudson Canal Company for the purpose of making an experiment of a plan for disposing of their coal which, in their opinion, will supply the consumers on the cheapest terms, have concluded on selling the ensuing season at the companys dock only and by the vessel load. The dock is on the Rondout, one mile from the North River, two miles below the termination of the canal, and about 90 miles from New York, and vessels drawing ten feet water can go up to it. The intention of the Managers is to open their coal business to general competition. They will therefore not engage to confine their sales to one person or house, in any one city or town . . . but will bind themselves not to engage in retailing their coal in any place.[135]

Construction of the railway had overstrained the company's resources, and it had to turn again to New York State for a loan. This application provoked more opposition than the first request. Representative Luther Bradish, speaking on behalf of the D&H, accused its foes of a corrupt plot to drive down the value of its stock so that they could later buy it up cheaply. Bradish's remarks, published in pamphlet form, contain many interesting details. Trying to demonstrate that completion of the D&H system would benefit the public, he argued that the substitution of anthracite for cordwood would save $1,440,000 for consumers in New York City alone. This calculation was based on an annual consumption in the city of 480,000 cords at $5 a cord, which could be replaced by 240,000 tons of coal selling at $6 (the correct figure at the beginning of 1830). Bradish also rebutted arguments that the D&H would be unable to compete effectively against the Lehigh and Schuylkill companies.[136]

Even Philip Hone had to spend time in Albany lobbying for the bill.[137] On April 30, 1829 it passed the House by the narrow vote of 49 to 42 and was signed into law on May 2. The act specified that the railway must be included in the company's mortgage to the state. Bolton must have performed valiantly, for the managers voted their thanks for his "zealous services and great exertions" and rewarded him with 20 shares of stock.[138] The closeness of the vote and the ferocity of the contest made it clear that the company could not dip its bucket in that well again; thereafter, attention was devoted to obtaining loans from private sources.

Century of Progress provides considerable detail about Allen's purchase of the four English locomotives and their journey across the Atlantic. On May 27, 1829 Philip Hone joined a party of men to see a demonstration of one of the locomotives at Abeel & Dunscombe's foundry in New York City. Mounted with its wheels raised, the engine ran successfully. A second locomotive was demonstrated with equal success a day later at Kemble's West Point Foundry on Water Street.[139] Garret Abeel, one of the proprietors, was a founder of the D&H and an original manager. His calculation that the canal company and his foundry would be mutually supportive was sound, but a lamentable family tragedy intervened. Deeply distressed by the death of a 20-year-old son and the dangerous illness of another, Garret Abeel committed suicide by jumping from the roof of his home at Park Place on December 21, 1829.[140]

On August 8 the two successfully tested locomotives were at Honesdale, as was Horatio Allen, ready for their date with destiny. One of the Foster, Rastrick products, named the *Stourbridge Lion* as it had been manufactured in Stourbridge, England, and someone had painted a lion's head on the front of its boiler, was under steam. Allen felt it was his duty to drive it—besides, no one else was volunteering. Allen had earlier been authorized to "employ two competent men to superintend the locomotive engines on the Rail Road," but this had not been done.[141] With the exception of John Stevens' experimental model, no one had operated a steam locomotive in the Western Hemisphere; nor had Allen had the opportunity to drive one in the Old World. Curiosity had brought out the sort of crowd that collected to observe public executions.[142]

As has been recounted many times, the *Lion* ran successfully and Allen returned safely, never again in his long life to operate a locomotive. Nevertheless, the experiment was a failure. As Jervis reported to the board, "the Iron plates were not fastened sufficiently firm on the wooden rails to resist the pressure of the Engine on the curved parts of the Road, and the consequence was that the Iron Plates were pressed from their places."[143] Jervis recommended that a horse path be made so that animal power could be used—a stunning if temporary setback for technology. The railway had been constructed in the flimsy manner characteristic of new enterprises in America. There was virtually no grading, and where the track could not be laid directly on the ground, it was supported on trestlework. What had happened, in brief, was that the locomotive was simply too heavy for the track and pressed the iron parts into the soft hemlock rails. Some hasty adjustments may have been made, but a trial on September 9 produced similar results.

Restrained and dutiful, Jervis kept his feelings to himself for many years—nearly fifty years in fact. It was only in 1877, during a wave of antiquarian interest in early railroading and when the national centennial had generated new awareness of history that Jervis, stung by newspaper implications that the railway had been poorly built, at last spoke out. He had calculated carefully the load-bearing capacity of the trestles and on April 23, 1828 wrote to Allen in England that a four-wheel locomotive should not weigh more than five and a half tons, preferably less.[144] For reasons never satisfactorily explained Allen ignored this clear instruction, and the *Stourbridge Lion* weighed seven tons exclusive of fuel and water. Always courteous, Jervis came as close as he ever did to personal criticism when he concluded "I did not think it reasonable to put the failure of the agent on the railway instead of the locomotive; and withal to give great credit to the man who ran the engine on trial, for his courage in a case in which no special courage would have been called for if the agent had executed his mission according to instructions."[145]

For an event that seemed so momentous, the run of the *Lion* was surprisingly devoid of lasting consequence. None of the four locomotives—probably the only locomotives in America at the time—is known to have run again, and the D&H did not fulfill its early promise of leadership in the new form of propulsion. Foster, Rastrick did not become a major locomotive builder, and the walking beam design

Scale model of *Stourbridge Lion* at the Smithsonian National Museum of American History.
CREDIT
National Canal Museum.

of its products soon became obsolete. Instead, it was Stephenson, maker of only one of the engines, who went on to great prominence. The imported Stephenson engine was apparently lighter, and there has been much speculation as to why it was not used or what the outcome would have been if it had been the one tried. If anything, the Honesdale fiasco had a dampening effect on locomotive development in America, and the best that can be said is that it did not prove to be a lasting discouragement. Jervis himself went on to achieve other successes in railroad design and construction and, despite his later clarification of the historical record, remained friendly with Horatio Allen. In 1881 Allen, at the close of a distinguished engineering career, made a pilgrimage to Honesdale. Alone with his thoughts, he visited the site of his epochal ride, which already belonged to a mythical age. He gloried in the distinction of having piloted the first commercial run of a steam locomotive in the United States; whether he accepted blame for the fact that the railway did not become viable will never be known.

One of the most puzzling aspects of the entire episode is that the D&H managers, normally so tight-fisted, did so little to salvage their premature investment. At first Jervis seemed to believe that the railway could be strengthened enough to support the locomotive, and on August 19, 1829 the managers authorized him "to make experiments for remedying any defects now existing, or that he hereafter discover on the Rail Road." Probably the second trial of the locomotive convinced Jervis that no quick fix was feasible, for according to *Century of Progress* Jervis later recommended that improvements to the railway be deferred.[146] In this way more than $12,000 the company had spent on the locomotives was lost.

A cylinder believed to be from the *America* and now in the Smithsonian.
CREDIT
National Canal Museum.

The fate of the locomotives has been the subject of considerable investigation and speculation among antiquarians. The *Lion* was stored in a nearby shed where horses, pulling cars over the track where it was supposed to have worked, presumably snorted in derision. In later years various parts were stolen or appropriated, and the boiler was converted to stationary use. Much the same fate probably befell the Stephenson product, whose name is given variously as *America* or *Pride of Newcastle*. The D&H minutes of November 26, 1832 contain a tantalizing reference to letters from George Farnham "relative to a lot at Honesdale and one of the locomotive engines," but the letters themselves are not included. One might surmise that the letter refers to using the locomotive as a stationary engine, but that is only a guess. Even less is known about the other two Foster, Rastrick engines. The fullest account is provided by James McEntee, who says they reached Rondout, were stored there for a time, and subsequently destroyed in a fire.[147] This must have occurred after 1834, as all four engines were still available for sale in that year.

Long afterward, the relics of the *Stourbridge Lion* were afforded a reverence the locomotive had not received in its lifetime. Eventually enough parts were collected to enable the Smithsonian to partially reconstruct the engine. In 1933 the D&H built a replica in its shops for display at the Chicago World's Fair. This veneration was the response of a later era, and at the time the most meaningful comment was provided by Wall Street, where D&H stock dropped from $82 to $74 when news of the unsuccessful trial reached it.[148]

Visions of Empire

IN 1826, with their canal far from finished and its future far from assured, the managers nonetheless considered a major territorial expansion. If successful, this scheme would have opened a great region of central New York and permanently altered the character of the D&H. The first formal acknowledgement of these aspirations appeared in the company minutes of March 8, 1826, which presented what amounts to an annual report. It directed attention up the Delaware beyond the mouth of the Lackawaxen, which was as far as the company's existing privileges reached. After noting that navigation of the Delaware seemed to be relatively free of obstructions for 100 miles further and in that distance the Susquehanna approached within 12 miles, the report developed the economic case for an extension:

> One of the State Surveyors appointed to explore a Southern route for the contemplated State Road, informed one of your Managers, that a road might be made between the two rivers at the point designated above, with an inclination not exceeding 1½ degrees, and stated his belief that a canal could be made to unite those rivers. The Susquehanna up to this point is represented to be of easy ascent and free from obstructions for more than One hundred miles. Our canal extending above the most formidable difficulties in the navigation of the Delaware will present inducements for improving that river above our work and for constructing a canal or rail road between the Susquehanna and the Delaware . . . . A great extent of fertile country will thus find its shortest cheapest and most certain route for the transportation of its products and of the foreign supplies requisite for its consumption through our Canal. Its population will rapidly increase and with it, the products of the soil, and the consumption of foreign supplies, furnishing a large and yearly increasing amount of transportation.

In a characteristic response the managers on September 30, 1826 requested Wright to survey for a canal from the mouth of the Lackawaxen to Deposit, New

York, the closest point to the Susquehanna.[149] As was customary, Wright dispatched John B. Mills to the area to investigate and later followed the route in person. Wright's career took him through vast areas of interior New York when it was still nearly virgin territory, and his surveying instruments were the instruments of its change. Mills, and then Wright, continued the examination to a junction with the Susquehanna at Bettsburg, now, its fleeting brush with importance forgotten, an inconspicuous locale in the town of Afton. Manville Wakefield discovered this survey in the D&H archives, and it revealed a project of impressive magnitude. At 83 miles it was comparable to the original D&H and might have posed greater difficulty, for the plan called for 58 locks, five inclined planes and a mile-long tunnel beneath the divide of the two rivers.[150] The planes probably would have been similar to those used to surmount the Alleghenies on the Pennsylvania state system, but the tunnel would have been the longest constructed in America to that date. Wright's cost estimates confirm the scope of the project: $870,237 for the portion up the Delaware to Deposit, and $771,430 for the extension to Bettsburg, of which $300,000 would be needed for a tunnel 18 feet in diameter.[151]

The managers were aware that in the previous year a charter had been granted to the Delaware and Susquehannah Navigation Co. to accomplish the same purpose.[152] On November 22, 1826, while Wright was still preparing his report, the managers reached an agreement with Edward Clark to obtain the D&SN charter. Clark and an associate reserved the right to take 100 shares of D&H stock if the project succeeded.[153] On January 10, 1827 Wright's survey and estimate were read to the board, and on January 27 "maps and profiles of the proposed canal to the village of Deposit, and from thence to Bettsburgh on the Susquehanna" were presented.

These documents made it obvious that the project would have been much more demanding than the casual estimate cited in the March 1826 report. In addition, mention of a tunnel revived unpleasant recollections of the Shawangunk controversy. Nevertheless, the managers seemed ready to press onward and forwarded Wright's report to President Bolton, then in Albany. It will be remembered that as one element of its planned request for state aid the D&H sought permission to extend to Deposit.

Thereafter, with many other matters on the minds of the managers, the Susquehanna proposal may have lost some of its urgency. In December 1827, the close of the year which had started with the company seemingly committed to the extension, the managers responded favorably to a proposal from a Sherman Page to obtain the charter of the Delaware & Susquehannah Navigation Co.[154] The transfer was not finalized at that time, for a year later the company minutes record that "The President was authorized to write to Sherman Page, saying that the right this company have in the Charter of the Delaware & Susquehannah Navigation Company shall not stand in the way of making the canal, for which it appears there is an intention on his part with others, to apply for an act of incorporation."[155]

By early 1830 the full cost of the route to Carbondale was known, as was the extent of their resources; nevertheless, the D&H managers still found the upper Delaware alluring. Necessity forced them to try a new tactic, and they decided to apply to Congress for aid in constructing the extension to Deposit.[156] A memorial asking for a subscription to $900,000 of D&H stock for this purpose was drafted, but at its February 17, 1830 session the board tabled it. No reason was given, but by then the Jackson administration, hateful to the interests that controlled the D&H, was entering its second year, and the managers may have concluded the proposal was hopeless in that political climate. Later, after the D&H prospered to the point where it could have reconsidered, there is no indication that the brilliant vision of the Susquehanna reappeared.

In his annual message of January 2, 1827, Governor DeWitt Clinton advocated a canal extending not only up the Delaware, but on to Hornell and perhaps even to Lake Erie and Pittsburgh. At that time the Chenango branch of the New York State canal system was not even in the planning stage, and Clinton's concept would have drained the traffic of much of central New York down the D&H. Clinton was surely as visionary a dreamer as ever walked a towpath in his imagination. Superficially it might seem that the D&H managers were examining the Delaware extension mainly to stay in the Governor's good graces, but the full record makes it clear that their interest was genuine and that they too were enthralled by the possibility of capturing the business of the rich inland empire. Wright's report noted that the southern route would add two weeks at each end of the navigation season compared to the Erie. This kind of competition might have been unwelcome even to Clinton, who never saw a canal he didn't like.

Another proposed extension occupied the board in 1827. This time the source was Maurice Wurts, who expressed interest in building a canal from the forks some distance up the Dyberry. Wurts thought there was potential for a "large business" up the Dyberry, although this was visionary, since the region was virtually uninhabited at the time.[157] Wurts saw an opening because, as he pointed out, the wording of the Pennsylvania legislation did not grant the company the right to build canals in other directions than toward its mines. Another appeal of the Dyberry canal was that it might provide access to the Lackawanna and ultimately offer another chance to intercept the traffic of the Susquehanna, which exercised an almost magnetic attraction. The D&H 1828 annual report notes that the Dyberry canal "will present a strong inducement to connect by rail road . . . with the Susquehannah, at the great bend."

Since the D&H would have provided the only outlet of the Dyberry canal, Maurice Wurts asked the D&H to guarantee equality of tolls on traffic to and from the Dyberry. At a meeting on September 1, 1827 the managers agreed, but imposed other requirements on Wurts, among them that the locks on the Dyberry should be the same dimensions as those on the D&H, that the canal should be at least ten miles long, that it should be completed within four years, and that the junction point with the D&H should be approved by the D&H engineer.[158] Some of these stipulations seem to be gratuitous interference, and Maurice Wurts thought so, as he expressed in his letter of September 18: "It appears to me that the preamble & Resolution contain all that is necessary to secure the interests of the Company."[159] In consequence, Wurts concluded, in diplomatic phrasing, that he did not consider the policy of the board "sufficient to induce him to become a party to the prosecution of a canal up the Valley of the Dyberry."[160] This rejection may not have been considered final, since the 1828 annual report still treats the Dyberry canal as a live possibility.

Thereafter, the thought of extensions lost whatever appeal it had to the company. In 1830 Charles Miner, a Wilkes-Barre newspaper editor and later historian, asked the D&H if it would be interested in building a canal or railroad down the Lackawanna Valley. The D&H was then in a period of deepening financial stress, and the managers were being no more than honest when they responded "the company at present could not embark in any plan for extending their work."[161] Perhaps the "at present" was a key qualification, for in later years the company's ambitions certainly turned in that direction. The unfulfilled plans of the 1820s pointed out the course of the company's later growth. It is unlikely that individuals who were prominent in 1827 still occupied positions of authority in 1870, when the D&H leased the Albany & Susquehanna RR. Yet some mysterious sort of corporate memory may have been at work to bring the D&H back into the area staked out by Wright when it was still largely a wilderness.

A Developmental Canal?

SINCE THEY WENT NOWHERE, it is easy to dismiss the expansion proposals. Because the Susquehanna project in particular exceeded the company's capabilities, they also seem faintly ludicrous. Nevertheless, it would be a mistake to laugh at these proposals, however much they resembled balloons with nail holes. While they fizzled, they were taken seriously at the time and reflected the direction of the company's thinking. Their failure may have helped define the nature of the company. The riches of central New York were obvious, but also undeveloped. If the D&H had been able to tap this region in the 1830s its place in the canal categorization would have become much different: like the Erie, it would have become a true developmental canal.

The distinction between "developmental" and "exploitative" canals, originated by H. Jerome Cranmer, attempts to create more meaningful categories than the traditional division by state or region. It refines a method of classification developed as early as 1823, when Army engineers divided canals into two classes: those which were devoted to the "general interest of the country" and those whose main purpose was producing revenue.[162] This approach may represent a theoretical rationale for the proposals made by Treasury Secretary Albert Gallatin in his 1808 report on public improvements. Responding to a congressional request, Gallatin proposed

Rosendale: an example of a town that prospered with the canal.
CREDIT
Kenneth A. Shuker.

canals through four "necks of land" to provide what amounted to an intercoastal waterway along the Atlantic seaboard, as well as canals linking four pairs of rivers to breach the Appalachian barrier.

In his revision of the engineers' classification, Cranmer acknowledged that there were relatively few "exploitative" canals, and of course all such arbitrary classification systems, while improving on a simple geographic arrangement, are imperfect. No canal promoter would have dared admit that a proposed waterway would be anything but profitable; so in that sense all canals offered at least the pretense of being "revenue producing." As with any system of classification there are always going to be mixed or debatable examples, but that should not deter us from applying a scheme that promises a better understanding of any individual canal.

Substituting the term "navigational" for "exploitative" may be productive. A navigational canal may be defined as one that makes it easier to travel from point to point with little regard for the country that lies between. Examples would include the Delaware & Raritan, the Chesapeake & Delaware and the later Cape Cod Canals, but this category is undeniably smaller. Some of the early "bypass" canals such as the Patowmack, the canals at Enfield and South Hadley on the Connecticut River and at Fort Stanwix and Little Falls in New York State at first glance seem difficult to classify. They attempted to improve navigation on a river, but their intention was really of a developmental nature—to open up an area whose growth had been retarded by lack of good transportation. The proof of this is that several bypass channels were precursors of major developmental canals. A similar progression can be seen in the Lehigh Valley.

In this typology the D&H falls into the developmental or colonization category because it was attempting to unlock an area that had been handicapped by inadequate transportation. Superficially the D&H shares one characteristic of the navigational canals in that it had relatively little concern for the territory it passed through. This points up the fact that the D&H falls into a specialized subcategory within the large family of developmental canals. Unlike the more typical representatives—the Erie, the Chesapeake & Ohio, the Pennsylvania State Canals and the canals of Ohio and Indiana, the D&H was not primarily concerned with opening up a vast new region. This is true even though the area it penetrated was as much a frontier as the others. The D&H, with a few close relatives, had the more limited purpose of transporting one significant commodity—anthracite coal—from its source to tidewater markets. In this sense—though the difference is only one of degree—canals like the D&H were more inward-looking, seeking to serve or enlarge existing markets in the coastal cities, as opposed to creating new markets in previously unsettled areas. The relatively small but vital subcategory of anthracite canals was recognized as long ago as 1908 by Chester Lloyd Jones in *The Economic History of the Anthracite----Tidewater Canals*, a work that is still valuable. Jones adds the Lehigh Navigation, the Delaware Division Canal, the Morris Canal and the Schuylkill Navigation to the D&H in his class of anthracite canals.[163] He treats the Delaware Division essentially as an extension of the Lehigh. None of these canals figured in Gallatin's 1808 national program.

As the failure of the Orange & Sussex charter partially confirms, the counties of Ulster, Orange and Sullivan and the Lackawaxen Valley could not have supported a canal on their own merits. However, once the D&H was compelled by geographical necessity to enter that territory it tried to squeeze the maximum advantage out of it. If a slurry technology for anthracite had existed in the 1820s, the D&H probably would have built a direct pipeline to New York City. Since that was

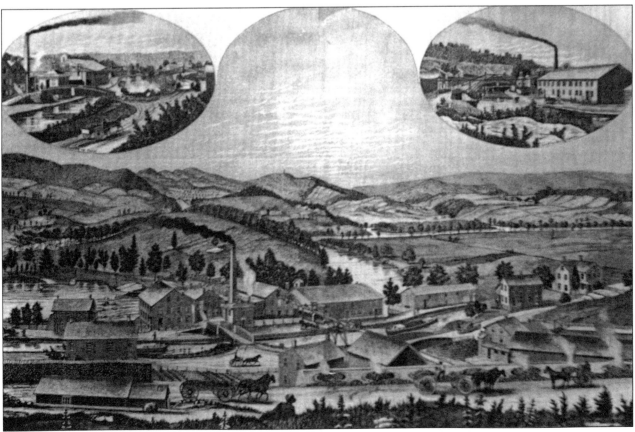

Linking the Delaware and the Hudson ◆ 85

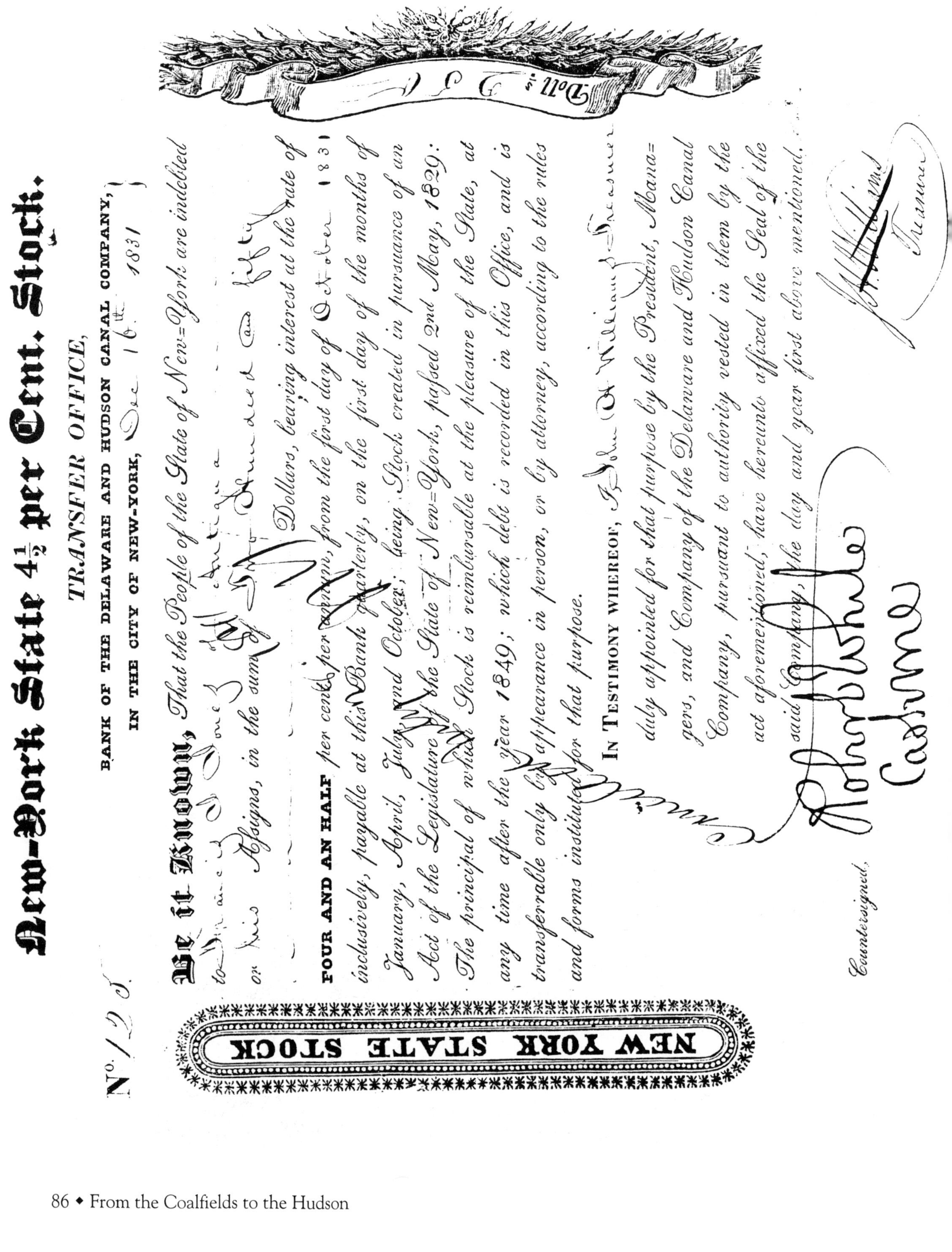

New-York State 4½ per Cent. Stock.

TRANSFER OFFICE,

BANK OF THE DELAWARE AND HUDSON CANAL COMPANY,

IN THE CITY OF NEW-YORK, *Dec. 16th 1831*

Nº *125*

Be it Known, That the People of the State of New-York are indebted to _____ or his Assigns, in the sum of _____ Dollars, bearing interest at the rate of

FOUR AND AN HALF per cent. per annum, from the first day of October 1831, inclusively, payable at this Bank Quarterly, on the first day of the months of January, April, July, and October; being Stock created in pursuance of an Act of the Legislature of the State of New-York, passed 2nd May, 1829: The principal of which Stock is reimbursable at the pleasure of the State, at any time after the year 1849; which debt is recorded in this Office, and is transferrable only by appearance in person, or by attorney, according to the rules and forms instituted for that purpose.

In Testimony Whereof, John A. Williams, Treasurer duly appointed for that purpose by the President, Managers, and Company of the Delaware and Hudson Canal Company, pursuant to authority vested in them by the act aforementioned, have hereunto affixed the Seal of the said Company, the day and year first above mentioned.

Treasurer

Countersigned,

Cashier

NEW YORK STATE STOCK

impossible, the managers, with characteristic thrift, decided to treat the intervening counties as more than just a run of pipe between well and faucet. This attitude of enlightened self-interest was evident in the decision to open stock subscription books at Goshen and Kingston.

Hone, as noted, spoke at some length of the canal's potential to enrich the surrounding region when turning the ceremonial first spadeful of earth. Some of this can undoubtedly be dismissed as public relations, but he and the other New York managers genuinely believed in the canal's importance as a developmental artery. The annual report presented March 1826 enumerates in considerable detail the natural resources that could be transported by the yet-unbuilt waterway: "Esopus mill stones," black marble, freestone, building marble, oak timber suitable for shipbuilding and tanners bark, and pine, as well as limestone, clay, and natural cement. The black marble, said to be "equal to that of Kilkenny in Ireland," was the only one of these resources that seems not to have been exploited significantly; all the others became lucrative sources of traffic.

Events proved the accuracy of what might have seemed to be extravagant forecasts. It was astonishing how quickly the economic effects of the canal were felt, even before the Pennsylvania section was fully operational. A newspaper ad in May 1827 noted that James J. Morison & Co. had opened a store on the canal basin at what was still called Mamakating.[164] In the following year a new establishment selling a diverse assortment of merchandise: "dry goods, hardware, crockery and glassware, Iron & Steel, Cut & Wrought Nails, Pork, Fish, Flower &c." was opened on the D&H dock at Kingston Landing. Canal engineer James McEntee became a partner in this enterprise.[165] During the summer of 1828, the first season of full operation, James W. Philips & Co. had already established a freight line on the canal. With the boats *Liberty*, *Gold Hunter* and *Royal Oak*, Philips planned to make at least three trips a week between Phillipsport and the Hudson.[166] Nor was incipient industry, still dependent on natural resources, ignored. The 1826 annual report cited factories in Sullivan County manufacturing leather, card backs, bed steads, chair frames, etc. In January 1828 owner Jacob L. Snyder sought to take advantage of rising property values by selling his mill and factory comprising a grist mill, cording machine, fulling mill and cloth dressing establishment. Snyder was careful to note that his complex was located "on the bank of the D&H Canal . . . about six miles from tide water."[167] Perhaps a newspaper columnist was not exaggerating when he wrote of what he called the Rundout Valley: "With all these advantages of nature and art, and with a population distinguished for wealth, intelligence, and industry, who shall set bounds to the improvement of the valley?"[168]

Eng.d by J Rogers

Philip Hone

IS THERE an individual but has witnessed with feelings of pride and satisfaction the prospects of incalculable advantages to this section of the country from these works . . . —Bethany (Pennsylvania) Enquirer

Coming of Age

I N THE FALL OF 1829 the D&H had what amounted to its commencement: its long period of preparation was at an end, and it was ready to go out into the world. The system was complete: coal moved from the mines at Carbondale over the rollercoaster "gravity" railway and was loaded into canal boats at Honesdale. Stair-stepping over the terrain through 108 lift locks, crossing the pooled Delaware along a rope, towed by steamboat the last miles down the Rondout, canal boats brought the coal to Bolton, where it was transferred again to ships for consumers in New York, Albany and other river ports. Like any vigorous, ambitious youth the D&H entered a business world alive with opportunity, but also populated by rivals who were ready to pounce on any mistake. Inexperienced and engaged in a largely untried business filled with unforeseen perils, the young company battled to survive.

When Philip Hone toured the company's works in mid-October 1829, his fondest expectations seemed to be realized. On October 14 the railway, which had been transporting 60 tons of coal a day, began carrying 120 tons. Jervis believed it could soon be increased to 180 tons. Hone described the system in some detail and actually rode the cars over the planes. The ride, he found, "was delightful, its pleasure being occasionally heightened by a feeling of apprehension in places where we found ourselves elevated 30 or 40 feet from the ground in the midst of wild uncultivated forests."[1] On the level where steam locomotives were supposed to have been used, Hone found horses at work, each pulling four wagons loaded with 2½ tons of coal. "The whole appears to be in complete and successful operation," he concluded.

The rosy conditions described by the ex-mayor proved to be of short duration. Soon after his visit, problems with the iron chains on the planes threatened literally to wreck the company's fortunes. On December 1 an alarmed Maurice Wurts wrote from his headquarters in Clarksville that "all dependence on the chains should be abandoned." So many wagons had been wrecked by chains breaking that only 125 tons a day could be carried, instead of the 180 that was feasible.[2] Wurts listed some of the wrecks and concluded that "the evidence is no longer to be resisted that the chains cannot be depended upon for our next years business."

Jervis's position was ambiguous. In his *Reminiscences* he has little to say beyond acknowledging the failure of the chains. Maurice Wurts's letter notes "a strong desire on the part of Mr. Jervis to adhere to the chains."[3] Like most inventors he was probably reluctant to give up on his creation. In attributing the failures to faulty manufacture of the links he was undoubtedly correct, but it made no difference.[4]

The board agreed with Maurice that sufficient evidence lay piled at the foot of the planes. By return mail Treasurer Flewelling informed Wurts that ropes "without tar of 6½ & 8 inches circumference" had been ordered and were being sent up on the steamboat *Congress* for use on the descending planes. Bowing to Jervis, the board deferred action on replacing the chains on the ascending planes while the engineer tried "new appendages fixed to the waggons" to solve the problem.[5]

Plane on the gravity railway.
CREDIT
National Canal Museum.

This device apparently did not help, for on January 6, 1830 the board resolved to use rope in place of chains on all but ascending Plane No.1. In the following month, after receiving a letter from ironworkers Blackwell & McFarlane that they were "unwilling to undertake the making of chain for Plane No.1 and guaranteeing to pay damages which might result from breaking," the managers decided to use rope on that plane as well.[6] The ropes, while cumbersome, greatly reduced the losses from breakage, and in 1830 the company was able to carry 43,600 tons. The wagons seemed entirely safe for travel, even by female passengers. Defending the road from criticism by another newspaper, the Bethany *Enquirer* reported that "Parties of *ladies* have traveled from Honesdale to Carbondale . . . and have found nothing very *astonishing* or alarming in the *velocity* of the transportation."[7] It had been daring for the managers and engineers to test the limits of technology, but now instead of steam locomotives and iron chains they had been forced to fall back on the safe but conventional methods of horsepower and ropes—natural in place of manufactured substances.

A novel braking method relying on fans that Jervis had invented for use on the planes does not appear to endured for long, although Josiah White found it still in use when he visited the area in July 1830.[8] Disappointment over the failure of his innovations, along with the fact that the transportation system was fully operational, if on a simpler basis, may have contributed to Jervis's resignation from the company in May 1830.[9] His departure symbolically marked the end of the developmental phase. Thereafter responsibility was divided, and with one brief exception no individual held the position of chief engineer for the entire system. On Jervis's recommendation James Archbald was put in charge of the railway and mines, while the canal was placed under the supervision of Russel F. Lord. Both were young men who had, like Jervis, started as rodmen and had gained field experience under his watchful eye. The departing engineer described Archbald as having "an excellent engineering mind and great practical sagacity and . . . eminently upright in purpose," while Lord "was a man of good executive ability and indefatigable in industry."[10] This direct line of descent from Wright through Jervis, from the Erie to the D&H, lasted into the 1850s.

The setbacks on the railway could be attributed to the unpredictable outcome of an otherwise admirable attempt to push the frontiers of technology. Another problem of the early years was largely of the company's own making. It was foreshadowed in a report by Maurice Wurts dated September 18, 1827, in which, responding to Bolton's request to insure the delivery of coal at the canal during the coming winter, "I have desired Mr. Young to make immediate preparation & commence uncovering and quarrying where the last coal was taken out, & where from 1,000 to 2,000 Tons can readily be got out . . . ."[11] Maurice was also hoping to justify the money spent on road building by sending this coal over the new highway.

The term "quarrying" was significant, for it meant that the product was surface coal, weathered and impure. When consumers discovered it would not burn properly, the entire reputation of the company was threatened. If the Lackawanna coal would not burn successfully, the five-year effort to bring it to market would be wasted. Competitors jumped at the chance to discredit the D&H, and their criticism was effective because it was already recognized that there were differences in the burning characteristics and the ash of coal from the different anthracite districts. The Wurtses themselves had exploited this situation in 1824 by obtaining a testimonial to the effect that "The Lehigh Coal are harder, and therefore more difficult to ignite."[12] In the imperfect state of knowledge at the time, a plausible case could be made that the product of an entire region was inferior. It required a great deal of scrambling for the D&H to restore its damaged reputation, and in the end the most successful tactic was giving partial refunds to people who had bought the defective coal.[13]

The Anthracite Rivals

IF WE LIKEN THE D&H IN THE FALL OF 1829 to a fresh-faced graduate, he was carrying his diploma into a tough neighborhood, perhaps whistling cheerfully to keep up appearances. The early signs of harmony and a possible division of markets represented by the journey of Josiah White and William Wurts proved deceptive, and the relationship among the anthracite districts became one of unremitting hostility. In July 1830 Josiah White's journal records another visit to the D&H mines and railway, but does not elaborate on whether he met with any of the Wurtses or company officials.[14] The Wurts correspondence contains frequent nervous references to their rivals in the Lehigh and Schuylkill, especially the former, which seemed to be a more serious threat in the New York market. Paradoxically, the Lehigh principals seemed more worried about the Schuylkill than the D&H, which was no danger in the Philadelphia market.[15] The quarrelsome family of anthracite canals was a self-defined grouping composed of the D&H and the companies it kept a wary eye on: the Schuylkill and Lehigh primarily, but also connections such as the Delaware, Delaware & Raritan, and Morris canals. The Morris was a mixed example: it was not a pure anthracite canal since it did not directly reach the coal fields; and it had characteristics of a developmental canal, intended to exploit the iron ore and agricultural resources of northern New Jersey. Yet as a functional extension of the Lehigh reaching directly into the New York market, it threatened the D&H.

The Wurtses watched developments in the Lehigh anxiously. Benjamin Wright had apparently visited the Lehigh in 1825, whereupon John Wurts inquired "What does [he] say about the Lehigh works?"[16] John expressed his feelings toward the competitor in vivid terms when he referred to "The Lehigh Company, whose opposition we have encountered at every turn, and who have ever acted with an illiberality and meanness characteristic of little minds."[17] What had particularly aroused John Wurts's animosity was his belief that the Lehigh had established a separate coal company in New York and was preparing to apply for a bank charter in that state. John pleaded with Maurice to persuade strong men from Ulster and Sullivan to serve in the legislature, "men who will be prompt to perceive and repel an enemy."[18] These concerns probably account for a resolution by the D&H managers in January 1826 requesting "Mr. Wurts" [presumably Maurice] 'to proceed to Albany to attend to the interests of this company and to oppose the application of the Morris Canal Co. and the Lehigh Co. for privileges which are considered as invasions of the vested rights of this Company."[19] The D&H had no credit in New Jersey and could not stand up to the Lehigh and Schuylkill in Pennsylvania, but in New York there was hope of bringing its influence to bear.

The conflict between the Lehigh and the D&H took the form of a race to complete their system first, in the belief that whichever gained a solid foothold in New York City would have a lasting advantage. This was stated explicitly by Nathan Smith, the canny insider, in a letter to President Bolton. Smith wrote that "one of the principal advantages the Lackawaxen has over other coal projects will be found in the certainty of the Delaware & Hudson Canal Co. possessing a perfected line of communication between the mines and the market, before any other company which deserve to be mentioned." He added that the D&H, by selling at favorable prices, would expand the consumption of coal and "secure the New York market against all possible competition." In case Bolton had missed the point, Smith observed that "the Lehigh Co. dreading such a result are making great exertion in the money market to obtain funds sufficient to complete their slack water navigation."[20] Having learned in November 1827 that the D&H Canal was essentially complete, the usually somber John Wurts, in a memorable and revealing quote, said he would prepare a newspaper article "by way of gratifying our Lehigh friends, who would as soon see a viper in their path, as meet with such a paragraph in the papers."[21]

A Battle for the Rivers

AS THEY HAD TAKEN ADVANTAGE of the D&H's lapse in marketing inferior coal, the anthracite rivals rejoiced in—possibly even abetted—a controversy that arose between the company and lumber raftsmen. This battle over control of the rivers was in many respects a classic conflict between the frontier and advancing civilization. Both the D&H and the raftsmen exploited a natural resource; but the D&H represented industrialization and permanence, while the raftsmen were engaged in one-time devastation, almost random except as it depended on access to suitable rivers. The raftsmen were unsupervised, untamed individualists; the D&H represented the rising system of organized corporate capitalism.

Like some present-day truckers, the raftsmen were vocal when they felt their interests were threatened. They rumbled with the potential of violence, and because they embodied the only economic activity in some of the backwoods areas, they could make their voices heard politically. Their concerns had been written pointedly into the Lackawaxen charter, which stated that it was the duty of Maurice Wurts "to make, construct and fix suitable and sufficient slopes and aprons, or other devices at each and every dam . . . in such manner as shall enable rafts of any description that can now be run in the other parts of the stream, when the same is in good rafting condition, to pass with safety over such dams." The 1825 amendment which permitted the merger of the D&H and Lackawaxen interests extended the protection for rafting, providing that improvements must "leave the channel . . . as safe and as convenient for the descent of rafts as it now is."[22] Like the "Don't Tread on Me" flags of colonial rebels, these clauses served as a clear warning to the D&H, but they also created a potential for exploitation by the company's enemies.

Perhaps because the earlier legislation applied only to the Lackawaxen, the D&H was initially less concerned about creating obstructions in the Delaware. Complaints that the Delaware dam was hampering rafting arose, and in February 1829 the board's Canal Committee recommended instructing Jervis to make

Lumber rafting on the Delaware, though much diminished, outlasted the canal by several years. Matamoras, PA, opposite Port Jervis, is on the left.
CREDIT
Minisink Valley Historical Soc.

whatever improvements were necessary to "prevent loss or inconvenience to those rafting on said rivers."[23] Jervis offered to meet with a committee of raftsmen to "make such improvements upon the aprons of the dams as they shall deem necessary" at the expense of the company.[24] When nothing was done, perhaps because the committee was never formed, the raftsmen resorted to their own solutions. In April 1829 Maurice Wurts informed the managers that they had cut down part of the dam.[25] Maurice must have negotiated with the raftsmen, for in December he forwarded "an engagement signed by twenty-one persons interested in the Lumber and Rafting business on the Delaware river to lend all the aid in their power to protect the works of the Company." The board then resolved to exonerate the signers from prosecution for the earlier damage.[26] This acknowledges the fact that at the same time it protected the rafting interest, the Pennsylvania charter had given Maurice Wurts a powerful weapon by providing a penalty of four times damages for anyone impeding navigation. John Wurts later acknowledged that the company had been able to arrest one of the men responsible for the damage. Furthermore, the man was arrested in New York although the destruction had occurred on the Pennsylvania side of the river, because the D&H conveniently assented to New York's claim of jurisdiction over the full width of the river.[27]

It was almost impossible to keep a contentious issue like this out of politics; on February 3, 1830 Pennsylvania appointed a commission of engineers to investigate "the effect of the D&H works on the lumbermen."[28] On its part, the D&H board named Maurice Wurts and Philip Hone to meet with the state engineers. A few days later Maurice begged off on account of ill health and was replaced by another board member, banker Thomas Tileston.[29] With his prestige and diplomatic skills, Hone was a good choice, although he consented to go only "reluctantly."[30]

When it appeared that a powerful and dangerous current was running against the D&H, sober second thoughts began to appear. The influential Bethany *Enquirer*, while acknowledging that it did not approve of the D&H actions toward the lumbermen, reminded its readers that

> This is not a question for adjustment between the raftsmen and the Canal Company; it has gone far beyond that, and it is now a matter between the Counties of Wayne, Susquehanna and Luzerne, and the State of Pennsylvania *whether the Delaware and Hudson Canal Company shall exist or not*. Is there a man among us who would not deprecate the destruction of this Company? Is there an individual but has witnessed with feelings of pride and satisfaction the prospects of incalculable advantages to this section of the country from these works—nay, the benefits which have already accrued? We put it to everyone, whether the sacrifice of the Delaware and Hudson Canal at this time would not carry with it the ruin of the County.... Those who were in this country some years ago when the sole source of revenue was lumber, and the only dependence for a market was on the precarious event of freshets at a particular season of the year, can well realize the change in the prospect—And they will unhesitatingly admit that our interests are so closely allied with those of the Canal Company as to excite our alarm upon the least appearance of evil to it.

In a similar vein, delegates from Wayne County adopted a resolution on February 9 which, shunning rhetorical moderation, asked: "Shall we permit ourselves by one mighty blow to be struck into that dark abyss of a confined interior, from which we have just emerged, without exerting every nerve to prevent it[?]"[31]

Hone and Tileston arrived at Honesdale February 14, 1830. They found that "the excitement which has been raised by the vile misrepresentations of Mr

Meredith and others of our Ennemies [*sic*], has been turned completely in our favour and the whole of this and the neighbouring Counties have risen in mass and forwarded counter memorials to the Legislature."[32] On the following day a "cavalcade" of some 50 people, including the engineers, raftsmen, and the D&H's accusers, set off down the Lackawaxen. Hone said that even the raftsmen, who "had been induced by misrepresentations to sign the memorials against our Company, are now ready to a man to fight for us if necessary." He added that "The Raftsmen declare the navigation is safer than it was before the Canal was constructed."[33]

Members of the party concluded their work on February 16 and went their separate ways. Meredith and his allies chose to return by another road, which Hone considered fortunate, as "the odium which his false charges have created against him is so great that it is doubtful if his personal safety might not have been endangered." According to Hone, Meredith had been hung in effigy in several places.[34] It might appear that Hone was seeing what he wanted to see, but his observations were confirmed by events. The legislative inquiry turned out to be entirely favorable to the D&H. Meanwhile, the company had defanged hostility by offering to meet with a committee of raftsmen and make whatever improvements were necessary to provide safe passage over the dams.[35] The D&H had originally been expected to build a river lock in the Delaware dam, but made a deal with Pennsylvania to avoid this obligation: in return for allowing a connection with the proposed extension of the state's Delaware Canal to Carpenter's Point, the D&H was excused from constructing the potentially challenging river lock.[36]

Hone was correct in blaming Thomas Meredith for instigating the dispute. The *Enquirer* said that one disgruntled individual (unnamed, but almost certainly Meredith) had opposed and undermined the D&H at every turn, culminating in inciting the raftsmen.[37] Meredith was the son of a prominent Philadelphian, and his

In the Narrows of the Lackawaxen, a "must see" for tourists, a costly stone wall separated the canal from the river, partly to avoid offending the raftsmen.
CREDIT
National Canal Museum.

relationship with the Wurtses may have been older—and perhaps originally friend-lier. Steers concludes, probably with good reason, that "The Merediths, although men of considerable strength of character, were somewhat eccentric."[38] The reasons for his vitriolic hostility are not altogether clear, but it seems that Meredith owned coal beds which he sought to exploit. If the D&H were declared a public highway, it would provide an outlet for his coal. The D&H Minutes report receipt of a letter from Meredith on January 21, 1829, in which he inquired about the "toll to be paid on coal to be transported on the canal from mines owned by individuals." No response is recorded.

These circumstances make it likely that Meredith was responsible for a remark-able polemic entitled "MONOPOLY IS TYRANNY: An Appeal to the People and Legislature from the Oppression of the Delaware & Hudson Canal Company," which was published anonymously at Dundaff, Pennsylvania, sometime in 1830.[39] The author argues that the D&H, which had been granted the right to improve transportation, had instead created a monopoly of coal traffic. He notes that he had asked Bolton about setting rates—further evidence that Meredith is the author—but had received no satisfaction. While the harsh and one-sided nature of the pamphlet makes it suspect, the author perceived some of the contradictions in the character of the D&H which would soon have to be resolved. Though it offered no more than wry consolation to the D&H, their Lehigh rivals ran afoul of similar hostility and were violently condemned as monopolists.[40] With the rise of the Jacksonian Democrats, who inflamed and exploited resentment of the propertied classes, partisan politics were kept at a brisk boil.

Troublesome Phantoms

THE D&H WAS A YOUNG COMPANY in a young country in a young economy shaped by youthful attitudes. It was a dynamic, unruly time in American history. The expansionist impulse had become irresistible and was no longer unrealistic: the land was there; its resources were known, and it was inevitable that they would be developed. Meanwhile the example of the Erie Canal gleamed like a beacon, but perhaps a mooncusser's treacherous light, showing the spectacular success that could be won under the banner of "internal improvement." The country buzzed with imaginative schemes to open new transportation routes; yet the capital available was inadequate to complete even a few of them. Thus it was an agonizing period for visionary promoters who were unable to pursue plans they believed in with all their heart. Desperate competition resulted. As in a card game, the hand one was dealt often did not matter as much as how shrewdly and cold-bloodedly one played it.

For established companies like the D&H the enthusiasm for improvements added to their problems. At the same time it was trying to hold a front against its competitors and perhaps launch an offensive into new areas, it was threatened by the proliferation of new transportation schemes, like brushfires springing up without warning in its rear. In early 1830 the D&H, clinging to the fading vision of expansion, was considering an appeal to Congress to aid in financing the extension up the Delaware. At the same moment it was being threatened by hostile interests on its home ground. The Orange & Sussex (largely Newburgh) backers, having failed to persuade the D&H to adopt their preferred route, continued their campaign. They had obtained a charter for a canal in 1824—only a year after the D&H itself was authorized. An 1828 New York amendment gave them rights to construct a railroad, although it is not certain that a similar charter was granted in New Jersey.[41] The Orange businessmen who supported this proposal were not able to generate financing, but the concept smoldered behind the D&H, one more nightmare.

When the Orange & Sussex seemed to be stalled, Orangemen secured another charter, the Hudson & Delaware, in April 1830. This presented a more potent threat because it was allied with projects in the neighboring states. As its name implied, it represented an open challenge to the D&H. New York granted it rights to build a railroad from Newburgh to strike the Delaware "at or near Carpenter's Point."[42] Thereafter, it was expected to link up with a Pennsylvania company to reach the Lackawanna valley "in the very heart of the coal region." According to Booth this would have been a "gravity" road something like the D&H, powered by stationary steam engines.

The danger to the D&H was increased immensely in 1832 when the New Jersey, Hudson and Delaware RR was chartered, largely by Paterson manufacturers. New Jersey showed that it took this concession seriously by allowing it to issue $1 million of stock and to increase to $2 million. The company was given the right to build across the state, from the Hudson to a point on the Delaware between the New York State line and the mouth of the Paulinskill.[43] With good reason the *Newton* (New Jersey) *Herald* described its charter as "perhaps the most liberal ever granted by the State."[44] This concept had its origins in a survey performed by none other than John Langdon Sullivan in 1828 at the request of the Society for the Establishment of Useful Manufactures (SEUM), an organization formed by Alexander Hamilton and others in 1791 to exploit the enormous water power potential of Paterson, New Jersey.

Sullivan's study contributed to a fierce controversy between the Society and the Morris Canal over water rights, which may explain why no progress was made for several years.[45] In 1831 Sullivan ran several more surveys between Paterson and the Delaware Water Gap. His report was addressed to Roswell L. Colt, president of the SEUM, indicating that the organization had maintained its active interest in the Delaware railroad.[46] Whether the Hudson & Delaware charter was the product of these surveys, which would indicate that members of the SEUM were responsible, is less certain: Lucas states that "Paterson manufacturers" obtained the Hudson & Delaware charter; while Kalata says that "Sussex County" was responsible.[47] An important consideration is that the earlier SEUM surveys did not result in a railroad charter; the NJH&D appears to have been the first railroad authorized to pass through the region. This suggests at least some connection to the SEUM. Furthermore, Sullivan's various lines all brought the route to the Delaware between the Paulinskill and the state line, as specified in the NJH&D charter.[48]

Sullivan's 1828 report envisioned a novel system of track in which the rails would be mounted on timber posts set at various heights above the ground, to even out the grade without filling. Ever the promoter, he had acquired rights to this system, which was probably never employed in its original design, but which resembles the method first used in constructing part of the Erie RR. Presumably the engineer proposed to use horse power on this line, but technology was advancing so rapidly that by 1831 he was able to advocate locomotive power with great conviction. He argued that a locomotive route, although longer, would be faster than relying on planes (the "post road" concept seems to have been dismissed by then).[49] The Newton *Herald*'s description of the NJH&D route notes that "actual survey" had found that the route, with one possible exception, could be operated

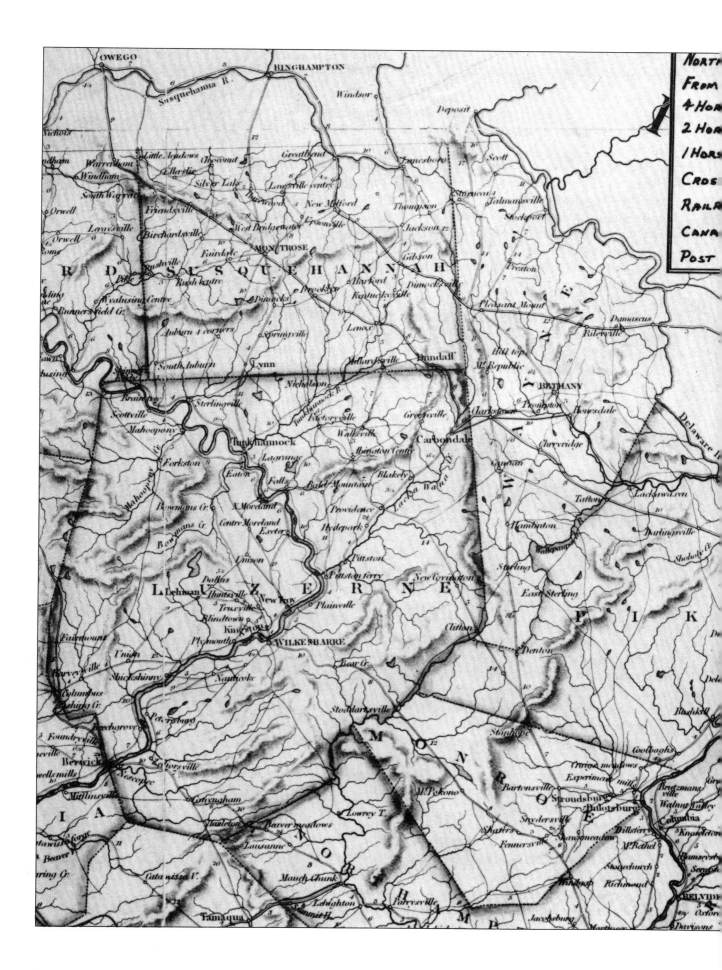

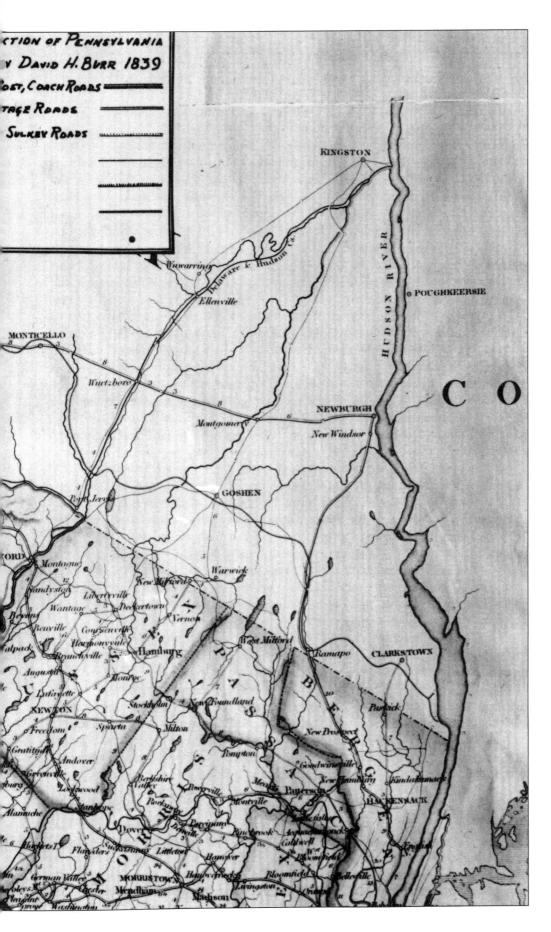

Map after David H. Burr, 1839.
CREDIT
National Canal Museum.

by locomotives—another clue that Sullivan's survey for the SEUM was synonymous with the NJH&D.

To the D&H the impact of all these proposals in New York and New Jersey was bad enough, but greater danger lay in the plans to extend into Pennsylvania. Each of them spoke openly of penetrating to "the heart of the anthracite country," or some such language. In Pennsylvania they could link up with the sworn enemies of the D&H. None other than Thomas Meredith had obtained a charter for the Lackawannock & Susquehanna RR in 1826. This line was supposed to run from Leggetts's Creek in the township of Providence (now part of Scranton) about 47½ miles to the Great Bend of the Susquehanna.[50] There, as in the D&H schemes, it could open up the rich interior of New York State. Hollister says, with considerable restraint, that this project was "conceived more in a spirit of opposition to the Delaware and Hudson Canal Company than to promote the interests of the Lackawanna Valley."[51]

The danger of Meredith's charter was increased because it was, in turn, part of a larger plan. Between the Lackawanna Valley and the Delaware lay the proposed Susquehanna & Delaware Canal and Railroad Co. This entity had been chartered in 1826 by the redoubtable Henry W. Drinker, one of those improbable individuals who sometimes alight in the frontier like a bird blown off course. A member of the Philadelphia aristocracy and a former surveyor-general of the state, Drinker had acquired enormous land holdings east of present-day Scranton. Jason Torrey had helped him locate land and had been rewarded with a 400-acre tract.[52] Drinker dwelled in splendid isolation; but in effect he was land-poor, for his sprawling acreage remained largely worthless until it could be opened to development. In 1819 he took an important step in that direction by laying out a turnpike road from Tobyhanna to the Delaware Water Gap. His railroad charter was even bolder, reaching to Wilkes-Barre on the Susquehanna.[53] Powell maintains that this concept predates Drinker, having been originated by Jacob Cist sometime between 1815 and 1825 and refined in correspondence with George MacCulloch of Morristown, New Jersey, remembered as the main proponent of the Morris Canal.[54] While Drinker may not have been responsible for conceiving the precise route followed by his 1826 charter, his turnpike demonstrates an equally early recognition of the importance of transportation.

After several years of inactivity, interest in these projects revived in 1831, perhaps energized by Sullivan's work for the SEUM. Concern with linking the various schemes culminated in a railroad convention at Ithaca, New York, on May 11, 1831. At a time when only a few miles of railway were in operation in North America, serious talk was heard of a "great chain of Rail Road communication between Lake Erie and New York."[55] A meeting held in the court house at Bethany on January 23, 1832 endorsed this "grand project."[56] Even this conception was not sweeping enough to satisfy every dreamer. Sullivan had sought an endorsement from Drinker, and in his testimonial the ebullient Pennsylvanian speculated that their projects could be incorporated into a railroad reaching from the Hudson to the Mississippi Valley![57] Several actions were taken to give substance to these airy visions. For the first time surveys were conducted of the Drinker and Meredith routes, and also of the Hudson & Delaware from Newburgh to Carpenter's Point. The Lackawannock & Susquehanna RR was organized at Milford on September 27, 1831, with Meredith elected president. Drinker's Susquehanna & Delaware project was surveyed by Ephraim Beach, chief engineer of the Morris Canal.[58] This collaboration of opponents could not have been a cheering prospect for the D&H.

Already the issue was becoming complicated by an excess of alternatives. In 1833 was added a precocious proposal to extend the Elizabethtown & Somerville, an ancestor of the Central RR of New Jersey, to Belvidere, New Jersey, and from there to the Water Gap. It could then link up with the Drinker road and become part of the "great chain." As the report noted, the route would pass directly through Carbondale—the heart of D&H country.[59] Inevitably the question arose: how would all these brilliant plans affect the already shaky D&H? In his 1831 report Sullivan, despite his disputes with his former employers, tried to put a positive face on the matter, noting that the extension of his survey to the Great Bend and beyond "will greatly benefit the Hudson and Delaware [sic] Company, by opening a vent for their Coal to the western counties of New-York."[60] One of the organizers of the "Lackawanna RR" was Lynde Catlin, who had been ousted as manager of the D&H, supposedly because he lived too far from New York City. Jason Torrey and Nathaniel B. Eldred, active supporters of the D&H, signed the resolution supporting the Lackawanna project at the Bethany meeting.[61]

The response of the D&H itself was ambiguous. On June 20, 1831 the board declared that it felt "the liveliest interest in the success of the Lackawanna Rail Road and regard it as a project, the execution of which would be eminently beneficial to the Delaware and Hudson Canal Co., but while they entertain such views in relation to this work, and feel anxious for its accomplishment they apprehend that this company has no power to aid it by a subscription to its stock."[62] Undoubtedly, as Sullivan had pointed out, an extension to the west would open new markets for the D&H. After all, the company had sought to accomplish this on its own; nevertheless, an association with Meredith must have raised warning flags.

Broader schemes to open new routes to New York could not have been viewed with favor by the D&H. Any such proposal called attention to the fundamental weakness of the company: its indirect route to that market. On the map Carbondale was only about 95 miles from lower Manhattan, but the D&H route extended this to around 215 miles. Furthermore, even this elongated route was not exceptionally advantageous. The "slope" of the D&H Canal, measured in feet of rise and fall per mile, made it the ninth steepest in the country. In effect, this was a measurement of the resistance of the terrain to canal operation. Compared to the Erie Canal slope of 1.9 feet per mile—admittedly an exceptional example—the D&H figure was 9.9 feet. This substantially exceeded the Lehigh (7.4 feet) and the Schuylkill (5.4 feet,) but was, in turn, much less than the competing Morris Canal at 16.2 feet.[63]

The long overland haul to Rondout created an enduring temptation to competitors and a chronic source of worry for the D&H. For the managers, there was no choice but to maintain that in the formative years of the company its engineers had examined all possible routes and had chosen the most favorable one. In their 1828 annual report, amid what should have been the unalloyed enthusiasm of the first year of partial operation, the D&H managers remained intensely aware of competition. Almost like small boys looking over their shoulders while boasting, they asked, "is it assuming too much to claim for this Company a decided superiority over all others that look to this market for the sale of their Coal?" In case the embryonic security analysis of the era missed the point, the managers went on to make explicit comparisons with the Morris and the Delaware & Raritan canals, to the detriment of the New Jersey waterways. As with the failure of the locomotive, the stock market provided the most telling commentary. *Century of Progress* notes that the act incorporating the Hudson & Delaware RR on April 19,

1830 "was enough to disturb seriously the management of the [D&H] and to depress the market quotations for its stock."[64]

Fortunately for the D&H, the threats presented by the various railroad proposals never materialized. Even Drinker, a persuasive man with good connections, was unable to secure financing. In 1835 a compilation of transportation projects continued to list the New York Hudson & Delaware as "proposed to connect the work with another, to extend to Lackawanna coal-mines."[65] A year later James B. Sargent extended this company's survey 42 miles from the New York state line to the Delaware Water Gap. His report administered a direct slap at the D&H: "The main . . . advantages to be gained by the proposed connection with the Delaware and Susquehanna Railroad and the Hudson and Delaware [Railroad] in New-York will be found in the transportation of the Anthracite Coal, from the Lackawanna valley . . . . To the citizens of New-York in particular, who have been accustomed to observe the difficulty in obtaining it, and the constant and uniformly increasing price that it demands, a supply of fuel is becoming an object of the most anxious solicitude."[66]

But, as with the proposed connections, the laborious survey remained on the shelf; capital was scarce in the early 1830s, and the depression of 1837 made matters immeasurably worse. The rapid evolution of technology may have been another hinderance: even after promoters had decided on a railway in preference to a canal, they could not be sure whether a steam railroad, a horse railway, a gravity system, or some combination would be best. In a sense, the D&H was fortunate to have been conceived just before this overabundance of choices. The dismal failure of its potential rivals makes its own achievement all the more impressive. The stillborn charters of the early 1830s outlined the direction of future growth, but it was only in the 1850s that a great surge of railroad construction brought the early plans to fulfillment. By then technical advances had confirmed the superiority of steam railroads. Only a few individuals, such as John I. Blair, spanned both eras.

The Crisis

IN ANY SAGA OF YOUTHFUL PROGRESS, the hero must pass through a time of trial, and the D&H held true to form. There are scattered hints in the Wurts correspondence that the brothers had never been happy with John Bolton as president. The strains that beset the company in its first years of operation heightened their frustration. An letter from "N. T. E———d," presumably Eldred, to Maurice Wurts on January 9, 1830 shows that Maurice was receptive to criticism of Bolton. The writer describes how Hone showed the president a letter from John Wurts, adding that it "contained a great deal of good sense." This "threw Mr. Bolton immediately into a fret, and caused him to make some hasty remarks, which I thought did not please Mr. Hone."[67]

Several months later Maurice delivered a passionate indictment of Bolton. No longer attempting to preserve civility, he enumerated his grievances with bitter sarcasm. "It seems as if a nightmare rested upon the man & all his measures," Maurice exclaimed. Specifically, he accused Bolton of neglecting practical matters such as providing boats and wagons—"matters of too small moment for the great man's attention"—while occupying himself with "getting another Loan to be squandered as much as the last was at Bolton." In addition, Wurts blamed Bolton for causing needless "disgust" against the D&H in Ulster County.[68] The reference to loans is accurate, for the company minutes record many attempts to borrow from various sources during this period. Beyond its questionable purposes, the mere fact of borrowing was objectionable to the Wurtses because it would reduce earnings and therefore delay issuance of the deferred stock.

Bolton's animosity toward the Wurtses did not in itself threaten his position, for what one correspondent called an "unholy jealousy" against Maurice Wurts already existed on the D&H board.[69] However, Bolton's days would be numbered from the moment he antagonized Philip Hone, although the wheels might grind slowly. It was a sensitive issue, and in that dawn of corporate capitalism there were few precedents for removing a chief executive. Meanwhile the condition of the company was apparently worsening. The board finally determined that Bolton must depart, and after being visited by two of the members he tendered his resignation on April 8, 1831. He was allowed the diplomatic refuge of illness: his letter refers to "my impaired state of Health," and in accepting the resignation on April 13 the board expressed the wish "that his health may be speedily and permanently restored."[70] In his diary Hone merely reproduces Bolton's letter without comment. Samuel Flewelling, who must have been a close ally of Bolton, resigned as treasurer later in the same month.

What is often overlooked is that the board that disposed of Bolton was much different than the one that had existed a year earlier. Five members, four of whom were original managers, had not been returned in the election of March 1, 1831. A quiet revolution had thus already taken place, so that Bolton's ouster was probably predetermined. Bolton was succeeded immediately by John Wurts, who had been elected to the board in the same pivotal March 1 vote, at a salary of $3000 per annum. This marked the first time a member of the Wurts family had sat on the board since 1826. John Bolton, who had been president of the company during the demanding years of its construction and initial operation, spent the remaining years of his life in obscurity. He died in Baltimore in October 1838. As a final indignity, Bolton was the one D&H-bestowed place name that did not stick. The Wurtses found it distasteful, and John Wurts seemed to take pains to avoid using it. Today one could stay a long while in Rondout without finding anyone who knew the place had once been called Bolton.[71]

In true novelistic style, John Wurts moved into the president's chair at the hour of crisis for the D&H. According to one account, Dr. H. Hollister's unpublished history of the D&H, the managers had actually decided to dissolve. This calamity was averted only by a selfless act of Philip Hone. Brooding about the terrible decision, Hone "reflected upon the distress the failure would bring upon widows and orphans who had been led perhaps by the appearance of his name among the Managers to invest in its stock. This reflection so preyed upon his sensitive organization during the night that the next morning before ten o'clock he raised

Portrait of John Wurts.
CREDIT
D&H Canal Museum.

the whole sum needed to save the company and handed it to the President without security."[72] Johnston repeats this story and adds the actual amount Hone furnished ($50,000).[73] These accounts sound too melodramatic to be true, and probably are. There is no confirmation in other sources; and Hone does not mention the incident in his diary, although it would not be in character for him to take credit for such a deed. Hollister does not give a date for the supposed rescue; since he mentions Wurts but not Bolton it would seem to have been after the change of presidents, but he displays other points of confusion about D&H chronology.

Many years later a special committee of the board reviewed the history of the company in a report and described this period in lurid terms:

> [T]he competition of older and rival coal interests . . . was by no means the smallest obstacle in its path. Immense speculations were daily occurring in its stock; and a powerful party thereby created, who were untiring in their efforts and unscrupulous in their acts, to destroy an enterprise, that should from its nature have commended itself to the good will and fostering care of every man in the community. The credit of the Company was assailed, in every possible way that ingenuity and falsehood stimulated by cupidity could devise. Its coal, to place within reach of the New York market, it had expended millions, was loudly proclaimed to be valueless; or if it were otherwise, it was boldly asserted, that the works of the Company were so imperfect in their construction, and so perishable in their character as not to be capable of passing a sufficient amount of tonnage to pay an interest on their cost.[74]

From its style it is probable that this outburst was composed by John Wurts, who was a member of the committee; furthermore, he was one of only four members of the 1845 board who had also been on it in the early 1830s. The others, one of whom was Philip Hone, were not the likely authors of a polemic that displayed an intensity of feeling not moderated by the passage of nearly 15 years. Still, there is an element of irony in John Wurts condemning so vehemently the sort of speculation he and his brothers would have conducted at one time, if they had been able.

The replacement of Bolton by John Wurts, by bringing an end to the divergence of interest between the New York and Pennsylvania factions, at last reconciled the inherent conflict that had torn the D&H since its beginning. The nagging uncertainty over the deferred stock and the Wurts's resultant distrust of the D&H management was removed as an issue. With a Wurts sitting at the head of the D&H table, questions of speculation in the company's stock or leasing the system were no longer pertinent.

It is noteworthy that these schemes and controversies had continued almost to the day of Bolton's ouster. Prior to John Wurts's elevation, Maurice's position as agent gave the family virtually its only means of influencing the D&H. Often this must have been a distasteful duty, with ill feeling lingering from the board's rejection of the Dyberry canal and probably a variety of other irritations. In late 1828, with the conversion of the Lehigh system into a conventional lift-lock canal approaching completion, William Wurts pleaded with Maurice to remain in the post another few years "disagreeable as it may be" to protect the family interest.[75] About a month later John, probably responding to a letter from Maurice, observed "it would seem that things can hardly be worse between you and the Company." In this revealing letter John referred repeatedly to the D&H as "they," as in "I hope they will hold the key & lock up every ton of coal in that region but their own," (maintaining the monopoly the Wurtses had always sought). This language confirms how little influence the Wurtses then had on the management of the D&H.[76]

Given this sense of detachment, the Wurtses felt no compunction about indulging in another speculation in D&H stock. In December 1829 John, convinced "that a great deal of money is to be made in that way," proposed an elaborate speculation to Maurice. This was a carefully planned maneuver, relying heavily on stock purchases on margin. John calculated that with $10,000, which he believed he could obtain, they could gain control of $80,000 to $100,000 in stock. It was even possible that Philadelphians would buy enough to gain effective control of the company. "If we undertake it we should do it in a business like way, and on a broad scale," John advised. He added figures on the performance of the Schuylkill Navigation, demonstrating that he was following developments in the industry closely. In a revealing postscript, William Wurts added "an opportunity is before us for an elegant operation, money is wanting but perhaps a good head, plenty of nerve & good credit may supply the deficiency of capital." Once again the frustrating lack of ready money hobbled the Wurts's schemes.[77]

There is no firm evidence that this speculation was ever carried out, and the reason may be that almost simultaneously, but unknown to his brothers, the company had given Maurice a cash advance on his stock. Acknowledging this gesture, Maurice wrote Treasurer Flewelling that he was gratified "by the friendly disposition of the Board in loaning me the amt."[78] This loan may have lubricated the friction between Maurice and the board and thereby removed much of the incentive for a predatory stock-jobbing campaign.

In a similar vein, the earlier notion of dividing the company by disposing of the Pennsylvania portion surfaced again. The D&H minutes record a proposal by Eldred to sell the works in Pennsylvania to that state. At a board meeting on February 17, 1830 the idea "met with the approbation of the members present," but no decision was taken due to the absence of several influential members (notably Hone). Bolton, however, was present, supporting other evidence that he favored a divestiture. Thereafter, although the minutes had concluded that "there is every reason to believe the board will agree to the measure," the proposal seems to have been dropped. One can surmise that Hone's unwillingness to lend his support averted a permanent shift in the company's direction. If, as has been assumed, Bolton favored the proposal, the rejection was a sign that his influence was drawing to a close.

John Wurts, then 38, began his administration with a series of conspicuous cost-cutting measures, which not only saved a little money but had considerable symbolic value. One had already begun in March 1831 while Bolton was still president, when the D&H petitioned the New York City Common Council to be relieved of taxes on its stock.[79] In his first days in office Wurts attempted to sell or lease the packet boats, *Silas Wright, Jr.*, and *Luther Bradish*, both named for New York legislators who had aided the D&H. These boats had begun running only in October 1829.[80] Soon the following advertisement appeared:

FOR SALE OR TO LET
The Delaware and Hudson Canal Company offer their Packet Boats . . . for sale or to Let; the Boats are in good order being nearly new, and built of first rate materials, well fitted for the comfort and convenience of passengers, affording 20 births, [sic] exclusive of the Ladies apartment. The kitchen is furnished with a cooking stove on the plan for burning coal. The Boats will be let or sold with all the furniture belonging to them, being a complete set of every article necessary to accommodate passengers.[81]

Early efforts to dispose of the boats were unsuccessful, since on September 12, 1831 Maurice Wurts was authorized to sell them "on condition that the boats are run on the canal and kept in good order for the accommodation of passengers."[82] By 1833 they had finally been sold, for a man named Washington Swart was advertising them in a freight service he had established on the canal to connect with a river freight line he operated.[83] This brought an end to packet service on the canal for many years.

In a similar move, the president was authorized on April 23, 1831 to sell the four locomotives for "the best price that can be obtained."[84] Some efforts were made in this direction, for a letter has been found in which Charles S. Wurts offered the engines to the Pennsylvania Board of Canal Commissioners for use on their Columbia and Philadelphia Railroad in 1834.[85] Further discussion took place, but no sale is recorded. Though only a few years old, the three Foster-Rastrick products must have been hopelessly obsolete. Some early engines had astonishingly long careers: three primitive-appearing "grasshoppers" built for the Baltimore & Ohio in the 1830s were still in yard service in 1892, but these were of a somewhat more advanced design.[86]

The D&H made a concerted effort to sell residential lots in the company towns of Honesdale, Carbondale, and Rondout and to obtain prompt payment for those that had already been sold. Only gradual returns came from this source, and for years afterward the managers were occupied with the laborious process of approving sales of individual lots. The company began donating lots on request to religious societies and schools, a practice that was both good public relations and enhanced the value of the neighboring property. To its credit, the company seems to have treated all denominations even-handedly. At first requests were granted to Episcopal and Methodist congregations and to a Welsh society; later several Catholic parishes and a Jewish congregation in Honesdale were aided.[87]

The "president's house" that John Bolton had built in his namesake town became the subject of a conspicuous push to unload real estate. For personal and business reasons John Wurts preferred to live in New York City; furthermore, the house, lording it over the company's works at Rondout, furnished an unwelcome reminder of what Maurice Wurts had termed Bolton's "vanity". Soon after taking office John Wurts obtained approval to rent the president's house, and on March 19, 1832 the board authorized its sale. Thus, as the Wurtses probably hoped, the memory of John Bolton was effaced from the land.

In another economy move, dear to the hearts of the old-fashioned members of the board, Benjamin Wright was brought back, as he expressed it, to "go through all their work, and examine into every expenditure . . . to economize in mining the coal, in transporting over the railroad and along the canal." Wright and a colleague were given full power to investigate every item and "to call on every man in their employ."[88] It is not clear whether Wright was able to press any more juice out of the cost side, although his finding that the railway was three times more expensive per ton mile than the canal was promptly seized by canal advocates.

One unexpected result of Wright's participation in this exercise was to provoke a rare outburst by his former pupil, John B. Jervis. Although Jervis by then had left the employ of the D&H, what he called his "Boys" were still in charge, and Jervis took the investigation as a personal affront. To Jervis's highly refined sense of loyalty and integrity, Wright's role was a betrayal, although he conceded it was in accord "with his protestations and those of the Board made at the time." Bitterly Jervis exclaimed "What magnanimity!! for a great man to build up his reputation by doing injustice to another. I hope I may never be so lost to honourable dealing."[89] If Jervis had ever bowed to Wright as a respected mentor, those days had certainly passed. On the other hand this letter, written to his own pupil Russel Lord, shows a fraternal cordiality among the "Boys." Jervis even bought instruments on Lord's account. The D&H was fortunate, he said, to be "conducted by Boys pretty much."

Another step that helped the company finances while settling old accounts for John Wurts was the downgrading of the banking operation. On April 21, 1831 the managers determined to rent their "banking house" at 13 Wall Street to the National Bank for $2500 per year, reserving only two rooms in the second story and one in the third for its use. Later, in November 1832, the building was sold for $47,000.[90] In the interim, on January 19, 1832, the managers passed a resolution that the Bank "should be separated from the coal business of the company as soon as practicable." While the board's attitude toward it did not improve, the bank seemed to have a life of its own. Fully ten years later, in 1842, the managers, declaring that "Very little if any benefit results to the company from its present mixed character of a Bank and Canal & coal company beyond that derived from the circulation of its paper," again tried to unload it.[91] A proposed arrangement to transfer assets and operations to another bank did not succeed, and the D&H finally escaped from the once lucrative banking business only when its 20-year charter expired on November 19, 1844.

The Wurtses had always viewed the bank with suspicion, although when a separation was being discussed in 1829 they were unsure whether it would be advantageous, since it would make it more confusing to calculate the company's profit and thereby determine if they were entitled to the deferred stock.[92] When trying again in 1842 to eliminate the bank the board, reflecting John Wurts's thinking, observed that "The change would be a positive benefit to the company, by relieving its officers and clerks from the labour and time now necessarily devoted to the daily details of the Banking operation, and enabling them to devote their entire time and attention to the canal and coal business." While Wurts was unable to terminate the bank's existence prematurely, there is no doubt that its importance diminished.

There was nothing phony about a $3-D&H bank note. At a time of great individualism, an immense variety of bank notes circulated, few of which traded at their face value.
CREDIT
D&H Canal Museum.

Added to their other objections to the bank, the Wurtses probably associated it with the discord that constantly seemed to swirl around the D&H. In 1838 the *Ulster Republican* of Kingston, under editor Rodney A. Chipp, began to espouse the radical political doctrine known as Locofocoism, based on hostility toward banks and other corporations. Being both a bank and a corporation, the D&H was doubly condemned. It was called to the *Republican*'s attention that the D&H was circulating notes inscribed "payable on demand," but with the phrase "six months after date" added. These "post notes" amounted to an interest-free loan to the company, and the *Republican* wondered whether it was due to "knavery induced by the lust of gain, or knavery induced by the emptiness of its vaults."[93]

Opposition journals, fearing the economic effects of crippling the D&H, rallied to its defense, although it is interesting that they did not deny the existence of the post notes. A paper known as the *Political Reformer* sputtered that "The fell spirit of destructiveness which has instigated the tirades which have appeared in the REPUBLICAN against the Canal Co., would be satisfied with nothing short of the overthrow of our system of Improvements."[94] Earlier the *Republican* gloated that a memorial had been introduced in the state senate calling for an investigation of the D&H. This request was quickly referred to committee, where it evidently died in obscurity.[95] The campaign gradually subsided, as it proved difficult to sustain indignation over a long period, and the local political need for it abated. For John Wurts it had been another acrid breath of the dissension that seemed to hang over the D&H like the polluted fogs of a later coal era.

It is strange that John Wurts, who had thought of his involvement with the D&H as only a temporary interruption in his career, a transient fraternal service, ended by devoting the remainder of his life to the company. Meanwhile, the brothers who had initiated the involvement became relatively less prominent. Maurice also devoted his working life to the company, but it was as agent at Rondout—an important position, to be sure, but not vital in the company councils. There seemed to be in Maurice some sort of flagging of ambition, an aura of disappointment. The family genealogy records that "he had had, in early life, an affaire d'amour, which had resulted unhappily; hence his persistence in remaining celibate until the end of his days."

William, who was at least the intellectual father of the D&H, never held office in the company and seemed to have little to do with it after it became a going concern. According to the genealogy, he set up a branch of the Philadelphia company in New York City, amassed a fortune, and was able to retire at a relatively young age. The genealogy provides an interesting capsule description of his character, depicting him as

> a man of indomitable will and great tenacity of purpose; ready to encounter great risks in overcoming obstacles; enthusiastic and sanguine of success to such a degree as to need and often profit by the advice and restraint of his more moderate and cautious brothers, Charles and John. He was a man of warm affections and of an earnest Christian character, and although as he advanced in years his ill health made him sometimes irascible, his outbursts of temper were always succeeded by acts of loving impulse.

Given the tendency of these family chronicles to gloss over faults, he must have been difficult company in his later years. Charles Stewart Wurts had never been more than marginally involved with the D&H, or the quest for anthracite.

Some members of the next Wurts generation became active in the affairs of the D&H, though not for extended periods nor at a high level. Although John was the first member of the family to attend college, it is remarkable how many male representatives of the subsequent generations pursued professional careers. None amassed great wealth, but they seemed to live comfortably and were praised as useful members of society. The strongest association with the D&H in the later generations was Charles Pemberton Wurts (1824-92), a nephew of the four D&H brothers. He began working for the D&H at Carbondale when he was 19 years of age, left the company for a number of years, but returned in 1853 to become its chief engineer. He left the company and Carbondale in 1865 and moved to Nice, France. He had a brother named Maurice (1808-73) who had been a merchant at Rondout, Chicago and Carbondale and became paymaster for the D&H for ten years beginning around 1850. Another brother, William (1809-58), was a lawyer in Carbondale. One of Charles Stewart's sons and namesake (1830-1907) was at one time a vice-president of the Cambria Iron & Steel Co.[96]

In his youth the William who was a nephew of the D&H Wurtses had worked for a short time under Lorenzo A. Sykes on the Morris Canal. This outdoor activity was intended to restore his health. His uncle Maurice offered him an engineering position on the D&H, but William's father, George, demurred. "There are too many young men already too far advanced in the art, to leave him an opportunity to profit much by it,"[97] he declared. Fortunately George, an older brother of the D&H founders and a successful physician in New Jersey, was not involved in managing the D&H.

The original New York directors, under the leadership of Bolton, had nearly run the company aground. Having been forced to turn to John Wurts, they had no choice but to accept his priorities, as the bank situation illustrates. He then proceeded to resolve the conflicts that a divided interest had inflicted. The symbolic seal of Wurts control was applied on September 26, 1833 when the board voted to put into effect the 1825 agreement and issue the $200,000 deferred stock. This ended the divergence of interest that had always presented such a fertile source of mischief. The corollary was that the Wurts family had now acquired the burdens of management and could no longer criticize from the sidelines. In June 1832, fifteen months into the Wurts presidency, Charles Wurts summarized: "He that has to do with the coal business will never be free of trouble."[98]

Turning the reins over to John Wurts meant that the other board members had to accept his definition of the company's nature and purpose. Board members who were not in sympathy with this turn of events had little choice but to depart. Several had done so at the time Wurts was elected. It is probably no coincidence that Rufus Lord, an original incorporator, resigned on June 20, 1831. Another original manager, Hezekiah B. Pierrepont, lasted until the election of March 1832. After his departure, Hone was left as the only one of the 13 original managers to remain on the board. The "up-country" directors had been pushed out in 1826, and the others had exited at the time John Wurts acceded, or soon after.[99] Thus a little-noticed revolution had occurred; in seven years the board, again with no precedent to guide it, had almost completely overturned its membership. With only Philip Hone to provide continuity, it was able to deal with the stresses brought by rapid change. In the absence of stock registers one can only speculate, but it is likely that the ownership of the company showed a similar upheaval.

The character of the D&H as a coal company with a controlled transportation outlet, rather than a transportation company, was established irrevocably. Just as

RECEIVED of the President, Managers and Company of the Delaware &
Hudson Canal Company, on board the *Sloop West Chester*
———— whereof I am Master.

$104.10.0.26

Sloop West
Chester

*One hundred & four tons
Ten cwt & Twenty Six pounds*

which I promise to deliver to *[illegible] J & B Townsend*
or order, at *their Nail works near Troy* paying freight for
the same. *at fifty Cents pr Ton* ————
(Signed in duplicate) and

———— day of *June* 1830

Dated at Bolton. this *Twenty Second*

John Sherwood

John Sherwood

Received of the President, Managers and Company of the DELAWARE AND
HUDSON CANAL COMPANY, on board the *Sloop Ann Eliza*
of Brookhaven ———— whereof I am Master,
Ninety five & 13/20 T Lackn Coal
of which abt 20 T Tons on deck

95 13/20

which I promise to deliver to *Collins Co & N Beecher Son*
———— or order, at *New Haven* they
paying freight for the same *at one dollar pr ton* ————

Signed in Duplicate.

Dangers of the sea excepted.

OFFICE OF THE DELAWARE AND HUDSON CANAL COMPANY,
RONDOUT, *October 23* 184[ ]

John Edwards

The Collins Company
Dr to Del & Hud Canal Co
To 95 13/20 Tns Lump Coal, @ [illegible] Ton $194.56

there was no further discussion of selling the Pennsylvania assets, it is no accident that all talk of expansion up the Delaware came to an end. As late as March 13, 1830 the board had voted to ask Congress to subscribe to $200,000 of D&H stock in order to fund the extension to Deposit.[100] This was at best a forlorn hope even if John Wurts had been supportive, but it is not likely that he was.

The Gospel of Anthracite

Wurts was also expansion-minded, but his effort to enlarge the business took a different form: rather than making a costly investment to extend the transportation system, he sought to increase the market for Lackawanna coal both geographically and functionally. In fairness to Bolton, some of the effort to extend the market beyond New York City had begun during his tenure. As Hone reported in his diary, 50 tons of the first D&H coal to reach tidewater in December 1828 was consigned to the Townsends at Albany.[101] The Townsends were apparently good customers and supporters of the D&H; Hone recorded visiting their nail factory near Troy in March 1829.[102] While Bolton was still president the managers wrote to the New York City Common Council "offering a supply of Lackawana[sic] coal for Public use."[103]

The first year of full operation of the canal and railroad saw a determined push into the New England market. At the February 17, 1830 meeting N. T. Eldridge proposed to become the D&H agent in Boston and was given permission to investigate at company expense. His inquiry must have been promising, for on March 13 the board decided to set up agencies to sell coal at Boston and Providence and sent 50 tons of "good quality" coal to Boston as a sample. In September approval was given for an agent at New Haven.[104] With John Wurts as president, Eldridge was given an exclusive agency for Massachusetts and Rhode Island. Another individual, Endicott, was allowed to run his own boats on the canal but permitted to sell only in the area "east of Cape Cod" (using the mariner's geography in which Maine is "down east").[105]

When John Wurts took over he continued and expanded this strategy. On February 7, 1832 he was authorized "to employ one or more agents to make sales of coal in the New England States," and in April of the following year approval was given to establish an agency in Albany.[106] It was only in Albany that the company had an unassailable position. Otherwise, the map was deceptive; although Rondout is close to central New England, there was no practical method of overland transport of a bulky item like coal. To serve the new agencies in the coastal cities of New England, Lackawanna coal had to be loaded into sloops and sailed down the Hudson. This probably removed much of the advantage over supplies that reached tidewater at New York City or Philadelphia. Little is known about what must have been a sizable fleet of coal vessels; they worked before photography became commonplace, and there was so little about them to capture the imagination that they must have been nearly invisible.

Modern historians would be wise to emulate the D&H managers and follow the movement of coal beyond Rondout. Depositing one's attention with the coal in Rondout is a mistake akin to viewing the railway and canal as separate entities. The managers were surely concerned to keep transportation costs to Rondout as low as possible, but their interest did not end there; the only meaningful measure of their competitive position was the final cost to the consumer. In this regard, it is startling to think how many times the coal was handled between mine and stove.

FACING PAGE TOP
This early receipt shows a coal delivery to the Townsends at Albany.
CREDIT
J. M. Ransom.

FACING PAGE BOTTOM
Receipt for coal delivery to New Haven.
CREDIT
D&H Canal Museum.

After traveling over the railway to Honesdale, it could have been transferred directly to a canal boat; but since the railway operated year-round but at a lower capacity, it would be more usual for the coal to be piled up at Honesdale before being loaded on a boat. At Rondout, since the canal boats were not seaworthy enough to go out onto the Hudson, the coal might have been loaded into a barge, but more commonly was probably piled up to be reloaded later into a barge or sailing vessel. This would transport it to New York City or some port on the Hudson River or the coast of New England. From there it might conceivably be transferred to a smaller vessel to go up a coastal river, or might be carted to the final consumer. With little machinery in existence, almost all of this movement was accomplished by hand shoveling. Obviously it was in the company's interest to reduce the number of times their coal slid down a shovel, but such improvements were hard to achieve.

A mountain of coal at Honesdale.
CREDIT
D&H Canal Museum.

Ever mindful of their interests, the managers tried to watch and control the movement of coal beyond Rondout. They had earlier purchased the sidewheeler *Rondout* for use in towing between Eddyville and their coal yard, which gave them some experience in steamboating. To facilitate its operation, they employed an "Albany Dredging Machine" in Rondout Creek.[107] In 1831-32 they purchased the barges *Lackawanna* and *James Kent*, as well as "an elderly sidewheeler" named *Delaware* to tow them on the river.[108] During the previous season they had hired the steamboat *Legislator* to tow the *Lackawanna*.[109] In 1833 they added another steamboat and two barges, one of which was named *Philip Hone*. Several of the barges were built on the hulls of former steamboats, and some of the steamboats were weary veterans of distinguished service on the Hudson or Long Island Sound. One, the *Fulton*, built during the lifetime of the great inventor, had been the first steamboat to offer regular commercial service on the Sound.[110] In a memorable phrase, Ringwald summarizes the results of D&H thrift by saying that the company's barge fleet "was to become a veritable floating marine museum with its relics of earlier days of steamboating."[111] In assembling this fleet, the D&H may have provided a model for the railroads which later operated sizable marine departments around New York harbor.

The second prong of market expansion consisted of demonstrating new uses for the company's coal. A vivid illustration occurred as early as May 20, 1829, when the managers gave permission "to have a cooking establishment (or apparatus) put up in the Kitchen part of the Banking house, for the purpose of burning therein the coal of the company."[112] This incident, mildly amusing on the surface, showed the company's attention to detail when it came to propagating the gospel of anthracite. Even after the value of anthracite for home heating had been convincingly established, an enduring prejudice made it necessary for "stone coal" to prove itself in each new application. This meant that the company managers and officers, even gentlemen like Philip Hone, became salesmen, promoting the product at every opportunity. A letter from John Wurts three months after he assumed the presidency is filled with mundane details of marketing coal.[113]

One thrust of the marketing campaign consisted simply of introducing coal into large institutions, with favorable prices as an inducement. In September 1832 the managers set a price of $6 a ton for an order of 200 tons from the Sing Sing state prison, where Lackawanna anthracite had been introduced the preceding year.[114] Earlier an order had been received from the state almshouse. In the fuel economy of that period, once large consumers switched to anthracite, there was little likelihood of their changing back. Whether they remained loyal to the Lackawanna brand was another matter. In December 1831 Hone observed that D&H coal was selling for $10 a ton in New York City, while the Schuylkill was $14.[115] For the moment that was an enormous advantage, but the company had to remain ever alert for changes in the balance. In addition, the Lehigh, which reportedly had sold 1000 tons on the North River in 1833, required close attention.[116]

Of greater importance in the long run were promotional efforts that sought to find new applications for hard coal. In June 1831 Nathan Smith, now a D&H insider following the Wurts accession, was employed at $200 a month "for the purpose of introducing the use of coal into manufactories and all establishments where steam engines are employed."[117] Thus the D&H caught early the powerful current toward the use of anthracite in steam generation.[118] Eldridge reported favorable results of an 1831 experiment in burning coal in the furnace of a boiler factory in Providence. Elsewhere, coal was finding successful applications in potash making and boiling soap in works at Hudson, New York.[119] John B. Jervis remembered his former employers and told his protege Archbald that he would soon want 100 tons "for the engines on the Mohawk and Hudson Railroad" on which he was chief engineer.[120]

Blacksmiths had been among the first successful users of anthracite, so it is not surprising that the D&H fostered this application. At the same time Smith was dispatched on his mission, the company agreed to pay R. Spencer $3 a day to introduce the use of coal to blacksmiths. This was an accepted use, but relatively small in volume; a wider expansion into iron manufacture was irresistibly attractive to the managers. In February 1830 the D&H received a request from a Mr. Mott of Auburn, New York, to establish an iron foundry at Carbondale if the company would give him half an acre.[121] The request was referred to committee and it is not clear if Mott attempted to carry out his plan. A letter from John Wurts in 1831 implies that Lackawanna anthracite was being used by the famed West Point foundry at Cold Spring, New York.[122]

It did not require a gift of prophecy to know that anthracite would someday be used in the smelting of iron; troublesome technical obstacles, however, made the moment of success uncertain. In January 1831 the Ulster Iron Co. asked the D&H to contribute $2000 worth of coal for an experiment in adapting its plant to the burning of anthracite. The managers, with the conservative Bolton still in office, agreed to provide some coal for preliminary experiments, but the records do not confirm that the Ulster Co. followed up on its proposal.[123] The timing was premature, for smelting with anthracite had not yet been perfected. Considerable progress had been made by November 1837 when the company received a proposition from L. & H. W. Howell of New York City to erect a furnace for "testing the discovery or successful application alleged to have been made in Wales of the use of Anthracite coal as the exclusive fuel in the smelting of Iron ores and the manufacture of pig iron."[124] This was surely a reference to the hot air blast, which at last made large-scale smelting with anthracite feasible. The managers decided to sell Howell up to 250 tons at the discount price of $4.50 a ton for the experiment; but once again the minutes are tantalizing, for it is not certain whether Howell accepted. By 1840 smelting with anthracite was firmly established and on its way to phenomenal growth.[125]

The strongest push by the D&H, and the one with the most colorful consequences, was the drive to introduce anthracite as the preferred fuel in steamboats. As early as 1827, before the canal was completed, the annual report adopted this objective. Frederick Moore Binder's conclusion that "The leader in the large-scale introduction of anthracite fuel for steamboats, particularly those on the Hudson River and Long Island Sound, was the Delaware and Hudson Company." is well founded.[126] This sustained emphasis paralleled the Lehigh Coal & Navigation Company's campaign to foster iron manufacturing. Each company ventured on occasion into the other's area of specialization but did not lose sight of its primary interest.

Robert Fulton's celebrated success with the *Clermont* in 1807 had opened the era of steam navigation on the waters around New York. In the 1830s, after Fulton's monopoly had been broken in a famous court case, steam navigation on the Hudson was both abundant and competitive. By 1832 anthracite was being used successfully in three New York City ferries.[127] This was gratifying, but the patronage of the sluggish ferries with their short runs could never be entirely satisfactory; the river steamers, with their compulsion for speed and resultant lavish consumption of coal, remained an irresistible target.

What Binder terms "the company's untiring efforts to promote the use of anthracite in steamboats," became widely known and stimulated all sorts of experimenters. In 1831 the D&H delivered coal to the steamboat *Victory* for trial runs between New York and Hartford.[128] In fact, the master of a rival vessel, the *McDonough*, also consulted the D&H about switching to anthracite, and a similar request came in from the *Chancellor Livingston*.[129] A year later, willing to pursue any prospects, the board offered to give the Troy Steamboat Co. a 5% discount if it would burn the company's coal exclusively.[130] In 1834 Hone reported making a short trip on the North River with engineer Robert Livingston Stevens and other D&H managers to observe the burning of Lackawanna coal in the steamboat *Delaware*.[131] This was an aged sidewheeler that the D&H had purchased as a towboat.[132] If any of these experiments was at all successful it would have only sharpened the managers' appetite.

In order to capture the market it craved, the company had to ally itself with the redoubtable inventor and professor Eliphalet Nott, president of Union College in Schenectady. Sharp, clever and slightly eccentric, the Connecticut-born Nott might have been a model for the stock Yankee character who was already beginning to populate American fiction. In the late 1820s, with other inventions to his credit, notably a coal-burning stove, he began attacking the problem of devising a boiler that could burn anthracite reliably and safely. By 1832 his experimental boat the *Novelty* was making speed records on the Hudson between Albany and New York City, although it does not appear that it was burning anthracite regularly.[133]

Nott approached the D&H board on January 5, 1835 proposing to use 30,000 tons of coal to supply a steamboat (the *Novelty* at that point having sunk while being towed). As Hone noted with customary restraint, this "will occasion an increased Consumption of anthracite coal to a very great amount."[134] After several years of experiments, half-measures and partial success, this move indicated a degree of confidence that would soon be justified. In March the ferry *Essex*, fitted with Nott's "patent tubular anthracite coal boilers" made a completely successful excursion of 40 or 50 miles on the Hudson and New York Bay. This breakthrough was considered so important that, even though it occurred after the annual meeting, it was inserted as a footnote in the annual report for fiscal 1834.[135]

Assured by an authoritative journal's conclusion that "the desideratum of generating steam by anthracite coal has at length been attained," the board on May 6, in a carefully phrased agreement, gave Nott the right to purchase up to 5000 tons of coal a year for six years at the bargain price of $4. Nott was required to begin running a regular passenger boat "as fast as any boat of the kind now on the River except the Champlain, exclusively with Anthracite coal, except so far as wood or other fuel may be necessary for kindling the fires and for bringing the Boat into port."[136] Later in the year, after rejecting an offer by the Hudson River Association to buy his patented boiler, Nott turned to the D&H for further assistance. On October 27, 1835 an agreement was approved under which the company gave him a one-year loan at 6%, secured by stock. There is some confusion about the terms of the various agreements, but it appears that the D&H was given the right to take up to six of Nott's boilers as payment for coal, while Nott stood to receive 1000 shares of D&H stock if he performed successfully.[137] Since Dr. Nott's son Howard had been elected to the D&H board in 1835, relations between the two companies amounted to a virtual partnership.

June 23, 1836 was a glorious summer day, and an impressive crowd had gathered at the foot of Chambers Street, New York City, to make the trial voyage to Albany on the refurbished *Novelty*. Hone, whose diary recorded the event, was joined by members of the board and other dignitaries to witness the first long run of a vessel burning anthracite in Nott's patented boilers. Despite unfavorable winds, current and tide, the journey to Albany was made in either 10 hours, 27 minutes or 12 hours, 8 minutes, according to different accounts.[138] Whatever the actual time, the trip was an unqualified success. Hone, venturing into more technical detail than was his custom, explained that

the great desideratum was to contrive the means of igniting the coal, and producing a flame sufficient to create the steam. This has been effected by condensing hot air, which by injection into the bottom of the furnaces, accomplishes this object, and forces the flame into a chamber in which are a great number of iron tubes of the size of gun barrels placed vertically. There are four of these furnaces. The quantity of coal consumed on this trip was twenty tons (something less) which at $5 pr ton amounts to $100. The same voyage would have consumed forty cords of pine wood the present price of which is $6, making a difference of more than one half.[139]

Philip Hone, perceiving that fulfillment was in sight, was ecstatic. Nott, he declared, had established "the certainty that coal will supercede wood in all our steam boats and the Delaware and Hudson Company will hereafter be able to sell all the coal they can bring down the Canal at an advanced price."[140] Eventually this optimism proved correct, but in 1836 it was premature. The *Novelty* was seaworthy, but Nott's finances could not ride out the depression of 1837. Apparently the doctor and his sons were unable to maintain their interest payments to the D&H. Although it did not benefit the inventor, by 1840 the D&H was able to proclaim in its annual report that the "unceasing effort to introduce anthracite coal into use in steamboats . . . may now be regarded as having been crowned with success; and it is a happy circumstance for the Company, that Lackawanna coal is found to be more peculiarly adapted to this extensive branch of consumption than any of the other kinds."[141] Around this time Philip Hone journeyed to Albany on the new steamer *North America*, designed to burn anthracite. He rejoiced in the fact that this fuel cost half as much as wood and asserted "The use of coal for steam navigation must inevitably become general." Perhaps anticipating the rise of the Hudson River Dayliners, he observed, "Passengers are conveyed 150 miles in a Vessel with every convenience and luxury and get a good breakfast and Dinner all for two Dollars. I wonder people do not live on board instead of going to the Astor House."[142] Hone and his colleagues had reason for satisfaction at the end, although the colorful, often vexing struggle to replace wood with anthracite on steamboats, set against the background of the Hudson's incomparable scenery, had occupied most of the decade of the 1830s.

Learning to Run the Thing

THE ERIE had served as a model in building the D&H, but as a state-owned facility was a less useful guide to operating it. In its early years the D&H was absorbed in learning how to run the system it had created. Many practices that later seemed routine and were taken for granted were adopted only after fumbling experimentation. Only long usage made them seem inevitable.

One issue was whether the company should act as a retailer. As noted in the previous chapter, it had initially tried to avoid this function. In 1831, however, it put in a bid to lease the North Battery, presumably for use as a coal yard.[143] This offer was apparently not accepted, for later in the year the company set up William G. Jones as its New York agent, with a coal yard at the corner of Chambers and Washington Streets on the Hudson waterfront.[144] Then on January 6, 1832 the managers reversed themselves and decided to discontinue retail sales. In the following month they reverted to the earlier system under which dealers in New York City would make their purchases at Rondout.[145] Several years later this decision too was reversed, for on January 19, 1839 the board appointed a committee to "hire or purchase a yard for retail business" in New York City. A report for 1840 indicated that the company operated yards in Brooklyn and at Beach Street, King Street and on the East River in Manhattan.[146]

Another issue that was critical in determining the character of the D&H was raised by Ransome D. Hall of Catskill, New York. In a letter of January 7, 1831

Hall, who had obtained a contract to ship 600,000 feet of boards from the Lackawanna Valley, inquired whether he could transport them over the D&H system. He also wondered whether the company would reduce the tolls on lumber "to the same rates as are charged on the Erie Canal." This revived in stark terms the question of whether the D&H was a public highway, and the managers, aware of the implications, replied cautiously. On January 18 they responded that "it is not expedient for the company to engage in transportation on the canal excepting coal and other articles for their own purposes" and flatly refused to match the Erie rates. This seemed to define the company as the monopoly the Wurtses had sought; but then, sensitive to the effect on public relations in the Lackawanna Valley, the managers drew back. They granted Hall favorable rates and allowed him to ship lumber whenever the collector at Honesdale determined that "the supply of coal shall be insufficient to furnish lading for the boats without detention."[147] This compromise did not address the question of how the lumber would be brought to Honesdale, but avoided handing more ammunition to the company's enemies.

A more critical matter was ownership of the canal boats, which was directly related to the status of the men who operated them. Here the company allegedly made a couple of false starts before settling on the method it employed during the remainder of its existence. In its initial approach the company seemingly meant to sell the boats outright. A notice in a local newspaper in April 1827—not long before the New York section was expected to open—offered to sell boats at cost in the yard at Mamakating where the company's first 21 freight boats had been built.[148] However, the cost of $360 would have been far beyond the means of anyone likely to be interested in the business, and the managers would have been seriously misguided if they thought otherwise. It almost seems that the managers were so absorbed in building the canal that they didn't think enough about how it would be run. Unfortunately, the board's minutes do not provide a complete account of the decision-making process, and the main source for this important episode is the opinionated John W. Johnston.

Under the first method described by Johnston, Elezar Townsend, who had held a construction contract for sections near Johnston's family home along the Delaware, contracted to operate the company's boats. He recruited and managed the boatmen, and the D&H provided the boats, lines, etc. D&H records confirm that on July 4, 1832 the company loaned Townsend $1500 to buy horses and harness in order to run a line of boats.[149] Townsend divided the canal into four sections. The captains stayed with their boat, but on each section boys of 12-16 were responsible for towing the boats with horses in their care. Soon the weakness of this system became apparent: the boys were idle until their turn came to take a boat in the opposite direction (Johnston says they sometimes waited one or two weeks, which is hard to believe.) As Johnston describes in his usual pungent language, "during all such idle time, a lot of boys 5 to 8 in number were acting without any control whatever, save their own wills and desires, deficient in judgment as to the feeding and usage of horses, and yet invested with absolute control."[150]

A printed "Terms of Boating for 1830" seems in part to confirm this, describing one method of operation as "'running Company boats in lines of Six boats with change of horses at each station that shall be designated by the Company."[151] As directed by the board on November 27, 1830, Bolton was allowed to make several types of contracts with individuals, paying up to $1.50 per ton to carry D&H coal. Some of these arrangements allowed boatmen to purchase company boats on instalment. Except for the stagecoach-like method of providing horsepower, this resembled the system that prevailed during most of the canal's history.

Johnston describes another variant, not well supported in the records, under which the company divided the canal into two-mile sections and contracted with individuals to make six round trips daily over their section. Later the sections were increased to 12 miles, but this did not eliminate the inherent flaw of making each contractor dependent on his neighbors, as well as a host of uncertain factors. Johnston says this system was put into effect in 1835, but he may be mistaken about the date. He is more certain about the result: as the contractors began to resent long periods of idleness followed by the necessity of working far into the night, they avenged themselves on the company by vandalizing the boats. "[T]hey would wreck and tear the boat cabins . . . deposit in them all manner of filth, write upon the walls the most vulgar sentences, draw the most rude obscene forms and pictures, tear the siding and roof from the cabin and the lining from the boat . . . until nearly every line boat on the canal became a most unseemly object to behold."[152]

The method employed during most of the canal's history provided for boatmen to pay the purchase price of their boats in installments. On each trip they were credited for the coal they had carried at a set rate per ton, and the installment was deducted, as well as necessary repairs. Thus the captains built up equity and hoped for at least a few years of running a paid-up boat. They were responsible for their animals, harness, and supplies; and this may be the main alteration in the system the D&H had adopted as early as 1830. In practice this meant that the managers, like the Federal Reserve today, engaged in constant fine tuning of rates so as to pay the smallest amount necessary to attract responsible boatmen. In the early days the company apparently had trouble recruiting men to an untried business, for it offered to advance 87½% of the cost of a boat "to any suitable person who may be inclined to purchase and run boats in the coal business."[153] Independents were allowed to use the canal under all the systems that were tried. Knowing that priority for coal shipments would be given to company boats, they took their chances on other traffic and the occasions when the company had a backlog of anthracite. In 1838 there were 200 private boats on the canal, half as many as the company owned.[154]

It became evident that the company needed to assist boat builders, as well as operators. In November 1833 it approved loaning a Mr. Spencer of Syracuse $200,000 to set up a boat building business at Rondout. In these measures, as with even the faulty boating experiments, the company displayed a youthful flexibility that was one of its most important attributes. Not hobbled by accumulated precedents and procedures, it was able to respond quickly and creatively to new situations. At the same time, the managers did not like to let control slip too far from their grasp. Each year they went through a laborious process of setting the price for coal at various points, and also determining tolls for a multitude of commodities. At the end of each year they set production targets for the following year, based on previous sales and remaining stockpiles; but they had no better luck at predicting the next season's weather than the popular almanacs. Corporate capitalism was still in its formative stage, and the concept of delegation of authority was not well developed. The military could have served as a model, but rate setting was apparently considered a strategic matter that could not be entrusted to officers.

To carry out this close style of management, the board decided on April 21, 1830 that one of its members should tour the company's works twice a month and make a written report of his findings. This policy, coupled with Philip Hone's resolute diary-keeping, has provided good descriptions of the company's early

ABOVE   D&H shops at Carbondale.
CREDIT   Carbondale Historical Soc.

RIGHT   Rough and functional, the interior of the loading
         chutes at Honesdale characterized the D&H.
CREDIT   National Canal Museum.

BELOW   Photo by Johnson
CREDIT   National Canal Museum.

period. He made his first official visit in June 1830 and another in August of the following year. In June 1833 he continued beyond the Lackawanna Valley into the other coal districts, reaching Mauch Chunk, which he described as "a miserable dirty place." Already the conflict between the romantic movement, with its worship of nature, and the industrialization Hone supported could not be ignored. At the "coal hole" of Mauch Chunk Hone observed "There is a great appearance of Business but nature's smiling face is sadly begrimed and every thing bears the Impress of Coal, Coal, Coal."[155]

Hone unfortunately does not elaborate on the system of running the boats he rode. On his 1831 tour he found that the Rondout operation "appears to be going on with great activity & good order." Reaching the mines three days later, he "was astonished at the immense deal of work which has been performed since my Visit last Summer. Seven or eight mines are in full occupation. Excavations have been formed in the mountain to the extent of 400 feet with Galleries and chambers branching off in various directions." Hone attended church the next day and was gratified to see that "The rattling of cars, the explosion of Gunpowder and the clinking of Pick-axes is now as still as the Tomb of the Capulets, and the miners who were Yesterday begrimed with Coal and looked like citizens of the Nether World are seen this morning on their way to church clean and well dressed with long coats and gilt Buttons, high shirt collars and Broaches in their Bosoms."[156]

Two years later Hone noted that the longest mine had progressed 1500 feet from its mouth. In another vivid comment, he observed of the miners: "What a hard life they have, and how exposed to dangerous accidents. But there is not one, Demon as he appears from the nature of his occupation, that does not look down with contempt on a Tailor or a Shoemaker, or any engaged in the more sedentary employments of life."[157] In reality, however, it proved difficult to recruit such men, and in 1835 the company appropriated $6000 to construct 24 houses for miners on the theory that it would be "likely to furnish the company with Miners who could be depended upon."[158] A shortage of miners forced the managers to reduce their target for coal production from 130,000 to 120,000 tons for 1836 and to seek to "import" 50 to 60 additional miners.[159] Many of this first generation of miners were experienced men from Wales and other parts of Great Britain.

Hone often remarked with pleasure on the vigorous growth of the town named for him, although on one occasion he acknowledged that Carbondale displayed "better taste" in the style of building. He was also pleased to note in 1833 a flurry of matrimonial activity on the part of the company's overseers and superintendents. "Sobriety, Industry and Zeal are still the characteristics of this fine Body of Men, and if the children equal their Fathers the more there are of them the better for the Country." More particularly he stated "I have been much pleased with Mrs. Archbald, the new Wife of our Superintendant. She is sensible, agreeable and well calculated to make him a good wife."[160] Whether this finding was included in Hone's written report cannot be determined.

In the 1830s John Wurts largely set the policy of the D&H, but Philip Hone determined its character. Although his financial stake meant that his voice would have to be heeded, one suspects that he would have exerted a massive influence even with a smaller investment. An American gentleman, he commanded by the gravity of his personality, his refined manners and his unshakable integrity. Hone was a capitalist, but he understood this in the old-fashioned sense that entailed an obligation to employ capital for the benefit of society. There was a wide streak of patriotism in his makeup; he expected to make a personal profit, but he also felt that capital carried with it a duty to develop the abundant resources nature had bestowed on the United States.

Hone watched the stock index, and there is no doubt that his sensitive nature was disappointed by the appraisal it gave to his efforts. At the "flourishing village" of Carbondale in 1830 he wrote: "When I first visited this spot about four years ago, it was a savage wilderness difficult of access to a man on foot, but impracticable for a Wheel Carriage. It is now a busy, animated place. Its population actively engaged and every body making a good living . . . and all this results from the enterprize and perseverence of the Delaware & Hudson Canal Company. Future Generations will award us the applause of which the present is so niggardly."[161] In a similar vein, he concluded in the following year: "I am proud of the Interest I have taken in this great work notwithstanding the arbiters of mens Fortunes in New York have decreed that the stock after the successful completion of the work is not worth more than 62 pr Cent."[162]

At times Hone bought and sold D&H stock, but that was not an end in itself. He was, in short, an investor, not a speculator, and his diary is filled with condemnations of the speculative spirit that was beginning to seize Wall Street even at that early date. In 1832 he turned down an invitation to the ground-breaking of the Harlem RR, the stock of which he felt had been oversubscribed due to "the prevailing spirit of Speculation and not from an expectation that this work if accomplished will be beneficial to the city or profitable to the Stockholders." In a scathing but characteristic comment, he noted that the Harlem's vice president "knows better how to make money and that as the World goes is a more important Talent."[163]

Manipulation of Morris Canal stock gave Hone ample opportunity to express righteous indignation. He described an effort to corner the stock in 1835 as "one of those Bubbles blown up in the stock of this company which now and then disgraces our city and astonishes those who are ignorant of the arts of the confraternity of brokers."[164] When the board of brokers passed a resolution not to honor ruinous contracts, Hone observed tartly "the persons who had thus burnt their fingers have been allowed as members of the Board to vote upon the Question in which they were so immediately interested, and have discharged themselves from all the penalties which are attached in that Board to a breach of contract by the Members. In other words they have decided (so far as Brokers can decide that point) that it is not dishonourable."[165]

Philip Hone would have been appalled by the era when Wall Street became the "Scarlet Woman;" but it was foreshadowed by trends of the 1830s, just as he saw glimmerings of the environmental disasters that would result from unrestrained industrialization. In his time, however, he helped keep the D&H on a path of rectitude. The speculative inclinations the Wurts brothers had displayed had no chance to flourish, even if they had wanted to do so after they became insiders. Similarly, perhaps unintentionally, Hone contributed to preserving the environment. By purchasing one of Thomas Cole's first landscapes he helped launch the "Hudson River School" of painting, America's first home-grown art movement. Glorifying native subjects, Cole and his followers assuaged the enormous cultural inferiority Americans felt toward Europe, and in calling attention to the glories of domestic scenery they planted the seeds of the conservation movement.

Even though he visited the canal only once or twice a year, Hone had ample opportunity to observe interruptions to navigation. In June 1830 he encountered a breach at Lock No.68 on the Delaware, and "a large Gang of Hands was employed

The famous Bolton Basin break of 1885 differed from many similar catastrophes mainly in that it was thoroughly recorded in photographs.
CREDIT
D&H Canal Museum.

in repairing it."[166] Three years later he found a longer lasting obstruction caused by heavy rains the month before. An accumulation of 15,000 tons of coal was being drawn down as rapidly as possible, with 90 boats reportedly being passed through one lock in a single day.[167]

There had been a more serious derangement in March of the previous year, when a flood on the Rondout devastated Eddyville. It was reported that the river created a new channel on the north side of the village, making Eddyville an island. The canal bridge was carried away, and water reached the second floor of houses.[168] It was feared that repairs to the canal would take at least three or four months, and John Wurts felt compelled to issue a prompt letter in which he declared that the damage was "much less than anticipated."[169] By then panicky stockholders who saw the extent of the damage and believed the canal would never revive had sold out at clearance prices.[170] This may have effectively eliminated Ulster County ownership of D&H stock and ended whatever influence the area had on management. To their chagrin, full operation was restored at the end of May, when "the running of the boats again infused life into the interior of our country."[171]

In the same year, as if the usual run of problems was not distressing enough, a cholera epidemic caused a severe slowdown. Early in the history of the canal the pattern was thus established that hardly a year passed without some serious interruption. This was typical of most canals, except possibly the Erie. Too much rain brought flooding; not enough caused drought; muskrat tunnels channeled water into places Russel F. Lord did not care to see it go. One could recite a history of these misfortunes, but it would be a tiresome and largely pointless litany. Floods at Eddyville and outbreaks of cholera became fairly regular events and lost much of their shock value. Each year the company calculated how many days of the possible total the canal had been navigable. If it ran without interruption 90% of the time it was doing well.

Whatever difficulties the D&H encountered, or whichever wrong directions it briefly pursued, most of the time the coal kept flowing as intended. In 1830, 43,600 tons of coal moved over the system. On one day that year 37 cars carrying between 90 and 100 tons (as well as 40 or 50 passengers) arrived in Honesdale in a single train.[172] A year later the total increased to 54,800 tons, and in 1832 jumped to 84,600 tons, despite the flood.[173] In one week of June 1832 between 12 and 20 vessels were loaded at Rondout as the supervisors worked down the backlog.[174] Weekly reports from the agent in Honesdale indicate that each railroad car, or wagon, carried about 2½ tons on average. In 1833 coal shipments leaped to 111,777 tons, but partly due to a mild winter this exceeded demand. The resulting surplus, accompanied by a general business downturn, drove the total in 1834 back to only 43,700 tons.[175] In 1836 shipments recovered to 106,270 tons. This constituted only about 15% of the total anthracite production, exceeded by the Schuylkill's 432,045 tons and 146,502 on the Lehigh.[176]

Hone, as noted, followed the stock quotations, and it was not a practice calculated to calm ones nerves. In January 1831, D&H fell to 64½, and a year later, when recovery from the flood was doubted, traded as low as 62.[177] Greater turbulence lay ahead: In what Hone termed "the most extraordinary freak which has ever been played in the stock market," D&H declined from 125 to par at the close of 1833. In one day it then plunged to 75, from which it recovered to 90 on the next trading day.[178] This movement, all too common in a thin, volatile market provoked a typical outburst by Hone, in which he declared, "These changes so destructive of public confidence and injurious to private property are the effect of Panic occasioned by the Gambling of the Brokers." After another year of gyrations, Hone expressed his feelings toward D&H stock, "which goes up and down like the piston Rod of a Steam Engine"—although an engine obeyed more predictable rules of physics. Hone's exasperation was tempered on this occasion by the fact that the stock was rising, and on March 19, 1835 he sold 40 shares at 108½.[179]

At the beginning of 1837 D&H stock was solid, but market quotes indicate it was not as highly regarded as its immediate rivals. With a par of 100, D&H was offered at 90½, while Lehigh Coal & Navigation, par 50, traded at 83 and Schuylkill Navigation showed an even greater premium. Its shares, par 50, were offered at 164½. Somewhat surprisingly, Morris Canal (96) traded higher than D&H. Railroad stocks showed a similar range; the market was already shrewd and unforgiving in its valuations.[180]

The year 1837 brought severe strains, as the first of the violent financial panics that punctuated American economic life in the nineteenth century took hold. According to Hone, D&H went down to 50 in May 1837. On May 9 most New York banks decided to suspend payments in specie. Relief at having escaped this potentially ruinous obligation had an immediate effect on the stock market: D&H jumped to 67 and the Morris Canal from 30 to 50. With as much detachment as he could muster, Hone opined that "the merchants are the most excitable class of men in the world" and called the stock market "the most volatile and effervescent of all things."[181] No bank could stand out against the crowd, and on May 10 the D&H joined the others in suspending specie payments.[182]

As with the later panics, the effect on economic activity persisted beyond the immediate financial crisis. In the spring of 1838 John Wurts advised Russel Lord that there was no need to rush work at Carbondale, or even hurry to open the canal because of the poor outlook. With 200,000 tons of coal left over from the previous year, he lamented that "the coal market and every other kind of business is as dull and dead as if they had been buried and the funeral service read over them."[183] On the other hand, the slump had predictable effects on wages. Lord wrote that common laborers were receiving 75 cents a day including board "except some on the Delaware and Lackawaxen sections which we shall have to pay 78 and perhaps some 80 cents." Foremen earned 90 cents to $1, and locktenders' wages had been reduced $1 to $15 per month.[184]

The following year brought signs of revival, but other problems intruded. Each spring Russel Lord compiled a detailed report on the damage done by winter freezing and spring floods. No year passed without some injury, and the winter of 1839 must have been especially devastating. Apparently no traffic moved over the canal in May, and in June John Wurts, always easily agitated, fumed that "since I have known any thing of this Company, I think its Canal and boating business was never in the month of June in so unpromising a state as it is now."[185] With good reason the president expressed "mortification" that he had to turn away customers ready to pay cash for D&H coal. While not wanting to burden Lord with apprehensions that "belong to my station," he could not resist the colorful reminder that "many a sleepless hour do I listen to the falling rain." Wurts even authorized Sunday operation to reduce the backlog, an extreme step in view of his religious scruples.

The crisis of 1837 was perhaps the last test of the youthful company before it could be admitted to the ranks of established, secure enterprises. Having weathered that ordeal, it passed into confident maturity. This firm self-assurance was demonstrated in January 1838 when the managers raised John Wurts's salary from $3000 to $4000, with an increase to $5000 approved for the following year.[186] Philip Hone shared this self-congratulatory mood. Looking back at the end of the turbulent but successful decade of the 1830s, he marveled at the increase in coal shipments over the preceding 20 years. In 1820, he wrote, the total amount of coal shipped to market was 365 tons (all from the Lehigh); in 1839 the total exceeded one million tons. The D&H's contribution was 122,000 tons, its largest annual shipment (though not enormously greater than the premature total of 1833). "What an argument is this in favour of internal improvements, and what a reproof to the miserable tools of party faction who to secure their election to the State Legislature have bound themselves by unholy pledges to break down these noble enterprizes and to check an experiment so eminently successful," he proclaimed.[187]

Are Now Thriving and Busy Towns

IN EARLY 1830, when the mischief instigated by Thomas Meredith seemed to threaten the survival of the D&H system, Wayne County delegates cried out "Shall we permit ourselves by one mighty blow to be struck into that dark abyss of a confined interior from which we have just emerged[?]" The canal had operated only one full season, and nothing better illustrates how quickly it had become essential. Almost overnight it revolutionized the way of life along its route in Pennsylvania. In their annual report for 1832 the managers boasted that "Carbondale and Honesdale, the sites of which, in 1827, were covered with forest trees, are now thriving and busy towns—the former containing a population of upwards of 2,000 and the latter of upwards to 1,200 persons." A degree of self-promotion has to be factored in, but the basic contention is accurate. This luxuriant growth resembled

ABOVE
D&H shop and office area,
Carbondale.
Photo by Johnson.
CREDIT
National Canal Museum.

RIGHT
Honesdale----a busy and
thriving place.
CREDIT
National Canal Museum.

that on the Erie Canal, where Lockport, the home of three families in 1821, had attained a population of 1500 by 1825.[188]

After the alarm created by Meredith had dissipated, the relieved editor of the Bethany *Enquirer* rejoiced on a visit to the canal "to witness the hum of business—and, in the midst of woods and mountains, to find oneself, as at Honesdale, at what might seem a *commercial port*."[189] Where a few years earlier had "stood the heavily timbered forest, traveled by none save the wild beast and the intrepid hunter," a visitor to Honesdale in 1832 found "a flourishing and beautiful village, numbering seven stores, three public houses, besides numerous private buildings of an imposing appearance, and a variety of shops for all kinds of mechanical business."[190] Mail coaches arrived daily from New York, Utica and Wilkes-Barre. Instead of the quiet of the forest the traveler experienced "feelings of confused pleasure" when confronted with the "noise occasioned by the coal dropping from the cars—the rattling as it passes into the boats, and the din of shovels used by the workmen." Since four boats could be loaded at the same time, the racket forcibly reminded Honesdale residents of the source of their prosperity. Seen first hand, the Industrial Revolution was both bewildering and exciting.

Honesdale quickly took on the attributes of a town, as related more fully by Vernon Leslie.[191] The first store was opened in May 1827 (Jason Torrey was a partner). A tavern or hotel appeared in the same year. By 1829 the rising settlement had 18 dwelling houses. Small shops and industries soon added their voice to the bustle of coal loading; a water-powered woodworking shop was in existence in 1832. Before long this expansion had an effect on municipal organization. In 1831 Carbondale was set off as a new township, and Honesdale petitioned to become a borough. Ten years later Honesdale replaced Bethany as the county seat, confirming the change in relative importance the D&H had set in motion. Knowing the conspiratorial tendencies of John Wurts, one might suspect that the D&H had a gloved hand in this maneuver, which would increase the value of lots at Honesdale. Although Wurts opined that the board would not be willing to contribute directly to the campaign to change the location, the legislation was introduced in the Pennsylvania Senate by E. Kingsbury, an ally of the D&H.[192] Later, Senator Kingsbury wondered whether the passage of the bill would "so increase the price of lots in town" that some speedy insider purchases might be worth while.

In assessing the impact of the D&H Canal on the New York side a logical approach is to look at the area before the first sons of Erin swung picks along the line John B. Jervis had staked out through what he called the Mamakating Valley, indeed even before the glowing embers in the Tontine had warmed the toes and souls of Manhattan financiers. Here one encounters the persistent legend of the Old Mine Road, which has beguiled a dismaying number of historians over the years. According to this durable piece of folklore, parties of Hollanders began working copper mines at a place called Pahaquarry along the Delaware in the vicinity of the Water Gap, transporting the ore overland to Esopus (Kingston) and then downriver to Manhattan before the English seized the New Netherlands colony in 1664. The route they hacked, said to be the first road intended for wheeled vehicles in what is now the United States, roughly paralleled the D&H and present Rt. 209 between the two rivers.

James Eldridge Quinlan, a historian of Sullivan County, deserves credit for resisting the all too easy temptation of local historians to perpetuate any story that inflates the marvels and importance of their region. In his 1873 history he debunks the myth of the Old Mine Road for reasons that remain valid. In modern times, in an essay that deserves wider circulation, Donald McTernan has shown that the supposed location of the mines in the upper Delaware Valley was based on confusion of names and that the account of the Old Mine Road originated only in 1828.[193] More recently Herbert C. Kraft, focusing on the Indian aspect, found further reason for debunking the resilient myth.[194] Between Quinlan and the contemporary writers, however, Charles Gilbert Hine penned an amusing little volume on the legendary road which, despite his best efforts, has been taken seriously by a disturbingly long list of historians.[195] Hine, who admitted to "an inability to grasp the truth," was willing to be accused of anything but dryness. For anyone tempted to fall into one of his snares, he put out plenty of warning flags: "It may seem to some that my capacity for marvels is remarkably well developed, but that is easily accounted for. My father used to remark that he could swallow anything that could get through his shirt collar, and one had but to see that shirt collar to appreciate how great was the old gentleman's ability," (p.118). It may be that readers have been so preoccupied scoffing at Hines's individual fables that they have neglected to question the underlying legend of the road that connected them.

Taking a detached view, it would require a collar of extraordinary dimensions to swallow the idea that in a rather shaky colony of a few thousand people enough manpower could be spared to mine ore at a remote, uninhabited site, lay out and improve a road more than 100 miles in length over which the ore was hauled by animal power and then transfer the ore to ships on which it was taken either to Manhattan or directly to Europe. No one has mentioned smelting or using the ore in America, so presumably it was shipped across the ocean in unrefined form. It is hard to imagine that any ore transported by this laborious enterprise could have offered a cost advantage over established sources.[196]

Whatever historical significance the legend of the Old Mine Road has may lie in the fact that it perpetuated the tradition of a geographical relationship that otherwise seemed puzzling. Rough sections of the Delaware River and the steep Kittatinny-Shawangunk ridge separating the Delaware Valley from New York City forced commerce out of its preferred channels and into the valley leading to Esopus/Kingston. The precise point at which the attraction of Esopus exceeded that of Philadelphia was variable and difficult to define, but in any case was closer to Philadelphia than the business interests of that city would have liked. There was always the danger that the trade of a large part of northeastern Pennsylvania and adjacent portions of New Jersey would flow away toward the Hudson. (The boundary between the two spheres of influence was reflected somewhat in the ancient division between East and West Jersey.) As late as 1734 inhabitants of West Jersey and Pennsylvania sent a petition to the New York Assembly requesting repair of the road to Esopus because they had "no other way to transport their produce than through the Minisink road."[197] Perhaps the legend of the Old Mine Road represents an effort to explain by folklore how the influence of Kingston once reached the Delaware.

Although the stern demands of historical accuracy may compel us to remove the signposts proclaiming the "Old Mine Road," there is little doubt that the highway in an ancient one. There is general agreement that it followed one of the main Indian paths converging at Esopus. Up this trail settlement spread slowly and steadily after the Indian war of 1663, but did not penetrate as far as present Sullivan County until the final decade of the seventeenth century. A petition dated 1743 asserted that the road to Esopus had been laid out at least 30 years before, indicating that the transition to a somewhat improved vehicular road occurred around 1710.[198]

This is an early date, but still 50-60 years later than the purported mine road.[199] Thus, by the time the D&H appeared on the scene, its prospective route across New York State was a long-established transportation corridor, whether or not it had been trodden by Dutch miners in the dim mists of history.

Maurice Wurts and the engineers who examined the Mamakating Valley with an inquisitive and measuring gaze found a region that was occupied but at a low population density. An account of James S. McEntee, the young engineer who went on to spend most of his life in the Kingston area, shows that the inhabitants along the line of the canal were so few that he could recall them individually nearly 50 years later. Only three families lived on the future site of Ellenville. "They were plain, substantial, well-to-do farmers," he wrote, "living in simple state, having most of the comforts but few of the luxuries of life."[200] Many place names and lock names along the canal perpetuate the identities of these solid farmers, most of whom shared a Dutch heritage even if their ethnic origins were not purely Dutch. Their secure stone dwellings testify to a profound rootedness to place and land.

Reaching back to childhood memories that must have been deeply affecting, John W. Johnston provides a vivid description of the impact that even survey parties had on the secluded rural populace. "Being the first public enterprise to penetrate the sequestered region; to lift the minds of the settlers from the lethargy of ages and to unfold to them something of the prior hidden resources of human genius, the power of money and the value of business, it is not surprising that the canal and its management wielded a dominant influence." The transformation brought by the canal was rapid and dramatic, introducing a new spirit of enterprise. In 1833, with canal operation scarcely five years old, the *Ulster Republican* proclaimed that "The attention of the public is directed to this section of country, to the numerous inviting locations along the line of this canal now unoccupied—to the natural advantages within our own county at present useless and unproductive, for the want of enterprising young men and the necessary supply of funds to forward and sustain improvements."[201]

The D&H had not built a canal primarily to serve the interests of Ulster, Orange and Sullivan Counties, however the managers, mostly bankers and merchants, were not about to overlook any source of revenue. Perhaps in an age when bookkeeping entries were made laboriously by pen and ink in ledger books and carried out to the cent and sometimes fractions of a cent, every penny had tangible meaning. Company policy, beginning as early as Hone's address at the groundbreaking, actively promoted economic development along the canal. The annual report for 1831 noted with satisfaction that "Various manufacturing establishments are going into operation at different points on the line of the work." In a possible reference to Ransome Hall, it added that "Arrangements have already been made by individuals to pass 3,000,000 feet of lumber over the railroad." The same 1833 annual report that boasted about Carbondale and Honesdale predicted that "an annual increase of revenue from tolls may confidently be anticipated, as the country through which the canal and railway pass, is steadily advancing in population and wealth, and new sources of business opening."

Two years later the annual report noted that "The agricultural products and the return supplies of a large extent of country must necessarily find their conveyance on the canal." There was already a solid basis for this belief. In the first two years the canal was in business, before the gravity railway was operational, shipments of cord wood exceeded anthracite.[202] By 1831, although coal tonnage exceeded all other merchandise by four to one, the non-anthracite traffic remained considerable. For the years 1834 through 1838, the combined general traffic made up a respectable 36% of the canal's tonnage.[203] Thus the D&H, almost in spite of itself, took on the attributes of a developmental canal. The company, true to form, began to keep detailed tallies of this traffic, excerpts of which are presented in Table 1.

In New York the canal greatly enlarged something that already existed, while in northeastern Pennsylvania it created a whole new economy, but similar astonishing growth could be observed in the New York side. This was most evident at Rondout, which like Honesdale and Carbondale, had exploded from an almost invisible nucleus. In 1820 the site, then loosely termed the Strand, contained three dwellings, three stores, an inn and a flour mill.[204] McEntee recalled that "With few exceptions both banks of the stream were thickly wooded from a point opposite the present office of the canal company to Eddyville." After the flood damage of 1832 had been repaired, a writer for the *Ulster Plebian* took a celebratory stroll along the Rondout wharf and observed that "a person is almost led to imagine himself in some city or seaport town, by the number of vessels from different and distant places—vessels from Maine, Rhode Island, Massachusetts, New Jersey, &c."[205] This was not just local puffery: in 1830 there had been 388 departures of vessels carrying coal from Rondout Creek.[206] In September 1833 a Kingston newspaper reported that since April 56 barges, 11 brigs, 166 schooners, 372 sloops and 42 canalboats had cleared the formerly placid Rondout Creek.[207] This averages to something like four a day and, incidentally, gives some idea of the diversity of craft that plied the Hudson in those days. Historian Nathaniel Bartlett Sylvester was not indulging in the literary excesses of his time when he concluded that "The impulse of this canal enterprise may be said to have created Rondout, as that place, now teeming with so many varied industries, and the seat of such extensive commercial enterprises, was a mere hamlet of a few buildings prior to the opening of this system."[208]

Ellenville seized the commercial opportunities the canal brought. The building on the left is the warehouse of Jacob Hermance, who purchased the Merchant & Tanners line of freight boats in 1869. Hunt & Donaldson took control of the warehouse several years after the canal ceased operating, and the building was commonly referred to by that name until it was razed in 1988.
CREDIT
Painting by unidentified artist in Ed LeRoy Collection, National Canal Museum.

ALTOGETHER, it is one of the most daring undertakings I have ever witnessed, to carry an artificial river over rocky mountains, and up the most savage and almost impracticable defiles. ---Washington Irving, 1841

Thunder Along the Delaware

IN JUNE 1839 THE D&H DECLARED A DIVIDEND OF 3½%, its first since 1833. This was an important milestone, marking the passage beyond the hazards of youth. Thereafter uninterrupted dividends were paid until 1877, when the company could no longer buck a prolonged depression. Survival in the harsh competitive climate of the 1830s, culminating in the financial storm of 1837, proved that the company rested on a solid footing. It would be unlikely to succumb to external forces; only failings of its own management could threaten it. In the 1840s, under the leadership of John Wurts, management was at the peak of its form. The company undertook a bold program to maintain and improve its relative position by increasing its capacity. At the same time, while pursuing policies that could serve as a model of active, forward-looking corporate management, the D&H continued to be afflicted by rivalry and contention more serious than it had yet encountered. Thus, while it attained a measure of security, it did not find lasting stability. Its history continued to be a succession of crises.

The feeling of jubilation at having weathered a long ordeal was expressed in a glorious episode in July 1841, when Washington Irving accompanied Philip Hone and D&H board members on a journey up the line to Honesdale. It was on this visit that a conspicuous cliff overlooking the town was named for Irving, contributing to the mistaken belief that the name Honesdale was bestowed at that time. Irving was then the most famous and beloved author in the country. With James Fenimore Cooper he had originated a distinctive American literature, paralleling what Cole and his followers had achieved in the visual arts. Hone, who delighted in the company of famous people and was a boyhood neighbor of Irving, was ecstatic. He confided in his diary that "Their whole voyage was one of mirth and good cheer. They took pleasure in the very inconveniences of the small canal boat, making their beds on the hard planks, eating in primitive fashion and traveling three miles an hour." Hone was deeply influenced by the belief, enunciated by Cole, Cooper, Irving, William Cullen Bryant and others, that wilderness was the key element of an emerging American cultural identity. A tolerable amount of physical hardship and exposure to the outdoors was already fashionable. Irving seemed genuinely to relish a reprise of his youthful wanderings. Hone noted that he "has enjoyed himself to the very top of his bent. He has been in perfect raptures all the way; I have never known him so entertaining; he jokes and laughs and tells stories and actually does not sleep in the day time."[1]

The view from Irving's Cliff appealed to the romantic sensibilities of city sophisticates Hone and Irving.
CREDIT
National Canal Museum.

Irving, moreover, seemed thoroughly impressed by his canal journey. Writing from Honesdale to his sister in England, he offered a characteristically polished description of the trip:

> I do not know when I have made a more gratifying excursion with respect to natural scenery, or more interesting from the stupendous works of art. The canal is laid a great part of the way along romantic valleys, watered by the Rondout, the Lackawaxen, &c. For many miles it is built along the face of perpendicular precipices, rising into stupendous cliffs with overhanging forests, or strutting out into vast promontories; while upon the other side you look down upon the Delaware, foaming and roaring below you, at the foot of an immense wall or embankment which supports the canal. Altogether, it is one of the most daring undertakings I have ever witnessed, to carry an artificial river over rocky mountains, and up the most savage and almost impracticable defiles; and all this, too, has been achieved by the funds of an association composed of a handful of individuals. For upward of ninety miles I went through a constant succession of scenery that would have been famous had it existed in any part of Europe; the Catskill Mountains to the north, the Shawangunk Mountains to the south, and between them lovely valleys, with the most luxuriant woodlands and picturesque streams. All this is a region about which I had heard nothing—a region entirely unknown to fame; but so it is in our country. We have some main routes for the fashionable traveller, along which he is hurried in steamboats and railroad cars; while on every side extend regions of beauty, about which he hears and knows nothing.[2]

Again, one sees the sensitivity to European opinion, the compulsive urge to measure up to the old continent, that tormented the young nation's few intellectuals.

At Carbondale, where the party inspected the mines, Irving's pleasure began to pall. Although he had established his reputation by writing American folk tales, he was probably the most cosmopolitan American of his day. Of Honesdale he confided to a favorite niece in Paris:

> Nothing can be more dull and monotonous than a Sunday in one of these little, commonplace orderly country towns. I have been to a commonplace little church of white boards, and seen a congregation of commonplace people and heard a commonplace sermon, and now cannot muster up any thing but commonplace ideas. . . . Good lord deliver me from the all pervading commonplace which is the curse of our country.[3]

Perhaps the author was already feeling the symptoms of a fever he contracted on the excursion.

It is not specifically recorded that John Wurts accompanied the holiday party; if he did, it is unlikely that he shared fully Philip Hone's elation. After the long period of privation, Hone rejoiced in the renewed dividend and the brilliant prospects for the use of anthracite in steamboats and manufacturing. None of this was lost on Wurts, but he was a chronic worrier, tormented by flickering shadows. In February 1840, even though dividends had been restored, Wurts wrote that the outlook for business was "much more gloomy and dull than this time last year." Pleading desperately with Russel Lord to hold down expenses, he wrote " 'Hope deferred maketh the heart rich,' and this I have experienced so long that I am almost weary of bearing up against it." Anxious not to present more bad news at the upcoming stockholders' meeting, he implored Lord "I must look to you entirely to guard us against another disappointment this year."[4]

Wurts became almost obsessive on the subject of cutting canal expenses: "The canal swallows up so much of our earnings that the attention of the Board and the

Stockholders is fixed on it with the greatest anxiety as being emphatically that part of our business on which more than any other our prosperity depends."[5] Like his modern counterparts, Wurts's cost-cutting focused on labor, which he regarded as purely a commodity. "Lock tenders are down as low perhaps as they can live," he told Russel Lord, but labor was plentiful and "we can doubtless send you as many men as you or Mr. Archbald may need if you are short now, or if the men you now have are not ready to come down to the standard of the times." This impersonal attitude toward labor shows up again in 1843, when Wurts sent Lord a clipping giving rates of pay for laborers on the Erie RR. Pay "must conform to the state of the times," he directed, although he allowed Lord to reduce the rates gradually "as circumstances will permit," rather than at once.[6]

The Erie Railroad

IN THE SUMMER OF 1841, while Irving and Hone were enjoying their cruise, Wurts's fears took more tangible form: the Erie RR was on his mind. This project, intended to create a direct route from the Hudson to the Great Lakes, originated as something of a political payback, in which Governor DeWitt Clinton rewarded the Southern Tier counties for their acquiescence in the Erie and Champlain canals. A charter for the New York & Erie RR was obtained April 4, 1832. Among other features, it provided that railroad operations be kept within New York State; later, the adoption of a broad (six foot) gauge was meant, in part, to discourage connections. The railroad duplicated and improved upon the proposed canal extension up the Delaware and offers one more reason why talk of that canal came to an end.

Redoubtable Ben Hendricks tended Lock No.32 (Sam Taylor's Lock) about a mile south of Ellenville. "Jake, I seem to be, er, busy just now. Could you go down and tell Ben Hendricks the company's decided to reduce his pay."
CREDIT
D&H Canal Museum.

The 1832 legislation had been prepared by John Duer, who had been counsel for the D&H and later became president of Columbia College. He and George D. Wickham were on the Erie's first board of directors. A more important connection with the D&H existed in the person of Benjamin Wright. Then Chief Engineer of the Erie Canal, he was detached by the state to make a rough survey for the projected railroad. Though only a preliminary study, it largely determined the future course of the railroad—another in the impressive list of Wright's contributions to public improvements in the youthful nation. In his report, presented January 1835, Wright was sensitive to the concerns of his former employer, noting that if the railroad entered the Delaware Valley it "might come into collision with the Delaware and Hudson Canal and perhaps divert some of its legitimate and fair business. In construction it might even interfere with the very important and useful work for the execution of which its enterprising proprietors deserve to be gratefully considered."[7] This concern did not pass unnoticed, and one of the D&H's vehement enemies criticized Wright for protecting the interest of the "odious monopoly."[8]

As work proceeded on the Erie RR it was found necessary not only to enter the Delaware Valley, but to cross into Pennsylvania. This violation of one of its cardinal principles brought on an agonizing legislative ordeal in each state. The standard modern history of the Erie RR states that the D&H "did everything possible to prevent [the railroad] from being placed through that valley."[9] Neither the D&H minutes nor its official history confirm that accusation, but it is entirely in keeping with the business practice of the times, in which there were many subtle methods of applying political pressure. With important influence in both states, the D&H was well equipped to pursue an obstructionist policy and probably contributed to imposing some of the restrictions that hindered the struggling railroad.

In the early 1830s there were no precedents for a railroad of its magnitude, and it took a long time for the Erie to get organized. By 1835 there were a number of railroads in successful operation, including three lines radiating out of Boston; railroading had passed beyond the experimental stage. Groundbreaking on the Erie took place at Deposit, New York, on November 7, 1835. Some construction followed, but by the end of 1836 had sputtered to a halt. A major effort to revive the project occurred in January 1837, when the mayor of New York City presided over a meeting at Clinton Hall. Many early backers of the Erie, before it became the plaything of scoundrels such as Daniel Drew, Jay Gould and "Jubilee Jim" Fisk, belonged to the same class as Philip Hone. He wrote in his diary that they "possess wealth and influence and zeal enough too in any thing in which themselves are engaged, however disposed they may have been at one time to throw difficulties in the way of enterprizes equally laudable . . . but from which they thought proper to stand aloof"—an acid reminder that the unwillingness of these wealthy men to aid the D&H years before still smarted. With his curious mixture of generosity and self-pity, Hone concluded, "I wish them all possible success in this great national work and that is more than they did me in regard to the Delaware & Hudson."[10]

Before this renewed effort could pick up steam the Panic of 1837 intervened. With seasoned enterprises pushed to the brink, there was no hope for a railroad that existed largely in the imagination of dreamers. If men like Hone and Wurts feared the Erie, one advantage of the depression was that the danger abated, leaving the D&H free to battle adversity on its own terms. In time the Erie stirred again, and on June 30, 1841 it began operating a small section of track. By September it was running between Piermont on the Hudson and Goshen. While placing this portion in service was a major accomplishment, the Erie could not ignore its western aspirations, and in the Delaware Valley this thrust brought it into collision with the D&H.

In the second phase of the relationship between the companies, the Erie became a tangible problem. No longer an abstract menace, it came into conflict with the D&H over practical physical issues of finding a route through the narrow, often steeply walled valley. There is no doubt that the D&H leaders were keenly aware of the looming threat. Writing to Russel Lord on January 4, 1841, John Wurts referred to the New York & Erie RR Co. "whom we have been watching for some time."[11] He was probably aware of an unpromising precedent in the Lehigh Valley in the early 1830s in which the Lehigh Navigation and the Beaver Meadow RR had resorted to arming their men with muskets during a confrontation over the railroad's location.[12] If the normally peaceable Josiah White, with his Quaker background, had been driven to this extreme, Wurts certainly had no desire to see the D&H put in a similar situation.

At first the two companies made a seemingly sincere effort to negotiate a solution. The presidents met, and each company appointed a committee to confer about the location of the railroad.[13] This committee held a long conference on January 8, 1841, but the D&H deferred a decision until it could consult with Lord, and with Archbald if he were available.[14] Subsequent sessions, while intense, turned out to be unsatisfactory. The railroad sought to enter canal property, cross it with bridges, and move material from the berm to the towpath side. In the opinion of the D&H committee this could "interrupt the navigation of the canal, and probably increase the risk of injury to it during floods." More disturbing to the D&H was the fact that the Erie offered "no plan to prevent the apprehended evils, and no indemnity against their consequences . . . other than the good intentions of that company and the liability of itself and its contractors."[15]

After another meeting of the engineers, the Erie offered a plan which would supposedly avoid interference with the canal. John Wurts, suspicious that this plan involved using the berm side, which "we consider as bad if not worse to us than to take the river side," warned Lord that "their movements must be closely watched." An exchange of letters had shown that the Erie was determined to remain in the Delaware Valley. It had not disclosed details of its new route to the D&H, and Wurts was beginning to speak of an injunction.[16] In April 1841 he requested particulars that could be used for this purpose, and in June he told Lord that a bill had been filed in chancery against the railroad.[17] Before the injunction could be granted the president of the Erie offered a new proposal under which a joint committee of the two companies would obtain a report from "skilful and disinterested engineers."[18]

Whether any of this was done is doubtful. By the end of 1841 the Erie's financial difficulties had accumulated, and once again work was virtually suspended. For nearly ten years the threat posed by this company had hung over the D&H without fully materializing, and now the canal company was granted another respite. John Wurts, deeply affected by the experience, took advantage of this interlude. The clash with the Erie was one of the factors that persuaded him to lead the company in a new direction.

Although the evidence is limited, it seems that Wurts was more concerned about the danger the Erie posed to the physical operation of the canal than to its traffic. Even a man with John Wurts's tendencies toward anxiety did not assume that the coming of a railroad would automatically doom nearby canals. Maurice Wurts expressed this point of view in a letter to his brother Charles:

What Mr. Smith says in relation to the New York and Erie R.R. being used as a competitor with us in the coal trade need cause no uneasiness. The situation of that Company—the high grade of their road—the poor construction of the work already done with what will be required to reach the coal region places them out of the question.[19]

Our perceptions are shaped by our knowledge of the eventual disappearance of the towpath canals, but in 1840 that outcome was not at all certain. The tendency to dismiss canals as hopelessly impractical erases a generation of fervent debate about which form of transportation was more efficient. Most early railroads initially emphasized passenger traffic, which was inconsequential on canals other than the Erie. Passenger business was like the salad course of a meal, but the canals were not ready to allow upstart railroads to sink knife and fork into the meat and potatoes of freight haulage without a duel.

Except within a small circle of enthusiasts, early railroads—perhaps deservedly—had relatively few advocates among engineers. Jervis was notable as one of the first prominent members of the profession who had an open mind toward the new form of transportation. Benjamin Wright, although he was willing to consider a railroad in the special circumstances of Moosic Mountain, was not in general a supporter of them. In presenting evidence to the House of Representatives relative to the debate between a railroad and a canal in the Potomac Valley, Wright said "In short, I place a railroad between a good turnpike and a canal."[20] It was in this document, as noted earlier, that Wright referred to his experience on the D&H and opined that the expense of a railroad was three times that of a canal. Josiah White, testifying in the same report, placed the ratio even higher, at about four to one, and pointedly refuted claims to the contrary by John L. Sullivan. In advocating railroads Sullivan was ahead of his time but, given his increasing reputation as a crank, his support may have been more of a handicap than a help. John Bolton, then living in Savannah, Georgia, and making perhaps his final appearance in the public eye, concurred in the anti-rail views of Wright and White. All of them believed that railroads were making inroads only because the true cost of operating them was not yet fully understood.

One of the most respected engineers of the 1840s, Charles Ellet, Jr., like his predecessors concluded that if the true costs of railroads were considered they would not only be uncompetitive with canals, but in many cases could not remain solvent. At that time the Schuylkill Navigation was engaged in a ferocious conflict with the parallel Philadelphia & Reading RR. After serving the interest of the waterway in less direct ways, Ellet agreed to accept its presidency. This was the only instance in his career in which he functioned primarily as a manager; apparently the chance to test his theories in practice overcame his usual reluctance.[21] The 1846 annual report of the Navigation, the only one composed during Ellet's brief tenure, shows the impact of his ideas and his knack as a propagandist: "A great issue is now to be tried for the determination of the relative merits of canals and railways in the transportation of an almost unlimited amount of heavy freight." Surely this was not the departing moan of an ebbing institution!

In point of fact, canals were almost always cheaper on a strict tonnage basis. Even as late as 1860, after 30 years of rapid railroad development, generally accepted figures showed average rates per ton mile at one cent for river travel, two cents for canals, and four cents for railroads—and that only where canal competition existed.[22] The reasons for choosing railroads were not based on pure cost comparisons but had to do with factors such as speed, directness, flexibility, dependability and year-round availability. A similar situation exists today, in which railroads (and the remaining waterways) are cheaper than trucks on a straight ton/mile basis, but trucks seem to offer other advantages and are certainly abundant, as anyone who has occasion to drive on the Interstate highways cannot help noticing. It is only in relatively recent times that the balanced concept of intermodal freight has made much headway. There was a precursor of this concept in the small railways that linked mines and factories to canal ports before an extensive system of railroads developed.

The Anthracite Rivals

AS IN THE 1830s when the D&H was faced with threats on several fronts, John Wurts had to keep his eye on ominous developments to the south. At the same time he was fending off the Erie RR his earlier foe, the Lehigh Coal & Navigation Co., began maneuvers that he found deeply disturbing. Chronically insecure, the D&H president believed he saw a systematic program by the Lehigh to seize a greater share of the anthracite market—inevitably at the expense of his company.

In late 1840 Wurts learned of a program to enlarge the Morris Canal, which had with difficulty weathered the crisis of 1837, so that it could handle boats of 50-ton capacity. To his way of thinking the Lehigh had "made common cause" with the Morris and would furnish the money for the work.[23] Later reports that 3000 men, paid by the Lehigh company, were working on the Morris confirmed this.[24] Josiah White of the Lehigh had, moreover, dispatched two of his engineers to supervise the New Jersey work.[25]

In Wurts's mind the plot went much deeper. White's real goal, he believed, was to secure an outlet lock on the Delaware Division Canal at Black's Eddy (now Point Pleasant). The Delaware canal, though built by the state, was essentially an extension of the Lehigh Navigation. For the state it was a worthwhile strategic investment to make sure that Philadelphia retained as much control as possible of the Lehigh Valley's resources. Building an outlet lock would allow White to cross the river and gain more direct access to the Delaware & Raritan Canal across the waist of New Jersey. (Otherwise Lehigh boats had to remain in the Delaware Division until its terminus at Bristol, then ascend some distance up the Delaware to enter the D&R, a roundabout path to the same point.) Using the D&R, straighter and more efficient than the hilly Morris Canal, could greatly improve the Lehigh's position in the New York market. Never prone to underestimate bad news, Wurts wrote that the Lehigh "grasps at all the world, and will not rest short of unrivalled possession of the coal market, if they can get it by hook or by crook."[26] From his perspective the Lehigh company was making an unrestrained bid for supremacy: "Its course in this and other matters seems to be dictated by the idea that it can break down all other concerns, and the power which it is concentrating renders the effort one that should not be dismissed as chimerical."[27]

Constructing a lock at Black's Eddy was at least as much a political as an engineering problem. Legislative approval was needed, and several interests were sure to oppose the request. Prominent among them in earlier episodes had been the Morris Canal, in which Philadelphia financial interests were represented. In Wurts's devious mind, Josiah White's assistance to the Morris Canal was mainly a means of appeasing that company so that he would be free to pursue what he was really after at Black's Eddy. The idea of an outlet lock went back virtually to the beginning of the Delaware Canal, and at one stage Josiah White had designed a crane to lift boats from the canal to the river. In arguing his case in the Pennsylvania Legislature, he stressed the ominous prospect that the Morris Canal would otherwise carry off the traffic of the Lehigh Valley.[28] Wurts's concern became more acute as it seemed that the Lehigh company had hit on a way to neutralize the previously potent opposition of the Morris Canal.

What John Wurts might have become under different circumstances is a matter of speculation, but a life experience comprised of law, political office and defending the D&H against a host of unscrupulous enemies had made him a profoundly suspicious individual. Nor had this experience inclined him toward a passive response. Once again he marshaled his forces to meet the new menace. Writing at a time when the boating season was ending and a legislative session would soon begin, he instructed Russel Lord to "consider how we may be able to counteract" the Lehigh company and its supporters.[29] In his next letter on the subject he vowed "We must stop that project if we can."[30]

This was one of the periods in the long history of the D&H when fortune smiled. Once again, as in the case of the Erie RR, the menace was removed by outside forces, in this case natural ones. On January 7 and 8, 1841, a devastating flood raged through the Lehigh Valley, sweeping away most of the works by which man had briefly tamed the river. Instead of assisting the Morris Canal, the Lehigh company had to reverse itself and request aid from the Morris directors in order to rebuild.[31] There was a definite logic to this, as the Lehigh was such an important generator of traffic for the New Jersey waterway.

After the flood crest had passed, John Wurts writhed in an agony of suspense while he awaited news as to whether the storm had been equally destructive to the D&H works; for it had affected a wide region. Almost as if writing with pins instead of pens, he begged Lord for a report and came close to berating him for the failure to provide prompt information.[32] Wurts, for his part, was being besieged by anxious stockholders. In a wry comment he noted that "formerly when they regarded the stock as less valuable, they did not trouble us on such occasions."[33] It was only on January 23 that Lord finally submitted a full report, which showed that while there had been considerable damage, especially in the Lackawaxen, it was not nearly comparable to the Lehigh destruction.

John Wurts was a pious man; under his leadership the D&H supplied each boat with a Bible, appropriated $300 in 1843 for "the promotion of Religion and morality among the Boatmen," and frequently donated land for churches. Yet the concept of generalized charity toward his fellow man seems not to have been highly developed, and he could hardly conceal his glee when describing the ruin of the Lehigh system. "[C]ompared with what has occurred on the Lehigh and elsewhere, we think that we have much cause for gratitude. On the Lehigh, if the accounts that have reached us be correct, the canal is not merely injured but destroyed; and it must be very late in the season, before any coal can come to market from that avenue—indeed it is doubted by many whether it will ever come again by that canal—Locks, dams, canal, lock houses, all are said to be gone. The Schuylkill canal is also much injured, and it is said cannot be ready for business before June."[34]

Wurts saw his great opportunity and seized it. He reminded Russel Lord with unmistakable clarity "how important it is for us to get every ton of coal that we can, and of course therefore to have our canal ready at the earliest possible day." He instructed Lord to put off meeting with the Erie RR people in order to concentrate on repairing the canal.[35] In his letter of January 15, 1841 Wurts noted that, because of the flood, the price of coal had already advanced $2 in Philadelphia and $1 to $2 in New York City. As if rubbing his hands while writing, he told Lord "We shall be able to get at Rondout $6 to $6.50 for all we can get down canal this year."[36] Still in a state of excitement a week later, he pressed Lord to work "with all the energy and industry that can be applied."[37] It was this year, with the national economy creeping with painful slowness out of the 1837 depression, that was the real turning point for the D&H. The company shipped over 192,000 tons of coal, achieved its greatest profit margin, and paid annual dividends of 8½%. Never was the adage about an ill wind better demonstrated.

It is no wonder that John Wurts often showed signs of strain and weariness, for even his successes never seemed permanent. In a remarkable achievement, the Lehigh Navigation rebuilt from the devastation of 1841 and by 1843 had revived the campaign for an outlet lock. The lock was such an attractive proposition that the Lehigh company could never let the idea die. In early 1843 a Pennsylvania Senate committee approved the outlet lock, reviving John Wurts's dire forebodings. "A harder blow could hardly be aimed" at Honesdale, Carbondale and the surrounding counties, he declared.[38] Ever cagey, he advised Russel Lord, "it would do no good, but harm for this Company openly to resist it. If we do any thing therefore, we must do it quietly and unobserved through third parties."[39] He was wary of the idea of staging mass meetings in D&H country, since it might call attention to the fact that the D&H, in carrying coal out of state, was no different than the Black's Eddy proposal. In writing to Lord, he recommended letters and quiet personal representation to legislators, even offering to cover the expenses of an expedition to Harrisburg.[40]

Despite the initial success of the outlet lock bill, it was ultimately stopped again. Kingsbury had gone to Harrisburg on behalf of the D&H, and his and other representations had apparently succeeded. By then John Wurts knew better than to believe the victory was final. "[T]his project seems to have many lives, and I begin to despair of its staying *killed, when it is killed.*[41] Events proved Wurts correct, for the outlet lock was completed in 1848, though at New Hope, rather than Black's Eddy.[42] By then much else had changed, and the outlet lock, though still disturbing, no longer seemed catastrophic.

The long-standing animosity Wurts felt toward the Lehigh company may have diverted his attention from another threat emanating from the Schuylkill. This third member of the anthracite canal triumvirate operated on more of a corporate style and was not identified with a single dominant individual like Josiah White. John Wurts may have viewed it as a more distant and less personalized rival; nevertheless, it was one more reason the D&H had no peace even after forsaking the dream of entering the Philadelphia market in favor of New York. In 1831 Lackawanna coal brought over the D&H undersold Schuylkill coal in New York by $4 a ton ($10 to $14) but this advantage was not permanent. In 1837 the first shipment of anthracite from the Schuylkill region was brought to New York over the Delaware & Raritan Canal, which had been completed in 1834. Because the D&R was one of the most easily navigable canals in the country, users of the Schuylkill system, despite a seemingly roundabout route, found they could compete with great effectiveness in New York. During the first two decades of the anthracite canal era the Schuylkill was the most highly developed and busiest of the group. In 1842 it carried more coal than the D&H and the Lehigh combined. This strength enabled it to become a major factor in the vast New York market. Of the 491,602 tons of anthracite it carried in 1842 only 26% was destined for New York, but that amount was equal to 62% of the D&H's total coal shipment. Meanwhile, John Wurts was disturbed further by the knowledge that at least for a time in the winter of 1843 Lehigh coal was selling in New York City at the same $4.50 a ton the D&H was charging.[43]

By 1853 market relationships had changed dramatically: Schuylkill producers had found New York so lucrative that coal shipped to that destination through the Delaware & Raritan Canal exceeded the amount delivered to Philadelphia by a 3-1 margin. This total of 474,105 tons was only about 20,000 tons less than the entire coal traffic of the D&H Canal.[44] Since not all D&H coal went to New York, this means that Schuylkill deliveries to that city actually exceeded those of the D&H. In that year the Morris Canal received 222,582 tons of Lehigh coal at Port Delaware, but much of that was delivered along the route in New Jersey and did not reach the metropolis.

Enlargement

Loading canal boats at Honesdale.
CREDIT
National Canal Museum.

LIKE BERRIES COMING RIPE ALL AT THE SAME TIME, a cluster of factors combined to convince John Wurts to lead the company in a bold new direction by enlarging the capacity of the transportation system. It had probably always been felt that original construction was not permanent. This was in accord with American practice in which construction was meant to be no more than minimally adequate to get the job done. Once again the Erie Canal set a precedent; only ten years after its completion a massive rebuilding and enlargement was begun and lasted more than 25 years.

Of more immediate concern, with the gradual recovery of the early 1840s, coal shipments were approaching the capacity of the railway and canal. In 1841 over 192,000 tons moved over the system, the capacity of which was considered to be only 200,000 tons.[45] In theory one option was for the company to stand still and remain content with this share of the market. It was the mark of John Wurts's leadership that he realized this course was impossible. As his analysis of the Lehigh/Morris relationship indicates, he had a conspiratorial, if not paranoid, turn of mind. Yet he was also able to understand the interconnections in the anthracite trade, to see how one event could bump into others. This kind of vision is the real contribution of a CEO and the distinguishing characteristic of effective leadership. More remarkable is that Wurts never lost sight of the panorama, even though no one was more distressed by transient problems and fluctuations.

From the lofty perch to which he was able to soar when he pulled free from the nervous worries that beset him, Wurts recognized that his company could not stagnate. Reading the events of the past couple of years made it apparent that his main rivals were bent on expansion—both of production and market share. It was accepted as a truism that efficiencies of scale would result, so that it would cost less to bring coal to the consumer. The Schuylkill Navigation, which under Ellet's guidance had responded to competition by enlargement, had set an example that could not be ignored, and the Morris Canal had followed. A later report to the board, probably composed by John Wurts, noted that "During the year 1841 events were maturing, that were calculated to exert an important influence on the coal trade. The Reading Rail Road was approaching its completion; and a struggle commencing between it and the Schuylkill Navigation Co. destined to affect very materially the price of coal."[46] No one made coal purchases out of sentiment; Lackawanna coal would not sell if its price was not competitive. The only market that might remain secure for the D&H was on the Hudson north of Rondout, but that was not large enough to provide adequate return on capital. Even that market could be threatened if schemes to link the New York and Pennsylvania state canal systems became reality. In sum, there was no reasonable prospect of the D&H becoming what we today call a niche player.

The factor that presented the most direct stimulus for enlargement was the Erie RR; not only because of the competition it might offer, but because it threatened to occupy the ground the D&H needed. On March 8, 1841 John Wurts sent a letter to Russel Lord that was laden with great and lasting consequences. This was the same revealing letter in which the president said that the movements of the Erie RR "must be closely watched." Wurts then went on to add:

> Let them go or attempt to go where they will, they would interfere more or less with our doing what at some day we must do, namely throw an aqueduct across the Delaware river and enlarge our canal. We deem it important that we should (before they attempt to occupy ground,) ourselves make a survey and mark the lines embracing the ground we should need for such alteration in our works from the Lackawaxen to Port Jervis.[47]

Wurts gave further instructions, telling Lord to claim as much territory "as would throw the Erie railroad or any other work entirely back and out of our way." Soon after, the president pulled the board along behind him, winning its endorsement to have Lord plan an aqueduct and survey for an enlargement between the Lackawaxen and Port Jervis. This part of the canal would expand to dimensions of 50 feet on top, 35 feet on the bottom, with a depth of five feet; the locks would be 13 feet wide and 80 feet long.[48] Since it would make little sense to have one section of the canal larger than the rest, this was in effect a commitment to enlarge the entire waterway.

Wurts had ordered the engineer to make his survey "immediately, if there is any indication of an intention on the part of the Erie Rl. Road Co. to take the berme side of our canal." As described earlier, the railroad did not move as rapidly as Wurts had feared. On June 4, 1841 Wurts instructed Lord to prepare a profile of his survey for the aqueduct and enlarged canal "at your leisure."[49] Meanwhile, Lord had reported in a letter of May 19 that a company had been formed to build a toll bridge across the Lackawaxen. This could relieve the D&H of the obligation to maintain a ford across the river, which had been the source of constant complaint.[50] It was an attractive prospect to the board, which voted to subscribe up to $1000 in the bridge company stock. When John Wurts, always thrifty, conveyed this to Lord he said the subscription should not exceed $800—"if less, so much the better."[51]

But not everyone shared John Wurts's sweeping vision of the anthracite industry. When the president made his first formal proposal to appropriate money for the enlargement, at a board meeting on August 9, 1842, Philip Hone proposed tabling the motion. This was a decisive parting of the ways; for Hone, whether or not he had rescued the company with his own fortune, had always been its buttress. Now approaching 60, with the lean years etched in his memory, he was probably content to collect his dividend and had little appetite for setting off in a new and risky direction. A substantial part of his fortune had melted away in the 1837 depression and in the failure of an insurance company, so that the dividend was important. By 1846 his worth of $100,000 barely qualified him for listing in a directory of the 1000 wealthiest citizens of New York.[52] More tellingly, Hone's motion was defeated, probably an event without precedent in the D&H board-room. It was one of those tangible moments of transition when the wind shifts to a new quarter. Thereafter Hone seemed to attend managers' meetings with less regularity; and since his stock ownership may have been diminished by then, his influence waned. In that same year Irad Hawley had been elected to the board for the first time, and his influence ascended—with portentous consequences.

From this inception in 1842 to the end of the decade, the work of enlargement was almost continuous, but it was divided into three distinct phases. The effort authorized in August 1842 was meant to deepen the canal from four to five feet, which would permit an increase in the capacity of boats from 30 to 40 tons. According to LeRoy, the nominal depth of four feet that was supposed to have been attained when the canal was opened was not achieved consistently until 1839.[53] This date seems excessively late for regular operation, and a contemporary source states that the full depth was achieved in 1832.[54] Work began with the close of navigation in November, continued through 1843 and concluded in the following year. The results were immediately apparent, for coal shipments in 1844 reached 250,000 tons for the first time, even though the increased depth had not been available during the entire season. Through the end of 1844 the company recorded spending $281,105 to increase the capacity of the canal and railroad. It calculated that there had been a saving of $209,228 resulting from the improvements; to some extent this is an imaginary figure, since the old system would not have been capable of carrying the increased volume.[55] Best of all, the improvement had been achieved without noticeable strain. The conservative management that had withheld dividends for several years until 1839 had continued this course into the early 1840s. As a result, even after paying annual dividends of 8% and repaying all debt except the state obligations, the company had accumulated by 1845 a surplus in the profit and loss account in excess of $750,000. More amazing, this account had continued to increase even though the costs of enlargement were taken from it rather than being capitalized, as conventional practice would dictate.[56]

Second Enlargement

NEXT, John Wurts brought before the board on October 14, 1844 a proposal to enlarge the canal to accommodate 50-ton boats. He could have paid for this out of the accumulated surplus, but by then the president had become aware that he needed to put the company's financial structure on a sounder foundation. Again, in the absence of useful examples, Wurts had little guidance but the dictates of common sense and equity. He was like a captain navigating through Arctic channels, in which charts were either non-existent or valueless.

One of many ways in which the D&H in that dewy morning of corporate capitalism differed from modern corporations was the lack of a Chief Financial Officer. The company had from the outset filled the office of treasurer, often combined with the position of secretary. But that person's function was limited to actually handling money, more like the duty of a cashier, rather than deciding financial policy. Except insofar as he might be prodded by other members of the board, John Wurts was responsible for noticing that corporate finances needed to be handled differently and recommending a course of action.

As he explained to the board in 1845, he was disturbed by the "very large, unusual and as the Board think unwise disparity between the amount of capital stock and the amount of permanent investment." At that time the cost of capital improvements totaled $3,463,686, while only $1,922,000 of stock had been issued. Most of the difference had been paid out of the operating surplus which, as Wurts said, "justly and of right belongs to stockholders." Meanwhile, the profits of the preceding five years had averaged 13½%. Drawing on experience reaching to the dawn of the anthracite age, with all the contention and hostility that churned in his memory, Wurts could foresee the ruinous consequences. There would be, he predicted, "no legitimate application of these earnings, other than dividends which must be so large, as to challenge a degree of public attention by no means desirable, because it might produce annoying and harassing measures to the Company—or induce competition that might not otherwise be thought of."[57] Although he did not mention it explicitly, he probably was thinking ahead to 1853, when the 30-year Pennsylvania charter would expire and the state would legally be able to assume control of the D&H works. No one else on the board would have been as keenly aware of this eventuality as John Wurts, who had been present at the creation and who had always tried to gloss over the implications of that provision. No one recognized as clearly the danger of presenting too tempting a target.[58]

In late 1844 President Wurts placed himself on a committee to review the company's financial situation. The first issue was whether the managers were authorized to issue additional stock. (One of the charges with which the Locofocos had blasted the company was that it had already issued stock beyond its authorization of $1,500,000.) In its report of November 19, the committee concluded that it was legally able to issue whatever stock was necessary to carry out its original purpose. Having dispatched that problem, the committee recommended an increase of stock from $1,922,000 to $2,600,000. About $339,000 of this would be used to establish a formal sinking fund to extinguish, or sink, the state debt, the first portion of which was coming due in less than four years. Another $413,000 would be used to continue the program of improvements to the system—increasing the capacity of the canal for boats of 50 tons, improving land at Rondout for coal deposit, extending the railway to additional mines, and buying new boats and railway cars.[59] Expansion also made the question of water supply, never far from the minds of canal managers, more acute. The record is not clear as to whether the canal in its early years had constructed reservoirs or relied on the natural flow of water. With every opening of the locks sending some 100,000 gallons of water downstream, the problem became more urgent. In December 1846 the board authorized Lord to purchase two ponds near Honesdale and one at the New York summit for reservoirs.[60]

Consideration of Wurts's proposal by the full board brought about some odd and probably unpredicted results. One member introduced a resolution for an immediate increase to $3,000,000. Wurts and the other two members of the committee that had drafted the first plan voted in the negative. Next, however, the increase proposed by the committee was also defeated. This shows a surprising independence on the board and Wurts's apparent failure to line up support in advance. As a compromise, the report was returned to the committee and two additional members were put on the committee. One of them was Irad Hawley. He had then been on the board less than three years, but had been named to the prestigious Finance Committee within his first year of service. Evidently he favored an even more vigorous plan of expansion than Wurts was advocating.

The enlarged committee brought forth a new report at the annual stockholders' meeting on March 4, 1845. It began with a lengthy and unusually frank description of the company's history and the stresses it had undergone. As has been noted, it explained the cautious management that had suspended dividends for several years and accumulated a surplus that had become troublesome. The committee proposed doubling the existing $1,922,000 of stock, to be used for the sinking fund, a program of improvements costing $613,000, and for funding $509,000 considered to have been borrowed from profit and loss for capital spending. This, it should be understood, was not a stock split; in effect, it was a 100% installment demanded of current stockholders (though a 25% stock dividend was declared in 1845). It was, however, voluntary; any new stock not taken by present share owners would eventually be sold on the market.[61] This time, with better preparation, the plan was approved by the board and by the stockholders.

The program of improvements showed that the company was committed to a continuing expansion of production. In 1844 the company had delivered more than 250,000 tons of coal. Nevertheless, it was obliged to reject requests for another 80 to 100,000 tons because the railroad would not be capable of moving that amount. Further improvements were proposed which would give the railroad a capacity of 450,000 to 500,000 tons. At the same time it was calculated that deepening the canal another six inches would expand its capacity from 700,000 to over 850,000 tons.[62] The increase in absolute numbers was important, but the continuing imbalance between the capacity of railroad and canal was to have a critical impact on the course of the D&H.

An insufficiently appreciated aspect of the enlargement is the effect it had on boats and boatmen. Prior to the enlargement the canal boats seemed perfectly adequate; afterwards they appeared almost toylike and were given the affectionate but condescending name of "flickers." The managers promptly sought to realize the gains the enlargement had allowed and reduced the rate they paid boatmen. Those boatmen who had paid off their boats and had hoped to run them at a profit a few years longer found they could no longer make money with them. Many of the boats were "hipped" by raising their sides to increase their capacity, but after the second enlargement even that was not sufficient. In the 1841 season, for the first time, Lord set up a sliding scale under which boatmen were paid a higher rate for shorter trips (for example, $1.40 per ton for trips of 9 days or less, $1.35 for ten days, and $1.30 for longer trips.)[63]

One result, probably not fully anticipated, was greater risk of a shortage of boats. Contributing factors were the rapid obsolescence of the older boats, and the sheer increase in production. The problem was a source of deep anxiety to Maurice Wurts, the company's agent at Rondout, and to Russel Lord who had overall responsibility for the canal. Each year the managers set production goals for the following year, but without boats these plans—which often were based on contractual obligations—were no more realistic than childhood doodles. In the summer of 1843 Maurice became alarmed by a shortage of boats, "especially as some of the individual [privately owned] boats are giving out, and the number diminishes daily."[64] This crisis cannot really be attributed to the enlargement, which was still in its early stages. In 1845 Maurice calculated that only 50 new boats would be needed, of which 25 could be built "on the canal" and the balance "here"—meaning at Rondout.[65] This seemed to be the customary ratio for boat building.

The correspondence between Maurice and Lord provides a revealing description of how the company conducted its operations. Each year the managers decided on an approximate production target, based in part on existing inventory, contracts, inquiries, and the general business climate. Archbald, who was responsible for the mines and railway, then committed to deliver a set amount of coal at Honesdale. Since only insignificant quantities were consumed at Honesdale or along the route, Russel Lord's duty was to bring the coal down the canal in a timely fashion. Maurice Wurts at Rondout had to be sure there was a smooth flow to the consumer.

In late 1846, for example, Maurice and Lord were busy planning for the coming year. They knew that Archbald had promised 450,000 tons. Assuming each boat would make 14 trips and carry 48 tons, Maurice calculated that 670 boats would be needed.[66] Only 520 were available, and it was estimated that 50 would be built along the canal.[67] Obviously, the company had to provide 100 new boats. A further complication arose because Maurice was suspicious that boats built during the summer and not used "may shrink and the seams become very open, and difficult to keep tight."[68] The agent was constantly concerned about the quality of boats and at one point seriously considered having boats built for the D&H on the Morris Canal and the Erie Canal. "I wish you to avoid contracts with all who build inferior boats," he told Lord. "[W]e had better go abroad for some of our Boats, than to employ men that give us inferior materials, or slight their work. I would particularly caution you against Hayes—and also Harden."[69]

Although there were sectional supervisors under him, Lord and Maurice Wurts had the primary responsibility for the "human resources" of the operation. While neither seems to have been a particularly sensitive person, they had to exercise enough diplomacy to keep traffic flowing smoothly. The boatmen were an independent lot, quick to take offense, and had to be handled with some delicacy. Trying to deplete an oversupply at Honesdale during summer 1846, the canal managers changed customary policy and kept the locks open until midnight. Maurice reported that the boatmen "demurred" at this plan, arguing that more time was lost during the day than was made up at night. Observing that "if Boatmen generally run until

12 at night, and start at 4 o'clock in the morning, I would think it must be so," Maurice recommended going back to the old policy.[70]

Rebuilding the Railway

JOHN WURTS KNEW BETTER than to consider the railway and the canal as separate entities. Insofar as it is possible for us to reconstruct his mental process, he divided the company's operations not at Honesdale between railway and canal, but at Carbondale between mining and transportation. He understood that any enlargement of capacity had to be system-wide. This meant that improvements to the canal had to be matched on the railway.

The railway at first was a flimsy piece of work, calculated to handle no more than 100,000 tons a year. For several years its limitations were of no concern; whether due to lack of demand or inability to mine more coal, the capacity was not approached. John Wurts later blamed the board for "timidly keeping back on coal" in 1831.[71] In 1833 production prematurely exceeded 100,000 tons, but it is uncertain how much of that amount passed over the railway that year.

In 1836 and 1837 the first notable alteration to the railway was made. It consisted of rebuilding the section leading to Plane #1, so that water power could be substituted for horses.[72] This effort, though limited in scope, may have improved operation to the extent that 1837 coal shipments reached a record high of 115,000 tons and thus inspired further change. In 1840 engineer Archbald was requested to make arrangements to increase coal production "by preparing for double tracks on the road at the summit level, increasing the number of wagons, and opening of such roads &c at the mines as in his judgment shall be necessary."[73] Although carefully limited and given a relatively small appropriation ($12,000 at first, later increased to $15,000,) this marked the first formal program of expansion. It preceded by several months the first canal enlargement.

Beginning in 1842 the railway was essentially reconstructed so that very little of the original system remained intact. For this reason anyone making assertions about the layout of the railway must be careful to specify the period being considered. (The mechanics of operating the railway have been so thoroughly explained in earlier publications that there is no need to repeat the description here.)[74] Although the line had previously been referred to as a gravity railway, Archbald's reconstruction made that label truly accurate for the first time. Most of the planes and levels from Carbondale to the summit were altered to take better advantage of gravity. From the summit to Honesdale the system was double-tracked, with each track operated by gravity. In this case, unlike conventional double-track railroads, the tracks were often a considerable distance apart. One descending plane was discontinued, leaving a continuous run of ten miles to the canal basin. On the return, or "light" track, five new planes operated by stationary steam engines or water power, eliminated all animal power. At the opposite end, the railway was extended several miles.

At the end of 1846 Archbald reported that the capacity of the railway had been increased to between 425,000 and 450,000 tons. He added that an alteration to one plane east of the summit could increase that to half a million, but "that would be the utmost limit of its capacity."[75] In his letter of February 5, 1847 Archbald calculated that the improvements to the railway had cost a total of $328,890.[76] Later, Wurts reported that the cost of the second canal enlargement had totalled about $265,000.[77] When he first proposed this work he estimated it would cost $100,000.[78]

Company figures present an interesting chart of the progress and extent of the capital improvements.[79] These numbers point up the greater relative impact of rebuilding the railway.[80] On February 26, 1842, before the beginning of the major program of improvement, the figures were:

Cost of Canal		
New York	$1,506,817	
Pennsylvania	693,824	
Total	2,200,641	
Cost of Railway	344,870	
Total	2,545,511	

On March 1, 1845, after the first enlargement of the canal had been essentially completed, the figures were:

Cost of Canal	$2,406,978
Cost of Railway	503,580
Total	2,910,558

Amounts as of March 1, 1848, after the second enlargement and the rebuilding of the railway had been completed:

Cost of Canal	$2,650,495
Cost of Railway	751,277
Total	3,401,772

The increases due to improvements were:

Canal	$ 369,854	(16%)
Railway	406,407	(118%)
Total	776,261	(30%)

The reconstruction of the railway was entrusted to Archbald, and he performed with distinction. James Archbald (1793-1870) had been selected, as noted, by Jervis. He was born in Scotland and had many character traits in common with Jervis, who was also of Scots descent. Archbald's name is often written "Archbold" or "Archibald," even in Wurts correspondence, indicating it was pronounced in these alternate ways. He was, by all evidence, deeply admired in the Lackawanna region. Hollister, who knew him well, testified to his integrity: "A man of few words, open, honest and sincere, he fraternized so readily with the workingmen under his superintendence that the man in and out of authority seemed as one, and yet everywhere and at all times he was esteemed for the accuracy of his judgment and the vigor of his intellect, and for his friendship for the industrious workingmen."[81]

Archbald had assumed responsibility for the mines and railway when he was still in his late twenties. Except for a brief period in 1837 when he left to pursue a private business venture, he remained with the D&H through the period of enlargement. For the first few years his energies were probably fully occupied making sure the rickety system functioned at all; only later could he start thinking about revisions. His task was much more challenging than Russel Lord's on the canal. Lord's work, since the size of the canal and locks were not changed, consisted mainly of raising the banks by steepening their slope and excavating the bottom. It thus did not differ enormously from the regular seasonal cleaning and maintaining of dimensions; and it was conducted during the time the canal was closed, so as not to interfere with navigation. Archbald, by contrast, had to develop a nearly new method of operation. His ingenious solutions showed technical mastery and placed his reputation on a lofty plane.

Jervis had proved himself a superb judge of character in recommending his two young protégés more than ten years earlier. His assessment of Archbald as having "an excellent engineering mind and great practical sagacity" was amply confirmed by his innovative remodelling of the railway. Jervis's praise of Lord—"a man of good executive ability"—seemed to place less emphasis on technical ability and more on his managerial skills. This had been demonstrated on the first two canal enlargements, and was soon to be tested again in supervising construction of the aqueducts and, later, the final and most demanding enlargement.

Suspension Aqueducts

IN 1845 THE QUESTION OF THE DELAWARE AQUEDUCT AROSE AGAIN, after a surprisingly long lull. Except for the purchase of land at the site, little had been done in the years since the subject was first broached. Lord reported to John Wurts in January 1843 that he had acquired 320 acres at the proposed location "when it is deemed nesisary [sic]."[82] Two years later necessity began knocking, for the Erie RR was awakening from one of its financial naps, reviving the urgency Wurts had felt when he first proposed the aqueduct. For the next several years Russel Lord was a busy man, involved with the aqueducts, the Erie RR route and, later, the last enlargement. Fortunately, when his "executive ability" was tested in this severe fashion, he was at the peak of his powers. Johnston, who was well acquainted with him, has testified to his formidable energy.

Lord submitted a more detailed proposal for the aqueduct in January 1845. By then it was becoming apparent that the Erie RR would win its battle to cross into Pennsylvania. Recognizing this, Wurts advised Lord "to do something there

Trying to improve his technical knowledge, Lord purchased an expensive engineer's encyclopedia in 1838.
CREDIT
Russel F. Lord papers, Minisink Valley Historical Soc.

immediately to demonstrate our intention to build an aqueduct." Lord responded by presenting fuller plans, though still for a conventional wooden aqueduct.[83] Early in 1846 Lord submitted estimates for this work:

Delaware aqueduct	$45,000
Lackawaxen aqueduct	15,000
3 new locks in New York	10,000
About 1½ miles of new canal	25,000 [84]

At this juncture John Wurts's sly pragmatism was again revealed. Although confessing that he had never understood what principle it rested on, Wurts said he had accepted New York's claim to have jurisdiction over the Delaware River up to the Pennsylvania shore. As the president explained, since "the Pennsylvanians indulged a bad temper towards our Delaware dam, which is rather *tolerated* than expressly authorised by the Penna. charter, I thought it was politic in us to do nothing that might by implication be regarded as admitting the claim of Penna. to the middle of the river."[85] By 1846 the situation was changed, and as Wurts put it, "the people of Penna. seem to be reconciled to it," so that it might be harmful to continue to acknowledge New York's claim to full jurisdiction of the river. Wurts directed Lord to begin keeping separate accounts for the two states of costs for the aqueduct.

Later in 1846 the name Roebling and the idea of making the aqueduct a suspension bridge came to the fore. The process by which this proposal originated is one of the annoying gaps in the history of the D&H, but John Roebling, a German immigrant who manufactured wire rope in western Pennsylvania, was already familiar to the company. Beginning in 1844 the D&H had purchased his wire rope to replace the cumbersome fiber ropes on the planes of the gravity railway. The first known correspondence between Roebling and Lord took place in November 1846.[86] This may not have been the initial contact, for in December John Wurts received a well-developed proposal from the wire manufacturer. Wurts's response to Lord shows his meticulous but far-sighted, process of decision-making:

> In regard to Roebling, I find that I have not information enough to enable me to make a comparison between his plan and the wooden aqueduct. In my memorandum book, it is assumed that "the superstructure of the two aqueducts if of wood, would be $38,000. On Roebling's plan the cost would be $60,000—difference $22,000. The wooden structure would require repairs in 12 years; what is perishable in Roebling's would require repairs in 17 years—difference in duration 5 years, difference in cost of repairs $17,000 in favor of Roebling." Now to make a calculation between the two it is necessary to compound the interest on $22,000 for 12 years to see what fund we would then have in hand to repair the superstructure of the wooden aqueduct. Against this on the other hand, we must put the $17,000 that would be saved in repairs the first time, on Roebling's plan, together with five years interest compounded, on the whole amount that it would require to repair the wooden structure at the end of 12 years. Now this amount I have not got—I have need of the difference between the two. If you will give me this amount I will make the calculation and then present the subject to the Board.[87]

It seems worth quoting this exposition at length to illustrate the precision of Wurts's thinking. As he was comfortable with the concept of amortization—a concept apparently unfamiliar to many managers of that era—one suspects he would have adapted with equal readiness to modern data processing capability.

At its meeting on December 28, 1846 the board appointed a committee to review the two aqueduct proposals.[88] On the next day Wurts wrote to Lord telling him to be ready for a trip to Pittsburgh to examine a suspension aqueduct Roebling had built for the Pennsylvania Canal.[89] A week later the committee presented a report tentatively favoring the suspension bridge. It compared a wooden aqueduct on stone piers, which was expected to last 36 years, versus the wire supported aqueduct, which was assumed a life expectancy of 60 years. With interest compounded, the

A startling look at the inside of the aqueduct after it had been converted to a highway bridge confirms its fundamental character as a trough to hold water.
CREDIT
D&H Canal Museum.

Since he was only a contractor, John Roebling's name does not appear on the plaque the company installed on one of the Delaware aqueduct piers.
CREDIT
Photo by Sandra S. Schultz.

wire was calculated to save over $55,000 in its 60 year duration—"provided the estimate of time that each will last is correct, that the wire is imperishable, never to be replaced, which the Committee must confess they have much doubt of."[90] One can certainly not accuse the capitalists and managers of that era of being unable to see beyond the next quarterly report. In fact, it was not even customary to publish quarterly performance data; men who created "bodies corporate" in those days assumed that they might be as eternal as their charters. The board need not have entertained any doubts about Roebling's cables; with restoration they have lasted more than 60 years, far outlasting the canal and outliving the D&H itself as an independent company.

The board had entrusted the final decision to its engineers, but only Lord made the trip to Pittsburgh, probably because the aqueducts fell within his area of supervision. In late January and early February he examined the project, which was Roebling's latest work and his first aqueduct. Lord returned with an enthusiastic report, and on February 12, 1847 Wurts accepted Roebling's proposal.[91] Stonework began almost immediately. The progress of construction is described by Vogel and Osborne.[92] There were the usual irritations and setbacks that are inevitable in projects of this scale, most of them seemingly involving the masonry, rather than Roebling's bridge work. Roebling's main effort on the aqueduct apparently began in late 1847 and was completed by April of the following year.[93]

As has been noted, the various proposals included an aqueduct over the Lackawaxen, as well as the main one across the Delaware. It would have seemed to make more sense to remain on the north side of the Lackawaxen and cross the Delaware above the confluence of the rivers. This would save not only the $18,650 direct cost of the Lackawaxen aqueduct and future maintenance expense, but would permit crossing the Delaware before its volume had been swollen by the sizable flow of the Lackawaxen. Until Peter Osborne began researching the Lord papers, various geographical and engineering speculations had been offered to explain the seemingly irrational decision. Lord's correspondence establishes that the additional aqueduct was built mainly because the land that would have been required on the north side of the Lackawaxen was owned by one Benjamin Holbert, who had a long record of hostility toward the D&H.[94] This is confirmed by an entry in the D&H minutes as early as 1841, when the discussion of enlargement was beginning. Lord's letter informing the board that a company had been incorporated to build a toll bridge at that point included the phrase that it would eliminate the ford the D&H was required to maintain "about which Benjamin Holbert & others have so much complained."[95]

In the conflict between the D&H and the Erie, Holbert had been a vigorous supporter of the railroad. Negotiations with him would be frustrating and costly. Furthermore, his property was improved by a tavern and outbuildings, as well as his house. Changes in the Pennsylvania constitution had made it less certain that the D&H retained the right of eminent domain; even if it did, the condemnation process was sure to be contentious. Any controversy in that section would not stop with the issue at hand, but would promptly drag in the old accusations about the D&H monopoly and its obstruction of the Erie RR. Considering these factors, the cost of the extra aqueduct probably seemed to be a bargain. When the board on December 10, 1845 authorized Lord to purchase land on the south side of the Lackawaxen it confirmed that conclusion.

Work on the Lackawaxen aqueduct proceeded a few months behind the Delaware. Both were ready for service when the canal season opened in April 1849.[96]

The two aqueducts, by raising the level of the canal above the river, necessitated a general reconfiguration. Three locks were eliminated on the Lackawaxen side, and three new ones were built so that the canal could step down on the New York side. Boats no longer had to pass through a guard lock on the New York shore.

It is to some degree curious that the Delaware aqueduct is now the best known feature associated with the D&H Canal. It does not date to the beginning of the system; nor, strictly speaking, was it essential, though it surely contributed to its efficiency. One can debate which is more astonishing: the excellence of the aqueduct, or the fact that it was possible to move up to 400,000 tons a year by the primitive method of pulling boats across the pooled Delaware. At 50 tons per boat, probably an overly favorable assumption, that would mean some 8000 loaded crossings in a season of about eight months in which interruptions almost invariably occurred.

The aqueduct has attracted a great deal of retroactive celebrity due to the fame the Roeblings went on to achieve with the Brooklyn Bridge. At the time they were constructed, the D&H aqueducts were regarded as proficient achievements, but not extraordinary. They were among many projects by which the Roeblings developed the reputation which culminated in the great East River bridge 30 years later. Due to a series of fortunate circumstances, the Delaware aqueduct has survived to demonstrate the durability of which all the Roebling suspension bridges were probably capable, and it is now the oldest known suspension bridge in the United States.

Restored by the National Park Service and reopened June 13, 1987, Roebling's suspension aqueduct remains the glory of the upper Delaware.
CREDIT
Photo by Sandra S. Schultz.

Settling with the Erie

AGAINST A BACKGROUND OF EXPANSION, competition with aggressive rivals and furious controversy in Pennsylvania, the problem of the Erie RR continued to oppress John Wurts. It was interwoven with these other issues so that it could neither be separated nor ignored. It nagged at the president like a chronic toothache, and not surprisingly he sought relief. On May 31, 1845 he wrote to his brothers "At present I am engaged in a negotiation with the Erie railroad company, which I hope to close to day in a way that will terminate all controversy between the two companies .... And if this troublesome matter can be put at rest, it will leave us at liberty to pursue our business in peace and quietness once more."[97]

By this time Wurts's policy toward the Erie had changed considerably. Railroads were advancing so rapidly, and capital, whether foreign or domestic, was so abundant, that there was no longer any reasonable hope of crushing it entirely. What would now be called damage control was the best the D&H could hope for. After conceding that they could not keep the railroad out of Pennsylvania, their immediate goal became to confine it to the Delaware Valley. "If they get up the valley of the Delaware as they propose, we do not want them up the Lackawaxen."[98]

Another change of attitude since the initial contacts may have been a growing fear of the fundamental harm the railroad could do. In early 1845 the D&H had sent remonstrances about the Erie to the New York Legislature. While these were limited to protests against physical encroachments on the canal, some of the D&H supporters saw more dire issues at stake. The Kingston *Democratic Journal* editorialized that the Erie promoters "now wish to prostrate a prosperous and well-managed company for the advantage of a horde of speculators." The D&H, it continued, had "opened a way through the wilderness, built up our populous region, triumphed by years of strenuous exertion over every obstacle, brought the anthracite regions of Pennsylvania to the portals of New York, and now, when they are reaping a reasonable reward for their exertions, a mere holiday company, one of the inflated offspring of moonshine legislation and theoretical financeering, is asking to be allowed to level the whole fabric to earth." Insofar as this represented D&H thinking—and with the prominence of Maurice Wurts in Rondout, one may assume it did—it was a recognition that for the first time a railroad had the potential to destroy the D&H. In what appeared to be an organized campaign, a number of companies and individuals sent similar remonstrances to the Assembly.

Meanwhile, an active, competent new president, Benjamin Loder, took over as head of the Erie in August 1845. Loder was anxious to remove any obstacles, such as the D&H, that blocked the railroad's progress. After considering other alternatives, the Erie had decided on a route that would remain between the canal and the river between Port Jervis and the mouth of the Shingle Kill (Bolton Basin on the canal—probably the only place that perpetuated the name of the departed president)—a stretch of a little over three miles. At that point the railroad would cross the canal to gain favorable curvature for the bridge that would carry it to the Pennsylvania side. John Wurts by then was willing to settle on reasonable terms and bring the prolonged struggle to an end. In a letter dated September 4, 1846 he told Russel Lord "it is in the interest of both companies to cultivate good feelings, and strive to get along in harmony." But while professing this benign policy, the old suspicion remained: "I would add that we must keep a vigilant eye to the location and construction of their work from Port Jervis to the point where they recross the Delaware above the mouth of the Lackawaxen, and we must hold them strictly to the provisions of the acts both in this state and Penna. . . . in every particular affecting our works or interest."[99]

Another issue concerned the parcel of land the D&H had purchased south of the Lackawaxen to accommodate the aqueduct. Lord had acquired this in his own name and had not yet transferred it to the company when the Erie inquired about it. Wurts was willing to sell a right-of-way at the right price, but hesitated to admit "that we had done secretly what we did not think it prudent to do openly."[100]

John Wurts continued to be concerned that railroad construction could interfere with canal operations by frightening the horses or filling the channel with debris. He was willing to negotiate, but only if the D&H obtained ironclad written guarantees. Otherwise, he was prepared to make a stand at the Shingle Kill: "we might as well begin the war there as any where."[101] On December 28, 1846 the D&H board approved a set of nine specifications, which would give the canal company a large degree of control over the railroad's location, and which the Erie would have to accept it wished to adopt its route by peaceful means.[102] Loder, who had made a commitment to bring a locomotive to Port Jervis by the end of 1847, was anxious to avoid a confrontation and apparently accepted D&H terms.

One provision called for the Erie to "take special care, that their contractors and their men so conduct themselves, and prosecute their work, as not to injure the canal & its appendages, nor disturb or impede those engaged in the navigation thereof."[103] This may have been the sincere intention of men at the top like Wurts

A loaded boat has crossed the Delaware aqueduct to the New York side. The canal had nearly right-angle turns at both ends of the aqueduct, creating a Z-shaped configuration. On the Pennsylvania side the Erie RR bridge over the canal is prominent.
CREDIT
Minisink Valley Historical Soc.

and Loder, but it did not always filter down to the working level. As Erie construction crews moved up the Delaware, severe clashes arose with D&H boatmen. The railroad workers, hardly members of the more refined elements of society, discovered that they could set off blasts on the Pennsylvania side that would cause stones to rain down on canal boats on the New York shore. In other cases they simply attacked boatmen directly. Tactically, the railroad gangs had an advantage, since the nature of canal operation made it difficult to concentrate numbers of men at one point. On one occasion the canal men succeeded in collecting a large force and fought a pitched battle with the railroad gang.[104]

The fullest and most vivid description of this tumultuous period is given by Russel Lord:

> The construction of [the Erie RR] has been a source of great trouble, perplexity and anxiety . . . from the inattention of their contractors or those in charge of their laborers. There have been frequent riots and conflicts among them, often resulting in the loss of life. It would not be reasonable to suppose that the large number of men employed on the canal, in sight of these acts and aggressions, could always be kept in subordination. The laborers on the railroad have had firearms and often made attacks on each other with them. Boatmen and others employed on the canal have frequently passed along the tow-path and canal while balls were flying amid them, the rioters on the railroad not designing to disturb them, but firing at each other without regard to who was in the way. On the 3d of June a large party of railroad hands, while returning from a turmoil, made an attack upon the boatmen, near the Mongaup, which resulted in a serious conflict, several of the men on both sides receiving serious personal injuries. Subsequent to that collision some of the police officers from the city of New York, together with the sheriffs of Sullivan and Pike counties, were employed by the Delaware and Hudson Canal Company, and remained on the Delaware section as peace officers until about the middle of November.
>
> In addition to the difficulties arising from the insubordination of the men, large fragments of rock were thrown by blasts across the Delaware river into the canal, often falling upon boats, buildings, locks, &c. All the foregoing difficulties continued to discourage boatmen and more or less disorganized the whole business. Parents withdrew their children from the boats, and many of the boatmen abandoned their boats in consequence of apprehended danger.[105]

Legal measures and militia patrols did not completely solve the problem, and things returned to normal only when the work crews moved out of the vicinity. Paradoxically, what seemed to be the most severe form of the conflict between railroad and canal occurred after the real issues had been resolved. It was a product of individual and random violence that did not express or affect the fundamental rivalry between the competing forms of transportation. On June 2, 1849, after the construction had moved out of D&H country and almost exactly a year after the worst of the incidents Lord described, the board approved his request to build a basin at the mouth of the Lackawaxen to facilitate a connection with the Erie.[106] There, at one of the vital positions in the former battleground, an uneasy peace was established.

It is doubted by many, whether in this or any county, there exists a more corrupt Incorporation than this Delaware & Hudson Canal Company----one whose policy is more similar to that of a bandit in acquiring power and influence, and like a tyrant and a despot in the use of it.

New Territory, New Trouble

BEGINNING IN 1845 the D&H entered a complex and troubled period which proved pivotal in the history of the company. Although this critical phase began with a forward-looking recognition that new approaches were needed to adjust to changes in the industry, the result was not what anyone had foreseen, or even intended. The best known product was a controversy of almost epic proportions—a result which no one had sought. This unsatisfactory outcome of what could have been a time of constructive transition was due to a variety of causes, some of which may have stemmed from innate contradictions in the nature of the company. The lack of a clear boundary between company and personal business was surely a factor, as was the difficulty in obtaining reliable scientific information. A more prosaic consideration was simply that the Wurts brothers were pushing deeper into middle age, feeling increasing infirmities. Yet probably the most direct cause of the devastating conflict was not some impersonal economic trend, but a misjudgment of character.

Rather startlingly, *Century of Progress* says of this tumultuous period that determined the future course of the company, "In the ordinary routine of the company's business during the years covered by this chapter [1842-1850], few changes occurred that were important."[1] If there is any validity to this singularly unperceptive assessment, it pertains only to the beginning of the period, which seemed routine enough. In 1843, as part of the program to rebuild the railway, the managers decided to extend it seven miles to a new mine at White Oak Run, now in the town of Archbald. This is another annoying gap in the history of the D&H, for it is not clear how this property was acquired. *Century of Progress* says that the mine was discovered only in 1843.[2] This is probably based on Hollister, who states that the deposit was discovered by Archbald and his assistant James Clarkson in that year.[3]

When work on the extension began in 1845 it was significant as marking the first geographical expansion in the company's 20-year history. Nevertheless, the managers had no reason to suspect the furious outburst that it would produce, in which, as Hollister says "there was displayed an acerbity of feeling and an intemperance of speech, action and resolution that provokes wonder after an elapse of more than a quarter of a century."[4] Archbald laid out a gravity railway on the same principles he was employing so brilliantly in rearranging the existing line. He calculated the various physical factors in the usual way, but had no way of anticipating the emotional storm that would prove more dangerous.

FACING PAGE
Although from a later date, this photo of empty boats at Honesdale basin symbolizes John Wurts's problem of matching canal and railway capacities while remaining competitive in price.
CREDIT
National Canal Museum.

Archbald and the D&H, as they probed southward, stumbled into an area that was already in a high state of agitation. The company was caught up in controversies not entirely of its own making. A strong and persistent movement in the upper townships of the Lackawanna Valley to carve a new county out of old Luzerne had emerged as early as 1837.[5] In many people's minds, all other issues were weighed against the effect they would have on the proposed separation. Around 1844 the Erie RR began making noises about crossing into Pennsylvania. This opened the alluring possibility that in passing from the Delaware to the Susquehanna Valleys it could cross through the heart of the Lackawanna coal district. Politics and economics aside, the map seemed to make this a tempting prospect. Underlying these concerns was the explosive growth of anthracite consumption, which created for the first time a boom in coal lands. At long last, it seemed, land values in the Lackawanna Valley would begin to realize their true potential.

Among those who sensed and exploited the mood of expansion were the Wurts brothers. It is quite likely that the initial interest in coal lands around Cobb's Gap was generated by the Wurtses individually, rather than the D&H as a company, recalling the divergence between personal and corporate interests that existed in the 1820s. In the absence of a significant body of Wurts papers for the period between 1830 and 1845 it is impossible to draw solid conclusions, but it seems that in the early 1840s William and Charles Stewart Wurts became more active in the coal business.[6] This represents a major contradiction of the family genealogy, which maintains that William had prospered to such a degree that he was able to retire from business by the early 1830s.

A letter in the Wurts correspondence presents quite a different picture, and indeed recalls the financial strains of an earlier period. On August 19, 1845 Maurice advised William that "considering your long past efforts to improve the business of your Market Street establishment without any apparent success and the strong desire of both you and Charles to withdraw from it, or at any rate not to engage actively in its business, with the inclination of your family for the country," he recommended getting out of it. The older brother, "in reference to the pecuniary circumstances of yourself and Brother Charles" added that he owned 600 shares of D&H stock, which provided more than an adequate income, and offered to transfer to the brothers "an amount of stock that will, with your own means, provide an income adequate to the supply of every want and enable you both to retire to the country and give your time to your families, without further care or concern about pecuniary matters." This was one of the most magnanimous expressions of the closeness that had always bound the four brothers. It did not carry over to the next generation as Maurice, then 62 and increasingly irascible, said he preferred to give the money to his brothers, rather than "leave it to a parcel of young folks, that have not heretofore furnished any evidence of their ability to either appreciate or preserve it."[7]

Regardless of their financial circumstances, something was afoot among the Wurtses. In February 1845 John wrote to Charles concerning "lands in Luzerne, that we purchased at the tax sale by N. Smith." The reason was that "If they have coal in them or if they are good arable lands, I think that the D & H Canal Company will in less than two years time be making an improvement that will give them value." In this context the "we" probably referred to the Wurtses personally, not the D&H. The improvement he had in mind was an extension of the railway "down from Wayne's Gap to Cobb's Gap, then . . . to the left of the gap, working by stationary power, and then by gravity to foot of Plane No.6, thence to Honesdale by the same power." Reverting to the secrecy that had characterized many of the family's dealings, he cautioned "this must not be spoken of."[8] This typically surreptitious approach was emphasized by Charles who, after inquiring about the location of coal deposits at various points, added "Cobbs is our more particular object and lands adjoining the D&H Company land at present, but remember that the Company have nothing to do with my present object *nor do I wish them to know anything about it*."[9] Wurts correspondence at this time contains many references to investigating and purchasing lands in Blakely.

James Archbald, after exploring a railway extension from White Oak Run to Cobb's Gap, reported it would be about 21 miles long and cost about $250,000, plus another $75,000 for 500 cars. Archbald added that "the public would be better satisfied to have the D.& Hudson Canal Co. make it, than any body else."[10] This was the genesis of the proposal for the D&H to extend a railway into that region. Archbald, however, preferred for someone else to build the road, as he "did not consider it desirable to carry for others." Although acknowledging talk of a new railroad to New York City, he was confident that "no route could be found that would . . . enable a rival to compete with us."[11]

In October 1845 Archbald and Clarkson conducted more detailed explorations of the east side of the valley, extending from White Oak Run to about two miles below the mouth of Roaring Brook in present Scranton. They found nothing in that region that seemed more promising than the field in Blakely "where our coal lands now are." Archbald also won the endorsement of Scranton and Grant, who were in the early stages of developing iron works at what became Scranton, for a rail line through Cobb's Gap to connect with the D&H along the Lackawaxen. More forcefully than usual Archbald recommended that "our company ought at once to say to these men and others in that vicinity that if a suitable charter can be got, that you will assist them in the construction of the road." Archbald was aware of the old Drinker and Meredith charters, which he believed would be revived, so that if the D&H did not act promptly "the ground may be occupied."[12]

Shortly after writing his optimistic assessment, Archbald must have reconsidered. He sent another letter to John Wurts on the same day in which he warned that it was "almost certain" another road would be built to connect with the Erie RR on the Delaware or, more ominously, through New Jersey. With less assurance than he had displayed earlier, he warned that a "road having its termination nearer the market than ours, may enter into a fair competition with us." He therefore asked "whether by giving proper encouragement to the people of the middle section of this valley *now*, we might not be able to direct and even entirely controul [*sic*] the whole matter." Recovering his earlier optimism, he added "There is not a question but if this company were to provide pecuniary aid, the people of Providence Township to a man would go for a Rail Road to intersect our Canal, and would most effectually prevent any other application."[13]

The D&H board had given a lukewarm response to John Wurts's first mention of a new railroad.[14] After receiving Archbald's follow-up, several members came to take a more favorable view of the proposal, perhaps alarmed that "The Erie Rail Road are already busy in manufacturing public opinion." This was the occasion on which Vice President Platt uttered the decisive remark "we do not want them up the Lackawaxen."[15] Maurice Wurts fully supported the proposal of a new railroad, adding that "we had better give it some help if necessary, by either subscribing to the stock, or loaning them money."[16] With the board now taking a more positive stance, Maurice advised William that "the purchase of lands with good working seams of coal in the vicinity of the proposed Cobbs Gap Road" was "safe even at a pretty liberal price."[17]

At a meeting on November 11, 1845 a committee of the D&H board reported that after "a social and interesting conference" with John and Maurice Wurts it "came to a conclusion somewhat at variance with the views which they had previously entertained" toward the Cobbs Gap rail line. The main reason for this change was Archbald's estimate that the road could be built for $350,000 including cars, instead of the $800,000 to $1 million that had been expected. "The small expenditure for a work of such importance and magnitude is, to the minds of your Committee, an additional inducement why this Company should control it by possessing a majority of the stock." The committee looked ahead and concluded that the "anticipated difficulty between the boatmen of the two companies" could be avoided. In bold and dramatic terms the committee found that Cobbs Gap "is apparently the key to the whole coal and iron region of the Wyoming Valley, and that control of it is of immense importance to this Company." The board responded to this call to arms by authorizing the committee to "unite with the people of the Wyoming Valley" to secure a railroad.[18]

Later in November the board met again to consider a revised estimate from Archbald. Having calculated that the line would be longer than originally believed, Archbald had raised his estimate to $450,000, "unless it is deemed best to use locomotive power." The engineer thought locomotive power would at least double the cost and advised strongly against it. Archbald had also held another conference with Scranton and Grant about the best means of securing a railroad charter. Archbald, now seeming to become more like John L. Sullivan, with his personal stake in the enterprise, showed signs of irritation. "I cannot see that any thing I can do here will make you much better prepared," he declared. He had calculated that a railway costing $450,000 would pay a return of at least 10% if it carried only 150,000 tons. Alarmed, he warned that subscriptions were being sought for Meredith's railroad and that many people believed the Erie RR was planning to come into the valley. "If so," he reminded the edgy board members, it may "be able to carry coal to market much cheaper than can be done on canal." In a negatively worded resolution, the board declared that the increased cost "is not deemed a good reason why this enterprise should be abandoned."[19]

At this juncture the movement toward a D&H-controlled railway through Cobbs Gap, which could open up the lower valley and give the company a position too dominant to be assaulted, seemed irresistible. Yet precisely at that moment things began to unravel. The first hint of cooling enthusiasm came on November 29, 1845, when John Wurts told brother Charles that he and Irad Hawley had decided against going to Carbondale to negotiate with "whoever might present themselves in relation to the road through Cobbs Gap." In his latest report Archbald, perhaps becoming more aware of the complexity of the situation he was entering, wrote "there are so many different interests involved in the occupancy of this route . . . that it will require those who negotiate [sic] to have tact and management, together with clear views both of what we want, and what is wanted."[20] Wurts and Hawley had changed their minds, according to the president, because they did not want it to seem that the road was "our measure." More ominously, John Wurts began to show signs of exasperation: "I am getting utterly tired of this [Cobbs Gap] matter. It bids fair to worry and harass me as the Erie rail road question did last winter. This I mean to avoid if I can—for I am no longer able to cope with such exciting matters."[21]

The new sensitivity toward public opinion revealed in the decision not to venture out to Carbondale was well founded. Less than two weeks later, on December 10, 1845, a mass meeting took place in Providence, "ostensibly in the interests of the New York & Erie Company," as Hollister says, "but really to frustrate, if possible, the entrance of the D&H."[22] This marked the first time since the conflict with the raftsmen 15 years before that a vehement public condemnation of the D&H was heard. Although the meeting resolved that it felt "no disposition to injure the prospects of the Delaware & Hudson Canal Company," it made its real feelings evident in saying "we cannot tamely submit to see this Company . . . intrude upon our rights by attempting to monopolize any interests which we as citizens, have a common right to claim and enjoy." Further resolutions expressed a lack of confidence in the D&H to build the Cobbs Gap road, adding "[We] shall regard any effort hereafter by them, to secure any railroad tract [sic] through Cobb's Gap as an interference with our rights, and a design on their part further to monopolize the exclusive coal trade of the Lackawanna, and will resist the attempt to the utmost of our power." After extending sincere good wishes to the D&H, another resolution claimed the right of seeking a different outlet "than by their peculiarly constructed works, one that will better promote the interests of the country; and better secure the confidence of the people; because we anticipate an improvement to be built upon more liberal and generous principles towards the public, by a more direct and better route, and in a more permanent manner."[23]

This marked the beginning of an extraordinary series of public meetings extending over more than a year, which were characterized by excess in expression, immoderation in policy, and unwillingness to compromise. A Wilkes-Barre newspaper, maintaining detachment amid this furor, said in a tone of judicious restraint that "No exertion will be spared to crush this serpent, before it shall have crawled, under legislative permission into the valley and struck poisonous death into all its hopes and prosperity."[24] Archbald's assessment of public attitudes was proven wildly inaccurate. He seemed to have little suspicion that the old animosity toward the D&H once incited by men like Thomas Meredith could be easily rekindled. Meredith was still living, and his railroad charter had been kept alive but, now dismissed as eccentric, he was no longer a leader. His place was taken—more effectively—by a more dangerous foe, Charles H. Silkman. This individual, a practicing lawyer, revived the early accusations of monopoly and turned them to a destructive purpose. Archbald's estimate of public opinion was clearly off the mark, but in his defense he had no way of guessing the extent to which Silkman could manipulate that opinion.

Hollister, who has provided the fullest account of this tumultuous era, said that Silkman "presented a remarkable compound of virtues and vices," and finally confessed that he "rather admired this erratic spirit."[25] Years later Hollister, although noting rather smugly that Silkman had died in the interim of "softening of the brain," was still grappling with the impact of this memorable personality. His vivid description is worth repeating at length, if only as a means of explaining how a man with Silkman's numerous contradictions could exert such a large and perverse influence on the D&H:

> Silkman was a lawyer of great social qualities, persuasive, fluent and incisive in speech, full of sophistry and sarcasm, and while his addresses bore an air of external sincerity, they were replete with subtleness and lack of candor. Seldom, if ever, was there a less scrupulous yet more gifted advocate pleading before a justice or jury within the border of Luzerne County. Educated but moderately, the

keenness of his intellect and the excellence of his judgment supplied in a measure the lack of greater study. In the heat of debate his tongue was viperous and his language venomous as the adder's bite. He was hospitable, even beyond his means, agreeable to his friends whom he could use, affable to all, unforgiving, jealous of his own rights while forgetting those of others, indolent to a degree bordering on laziness, and few men indeed had the faculty to insinuate false doctrines or to prejudice and pervert the public mind.[26]

Hollister, who was personally acquainted with most of the actors and had attended many of the meetings, is more reliable in describing this contentious period than he is for the origins of the D&H, which he did not witness. Although he tends to have a D&H bias, he is probably correct in asserting that Silkman was in the employ of the Erie.[27] Wurts ally Thomas Young agreed with this assessment, describing Silkman as "a man of corrupt principles & ready for any dirty work."[28] Stunned by the violent opposition it had aroused, the D&H leadership had no choice but to retreat. The committee on Cobbs Gap instructed Archbald to withdraw any proposition he had made to the inhabitants "and leave them to pursue their own interests in their own way." As Maurice Wurts put it the D&H "will not force it on to those interested, and will wait until *they* find that they want it."[29]

D&H supporters were active on their own account, although they could not match the numbers that Silkman's fiery oratory could muster. At least two pro-D&H meetings were held in the valley, although the Wurtses and members of the D&H board, maintaining the appearance of waiting to respond to popular initiative, remained at a distance. On one occasion William Wurts wrote a letter explaining his position and offering compromise to a man strongly identified with the opposing faction.[30] Nathan Smith, as ever active in serving the Wurts and D&H interests, continued to buy up land and sought to obtain a charter for a new railroad to be called the Luzerne & Wayne. Still, the D&H side seemed not to have the firepower (or the lack of restraint) of Charles Silkman. William Silkman, probably related to Charles, was a vigorous supporter of the D&H and said the company was submitting too tamely to the "slander and abuse" it was suffering. Impatiently he warned "there is a point where forbearance ceases to be a virtue and silence is taken for an admission of their declarations."[31]

Given the temper of the times, it is surprising to find that Charles Silkman wrote a superficially friendly letter to Nathan Smith in which he seemed to suggest compromise. He even appeared to hold out the lure of selling a lot he owned. Trying to insinuate himself into the good graces of Smith, Silkman portrayed himself as a peacemaker, willing "to refrain from anything calculated to agitate the people and produce discord." More to the point, he blamed the D&H supporters for breaking an understanding he believed he and Smith had reached "that these meetings were no longer to be called, to ferment the public mind."[32]

This cleared the way to justify the most virulent display of hostility toward the D&H seen yet. A mass "Railroad Meeting" held at Hyde Park March 12, 1846 discarded any pretense of moderation and condemned the D&H in the harshest terms: "It is doubted by many, whether in this or any county, there exists a more corrupt Incorporation than this Delaware & Hudson Canal Company——one whose policy is more similar to that of a bandit in acquiring power and influence, and like a tyrant and a despot in the use of it." The meeting was ostensibly intended to oppose the Luzerne & Wayne RR, and as a result Nathan Smith was personally vilified in unsparing terms: "the mere tool of the Delaware & Hudson Canal Company to deceive and humbug our citizens."[33]

If one discounts the exaggerated language, there is a certain validity to some of the accusations. Considering all the references in Wurts correspondence to secrecy, it is difficult to deny the accusation that the D&H "came into our valley by stealth." Similarly, looking back at John Wurts's maneuvers in the legislature, the statement that "Their chartered privileges were obtained by a species of fraud upon the Legislature" has a measure of accuracy, as does the claim that the charter was made up of "patches and shreds of legislative enactments." Though the D&H might deny it was seeking monopoly, that position was credible only as long as all the references to it in the Wurts correspondence remained hidden. Nathan Smith's quiet purchases of land before people realized who he was serving were not calculated to increase trust and goodwill, once his real purpose was known. John Wurts, with his cagey, conspiratorial mind had warned of this, writing in a note "You will see that Smith talks big to Archibald [sic] a little more so than is prudent when you reflect that it must soon be known that he is acting for you & William."[34]

Given this burden of suspicion, it is not surprising that the Luzerne & Wayne RR was seen as a devious means by which the D&H—"this soulless, unprincipled company"—was seeking to tighten its grip on the coal valley. This was true even though the Luzerne & Wayne received the support of men such as Selden T. Scranton. At that time the Scrantons were not nearly as influential as they later became; their iron venture was struggling to survive, and the Scrantons themselves were newcomers to the valley. In itself, the charter of the Luzerne & Wayne seemed designed to satisfy all interests. It proposed a rail line beginning on the Delaware at or near the mouth of the Lackawaxen and extending "thro' Roaring Brook gap, to the Lackawanna River; from thence down the river on the west side thereof where practicable, to the head of the North Branch Canal slack water navigation or railroad."[35] Not only would this allow a connection with the Erie, but the railroad would be the same wide gauge as the Erie. The fact that it was also authorized to connect with the D&H Canal was no more than a reasonable balance. It is possible, given the solicitude the Wurts brothers demonstrated toward Smith's efforts, that the Luzerne & Wayne scheme was conceived in their interest, rather than that of the D&H.[36]

After the March 12 gathering further inflamed passions, the pattern of alternating and increasingly vituperative meetings continued through the remainder of 1846 and into 1847. Historian J. R. Durfee predicted that "The proceedings of these counter meetings, held in Blakely and Providence during 1846-7, would fill a volume, and will do so one day."[37] Hollister's draft attempted to fulfill this prophecy, but was not completed. By now the overblown rhetoric of that overwrought time seems tiresome, if not irrational. The events of that era are best viewed within the parameters of mass psychology, rather than normal political discourse, and may be a product of the particular stage of historical development in which the valley then found itself. Having survived the uncertainty and deprivation of the frontier phase, the region had entered a period of greater affluence and security, but still lacking many of the refinements of advanced civilization. It was almost as though the energies needed to survive on the frontier no longer had a natural outlet and turned into the false channel of contrived political commotion. Hollister concludes as much, observing that "These meetings, in the absence of all other exciting topics and events of the day were always points of attraction and excitement to those who attended them."[38] The singular combination of characteristics and abilities that formed the personality of Charles Silkman was ideally suited to make him an effective demagogue during this strange period.

Never did all the sound and fury that filled meeting halls and newspaper columns week after week have a more futile outcome. It was difficult to sustain such intense animosity month after month; and, in Hollister's way of thinking, truth eventually prevailed. Silkman's powers were primarily destructive, although eventually a new county was formed out of old Luzerne. Efforts to bring the Erie RR deep into the Lackawanna Valley were probably doomed from the start because the D&H held cards whose value the local agitators could not fully appreciate. The Wurtses understood, as their rustic foes did not, that the Erie had obtained approval to enter Pennsylvania only grudgingly. The more it ventured into Pennsylvania, the more it risked antagonizing its home base in New York State. If the Erie tried to inflame opinion against the D&H in Pennsylvania, the D&H could retaliate in New York. This is probably the meaning of a cryptic letter from John to Charles S. Wurts on April 8, 1845, in which the president wrote "We shall take care to make this movement known at Albany, where it cannot but do harm to the railroad interest." However he added, significantly, "it is unfortunate that the Del. & Hud. Canal Co. has been obliged to be so prominent in the opposition—as it has created a strong excitement against us in the North East [of Pennsylvania] and undoubtedly will make us enemies both there and at Harrisburg." Almost as if anticipating the frenzy that would erupt a few months later, he warned "it is always bad for a company to stand in unfriendly relations with any part of the community."[39] It was only many years later, under greatly changed circumstances, that the Erie broke out of the valley of the Delaware. Meanwhile, the Luzerne & Wayne RR was never built with its own resources, and no railroad passed through Cobbs Gap for another decade. The D&H made toll and traffic proposals to representatives of the valley, but in the climate of rancorous discord the factions neutralized each other and no course of action could ever be agreed upon.

Another Approach

ALTHOUGH THE D&H ATTEMPT to collaborate with others in the valley had failed dismally, its economic imperatives remained unchanged. James Archbald, whose advisory role in the company went far beyond that of an ordinary engineer, came up with a different approach. According to the Wurts correspondence, he suggested that "an association might be formed under the Pennsylvania statute in relation to limited partnerships to mine coal and make a railroad to our Canal &c and thus held [?] independent of the Legislature and every body else."[40]

This concept had great appeal to the Wurts brothers and was incorporated in a formal proposal to the D&H board on July 23, 1846. At that time William and Charles Wurts presented a project to "take up" the dormant charter of the Washington Coal Co., which already possessed the right to construct a railway from Providence to connect with the D&H system. (It is not certain whether the brothers had gained control of the charter at this time, although they definitely held it a few months later.) Regrettably, the WCC, having been organized in the less expansive era of 1838, was limited to a capitalization of $300,000. Enlarging this would require another foray to Harrisburg, and another public exposure to the poisonous darts of Charles Silkman and his cohorts. The brothers, while assuring their proposal would "add much to the prosperity" of the D&H, estimated it would cost the company $800,000 to $1 million to complete the connection to Providence and otherwise develop the Washington Company's facilities. Anticipating expansion around Cobbs Gap, the Wurts brothers, and probably members of the D&H board, purchased lands in their own names.[41] Thus it may have come as a shock when the board informed them "it is not deemed advisable at the present time for the Delaware & Hudson Canal Company, with the information possessed by them at this time to extend their rail road as proposed, to Providence."[42]

The reasons for this startling turnabout are more complex than mere suspicion of any scheme cooked up by the Wurts brothers (although that may have been a factor) and introduce another of the unanticipated circumstances that shaped the course of the D&H in that critical period. During their frequent explorations of the Lackawanna Valley, James Archbald and his assistant James Clarkson, the "great coal savans of 1840" as Hollister termed them, had concluded that there were no commercially valuable coal lands in Providence, including later Scranton and Dunmore. As late as 1840, they believed that "there was no coal land a mile above or below Carbondale worthy of attention for its anthracite."[43] The extension to White Oak Run, initiated in 1843, marked a departure, but did not extend the horizon as far as Providence. In a striking perception, Hollister asserts that because of the long-standing hostility between Thomas Meredith and the Wurts brothers the opinion was "thus inculcated in Chief Archbald by these pioneer coal men that Thomas Meredith's fence defined the coal line down the Lackawanna."[44] Thus the ancient conflict continued to distort the development of the D&H.

As Hollister makes clear, the two D&H engineers were well-intentioned and could not be blamed for conclusions that were proved disastrously inaccurate. No comprehensive scientific study of the coal lands was performed until the 1850s, and even that may not have fully understood the structure of the formations. Archbald and Clarkson, as Hollister points out, had no training in geology or mineralogy; whatever knowledge of the coal deposits they had acquired was gained in the practical service of the D&H. Archbald recognized that there was coal in the Cobbs Gap area, but estimated the quantity at only 1,500,000 tons—not enough to justify the investment in mining and transportation.[45] At one point the D&H board considered naming a committee to accompany Archbald in his investigations, but "after mature consideration and knowing they could not add to the geological knowledge of our engineer it was deemed inexpedient to appoint one."[46] Curiously, John Wurts, though he had not spent a great amount of time in the Lackawanna Valley, intuitively questioned Archbald's assessment and was probably responsible for the talk of sending the special committee. But he was trapped in a paradox: he might suspect Archbald's geological knowledge, but had no one more expert to suggest. Two factors that could not have been foreseen: Charles Silkman's skill as a rabble-rouser and the limitations of James Archbald's knowledge of geology, had combined to push the D&H out of its normal path of expansion.

Archbald, whatever his failures in geology, was basically an innovative "can-do" person. After dismissing the vastly productive deposits in old Providence, he became a strong advocate of coal lands around Pittston, at the extreme southern end of the valley. As early as February 1846 he proposed extending the Cobbs Gap railway, then under consideration, into that district. Responding to this cue, Maurice Wurts suggested to brother William "perhaps it will be wise for you to stop all further purchases south and east of the Lackawanna and go down to the heavier formations of coal where the mining will be much cheaper."[47] By October 1846 a D&H committee advocated an unspecified "project" to exploit "veins of coal of superior quality and great thickness which can be mined at a low rate and brought to the canal by railway at a cost of from $600,000 to $700,000."[48] John

Wurts was won over to this belief: "whoever owns the coal at or near Pittston will control the trade," he proclaimed Napoleonically.[49]

At the close of 1846 President Wurts looked back over a year that had brought exhausting turmoil, yet had produced no visible movement toward meeting the challenges he perceived. He thereupon sent to the D&H board a letter that proved to one of the most decisive in the history of the company. He began with a sweeping review of the company's position: the massive improvements to railway and canal were nearly complete, yet after two years of discussing an increased coal supply "no practical result" had followed. The rebuilding had given the railway a capacity that could not be expanded beyond 500,000 tons, while the limit of the canal could easily be increased to a million tons. Since he believed a market existed at Rondout "for all the coal that our canal would deliver at 37½ to 50 cents a ton above the price at which coal may be sold at the Schuylkill or Delaware wharves," the obvious conclusion was to "make arrangements in some way, without delay, for an increased quantity of coal through the canal."[50]

That was the positive aspect. The president then went on to discuss the fears that preyed on his mind. The anthracite rivals were moving to increase the supply which, he was convinced, would bring down the retail price to a level the D&H would find hard to match. Of more dire concern, if the D&H did not stake out a dominant position in the lower part of the Lackawanna, that field "will soon be penetrated by a rail road terminating at a favorable point on tide water, by which the increased quantity of Lackawanna coal called for by the market, will be supplied; thereby not merely cutting us off from the opportunity of deriving revenue from it, but also introducing an inconvenient and perhaps dangerous rival . . . from whom we can expect nothing but keen competition." Referring to the stresses of the year just ending, Wurts conceded that he had sometimes expressed his views "with more earnestness than was deemed suitable." A cryptic remark that "circumstances then existed which brought into question the singleness of purpose, with which I asked," may imply that his brothers' personal involvement had aroused suspicion.[51] In this way the shadow of the 1820s lingered, although no one on the board but Philip Hone, now largely inactive, personally recalled the old dichotomy between the Wurtses and the D&H.

Beyond stressing the urgency of the situation, John Wurts had not recommended any specific course of action. The board responded in accustomed style by appointing a committee to consider his letter. At the next board meeting this committee reviewed the two main, unsuccessful, proposals that had occupied most of 1846 and decided to await further study by Archbald.[52] Wurts was not dismayed by this further delay, and after another meeting later in the month took satisfaction that "The Board is now in the right mood." The increasing intensity of the conflict between the Reading RR and the Schuylkill Navigation, which threatened to cause wider strife in the industry, was convincing some members that the D&H needed "to hold a more commanding position in the coal trade."[53] The president felt that the members were moving in the proper direction of opening the canal to other users through a satisfactory toll structure. Still, the problem remained, "who are we to negotiate with"—in other words, who was going to build a new railway feeder to the D&H? This vital question became the main order of business in 1847.

At first John Wurts felt that the board would leave the resolution of the issue largely to the Wurts brothers. However, he told Maurice, they could expect little help because "We have opposed the views of many members . . . so stoutly."[54] If John Wurts was looking for a reprise of the 1820s, when his older brothers, in their full vigor, wandered through a nearly empty land and conjured up its destiny, he was mistaken. Maurice was in his sixties, long settled at Rondout on the margin of the company's affairs and probably little acquainted with conditions in the coal fields. William and Charles Stewart, who had probably returned to the coal business only after many years of relative absence, lacked the resources and probably the credibility to carry off such a project. Increasingly, the brothers' correspondence becomes occupied with their physical ailments. Their beginnings, when anthracite was a speculative, almost laughable, business belonged to an era that was receding into legend. Now it was an industry with seemingly limitless prospects for wealth, and its future was seized by men with stronger and more grasping hands.

Almost immediately a movement arose to form an association along the lines Archbald had suggested. As early as April 20, 1847 Irad Hawley was able to report the formation of the Wyoming Coal Association, although the company was not formally organized until June 24.[55] With Maurice Wurts acting as middleman, Hawley and his allies made it clear that they intended to include the brothers in their plans. Whether this was a matter of genuine solicitousness, or sheer necessity is a matter of speculation. Charles and William controlled the Washington Coal Co. charter, which carried rights to hold 2000 acres of coal land; in addition they owned land around Cobbs Gap that almost certainly would be needed for a railway from the lower valley.[56] Another concern was that Nathan Smith, in his inimitable style, was prowling around Pittston quietly acquiring potential coal lands. In renewing the offer of participation in the prospective association, Hawley pointedly observed that Smith's activity "might have a tendency to create a competition for lands in that valley & of course an advance in price."[57]

Irad Hawley (1793-1865) had emerged as the dominant personality not only in the D&H, but more broadly in determining the future of the Lackawanna coal district. After joining the board in 1842 he influenced the character of the company much as Philip Hone had earlier. He was named to virtually every committee that considered expansion. Later developments followed the course he had outlined so closely that it is tempting to think he had anticipated the outcome from the start. Yet in many respects he is a puzzling figure who seems not to have received the historical recognition he deserves.

Hawley was born in the ancestral homestead in Ridgefield, Connecticut, property which had been in the family since the first settlement of the town in 1713. His great-grandfather had migrated to Ridgefield from Northampton, Massachusetts, to become the town's first minister. Irad moved to New York City when he was 14, perhaps to join an older brother, and by his twentieth birthday had become a partner in a prosperous West India trading house. In this the Hawleys were obscure marchers in a large contingent of New Englanders "whose accumulated mercantile skill served New York at the expense of its Yankee rival, Boston," according to one historian, who added "Boastfulness aside, it was true that the New Englanders and their descendants contributed heavily to the growth and welfare of the city, giving them a stronghold not only on business but also on social and political matters."[58] The Hawley firm must have been successful, for Irad was able to retire in 1839 despite having six young children (another was born later).[59] According to Beach's directory, he was worth $150,000 in 1846.[60]

There are parallels to the career of some of the Wurts brothers, and a similar mystery concerns the beginning of Hawley's involvement in the coal trade. Nothing in Irad Hawley's early life seems to suggest an interest in that business; nor does it appear that he belonged to one of the Connecticut families that had attempted to settle the Wyoming Valley. One difference is that Hawley became active in anthracite at a later age and when the industry was prospering at a fabulous rate. Probably he saw it merely as an investment—one of the best that could be found at the time. He could be as conspiratorial as the Wurtses, at least as tough-minded; and he commanded financial strength the Wurtses never seemed able to develop.

Over a span of two years Irad Hawley engineered a consolidation of the Lackawanna Valley coal industry and created a new feeder for the D&H. It seemed to be just the sort of setup John Wurts had sought, except that it slipped out of his control. First was the organization of the Wyoming Coal Association, with a capital of $250,000. This done, the next step was the acquisition of the Washington Coal Co. Although nearly ten years old, the WCC was essentially a shell. Hawley believed it was desirable to organize the company and fill its stock subscription before combining it with the Wyoming Coal Association.[61] There had been a nasty but brief spat between Hawley and Charles Wurts in April; after that was patched up, they worked harmoniously to arrange the merger without attracting notice. The organization of the Washington Coal Co. was completed early in September 1847. Control of the company rested overwhelmingly in the hands of D&H board members, though no single individual owned as much as 10% of the stock. Collectively, the four Wurts brothers owned just over this amount, while another $50,000 was reserved for Wurts associates in Philadelphia.[62] Much of the Wurts holding probably resulted from taking stock in exchange for their land.[63]

In its first year of existence the Wyoming Coal Association purchased coal lands near Pittston totaling 2146 acres at a cost of $220,622, in addition to absorbing the Washington Coal Co. property. All lands had been purchased on the recommen- dation of James Archbald. In another vital combination, the association had acquired all 4000 shares of the Pennsylvania Coal Co. This company, despite its expansive name, was authorized only to hold 1000 acres of land in Pittston. It made somewhat more progress than the Washington company, opening a mine and shipping a small amount of coal down the North Branch Canal, an extension of the state system that terminated in Pittston.[64] There was some sort of conceptual, if not financial, linkage between the Pennsylvania and the Washington Coal companies. They were formed in the same year, 1838, with similar but not overlapping charters. There does not seem to have been a direct D&H influence, although one of the incorporators of the WCC was William H. Dimmick, a state representative and D&H attorney.[65] While not allied with the D&H, it also does not seem that any of the men connected with the Pennsylvania or Washington companies joined in the frenzy against the company; in fact at least one of the PCC incorporators, Lewis S. Watres, was cited as a defender of the D&H during the height of the agitation.[66]

For legal reasons the charter of the Pennsylvania Coal Co. came to be more important than any of the company's other assets or accomplishments, and this has created a misconception about the PCC's role in the development of anthracite. Although the association form of organization had seemed appealing to evade some legal entanglements, it had created others. Some investors in the Wyoming Coal Association became concerned that they would be personally liable for the associa- tion's activities. To alleviate this worry, it was decided to shield them under the protection afforded by the corporate form and carry on mining and transportation under the charter of the Pennsylvania Coal Co.[67] The PCC, therefore, was not an independent source of power, but was like a frame that needed to have an engine installed before it could begin moving.

Over the next several years the Pennsylvania Coal Co., in effect a holding company, gradually went through the legal formalities to obtain the rights and property it needed. It acquired land from the Wyoming Coal Association; absorbed all assets of the Washington Coal Co., including the authorization to construct a railroad; and in 1849 assumed the charter of the Luzerne & Wayne RR.[68] The urge for secrecy that had driven the founders of the association no longer seemed compelling, even though many of the legal steps required formal state approval. A number of factors contributed to this changed attitude, even though "outside interests" were undeniably dominant; and it was obvious that among these outsiders were D&H board members, if not the company itself. The uproar incited by Charles Silkman, like a sudden blast from a bellows, proved difficult to sustain; and it is likely that some of his followers became embarrassed by their excess enthusiasm. It was also apparent that the Erie RR was not soon going to enter the Lackawanna Valley; nor had the locals been able to devise an alternative of their own. There was little choice but to acquiesce in the fact that if the coal reserves of the Lackawanna Valley were going to be developed, it would be done by men associated with the "base and detestable" D&H monopoly.

During the first weeks of its existence in 1847, the Wyoming Coal Association had few points of direct contact with the D&H, even though most of its leaders sat on the board of the older company. The first true intersection of interests arrived when the WCA reached the point of negotiating toll rates on the D&H. Here, unexpectedly, a serious difference of opinion arose. In its negotiating strategy the D&H had taken the position that if it enlarged its canal part of the cost would be charged to the new connecting railway. This seemed to present the possibility that the D&H could sell its coal cheaper than the WCA. Members of the association made it clear that they could not accept this arrangement, while others hesitated to subscribe to Wyoming stock until the issue was resolved.[69]

John Wurts had told Hawley that he personally considered the offensive provision a mistake and that "it would be better to leave it out altogether."[70] It was a delicate issue, with negotiation made more difficult by the fact that the practice of spending the summer "in the country" had already become fashionable, so that many of the participants were not available. It was only on August 1, 1847 that agreement was finalized, based on a draft prepared by lawyer Samuel Tilden. The problem of transferring the cost of canal enlargement was postponed.[71] After John Wurts allowed "It meets my approbation," the Wyoming Coal Association pro-ceeded to open its stock subscription books and took the other steps to complete its organization.[72] Since there was a "community of interest"—to put it mildly—between the two companies, the sharpness of the disagreement was startling and a grim portent. If the Wyoming Coal Association was an offspring of the D&H, it was already beginning to look like a rebellious child.

Third Enlargement

IT MAY HAVE BEEN ONLY COINCIDENCE, but just at the critical point in the discussion of toll rates, Russel Lord delivered a major report on the further enlargement of the canal. John Wurts, thinking of the future as always, had requested the study during the previous winter. Lord's plan called for a far more extensive reworking of the system than the two earlier phases. For the first time, in addition to deepening the channel, the locks would have to be enlarged. Since, unlike the banks, locks could not be widened by scraping and straightening, true rebuilding was needed. In keeping with the magnitude of the project, the estimated cost would be much greater: at $1,105,000 it would exceed the first two stages combined.[73]

Since the capacity of the canal was already roughly twice that of the railway, enlarging it was purely an exercise in expansion, an expression of John Wurts's guiding principle that continued reduction of the unit cost of coal was necessary to keep pace with ruthless competitors. Lord spent almost as much time on the economic aspects of his plan as on the engineering side. He calculated that transportation could be lowered to 50 cents a ton, or 40 cents lower than it had ever been. This reminder of the stark imperatives that governed the company's position, coming just when it did, may have made the president more amenable to approving the agreement with the Wyoming Coal Association. He later testified that he had accepted the amount proposed by the WCA so as not to appear "too tenacious of my opinion."[74]

In September 1847 Lord amended his plan on the basis of building all locks to the largest dimension he had considered (his initial estimate had offered four alternatives).[75] At the board meeting of November 17, 1847 President Wurts reported completion of the second enlargement to accommodate boats of 50 tons, at a cost of $265,000. By the company's method of calculating, as presented in the annual report for 1847, the improvements had saved $232,000. Janus-like, the president then looked to the future and proposed the further enlargement, according to Lord's estimate. In the competitive atmosphere of the time, it was easy to make a case that relentless rivals were waiting to seize any opening, and the board approved Wurts's proposal. In March 1848 a special report to stockholders explained and justified the enlargement. With the demand for Lackawanna coal growing without visible limit, the report argued that "the surest way of extinguishing all motives for the prosecution" of competitive schemes, described as still "crude and undefined" was for the D&H to satisfy the demand itself.

Except in High Falls, where a new route for the canal was planned, work on the enlargement again had to be conducted during the off season. On October 28, 1848, after as much preparatory work as possible had been completed, Maurice Wurts was authorized to begin contracting for the enlargement.[76] Two more suspension aqueducts were required, over the Neversink and the Rondout; Roebling's plan for them was approved on December 2.[77] Not long after work started a riot erupted among Irish workers at High Falls. The cause was explained as another bout in the long-running match between Corkonians and Fardowners, which seems to have been something of a traveling sports rivalry in Irish work camps. In 1849 a vigorous temperance movement added another dimension: "Without knowing or caring what are the abstract grounds of difference between the Corkonians and Fardowns, we do know that the grog shops are the parents of the fight. . . . Whatever are the discordant traits of the factions, they won't fight about them without whiskey."[78]

In the spring of 1850 Eddyville was the scene of immense labor to finish the new tidewater guard lock and the weigh lock:

> The lower "village" from the tide water lock to the bridge is a vast workshop, where hundreds of horses are digging and wheeling, picking and cutting stone and building massive walls, and where steam engines and horses are pumping water, and huge cranes are doing the lifting and hoisting, and cars and temporary railroads carry the ponderous blocks of stone to and fro.

The solidity and neatness of the walls are worthy of remark. The stone used is a kind of limestone from Lawrenceville, generally very compact, and dressed with great precision, so as to close joints with scarce a fissure.[79]

This was thought to be the final stage of the enlargement, but work extended into another season. As a result, boating during the 1850 season was more confused and disrupted than usual. It was later reported that boatmen "met with so many obstructions and detentions . . . in consequence of the unfinished state of the enlarged canal, much of it being so narrow that two boats could not pass, and the depth of water not being sufficient to allow them to take as large cargoes as they expected" that some became "very refractory," and the company had to raise the rate to compensate them for delays and other losses.[80] Only slightly more coal was transported in 1850 than in 1849.

Not only did the work take longer than expected, but an enormous overrun developed, so that the project cost twice as much as Lord's initial estimate. On February 10, 1848 the board had approved an increase to $1,900,000, but the final cost exceeded even that. In a letter of October 21, 1850 the engineer went to great lengths to account for the discrepancy. Unfavorable weather was a factor. Lord also admitted overestimating the amount of material that could be salvaged from the old locks. He also ran afoul of the construction methods used on the old canal, although he had been around long enough that he should not have been surprised. "It was found in making the excavation on the Berm, that the canal in its original construction had been located extensively so as to just pass clear of rock excavation, and when rock had been discovered the line was more or less changed to avoid it." During the enlargement the rock was rediscovered, and this time could not be dodged.[81] In this respect, canals were structurally more rigid than railroads. There was usually less opportunity for rerouting, so that it became more difficult to compensate for the shortcuts taken by the early builders.

At High Falls more wet weather than expected turned ordinary soil to quicksand, so that the cost of excavation jumped from $136,000 to $244,000. In addition, aqueducts over small streams were widened, while Roebling's suspension aqueducts required more masonry than had been allowed in the estimate. Lord concluded his litany with a rather abject apology: "I regret that I was not able to estimate the cost more correctly, but it required more experience than I had, to anticipate the embarrassments contingent to the accomplishment of such an amount of work, while sustaining an uninterrupted navigation."[82] Another, and characteristically less charitable, explanation was offered by John W. Johnston: "such a ravenous, greedy system of plunder upon the resources of a corporation has been rarely witnessed among the peculating proceedings of mankind."[83] While such abuses are hardly unknown in large, hurried construction projects, it is unlikely they could account for an overrun of the size that occurred.

While the negative aspects need to be acknowledged, we should not lose sight of the enormous achievements of the D&H during the 1840s. In 1842 the canal still operated within its original dimensions: 32 feet wide at the top, 20 feet at the bottom, with a depth of four feet; locks measured 75 feet in length and nine feet in width. By the 1851 season these figures had increased to 48-50 feet on top, 32 feet on the bottom, with a six foot depth of water. The locks had been enlarged to 100 by 15 feet and improved with paddle gates that made it possible to float boats out. In addition, four locks (three at Phillipsport and one at High Falls) had been eliminated, leaving a total of 108 (106 lift and two guard locks). In 1842 the capacity of the railway stood at about 100,000 tons per year and the canal about twice that;

after the enlargement these figures were multiplied five-fold. Before the campaign of improvements began, less than $2 million of stock had been issued; by the end of 1847 the full allowed amount of $6 million was outstanding, and a further increase to $7.5 million was approved in November 1850. Despite this rapid increase, dividends had been paid at a gratifying rate: 34% in 1845 (including a 25% stock dividend), 16% in 1846, 20% in 1847, 18% in 1848, 16% in 1849, 14% in 1850. This performance was remarkable enough, but in addition the company easily repaid in 1848 and 1850 the state loans when they came due. It is fashionable to criticize public investments, but any glance at the economic results would confirm that the loan which enabled the D&H to be completed was a productive use of state funds.

The canal in its final dimension, probably south of Ellenville.
CREDIT
Minisink Valley Historical Soc.

During the time the third enlargement was proceeding, work was also underway on the Pennsylvania Coal Company's railway from Pittston to meet the D&H Canal at a point called Middle Fork (of the Lackawaxen), soon renamed Hawley. On November 16, 1847 Archbald's request to devote a quarter of his time to construct the railway was approved by the D&H board, illustrating the close relationship that then prevailed.[84] In planning this railway Archbald was able to take advantage of the experience he had gained on the D&H without being restricted by earlier errors and compromises. He laid out two tracks, each about 27 miles long, but often a considerable distance apart. The railway (really two railways) was operated entirely by gravity, with the planes powered by water or steam, depending on circumstances. It was another brilliant achievement, which established James Archbald as the country's master of the gravity railway.[85] He had carried the concept to its highest level of perfection, although it was a technological dead end. The railway was completed in 1850, and the first PCC boat cleared Hawley on June 8. Unfortunately, this was just in time to be caught up in the confusion caused by the incomplete enlargement.

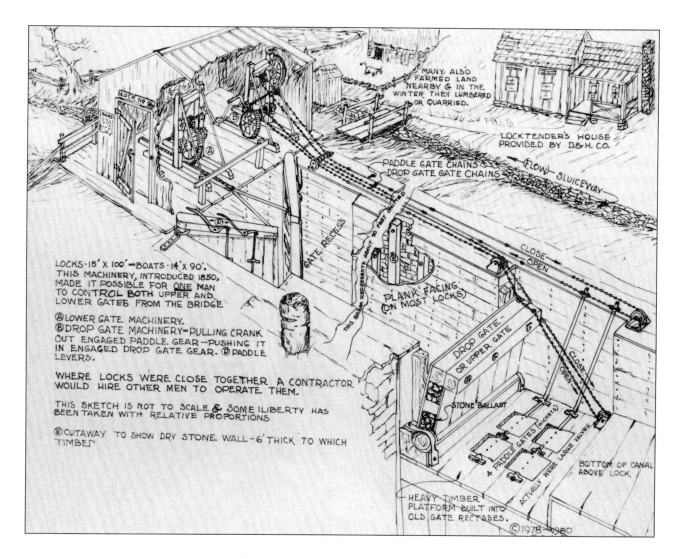

Inside the drawing:

MANY ALSO FARMED LAND NEARBY & IN THE WINTER THEY LUMBERED OR QUARRIED.

LOCK NO 2

RAILS

LOCKTENDER'S HOUSE PROVIDED BY D.&H. CO.

PADDLE GATE CHAINS
DROP GATE GATE CHAINS

FLOW SLUICEWAY

GATE RECESS

THIS BREAK REPRESENTS ABOUT 30 FEET OMITTED

CLOSE OPEN

PLANK FACING (ON MOST LOCKS)

DROP GATE OR UPPER GATE

CLOSE OPEN

LOCKS·15'X 100'—BOATS·14'X 90'.
THIS MACHINERY, INTRODUCED 1850,
MADE IT POSSIBLE FOR ONE MAN
TO CONTROL BOTH UPPER AND
LOWER GATES FROM THE BRIDGE

Ⓐ LOWER GATE MACHINERY.
Ⓑ DROP GATE MACHINERY—PULLING CRANK
OUT ENGAGED PADDLE GEAR—PUSHING IT
IN ENGAGED DROP GATE GEAR. Ⓓ PADDLE
LEVERS.

WHERE LOCKS WERE CLOSE TOGETHER A CONTRACTOR
WOULD HIRE OTHER MEN TO OPERATE THEM.

THIS SKETCH IS NOT TO SCALE & SOME LIBERTY HAS
BEEN TAKEN WITH RELATIVE PROPORTIONS

Ⓔ CUTAWAY TO SHOW DRY STONE WALL - 6' THICK TO WHICH
TIMBER

STONE BALLAST

4 PADDLE GATES (WICKET)

ACTUALLY WERE LARGE VALVES

BOTTOM OF CANAL ABOVE LOCK

HEAVY TIMBER PLATFORM BUILT INTO OLD GATE RECESSES

©1978 1980

Familiar Themes Replayed

Drawing by Ed LeRoy.
CREDIT
National Canal Museum.

RECOVERY FROM THE DEPRESSION OF 1837, complete by the mid-1840s, brought a reappearance of trends that had characterized the early years of the D&H. The harsh defensive struggles of the 1830s, which for the D&H began long before 1837, seemed like a shadowy valley that had been left behind as the economy regained the heights of confidence and ambition.

For the D&H the occasional replay of familiar themes brought almost nostalgic reminders of the company's youthful striving. The persistent, imaginative drive to find new uses for anthracite was recalled in 1848 when the board appropriated $10,000 to encourage the use of coal in the manufacture of salt at Syracuse.[86] Unfortunately, as with most of the earlier experiments, the minutes do not record the outcome. An openness to new technology, one of the company's most admirable traits, recurred in the same year when the board subscribed up to $300 to construct a telegraph line from Lake Erie to New York City through Carbondale. This was done at the specific request of James Archbald.[87]

Expansion, both geographically and functionally, was in the air again. In one of the boldest examples the Wurtses considered becoming iron manufacturers. In July and August 1845 William Wurts obtained information from several individuals about taking an interest in an iron furnace at Danville, Pennsylvania. Four blast furnaces had been erected in this Susquehanna Valley town between 1840 and 1842, and a major puddling and rolling mill, the Montour Iron Works, was completed in 1845.[89] It was an appealing location because the North Branch Canal, perhaps in conjunction with the Pennsylvania Coal Co. or Washington Coal Co. railroad charters could provide ready access to the Lackawanna coal fields.

In examining this prospect William Wurts was following the example of the Scranton brothers, who a few years before had built an iron works at a site then called Slocum's Hollow. The Wurts papers show that they were acquainted with the Scrantons, although they can by no means be described as allies or associates. On one occasion Selden T. Scranton signed one of Charles Silkman's inflammatory petitions, but that was more likely due to his eagerness to obtain a rail outlet than to hostility toward the Wurtses.[90] A more direct connection was through William Henry, the well known geologist who had guided the Scrantons to the site of their operation. Henry provided the Wurtses an analysis of iron manufacturing prospects at Danville and also compared it to the Lehigh Valley. He advised that it would cost about $50,000 to build a furnace and offered to act as agent.[91] Ultimately William and other members of the family decided against plunging into the iron industry. The reasons are not clear, but John Wurts's lack of support may have dumped cold water on the idea. John apparently accepted the opinion of a presumed expert who remarked that "He expects to see this business *over done* in the course of the next twelve months, in consequence of the numbers that are rushing into it."[92]

Map by Ed LeRoy.
CREDIT
National Canal Museum.

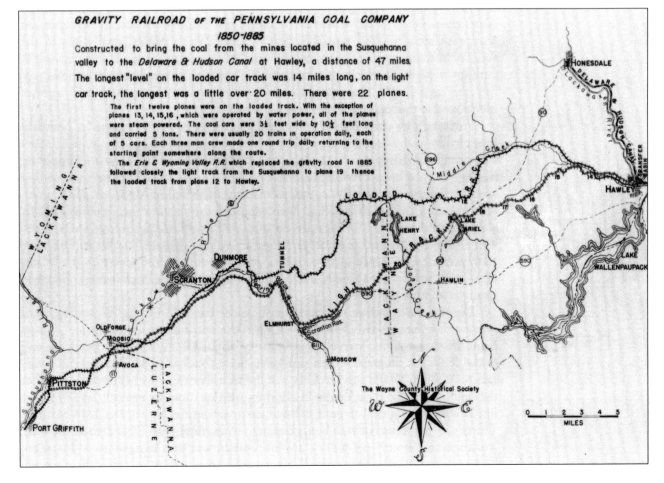

An unwelcome reminder of bygone times was a revival of interest in a rail line across New Jersey. Railroad technology had advanced so rapidly in the interim that it posed an even more acute danger. In late 1845 talk of a railroad through Cobbs Gap all the way to Jersey City was arousing the Lackawanna Valley. Irad Hawley opined—correctly at the time—that such a railroad would cost $6 million, a sum that could not be raised.[93] Another member of the Wurts family, Alexander, kept track of railroad matters in New Jersey. He was probably a son of Samuel Grandin Wurts, the oldest brother of the D&H Wurtses. A lawyer and member of the state legislature, he wrote a letter in March 1846 in which he described railroad developments at Trenton. At that time the Morris & Essex RR and a railroad from Paterson both had permission to extend to Dover. Neither was authorized to continue to the Delaware; but the old Hudson & Delaware RR charter had been kept alive, and people in Sussex County seemed confident it would be built. What Alexander called "the Somerville Railroad" (really the Somerville & Easton) was still alive although he knew nothing definite about it.[94] This letter, which may hint at a larger correspondence, indicates that the D&H Wurtses were keeping close watch on railroad developments which threatened to reawaken the troublesome specters of the 1820s.

In an incongruous but informative letter in April 1847 William Henry informed William Wurts of several railroad projects that were then bubbling. This letter was accompanied by a fascinating sketch of the proposed or actual railroads. Drinker's old Delaware & Susquehanna charter to the Delaware Water Gap was still alive. It had always been handicapped to a degree by the lack of a definite connection in New Jersey, but now active interest by the Morris & Essex RR had given it renewed energy. After a pointed reminder that William Wurts owned coal lands in the vicinity of Roaring Brook, Henry inquired "what amount of stock will yourself & perhaps some of your friends take upon the opening of the Books of the Susq. & Del. rail road Co."[95] This showed considerable temerity, since the D&H was not mentioned in the letter or illustrated on Henry's map.

Not long afterward John Wurts learned that books would be opened at Newark, Branchville and Newton, New Jersey, for a railroad across the state. Rather surprisingly, he added that "I think it was called the Hudson & Delaware," implying that he had not been aware, or did not remember, the earlier competitor of that name.[96] Renewed activity was indeed evident: after failing to accomplish much during the 1830s, the charter had been extended for another ten years in 1842. It was apparently only in 1847 that the economic recovery had progressed to the point where a revival seemed feasible. Another amendment to the charter in February 1847 permitted a choice of two routes, reaching either Port Jervis or the Water Gap—two arrows aimed at the D&H, but again no one had enough financial strength to draw the bow.[97]

Despite the purchase of more coal lands, the sale to the Wyoming Coal Association, the consideration of investing in the iron industry, the transfer of assets from Maurice and the marvelous prosperity of the D&H, the Wurtses at the end of the 1840s felt financial strains similar to those that had bedeviled them 20 years earlier. William Wurts was certainly not the secure retired businessman depicted in the family genealogy; and with 14 children, the last born as recently as 1843, was not in a strong position to endure financial pressures. In November 1848 Maurice Wurts's former sense of well-being began to evaporate; with D&H stock showing weakness and money needed for another installment on the new stock, he wrote "I fear we are all in a bad scrape." He was also troubled by margin calls on stock he had used as collateral. Anxiously the aging explorer of the D&H planned "to sell first all my Washington, and then if further sacrifice is necessary, my New Haven R Road." Recognizing a problem familiar to big stock traders today, he added "it will require time to sell Washington without breaking down the market."[94]

Several months later, in what must have been an agonizing humiliation, William Wurts, "being a little poor just now," had to ask Irad Hawley for an extension of time to pay an installment on the Pennsylvania Coal Co.[99] Later, John Wurts advised that the best thing for Charles and William to sell "if I needed money" would be Pennsylvania Coal Co. In explanation, he described PCC as "an article that will not in any event yield revenue for some time, and may be so mismanaged as to make the profit very small. Indeed I think this will be the case. Hawley will be left at the head of it, and he is entirely unfit."[100] Finally, in what amounts to an epitaph on his long but stressful involvement in the coal business, Charles Stewart Wurts concluded "it is not wise for me to risk all I have on the prosperity of the coal trade, whatever may be the prospect of future gain. And I am in no condition to encounter the wiles of poverty. With these views, I must cut down my coal stocks to my means, and I think it best to sell, but without crowding the market."[101]

In an earlier period the Wurtses could count on time and energy to pull them out of the tight spots into which their speculative inclinations had drawn them. One obvious difference in the late 1840s was that this was no longer true. Burdened by family responsibilities and declining health, the brothers could not readily overcome renewed but more complex challenges. Their most important asset remained their extraordinary closeness, tested in the crucible of several decades' survival in a cutthroat market.

These pressures bore most heavily on John Wurts, on whom the older brothers, and for that matter the entire D&H, placed an inordinate dependence. As the company grew in size and complexity, its management structure did not keep pace. In 1844 Isaac Platt was appointed vice president at a salary of $3000, the first time in company annals that office had been filled.[102] Platt seems to have been competent and relieved some of the burden on the president; but the company still lacked a developed bureaucracy, and the board's tendency toward micro-management placed enormous demands on the chief executive. By 1848 he was simply worn out by the strain of expansion and forming a new affiliate in the Lackawanna Valley. If he did not actually experience a breakdown, he felt one approaching and on May 16, 1848 expressed the desire to retire due to ill health. After considering for several days, the board asked him to continue in office, but requested that he "absent himself" six to twelve months to recover his health. Platt having left earlier, John Ewen was named vice president.[103] Ewen, previously not prominent in the affairs of the D&H, stepped down after about a year in office.[104] With John Wurts still requiring a "respite," Maurice was appointed president pro-tem, a curious testimony to the dependence on the family or the inability to separate the concepts of Wurts and presidency.[105]

John Wurts was back at his post by the autumn of 1849 and was becoming aware of a situation that was certain to undo any benefits of his vacation. "The more I hear of the movements of the Washington Company," he confessed, "the stronger is my fear of ultimate trouble from it. They seem to be marking out their course as a *rival* concern, and are imprudent enough to hold such language."[106] Later, he observed that Hawley had purchased land on Rondout Creek, which would not be necessary if the Pennsylvania Coal Co. allowed the D&H to transport its coal. Wurts was forced to acknowledge "a pregone conclusion on the part of the Pennsylvania Co. to do its own business after 1850."[107]

As negotiations between the two companies proceeded with painful slowness and considerable irritation, the Wurtses tended to place much of the blame on Irad Hawley. John Wurts's remark on his unfitness has been noted. Not long afterward he described Hawley as "the most impracticable and mulish man I ever met with."[108] Maurice Wurts seconded this opinion, remarking "it is most unfortunate that such a man as Hawley should occupy a station for which he is so little qualified."[109]

These developments must have been profoundly distressing to John Wurts. They signified not only a grave misjudgment of Hawley but a recognition that his entire strategy of creating a congenial associate to fill the capacity of the canal was failing. The fact that it was not intrinsically a flawed strategy was little consolation. These disappointments deepened the tendency toward gloom and anxiety that was always present in Wurts's character:

> I have little hope of any thing but trouble from the Washington Co. The disadvantages resulting from it will I fear ere long counterbalance all the good that was looked for, if not even worse than that. My own conviction is very strong, that the Del. & Hud. Co. has reached its highest point of prosperity. But my judgment may be affected by depressed feelings arising from a multitude of perplexing things, which I do not feel able to cope with; and I see no way to provide efficiently for the due administration of the affairs of the Company . . . .[110]

Given this attitude, it is not surprising that the brothers were considering disposal of their coal stocks. Of greater importance for the future was John Wurts's unfortunate combination of a clear perception of the perils that awaited the company with, in his weakened physical and mental state, a lack of confidence in his ability to deal with them.

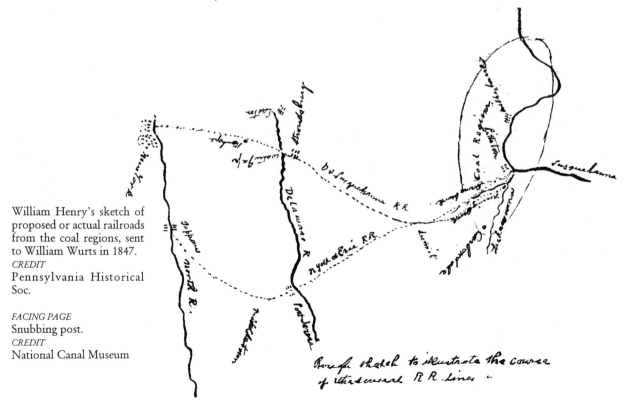

William Henry's sketch of proposed or actual railroads from the coal regions, sent to William Wurts in 1847.
CREDIT
Pennsylvania Historical Soc.

FACING PAGE
Snubbing post.
CREDIT
National Canal Museum

To those who love to contemplate nature in its grand, beautiful and picturesque features, these boats afford the greatest facilities; while the hills encircle you, you may see, now and then, in the valleys, . . . beautiful villages resounding with the voice of thriving industry and exhibiting marks of the successful enterprise of its inhabitants.

The First Skirmishes

AS JOHN WURTS HAD FORESEEN, the next few years, which proved to be the last years of his family's association with the D&H, were dominated by the gradual descent through misunderstanding to outright hostility with the Pennsylvania Coal Co. It proved to be the bitterest and most prolonged of the crises that divide the history of the D&H, although it did not threaten the survival of the company as had those when the company was younger and more vulnerable. It was also a conflict that the president, in declining health, was less able to deal with.

John Wurts had taken to spending long intervals in Europe—on one of them he indulged himself by visiting his family's ancestral haunts in Switzerland. In October 1850 he announced his desire to take a leave of absence from the presidency to recuperate in Europe. This climaxed a letter in which he outlined the company's position and concluded "I apprehend neither injury nor inconvenience (as likely to result from my absence) to the business of the company."[1] Several months earlier William Musgrave of Philadelphia had been appointed vice president at a salary of $5000.[2] This was another strange choice, since Musgrave's qualifications consisted of being a partner in the Wurts Brothers business, and he had no known direct experience with the coal trade. It was almost as if he was chosen under a divine right concept in which the presidency resided in the Wurts family or their associates.

During the president's long absences Musgrave, lacking both title and experience, filled in as best he could. This testifies to a deeper and more ominous problem: lack of strong leadership on the board. As no forceful substitute appeared, John Wurts's increasing infirmity led to chronic indecisiveness. His successor later said that "for some years" Wurts had been "a confirmed invalid, and he had with the consent of the Board, substantially withdrawn from the active management of the Company's affairs."[3] Isaac Platt had considerable experience and remained on the board until 1852, but the Wurtses had already dismissed him as hopelessly "under the influence" of Hawley.[4] The fact that he left the board a month after Hawley chose not to stand for reelection supports this conclusion. Even Archbald, though not a member of the board, suffered some kind of collapse and was not available to provide guidance. (John Wurts noted in his letter that during 1850 Archbald "was entirely unable to counsel or direct.")[5]

Wurts returned from Europe in late 1851. The board generously credited him with his salary for the period of his absence: October 12, 1850 through October 26, 1851.[6] Thereafter relations with the PCC deteriorated steadily. As noted, Wurts had expressed forebodings as early as 1849, but this was not reflected in the company minutes for another year; probably they tried to put a good face on things as long as possible. In late 1849 the two companies managed to reach an agreement for the D&H to sell coal produced by the PCC in 1850, but this was a temporary measure that did not address the fundamental issues.[7] The first open sign of discord in the minutes was a reference to "some contrariety of views" on tolls between the D&H and Irad Hawley of the PCC.[8] Meanwhile, the PCC was steadily consolidating the companies it had absorbed. This process culminated in May 1851 when the Wyoming Coal Association transferred all property, rights and interest to the PCC.[9] Earlier the PCC had formally assumed the contract made between the WCA and the D&H in 1847. After discussion between committees of the D&H and the PCC, transfer of the contract was accepted.[10]

The core of the emerging dispute no longer concerned precisely the issues that had arisen during the first disagreement between the D&H and the WCA in 1847. Under the proposal discussed at that time, tolls would be based on the cost of bringing coal to Rondout. The D&H held out for $2.50 a ton, while the WCA, arguing that its costs would be higher because of having to operate a longer railway, was adamant for $2.60. Eventually, as noted, John Wurts yielded so as not to seem too obstinate (and also not wishing to have the arrangement fall apart). If nothing else, this debate illustrates the close and careful calculations that already characterized the coal industry. Wurts correspondence and other documents display a fundamental conception of the coal market as a unit. Recognizing this resulted in an almost morbid attention to prices set by rival companies. The D&H, as an important but relatively small player, understood that it could not resist pricing trends set by the larger companies. A concomitant was that the coal men, driven by an acute sense of profit margins and break-even points, made exceedingly fine calculations of costs.

The developing dispute focused on a clause in the agreement that required the PCC to pay half of the cost savings brought about by the enlargement of the D&H Canal. This is why the intensity of the conflict shot up once the enlargement was finished and the D&H had a basis for computing its cost. From the D&H perspective this seemed perfectly reasonable. It had always been an article of faith that increased capacity would produce savings in transportation costs. Nor is it likely that the D&H would have begun the third enlargement without considerable certainty that the extra capacity would be absorbed by another producer. The PCC, and the WCA before it, had accepted the idea in principle. Whether they signed in good faith can only be speculated upon; all that is certain is that the D&H efforts to apply the principle met with immediate resistance.

In April 1852 a disagreement between the two companies arose over the method of weighing PCC coal.[11] This clash was of no lasting consequence except to illustrate how difficult it had become for the supposed partners to work harmoniously. Less than a month later, with an agreement on tolls still elusive, the D&H informed the PCC that it would begin collecting tolls of 50 cents a ton, per an informal arrangement worked out by some of the managers of each company.[12] The D&H board seemed to be making a special effort to accommodate the PCC and accepted the latter's request to collect tolls once a week rather than on each cargo.[13]

After another year of inaction and tiresome correspondence, relations descended another level in July 1853. Advised by its lawyers, the D&H notified the PCC that it would "hereafter charge and collect the additional toll on coal, to which it is entitled by said contract, in consideration of such enlargement." It also threw down the gauntlet by determining that the saving resulting from the enlargement was not less than 40 cents a ton, meaning that the PCC share would be at least 20

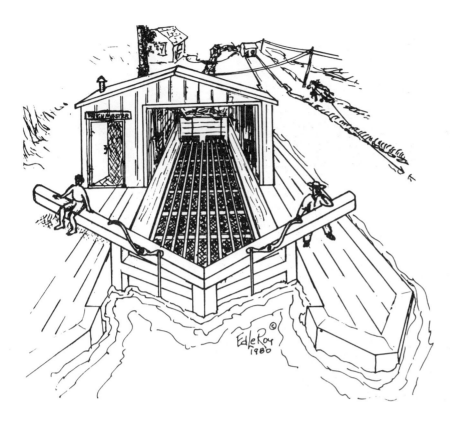

Drawing by Ed LeRoy of the D&H weigh lock located a quarter of a mile east of the Hawley basin. It was built to gauge tolls to be charged for coal shipped by the Pennsylvania Coal Co. A boat was floated into the weigh lock and the water drained out so that the boat rested on a grid or cradle which, through linkage overhead, was connected to balances within the building. After weighing, the captain was given a clearance ticket, the lock was refilled, and the boat was backed out.
CREDIT
National Canal Museum.

BELOW
A view of the Hawley weigh lock from the 1880s.
CREDIT
Pennsylvania State Archives.

The First Skirmishes ◆ 187

Interior of the weigh lock at Eddyville.
CREDIT
Patricia & DeWitt Clinton Collection.

cents.[14] President John Ewen of the PCC, as if waiting for this challenge, pounced immediately by denying that the enlargement had produced savings. Later he disputed the method of calculating the excess toll.[15] Thus the parameters of the monumental dispute were defined. Both sides agreed to arbitration, as provided in their contract; but mediation must have been unsuccessful, if it took place at all. With other possibilities exhausted, the D&H in 1856 resorted to legal action against the PCC.[16]

In some respects this outcome, though the result of six or more years of friction, remains difficult to understand. The PCC originated essentially as a holding company formed by men connected with the D&H, and the identity of interest did not suddenly disappear. As late as May 30, 1851 members of the D&H board and the Wurts brothers together owned more than 28% of the shares of the Wyoming Coal Association; the brothers alone held well over 10%.[17] Yet this apparently did not convey effective control; moreover, they may have had less of an interest in the PCC itself, although in the absence of stock ownership records it is impossible to be sure. Nor was it inevitable that Irad Hawley would instigate a quarrel and take the PCC side against the D&H. He was a large holder of PCC, but by no means had a controlling interest. He had sat on the D&H board for ten years, suggesting that he was heavily invested in that company as well. In fact, as the crisis intensified, Hawley's influence seemed to wane. He served only one year as president of the PCC and was then replaced by Ewen, a man who seems to have been a hardliner with no hesitation about pushing the dispute to the breaking point. It is not clear how Ewen entered the coal industry, much less how he developed such stubborn hostility toward the D&H. He had served as D&H vice president for about a year, and seemed to depart with good feelings. On that occasion the D&H board passed a resolution stating that it "cordially reciprocates the expressions of regard contained in his communication," and continued his salary for six months.[18]

A Thirty-Year Cloud Dissipates

DURING THE DREARY PERIOD when relations between the D&H and the PCC deteriorated toward a final split, another burden weighed on John Wurts's mind. This was the approaching 30-year deadline after which Pennsylvania could assume control of the D&H property in that state. Quite likely this threat, lurking in the background, distracted Wurts and kept him from pursuing more aggressive policies. Having been present when the provision was inserted and having tried to minimize its impact, he was more acutely troubled by it than anyone else. Perhaps this is why he chose to be absent in Europe in May 1851 when the Pennsylvania House of Representatives announced that it had appointed a committee "to investigate the affairs" of the D&H.[19]

The seriousness of this matter, as John Wurts understood, could hardly be overestimated. In the 30 years since a charter had been issued to an untested group in an unproven business, the D&H had prospered. Article 18 of the 1823 act had provided two eventualities under which the state could acquire the D&H property, and at that time they seemed equally likely. The charter in essence allowed the D&H to earn a steady 6% a year. If it did so over the 30-year term, the state could simply assume control of the company's assets. There was, however, a trick in the wording, which spoke not of earnings, but only of tolls. Since the company did not collect tolls on its own coal shipments, its toll receipts were actually limited.

The enemies of the D&H may not have been aware of the precise wording but knew that some sort of 30-year reckoning existed. "The days of this foul incorporation are numbered in 1853," declared Charles Silkman in one of his more inflamed pronouncements. "It must go before a tribunal of the sovereign people of this Commonwealth steeped in crime, festered with corruption, and running over with infamy, and, if then judged according to its merits, we feel well assured it will exist no longer, a pest to our citizens and a curse to the country."[20] This restrained utterance was vented on March 12, 1846—only seven years before the final numbering of days it awaited so avidly. If that level of intensity could be sustained, things would look bad for the company. Regardless of the wording of the legislation, public sentiment would make itself felt. Under pressure some legislator might come up with an imaginative solution such as charging an assumed or imputed toll on company shipments.

Fortunately for the D&H the largely artificial frenzy whipped up by Silkman and his minions had long since evaporated. In its years of struggle, beginning with the hard-won charter and amendments and extending through the battles to curb the Erie RR, the D&H had learned how to maneuver in the legislative arena. On January 18, 1852 the legislative committee reported that Pennsylvania would have to pay $1,246,438 to acquire the D&H property. The D&H board believed this was actually an underestimate, but even the stated amount was enough to give pause at a time when the state had absorbed enormous losses on its own canals.[21] Furthermore, owning assets in only one state would be like owning the front half of a cow. Representatives from its region strongly supported the D&H. One of them, Silas S. Benedict of Luzerne, managed to wangle the chairmanship of the committee on Internal Navigation in return for backing a representative from western Pennsylvania as speaker.[22]

With this kind of masterful management in the "tribunal of the sovereign people" the D&H had less to fear. In April 1852 the legislature passed an amendment to the 1823 act repealing the notorious Article 18.[23] The Pennsylvania charter finally

Scene at Rowlands along the Lackawaxen, part of the D&H properties in Pennsylvania.
CREDIT
D&H RR Collection, NYS Library.

became in reality what John Wurts had misleadingly termed it in 1823: perpetual. In reporting this the board was at last able to confess the fears that had haunted it, noting that the amendment "relieves it from doubt or hesitation that might otherwise exist." This fear must have been genuine, since as soon as the legislature had alleviated the anxiety the board approved several significant expenditures. It decided to complete the enlargement of the Pennsylvania portion of the canal, purchased land for additional reservoirs, and acquired more coal land. In another coincidental but striking example of closing the historical circle, the board also agreed to purchase coal lands that had belonged to its old nemesis Thomas Meredith.[24]

Other than the Wurts brothers, there were few people connected with the D&H in 1852 who remembered the uncertainties of 1823 or understood the passions recalled by the name Thomas Meredith. One who would have recalled without prompting was Philip Hone, though he probably would not have responded with equal emotional intensity. But that commendable individual was no longer present, having died May 4, 1851. He had remained on the D&H board, and his colleagues honored him with an effusive testimonial which largely concealed the diminished influence he had exerted in his last years. Hone had lived an admirable life; the list of his memberships, positions and friends could have filled an agate newspaper column. Change, already rushing with dizzying speed, had passed him by to a large extent. He represented a smaller, more congenial and perhaps more honorable New York, the cozy New York of the Tontine and a Wall Street of two-story town houses. In another mystical coincidence, Hone's death occurred only ten days after his namesake town of Honesdale was devastated by fire.

Next to depart as the founding generation passed from the scene was Maurice Wurts, who died December 29, 1854 at the age of 71. He was praised, deservedly, for his sagacity and perseverance. His moral character and "purity of life" were noted, as was his charitable nature; but there must have been a sharp side to his personality, as one article referred to "a decision which might have impressed the casual observer as sternness."[25] The harshness of his early struggles had etched his character, giving him a craggy image that frightened a smoother younger generation. Maurice had owned the "President's House" at Rondout, and in 1857 the D&H board agreed to purchase it from his executors for $6500.[26] Maurice Wurts had bought it in 1852 for the same price, leaving the questions of where he had lived previously and who had occupied the house that the long-departed John Bolton had erected to symbolize his grandeur.

The four Wurts brothers associated with the D&H enjoyed similar life spans. William died in Trenton December 25, 1858, aged 70; and Charles Stewart followed in June 1859, a few weeks short of his 69th birthday. John Wurts outlived them, but his leadership of the D&H did not. Encouraged by a board hesitant to take the decisive step, he clung to the presidency as long as he was able; but by March 12, 1858 he had reached the end of his capacity. In a tone of understandable regret he acknowledged "it seems to me that the limit to my usefulness has been reached— perhaps it has already passed. I have no longer health and strength to meet and dispose of the daily details of business." It was a poignant moment, and surely John Wurts was being truthful when he confessed "It will readily be believed by gentlemen of the Board, that after seven and twenty years of official toil, through varied scenes of adversity and prosperity in the Company's business, severance of my relations to it cannot take place without a struggle on my part."[27]

On previous occasions when Wurts had raised the subject the board had been reluctant to admit that so drastic a break was unavoidable, but now they saw it could no longer be deferred. In February 1855 the board had named one of its members, George Talbot Olyphant, acting president while John Wurts was absent. By 1858 his colleagues must have felt fully confident in Olyphant's executive abilities. The board made every effort to treat the departing president generously, offering him a gift of $6000 and appointment as counsel to the company.[28] Wurts at first balked at the gift, believing it was tied to accepting the counsel position. He explained, probably with good reason, that "after seven and twenty years with-drawal from active professional business, I do not feel competent to act as counsel of this company." After being informed that the gift was not dependent on taking the position, he eventually accepted both. His response to the offer provides revealing testimony about his financial situation, showing that in his years of involvement with the D&H and the coal industry in general he had never succeeded in amassing great wealth:

> [I]t is not my desire to live in idleness when I am able to labor, nor will my circumstances permit me to do so. These considerations make it incumbent on me to take some decided step for the improvement of my health, which may oblige me to absent myself for some time . . . . If I should return with improved health, so as to be able to resume labor, I would feel it necessary . . . to occupy my time in a way that would yield more than $3000 a year; or failing in that, to seek some less expensive residence than this city.[29]

Any hope John Wurts had of recovering his health was disappointed. He went abroad in 1859 and died in Rome, Italy, April 23, 1861 at the age of 68. He had remained a member of the D&H board until his death, but his long absences made that largely a courtesy. Vice President William Musgrave had died in 1856, meaning that with one exception the Wurts era on the D&H had come to an end. That exception was Charles Pemberton Wurts, the youngest of the 13 children of George Wurts. Born in 1824, he began working for the D&H at the age of 19. Later he made surveys for the New York, New Haven & Hartford RR.[30] (It will be recalled that at least one of the senior Wurts brothers owned stock in that company.) In 1853 C. P. Wurts became chief engineer of the D&H and remained in that capacity until 1865. With Thomas Dickson, another Maurice Wurts (an older brother of C. P.) and others he founded the Dickson Co. which became a successful manufacturer of locomotives in Scranton.[31]

In a poignant twist of history, in what proved to be John Wurts's last full year as president he was plagued by a recurrence of issues that had beset the early years of the company. In 1857, as in 1830, the company was troubled by inferior coal which, for reasons that are unclear, had been passed down the system. "We will be ruined in reputation if we go on as we have done for some time past, shipping coal that puts afloat such stories (and I suppose they are true) as you will find in a letter

Interior of a coal breaker. Engraving from *Harper's Magazine*.

View of coal breaker at Plane No.4 on the gravity railway, 1896.
CREDIT
National Canal Museum.

we received this morning from Providence," the president lamented.[32] This wholly unexpected problem must have revived dread memories. John Wurts was nearly the last individual who remembered the distress caused by defective coal—one of the factors in the crisis which brought him into the presidency.

Worse still was Wurts's tendency to internalize these problems. He admitted that the defective coal, which would make it impossible to fill contracts, was "a matter that presses heavily and sorely on me, and I hardly know how to deal with it."[33] A few days later he made an explicit connection to his physical condition, conceding that "I am sick at heart to think of the consequences to the company that must follow from scattering this wretched stuff through the market."[34] The stress burst through in a wrenching plea: "Do our dock masters know the difference between coal and slate or sulphur or other trash that should never have reached Rondout? If they do not pray teach them the difference."

Compounding the problem were developments in the coal market, with increasing specialization in the sizes of coal being sold and growing demand for the smaller types. As Wurts observed, demand for traditional "lump" coal was declining in favor of more refined varieties. Amazing as it may seem, whatever breaking of coal took place up to that time was performed by manual labor. Prior to 1857 most of this was apparently done at Waymart, on the railway. With poor prospects for lump coal, the president now advocated breaking coal at Rondout and Honesdale as well, admitting that "it will be expensive to do it."[35] To an aging and ill John Wurts these changes must have been dismaying, but he recognized necessity and reluctantly agreed to put up a breaker. Steam-powered coal breakers, which eventually gave the anthracite districts a distinctive and ominous appearance, originated in the Schuylkill field in the 1840s.[36] By the mid-1850s the D&H dared not resist them any longer; once again its policies were decided by larger trends in the industry.

Finally, in the latter part of 1857, another financial panic erupted. Earlier fears about not having a sufficient quantity of marketable coal became suddenly irrelevant. Advocating a reduced operation, John Wurts wrote "the times are such that it behooves the strongest to act with great prudence and caution."[37] Although this financial downturn did not prove as severe as the depression that began in 1837, it surely reminded the president of the earlier panic. If he had been acquainted with Hindu philosophy, he might have seen his career as condemned to endless cycles of corporate repetition. It is understandable that by 1858 he was ready to admit that he had worn himself out in the service of the Delaware and Hudson Canal Company.

Although he was probably too distracted by recurrent irritations to think in those terms, there were many grounds for the president to take satisfaction from his company's accomplishments. In 1853 total shipments from the anthracite region cracked the five million ton mark for the first time. The D&H contributed about 10% of this amount. The doubts that surrounded stone coal had long since been dispelled. An English visitor in 1854, adding to the prolific genre of travel accounts to the mysterious young nation, observed casually that "The houses are warmed by air heated from a furnace at the basement; and although in addition open fires are sometimes adopted, they are made of anthracite coal, which emits no smoke."[38] The industrial uses that the D&H and others had struggled to establish were fully accepted. Similarly, the D&H campaign to broaden the regional market had been crowned with phenomenal success. Shipments of anthracite from Philadelphia to Boston jumped from 63,000 tons in 1830 to a million tons in 1850. Coastwise shipping naturally kept pace, with the total of arrivals and clearances at Boston nearly doubling from 5000 in 1830 to 9300 in 1848.[39]

A valuable compilation by the *American Railroad Journal* in 1847 calculated that 417 miles of canals and 503 miles of railroads had been built to transport anthracite. Their total cost came to $34,060,000, of which the D&H accounted for $3,250,000—roughly in proportion to its market share. This amount was exceeded by the Lehigh Navigation ($4,455,000), the Schuylkill Navigation ($5,675,000), and the Morris Canal ($4,000,000), not to mention the Reading Railroad ($11,000,000). If the D&H had been the first million-dollar corporation in the country, by 1847 it was clearly no longer the largest.[40]

A coal schooner entering Newburyport Harbor, Massachusetts.

War with the PCC

WHATEVER THE PRECISE NATURE of John Wurts's chronic illness, the impending battle with the PCC, never out of his mind, surely contributed to his decline. Even though he might not be to blame for the dismal outcome, the failure of a policy he had pursued with unswerving determination must have been dispiriting. Operationally, the two companies had been able to work out a cautious coexistence. PCC coal flowed down the D&H Canal and in some years exceeded the D&H's own shipments. But lurking in the background was the dread certainty that their dispute would someday have to be settled in an all-out legal battle. Even if John Wurts had possessed his full health, it is difficult to see how the conflict could have been resolved by other means; indeed, his departure had no effect.

After what it considered sufficient preparation, the D&H filed suit against the PCC in early 1857, seeking to recover the additional tolls which it asserted were owed due to the lowered costs resulting from the enlargement. The subsequent case became one of the memorable legal battles of the nineteenth century, notable for its size and complexity, as well as the acerbity with which it was often conducted. Its initial phase of hearings alone lasted more than four years, called more than 200 witnesses and filled nearly 5000 pages published in eight bound volumes.[41] In this respect it proved to be a bonanza not only for lawyers, as expected, but also for printers, since the proceedings were published daily.

A separate study would be needed, but the case may form a landmark of American jurisprudence. It was noteworthy not only for its magnitude but for the extent of the reliance on expert testimony and statistical data and for the persistence with which this evidence was challenged. The parties seemingly had some awareness that the case would present unusual difficulties, for they met beforehand to set ground rules. They agreed on a referee, Jacob DuBois, determined a schedule—which proved wildly optimistic—and laid out rules of procedure. Standard court-room rules of examination were followed, and objections were allowed; but since it was not a trial and DuBois was not a judge, he could not rule on these objections. They were made for the record and accumulated for later decision; as the hearing progressed, they were inserted with tedious frequency.

Looking at the overall course of the hearing, probably the most critical factor was the failure of the D&H to anticipate the tenacity and effectiveness of the PCC defense. It seems that the D&H expected a fairly routine, almost perfunctory, process; and its lawyers were probably shocked by the resistance they encountered, especially the intensity with which witnesses were examined. As the case dragged on far longer than the D&H had expected, the exasperation of its lawyers became obvious. They accused the PCC of deliberately prolonging the process, and indeed it seems that the defense saw no advantage in bringing matters to a rapid close. On occasion President Ewen acted as counsel for his company and used his objections to insert long and provocative presentations of the PCC position, which made the D&H lawyers so livid that the musty pages still seem to glow after a lapse of 140 years. Other portions of the PCC case were handled by its counsel Samuel J. Tilden, who had drafted the articles of association for the Wyoming Coal Association, as well as the original agreement between that company and the D&H. He is better known as the Democratic candidate who many historians feel was cheated out of the presidency in the 1876 election.

The D&H side began confidently enough in December 1857 by introducing experts such as James McEntee and Russel Lord whose knowledge seemed unimpeachable. These witnesses established the central claim that a 125-ton boat on the enlarged canal could transport coal for about 40 cents a ton less than the 50-ton boats in use after the second enlargement. This line of reasoning was hardly unexpected, since the D&H had predicated the enlargement—and Lord had staked his career—on this principle. Lord's figures claimed that freight costs had dropped almost 43 cents a ton as a result of the 1842-46 enlargement, and it was assumed that the grander enlargement would produce a similar result.[42] What was unexpected was the persistence with which the PCC attacked the claim. It refused, first of all, to admit that there was any saving, sometimes even maintaining that the cost was actually higher on the enlarged canal.[43] In the process every item of expense was analyzed exhaustively, down to the cost and durability of ropes and candles. Issues such as the costs and requirements for animal fodder were sifted almost to the last oat. Although it was not the intent of the disputants, the proceeding gives historians an unrivaled mass of information on canal operations. In view of the way the proceedings were treated by judges in later appeals, this was virtually the only positive result.

The transcript of the hearings also provides an unexcelled insight into the lives of people who worked on the canal, from boatmen to supervisors to boat builders and shippers. In many cases it constitutes their only presence in recorded history.

Only a small proportion of individuals who worked on the canal over a ten-year period are humanized in this way, yet it is still a sampling that no other canal can match in its directness and immediacy. Much of the actual testimony is suspect, since it is obvious that each party's witnesses were carefully coached to present consistent stories. Nevertheless, the individuality of the boatmen occasionally shows through a process that must have seemed bewildering and threatening.

It is obvious that many of the boatmen had been only lightly brushed by formal education. Many were illiterate or nearly so—and these were men who had been selected as the most competent witnesses! Considering that they were being asked to make complex calculations of expenses and profit, their lack of arithmetical ability casts suspicion on the process. One boatman acknowledged "I can't figure"; another testified "I know figures when they are put down, but I can't add up and carry . . . when I want anything figured up, I get a man to do it for me." At one time a counsel for the plaintiffs exploded "it is entirely too expensive to the parties in the controversy to have the time of the hearing consumed in giving lessons to, or teaching the witness arithmetic."[44] It was easy enough for sharp lawyers to discredit the evidence of a man who testified "I can't read writing, but I know that in going both up and down at Hawley and at Eddyville my permits are taken to the offices and changed" or another who acknowledged "I know that the months have either 30 or 31 days, but I am not certain which of them only 30 days." Occasionally the irritation of these highly individualistic boatmen at being raked over in this way shows through, creating flashes of unintentional humor. In one instance a boatman, asked "Does it not require some considerable pains and time to teach the horse the rules of the canal?" responded dryly, "I never knew that it was necessary for a horse to know the rules and regulations of a canal." Upholding the equine side, another boatman declared "I mean to say that some of the horses knew more than the boys."[45]

Light boat and crew at Creek Locks late in the history of the canal. A generation earlier their predecessors had squirmed under cross-examination during the great legal battle.
CREDIT
D&H Canal Museum.

One can only guess at what is going on here. Is the well-dressed young man explaining the rules of the canal, or some deeper sentiment? One hopes that the women's effort in putting on their finery was intended for a more appreciative audience, as their companion could hardly seem less impressed.
CREDIT
D&H Canal Museum.

One point both sides accepted was the existence of a clear demarcation between the canal before and after enlargement—paralleling the distinction between the old and new Erie after the rebuilding of that canal was completed in 1862. The D&H attorneys were placed in the paradoxical position of arguing that boat captains had really not been able to make a profit while carrying coal for the company on the old canal. The surplus that supposedly remained at the end of a season was, they contended, largely imaginary and would have vanished if the captains had allowed reasonable compensation for their own services. Conversely, the PCC argued that the late 1840s—in other words before their company began shipping coal—was a halcyon period on the canal, a time when, as one boatmen testified, he was able to buy a lot and build a house with the proceeds of boating.[46] It was not necessarily a contradiction to maintain that boatmen fared better under the old system even while the cost per ton was less with larger boats, and if this had been an arbitration proceeding that might have furnished the basis of a settlement. The time for arbitration, however, was long past, and with the increasing animosity each day's testimony brought, any possibility of compromise disappeared.

The D&H approach was to compare large and small boats in the same year, which was hypothetical since, with the partial exception of 1853, the two never operated on the new waterway in its completed state. It might have seemed self-evident that larger boats would produce savings, but the heart of the PCC defense was the refusal to accept this proposition. Early in the proceedings the D&H introduced James F. Smith, who had been chief engineer of the Schuylkill Navigation for 21 years. His figures showed a savings of about 37 cents a ton between 50- and 125-ton boats; however his evidence could be dismissed to some extent because his system combined canal and slackwater. Of its 108 miles only 58 miles were a canal, and the 50 miles of slackwater could relieve crowding.[47] The massive enlargement of the Erie Canal was not completed until 1862 and thus could not offer a valid comparison. There had been a significant reduction in freight charges on the

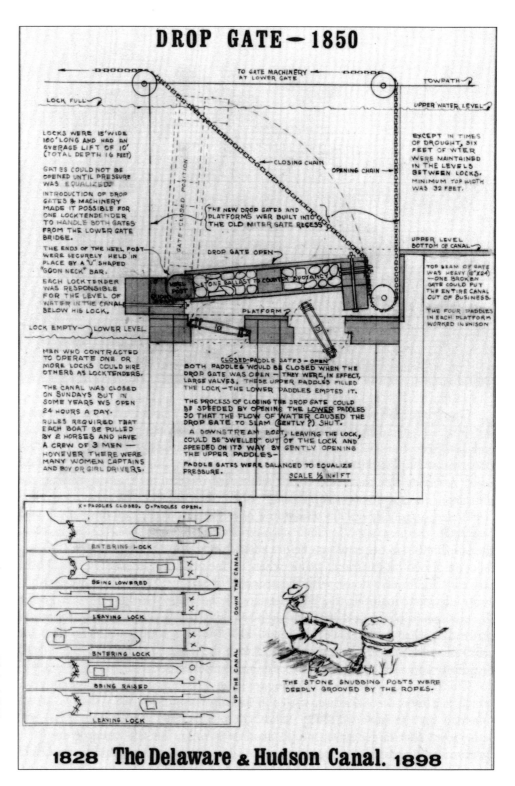

DROP GATE — 1850

TO GATE MACHINERY AT LOWER GATE

TOWPATH

LOCK FULL

UPPER WATER LEVEL

LOCKS WERE 15' WIDE 100' LONG AND HAD AN AVERAGE LIFT OF 10' (TOTAL DEPTH 16 FEET)

CLOSING CHAIN

OPENING CHAIN

GATES COULD NOT BE OPENED UNTIL PRESSURE WAS EQUALIZED.

INTRODUCTION OF DROP GATES & MACHINERY MADE IT POSSIBLE FOR ONE LOCKTENDER TO HANDLE BOTH GATES FROM THE LOWER GATE BRIDGE.

GATE-CLOSED POSITION

THE NEW DROP GATES AND PLATFORMS WER BUILT INTO THE OLD MITER GATE RECESS.

EXCEPT IN TIMES OF DROUGHT, SIX FEET OF WTER WERE MAINTAINED IN THE LEVELS BETWEEN LOCKS. MINIMUM TOP WIDTH WAS 32 FEET.

DROP GATE OPEN

UPPER LEVEL BOTTOM OF CANAL

THE ENDS OF THE HEEL POST WERE SECURELY HELD IN PLACE BY A "U" SHAPED "GOON NECK" BAR.

STONE BALLAST TO COUNTER BUOYANCY

HEEL POST

TOP BEAM OF GATE WAS HEAVY (12"X24) — ONE BROKEN GATE COULD PUT THE ENTIRE CANAL OUT OF BUSINESS.

EACH LOCKTENDER WAS RESPONSIBLE FOR THE LEVEL OF WATER IN THE CANAL BELOW HIS LOCK.

PLATFORM

THE FOUR PADDLES IN EACH PLATFORM WORKED IN UNISON

LOCK EMPTY — LOWER LEVEL

MEN WHO CONTRACTED TO OPERATE ONE OR MORE LOCKS COULD HIRE OTHERS AS LOCKTENDERS.

CLOSED-PADDLE GATES-OPEN BOTH PADDLES WOULD BE CLOSED WHEN THE DROP GATE WAS OPEN — THEY WERE, IN EFFECT, LARGE VALVES. THESE UPPER PADDLES FILLED THE LOCK — THE LOWER PADDLES EMPTED IT.

THE CANAL WAS CLOSED ON SUNDAYS BUT IN SOME YEARS WS OPEN 24 HOURS A DAY.

THE PROCESS OF CLOSING THE DROP GATE COULD BE SPEEDED BY OPENING THE LOWER PADDLES SO THAT THE FLOW OF WATER CAUSED THE DROP GATE TO SLAM (GENTLY?) SHUT.

RULES REQUIRED THAT EACH BOAT BE PULLED BY 2 HORSES AND HAVE A CREW OF 3 MEN — HOWEVER THERE WERE MANY WOMEN CAPTAINS AND BOY OR GIRL DRIVERS.

A DOWNSTREAM BOAT, LEAVING THE LOCK, COULD BE "SWELLED" OUT OF THE LOCK AND SPEEDED ON ITS WAY BY GENTLY OPENING THE UPPER PADDLES.

PADDLE GATES WERE BALANCED TO EQUALIZE PRESSURE.

SCALE ½ IN = 1 FT

X = PADDLES CLOSED. O = PADDLES OPEN.

ENTERING LOCK

BEING LOWERED

LEAVING LOCK

ENTERING LOCK

BEING RAISED

LEAVING LOCK

DOWN THE CANAL

UP THE CANAL

THE STONE SNUBBING POSTS WERE DEEPLY GROOVED BY THE ROPES.

1828 The Delaware & Hudson Canal. 1898

Drop-gates, newly designed on the enlarged canal, supposedly speeded operation by swelling boats out of the lock. Drawing by Ed LeRoy.
CREDIT
National Canal Museum.

Erie, with the fees on a barrel of flour dropping from $1 in 1832 to 64 cents in 1846.[48] While the size of boats had been increased during this period, tolls had been lowered, and it was difficult to separate the two effects. Other figures showed a reduction in eastbound freight charges from an average of $2.96 per ton in the years 1840-44 to $1.75 for 1855-59, exclusive of tolls.[49]

Later the PCC itself brought in a witness who confirmed that larger boats had generated savings on the Erie Canal. This person, New York State Engineer William J. McAlpine, a member of the Canal Board and a Railroad Commissioner, seemed to have unimpeachable credentials. McAlpine testified that, as a result of continuing enlargement on the Erie Canal, shipping costs per ton between Albany and Buffalo had dropped steadily from $3 in the period 1846-49 to $2.75 in 1853-56; $2 in 1857; $1.60 in 1858 and $1.55 in 1859. The average eastbound cargo had increased in the corresponding periods from 68 to 92½, 100, 126 and 143 tons.[50] McAlpine, however, denied that similar savings could be achieved on the D&H because the canal prism did not have proper proportions, resulting in excess friction. In McAlpine's words, delays resulted from the "diminished ratio which now exists between the immersed section of the boat and the section of the channel-way."[51]

Because of delays from this and other causes, the PCC, while conceding that savings were a theoretical possibility, argued they had not been realized because the smaller boats had been able to make significantly more trips per season. In response the D&H maintained that the excess number of boats due to the two companies operating simultaneously caused slower trips. That seemed to be beside the point, but actually went to the historical heart of the dispute. When the D&H under John Wurts's leadership adopted its policy of expanding traffic on the canal it apparently assumed that the additional cargo would be carried on company boats. It was probably not anticipated that another company would operate a separate fleet on the canal. There was a consensus among boatmen that boating was more demanding and difficult with the large boats. They were more likely to scrape the banks and become wedged, and there was greater danger of drowning or injury to horses. The gains attributed by the D&H to the practice of "swelling" boats out of the improved locks were not sufficient to compensate. One boatman summed up by saying "A boy ten years old could handle a small boat much easier than I could handle a large boat."[52]

More damaging to D&H sensibilities, the PCC introduced evidence that the enlarged canal had not actually attained its nominal dimensions, leading to the possibility of boats being "squeezed" at narrow points. This was a direct challenge to Russel Lord's competence, and he denied the accusations vigorously. In the spring of 1854 the PCC had sent a team of consultants over the canal to measure the prism, and it had documented many examples of inadequacy. In rebuttal, various D&H section supervisors argued that the measurements did not take into account the effects of a big snowstorm and had been made before the regular cleaning of the canal had been completed. Continuing the earlier paradox, they responded that the old canal was even more defective, with many places too narrow for boats to pass.

To the extreme distress of the D&H, the PCC introduced John B. Jervis as a witness. The D&H might have supposed that Jervis would place loyalty to his old employer and to his pupil Russel Lord first; but the engineer's rigid sense of integrity prevailed, and he testified that the canal contained many points of inadequacy. This evidence, along with the claims that the canal proportions were improper, appeared to tarnish Lord's professional reputation. It brought to mind Jervis's early endorsement of his students, in which he stressed Archbald's technical ability while citing managerial ability as Lord's strong point. The D&H lawyers were put in the unhappy position of trying to refute Jervis, making him admit that he had not always measured the canal and that visual observation could not determine the actual dimensions.[53] There must have been some substance to the PCC accusations, since in 1859——midway through the proceedings——the D&H had James McEntee experiment by passing two boats lashed together down the canal to demonstrate adequate width.[54] Further evidence is provided by the board's decision as late as 1857 to spend about $1000 to remove a projection of rock below the lock at Butler's Falls "to prevent boats wedging at that place."[55] The PCC contended (and the D&H denied) that many similar improvements had been necessary long after the enlargement was supposedly finished.

Like the European leaders who expected a quick seizure of the enemy capital despite knowing that the enemy had been preparing its defenses for years, the D&H attorneys were not initially prepared for a long campaign. Forced into trench warfare, they conducted a largely defensive battle. It was relatively easy to punch holes in the testimony of boatmen by revealing their lack of education and mathematical ability and pointing out inconsistencies once they were pulled away from the cover of their rehearsed presentation. On the other hand the D&H witnesses suffered equivalent casualties. Looking beyond the details, perhaps the most telling factor was that more than a hundred boatmen who had been contractors for the D&H were willing to testify against it. Whether or not they really believed they were faring worse on the enlarged canal (and many had not worked on both) they were clearly dissatisfied with their treatment by the company. Many had left home to try their luck boating coal on the Lehigh/Morris chain of canals.[56] The confusion on the unfinished D&H of 1850 with its abrupt changes of rates had been followed by drought in 1852 and nasty strikes among boatmen in 1853 and 1854. These walkouts, the most severe and best organized to date, emphasized economic issues. In a larger sense the boatmen, although many could not "figure," had some awareness that the company over the years had systematically fine-tuned rates to keep their compensation to a minimum. At the same time, although the amounts and the methods of calculating them were foreign, the boatmen had some knowledge of the company's lavish profits.

Again following the course of later military commanders, the D&H lawyers, sensing that they were losing, looked for a bold stroke or a secret weapon to reverse the course of events. In June 1860 they introduced the examination of John Wurts, which had been conducted two years earlier and held in reserve. The problem with this tactic was that the interrogatory had taken place in the early stages of the proceeding, before the direction and the doggedness of the PCC attack had become apparent. Wurts's responses were oddly detached, as if he wished to remain above the sordid fray. In many cases he was unable or unwilling to remember events. Because of his position, as well as his poor health, he was handled respectfully. It was not reasonable to expect that he would be able to provide additional enlightenment on topics such as the cost of towing lines, which had consumed several pages of transcript; but his recollection of negotiating the controversial agreement seemed hazy and did not improve with time. His greatest value was to lay out, as no one else could, the strategic considerations that produced the flawed alliance:

> I was anxious to have a railroad built through [Cobbs] gap, to connect with our canal, because there was agitation then in the Lackawanna Valley to have railroads built from the Valley in other directions, and a great deal of effort was made for such purpose; and our managing engineer there, Mr. Archbold [sic], expressed the opinion that if we didn't give encouragement to the proposed railroad . . . there would be a road built to reach the market in some other direction.[57]

At a special term the New York Supreme Court on September 25, 1860 limited the length of additional testimony and examination by each party.[58] It was probably only this ruling that kept the case from becoming literally interminable, and the final testimony was heard on May 17, 1861.[59] The actual judgment was not entirely satisfactory to either party and probably did not differ much from a compromise that could have been negotiated by the parties had they had the will to do so and had not personalities, especially Ewen's, interfered. In a decision handed down in 1863 the D&H was awarded 5 cents a ton additional toll for coal transported since July 28, 1853. By this decision, which *Century of Progress* delicately describes as "partly unfavorable" the D&H gained about $350,000 including interest, but lost over $700,000 it had sought to recover from the PCC.[60]

Often overlooked is the fact that this recognition of some savings from the enlargement was a partial defeat for the PCC, which had denied that concept altogether. Neither side was satisfied, and it appears that each appealed, extending the conflict more than a decade longer. Meanwhile the D&H brought additional actions, one of which was based on the claim that, by sending some of its coal over another route, the PCC was violating a commitment to make the D&H its sole outlet. These subsequent cases were an unmitigated disaster for the D&H, making the "partly unfavorable" assessment a ludicrous understatement. The issue of whether the PCC had committed a breach of contract by shipping some of its coal over a railroad reached the U. S. Supreme Court. There, however, it was dismissed so brusquely that it must have been embarrassing to the D&H lawyers.[61]

The core D&H argument fared no better in the various appeals courts. Judges interpreted the 1847 agreement as meaning that there had to be an overall saving in transportation costs before the provision that half the reduction attributable to the enlargement would be paid as tolls came into force. Since the overall cost had actually risen, there was no basis for attempting to calculate the effect of the enlargement. One judge conceded that there would have been a reduction except for general increases in the cost of labor and materials, but that was immaterial. In order to compare the old and new canals, the referee had followed what was termed an "uncertain, visionary, technical basis" to calculate what things *ought* to cost, rather than relying on the practical experience presented by actual freight rates. By this line of reasoning, the elaborate four-year, eight-volume effort to determine relative costs was utterly discarded; it had succeeded primarily in accumulating a massive midden for patient historians to dig. The last challenge by the D&H was blasted in 1872, fully 25 years after its agreement with the Wyoming Coal Association had been ratified.[62] This result was catastrophic for the D&H, although it is not possible to calculate the precise cost: in addition to losing the tolls it had hoped to collect, it had to pay court costs for its unsuccessful actions, as well as its legal expenses. Finally in 1874 the two companies negotiated a settlement. They dropped their various claims against one another, and the D&H refunded over $54,000 that it had collected between the time of the decision and its reversal.[63]

The Boats . . .

ONE OF THE MOST USEFUL CATEGORIES OF INFORMATION presented in the hearings concerns boats. It is also a subject that is less likely to be distorted by managed testimony. As with most aspects of operating the D&H Canal, the subject of boats is complex; one must be careful to specify which boats and which time period. In the years between the second and the last enlargement some 700-800 boats worked on the canal. These 50-ton boats measured 70 feet in length, 8 feet in width and about 5 feet in depth. They required about 175 days of labor and cost $400-450 to build. These boats were considered to have a service life of five years, which made it possible for some boatmen to pay them off and become owners. Between 1840 and 1853 it is estimated that one-fifth of the boats on the canal were privately owned in this way.

Boatbuilding at Booth-royd's dry dock, Phillip-sport. The man at the bow is holding a caulking hammer, more commonly pro-nounced "corking."
CREDIT
Minisink Valley Historical Soc.

During the winter of 1850-51 three to four hundred 50-ton boats were "hipped" to 14 foot width at a cost of $250 each. Although only a minimal installment was charged in 1852, and none in 1853, it proved difficult to find boatmen to take them. None remained in service after 1853. To the D&H this demonstrated in the most unequivocal way the cost advantage of the large boats. But the defense countered that it would simply have been unsafe as well as inefficient to run a small boat among the sluggish monsters that now populated the canal. A D&H official claimed that the company lost more than $237,000 on small boats that were scrapped when the canal was enlarged. The D&H was willing to experiment with different kinds of boats, but most of these trials were unsuccessful. It had 50 square-bowed section boats built to Lehigh Coal & Navigation standard design along the Lehigh Canal in the winter of 1849-50. Being made of pine they were cheap ($625) but unpopular with boatmen. The space between sections increased resistance and made the boats harder to maneuver and to free if they became stuck. In 1852 this style was "doubled" in an innovative way by making each half the stern section of a new scow. The second model scow, round-bowed and made of oak, was much more popular with boatmen after its introduction in 1854. Another test consisted of building what were called "lattice" boats due to their style of construction. No more than 28 of these were built, and they also proved unpopular.

While the hope that the enlargement would be finished in 1850 was not fulfilled, the impending completion created an enormous demand for boats. The PCC required 228 boats, and orders by the D&H brought the total to about 400. This far exceeded the capacity of yards along the canal, so many were built elsewhere. Boats built at Syracuse and Susquehanna, however, used unseasoned lumber and were considered to be "poor boats, both as to construction and materials." The PCC boats needed to be heavier because they were intended to be towed down the Hudson ("full river" boats). In 1853 boats of this type cost up to $1500, while the second-model scows cost about $900. Ordinarily the D&H sectional scows could be towed no farther than Rhinecliff, and that only in calm, fair weather; but as early as 1853 the company owned 132 boats capable of going onto the river. The 125-ton boats had a tare weight of 56 tons, obviously placing much greater strain on animals than the 14-tonners on the old canal. Like their small predecessors, these 125-ton boats were credited with a service life of five years, which was also assumed to be adequate to pay them off.

After the elimination of the last small boats in 1853, the number of boats on the canal during the remainder of the decade ranged from 1000 to 1100. In theory it would not seem to matter how many each company had, but a counsel for the D&H argued otherwise. In 1856, when the D&H and PCC together operated 1099 boats, he claimed that 684 would have been sufficient to handle the traffic. The excess was due to rival companies serving their immediate needs without attempting to coordinate. This seemed to summarize the hidden costs of a fierce rivalry that had not been anticipated and may not have been necessary.

Photographs of the D&H Canal are numerous, but almost all date from the last two decades of operation. As a result there are virtually no representations of several generations of early boats. Nor are any examples, or even major elements, likely to survive. Except insofar as there was a family resemblance among boats from any canal, there is no evidence of the thousands of boats which once served a risky and colorful pioneer enterprise.

. . . And Those Who Guided Them

As a statistical sample the cross-section presented in the hearings would not satisfy a rigorous sociologist. Having been made for tactical legal reasons, it is surely not a random sampling. At best it describes in detail only a 15- or 20-year segment of the canal's 70-year operating history. One boatman, Thomas Mathews, observed "There were many different people on the canal, and if they did not make money one season, they would try it again until some of them had to give it up entirely."[64] The hearings tended to emphasize people who had fairly long careers on the canal, ignoring those who drifted into boating only briefly. The reasons why people did not stay with it might have been instructive. Mathews regards them as failures, but some of them might have been clever enough to perceive that they were not making a good living on the canal. By the 1880s and 1890s anyone who attempted to build a career on the canal was certainly not making a wise economic choice.

One category of information that was explored exhaustively was wages. Sizable differences brought out in testimony are difficult to explain, except that they may be due to employing family members or the way board was calculated. After discarding figures at the extremes, wages for captains in the years 1847-49—the era

This Indenture, Made the *Thirteenth* day of *April* in the Year of our Lord One Thousand Eight Hundred and Fifty-*Five*, **BETWEEN** the President, Managers and Company of the **DELAWARE AND HUDSON CANAL COMPANY**, of the first part, by Russel F. Lord, their Attorney, and *R. L. Smith* of the town of *Mamakating* County of *Sullivan* and State of New York, of the second part.

Whereas, the said party of the second part has been appointed a Lock-Tender for Lock number (*48*) *Forty Eight* _____ on the New York Section of the Delaware and Hudson Canal, for and during the pleasure of said Company, and until the said appointment shall be revoked by a Notice for that purpose, from the President or Agent, or an Engineer or Superintendent of the said Company,

Now Therefore this Indenture Witnesseth, That the said party of the first part agree to pay to the said party of the second part, as and for his wages at and after the rate of *Forty Eight* Dollars per month, commencing at the opening of navigation and ending at its close, in each year, to be determined by the passage of the first canal boat in the Spring, and the last at the close of navigation, unless he shall be discharged from the said appointment and employment by the President, Agent, Engineer or Superindent, as aforesaid.

And the said party of the first part agree that the said party of the second part shall have the use and occupation of the Lock-House attached to said Lock during his continuance in the service of said Company as a Lock-Tender as aforesaid.

And the said Party of the second part Covenants and Agrees that he will well and faithfully discharge his duty as a Lock-Tender as aforesaid, and will safely keep and deliver up on demand, all such Property, Goods and Effects of said Company as may be put into his charge or custody, and during any suspension of the navigation by breaches or otherwise, if required, he will labor on the Canal under the direction of the Superintendents without extra compensation; that upon receiving a Notice of his discharge as above mentioned, he will immediately allow to such person as may be appointed and employed by the said Company to take charge of the said Lock as his successor, the use and occupation of a suitable room in the said Lock-House for his accommodation, and that within six days after receiving such Notice of his discharge as aforesaid, he will peaceably and quietly surrender the entire possession of the said Lock-House, with all Buildings, Garden and Appurtenances on the Lock, Embankments, or otherwise appertaining thereunto, without damage or injury thereto, unto the said party of the first part, or such other persons as may be appointed or authorized to receive the same.

And the said party of the second part further covenants and agrees for himself, his executors, administrators and assigns, that if he, they, or any of them shall remain in the possession or occupancy of the said Lock-House, or the Appurtenances, after the expiration of six days from his discharge from the service of the said Company as aforesaid, or if he, they, or any of them, shall refuse, neglect or fail to surrender the possession thereof peaceably as aforesaid, within six days after such discharge as aforesaid, that he or they, as the tenant or tenants of the said party of the first part, shall render and pay to them, the said party of the first part, at their office or place of business in the Village of Rondout, Ulster County, and State of New York, as and for the rent of the said Lock-House, the sum of five dollars for each and every day after the expiration of the said six days from the time of such discharge, the said rent to be paid daily at noon—the first payment to be made on the seventh day from and after such discharge as aforesaid—and the said party of the first part may distrain for the same without any previous demand, whenever any part shall be unpaid.

And the said party of the second part covenants and agrees, that in case he or any of his representatives or assigns shall fail or refuse after his discharge as aforesaid, immediately to allow to his successor a suitable room for his accommodation as above specified, then and in that case the above mentioned rent of five dollars per day for said Lock-House shall commence and become payable immediately upon such failure or refusal.

Signed and Delivered }
in Presence of }

Wm. C. Roe

THE PRESIDENT, MANAGERS AND COMPANY OF THE
DELAWARE AND HUDSON CANAL COMPANY,

By *R. F. Lord,* Attorney.

of 50-ton boats, range from $14 to $20 a month. Bowsmen earned $9 to $14 and drivers $4 to $8. In 1853, under the regime of 125-ton boats, captains made $18 to $30, bowsmen $14 to $17 and drivers $8 to $10. Another approach was taken by a boat owner in 1855, who paid a captain $130 a month, from which he had to cover all expenses. The duties of the bowsman, or second crewman, were described by one boatmen as including cooking, attending the bowline, steering in the morning if the captain had steered all night, and driving while the driver was eating.[65] Company regulations, on both the old and new canal, required three-man crews, but that provision was usually not enforced.

In most cases the wages included board. Again, there is a surprising range of data, with the monthly cost of board for a crew of three being given as $15 to $25 in 1849 and $18 in 1856. Some representative prices for edibles in 1849 were potatoes at 50 to 75 cents a bushel, butter 18 to 25 cents a pound, pork seven to eight cents a pound, and ham eight to ten cents. By 1853 many of these amounts had increased about 20%.[66] Boatmen who lived along the canal often brought their own supplies. It would be a serious error to assume that there was anything elegant about canal fare. The fact that the Culinary Institute of America is now located in the Hudson Valley has no connection with any foodways tradition carried over from the canal.

Another category of information that received great attention was the length of time required to make a round trip, with the resulting number of trips that could be made per season. This issue stimulated the parties, especially the PCC, to perform an accumulation and manipulation of statistics that may have had few precedents in legal history. Unfortunately, this same emphasis on data led to wrangling over

Winter hibernation at Rondout, where the towboat *Austin* and a flock of idle canal boats are shown locked in ice. Rondout contained a floating population of transient laborers, but most of the boatmen were probably local and spent the frozen season at domestic firesides in the canal towns, sometimes carrying on other trades or businesses or using their teams for carting. According to Bill McKelvey, the "Austin" was a 400-hp, 380-ton vessel built in 1853.
CREDIT
D&H RR Collection, NYS Library.

FACING PAGE
A D&H lock-tender contract signed by Russel Lord in 1855.
CREDIT
D&H Canal Museum.

Newspaper ad.
CREDIT
Bill McKelvey.

FACING PAGE TOP
The people walking the towpath, presumably crew members, appear to be black.
CREDIT
D&H Canal Museum.

FACING PAGE BOTTOM
A family boat tied up at the Delaware aqueduct.
CREDIT
D&H Canal Museum.

matters such as how to allow for detentions that makes it difficult to reach reliable conclusions. It seems fairly well established that on the "old canal" of the late 1840s it was possible for boatmen to make 14-16 round trips a season if they wished. Before the enlargements began it may have been possible to make as many as 18-20. With the large boats ten to twelve trips seems more common, although there was a great deal of disagreement. The fastest time listed for a round trip Eddyville-Hawley-Eddyville was seven days and seven hours, but that was a deliberate attempt to make a record. After an exhaustive processing of data a PCC expert witness concluded that the average trip of a small boat took 12.73 days, while a large one needed 18.23 days—a difference of 43%. A D&H expert, George F. Von Beck, who was paymaster and bookkeeper at Rondout, testified that in 1851, when both small and large boats operated on the canal, there was no essential difference in time: trips averaged slightly over 12 days. This appeared to confirm the PCC contention that fewer trips were being made than in the late 1840s and also seemed to support the argument that the large boats blocked the small ones from operating efficiently.

The D&H side, which had argued in effect that boatmen could scarcely make a living on the old canal, found no contradiction in stating that "There was a better class of boatmen, generally, on the old canal."[67] Presumably this was because in 1850, with 475 new boats commissioned, not enough experienced boatmen could be found along the line of the canal. The companies then "swept about six states to find boatmen, the greater number of whom were inexperienced in canal navigation."[68] Using even blunter language, D&H agent Lorenzo A. Sykes reported that most of the boatmen recruited from other canals "were of a class that were not able to get employment on the canals where they were, on account of their inefficiency and their bad character; they introduced insubordination and bad habits upon the line of our canal, the effects of which are still felt to a certain extent."[69] Nevertheless, other evidence indicates that a majority of the boatmen still originated along the D&H. Most of the boatmen called as witnesses bore family names familiar in the region. They were "anxious to have their boats near their homes," as one witness testified.[70] This was perfectly understandable, since they needed a place to live and a source of income during the four or more months the canal was frozen. Economic theory might suggest that living standards on all canals would approach equilibrium, since an individual dissatisfied on one could seek better opportunities elsewhere. On a largely isolated canal like the D&H such mobility seems to have been limited. Boatmen were tied down by a host of factors—among them roots in an area, investment in a boat, off-season employment, familiarity with the culture of a particular canal and a simple lack of imagination and lack of awareness of the world beyond the berm bank. The D&H thus can be classified as a "homeboy" canal, having little in common with the popular perception in which the "canawlers," almost like gypsies, were a breed apart, with a self-contained culture substituting for a settled community.

The increasing difficulty recruiting boatmen and growing economic pressures led to greater employment of female family members, a trend that became more pronounced in later decades. As might be expected, this development brought mixed reviews. A prominent D&H official who, however, did not actually operate

boats, observed that "both the small boats on the old canal, and the large boats on the new canal, substitute women and girls for men and boys, and we often find them the best boatmen."[71] In contrast a boatman acknowledged that women "that are naturally ingenious do steer canal boats," but added that in general "women are out of their element in steering boats, and it is more out of their sphere of business."[72] Other testimony confirms the presence of black ("colored") boatmen, although none were apparently called as witnesses.

Although some thought of themselves as equals, it would be an exaggeration to compare canal boat captains with sea captains. Many of the boat captains were semi-literate lads in their late teens or early twenties, although by then they had accumulated years of experience on the ditch. Just as people jocularly referred to the "raging Erie" or the "Morris Ocean," some boat captains assumed the ponderous dignity and self-importance of captains of proud liners. Even in the early 1900s, deep into the period of the canal's demoralization, Earl Mack recalls one boatman, "the fashion plate of the canal," who on Sunday tied his boat in a conspicuous place and went on deck dressed in all his finery so people could observe him in full splendor.[73]

Many young men were able to assume responsibility for a boat before they were 20 because by then they had been working on the canal more than ten years. There is abundant testimony that many boys began working as drivers before their tenth birthday. In their mid-teens they often graduated to bowsman. Many were members of farm families along the route, bringing in extra income——or at least providing their own subsistence. Perhaps there was an analogy to societies in which surplus boys went into the military or went away to sea. The system worked well enough as long as it remained a family matter, where the captain could look after younger brothers; under other conditions it offered potential for abuse.

This was especially troubling because it represented the kind of moral decay predicted by rustic skeptics when the canal was first announced. According to Johnston, "The canal was indeed a school for whatever was vile in human nature . . . . The tuition was chiefly to collect what they deemed smart vulgar words, sentences and defamations, to write lewd sentences and draw obscene pictures . . . in fact anything which they supposed offensive to decency."[74] Johnston's writing is so vivid and quotable that one is tempted to overlook his tendency to dip his pen in acid before applying it to paper. In this case, however, his denunciation receives support from a contemporary source. The writer of an 1851 travel guide presents the following description of the canal boys who labored on the D&H:

> . . . in a short time the mingled air of martyrdom and meditation stamped upon his visage on his first elevation to office gives way to an expression of blank stolidity, the result of his monotonous duties, while the constant exposure to the elements, and the corrupting intercourse of his older associates, make him, while still a child, old in constitution, morals, and disposition, taking from his young face every sign of boyish hilarity, and stamping there revolting traces of early dissipation of the vilest sort . . . . How listlessly he sits there, in a sort of *sun-struck* doze——his bloated young cheeks, his puffy eye-lids, and the glaring light nearly concealing his glazed eyes——a thing of hopeless inanition, save when he starts up to vent an imprecation upon his charger, or exchange a blackguard jest with some passing vagabond mounted like himself! No blithe country lad is he, with the exhilarating influences of nature's scenes acting upon young, excitable nerves and pulses! Premature bad brandy and tobacco have shriveled up such sensibilities.[75]

Mistreatment of canal boys became a recurrent scandal, but not one that was pursued to the point of eliminating the problem. A particularly deplorable incident in 1859, in which an orphan boy of 11 fell asleep from overwork and drowned in the canal, provoked editorial wrath:

> We have been credibly informed that many of the little sufferers are obliged to rise at four o'clock in the morning and remain at work until twelve at night . . . . This is beyond toleration even in adults. . . . The character of a large proportion of boatmen is noted as brutal and depraved to a degree. Many of the boys employed as drivers are orphans or worse than orphans, homeless, friendless, helpless, and entirely at the mercy of their employers. Is it strange, then, that in frequent cases these poor lads are cruelly overworked and abused? We say nothing of the terrible lessons of vice and depravity learned in their deplorable servitude.[76]

The editor concluded that the canal "affords a wide field for the philanthropist," but despite his wish "to soon hear of a reformation in this matter," no improvement was forthcoming. During the summer of 1870 three separate incidents of canal boys drowning occurred within a short space of time. In one instance a team of horses bolted, but the other two were the more frequent situation in which overtired boys walked or fell into the canal.[77]

Boys at work picking slate
in a coal breaker.
CREDIT
National Canal Museum.

There is no reason to believe that conditions improved as the canal entered its decline and the caliber of people working on it sank with it. Although the canal produced some material that would have delighted Horatio Alger, the fact that most children of canal families received only about three months of schooling a year was bound to be a limiting factor. One brilliant success story was Amos J. Cummings, a Honesdale boy who began his working career as a driver on the D&H and went on to become the editor of the *New York Sun*. This accounts for the relatively extensive coverage that paper gave the canal, but Cummings was only one of thousands of barefoot boys who trod the dusty towpath.

The company, with many moralistic men on its board, sought to counteract the tendencies toward depravity. It was characteristic for wealthy men at that time to accept an obligation to uplift the masses. Sanctimonious practices such as shutting down the canal on Sundays, placing a Bible on each boat, subsidizing a missionary to work among the boatmen, and donating land for churches gratified the Wurtses, with their ministerial heritage. In many respects the D&H displayed a "company town" image, vividly illustrated in 1836 when the board voted to donate $50 toward a bell for the Presbyterian congregation of Carbondale "upon condition that the Company shall have the privilege of using it at such hour during week days as it may deem necessary . . . in its business."[78] For these reasons the D&H differed from the boisterous, violence-prone folkways depicted by Walter Edmonds in his fictional accounts of the Erie Canal. Occasional violent incidents were recorded, as in 1873 when two boatmen, described as "large heavy men," while navigating through the Neversink Locks, attacked locktender Calvin Griffith, a man "considerably beyond the prime of life, and shamelessly beat him."[79] Then as now, it was the sensational exceptions that were recorded in the media, while the thousands of uneventful passages and even the majority of canal boys who labored within the observant confines of their families went unnoticed.

Despite periodic bursts of activity by missionaries, there could never be lasting reform as long as the number of saloons in canal towns remained at its extraordinary level. Even minuscule villages offered an impressive array of establishments: in 1835 Eddyville already listed three taverns.[80] In the 1850s Port Ben numbered four places where liquor was sold,[81] and even in the closing years of the canal there were said to be five saloons in High Falls and six in the otherwise undistinguished hamlet of Creek Locks.[82] Eddyville, an oasis which may have had as many as 14 watering holes, was by all accounts the champion of the sawdust league, and it is no wonder writers have referred to its "lusty, waterfront atmosphere."[83]

Perhaps the presence of so many of these taverns in close proximity to the canal contributed to the staggering number of drownings, considering that under normal conditions the depth of water never exceeded six feet. In 1872, by no means an exceptional year, 18 persons were drowned on the canal.[84] One cannot read nineteenth-century newspapers without concluding that the ability to swim was much less common than it is today. Since a vastly higher casualty toll on the railroads passed with little other than maudlin sentiment, fatalities on the canal did not lead to any corrective action. Similarly, pious hand-wringing over abuse of canal boys produced no improvements. With multitudes of "breaker boys" exhausting their childhood picking impurities out of coal, it was easy to rationalize that canal boys were no worse off. The Erie, a much more visible canal, was little better in this respect: generations of fervent moralizing had limited practical effect, although there may have been a more sustained effort to improve the lot of canal workers.[85]

Bluestone waiting shipment at the stone dock in Alligerville.
CREDIT
D&H Canal Museum.

An Artery of Commerce

IT WAS TYPICAL of the era that members of the privileged class were able to ignore the harsh and squalid aspects and direct their glance to the beauties of the passing scene. This was facilitated by the revival of a packet line in 1850, headed by the celebrated boat *The Fashion*. Although by then the expanding rail network intersected the canal at several points, there was still place for a passenger boat because no railroad paralleled the full route of the canal. In addition, a growing leisure class was able to travel simply for the novelty of the experience. One such person observed in 1856:

. . . there is a pleasure in sailing on this artificial river . . . . You glide along in this quick way for miles, at the base of a mountain, or by rocks, which rise perpendicularly at your side, to an elevation which throws into contempt the pigmy structures erected by man . . . . Thus you wind among the mountains, rising by locks you look out, expecting you are at or near the summit, but still around you and above you are eternal hills and still the water is of the same depth.

To those who love to contemplate nature in its grand, beautiful and picturesque features, these boats afford the greatest facilities; while the hills encircle you, you may see, now and then, in the valleys, . . . beautiful villages resounding with the voice of thriving industry and exhibiting marks of the successful enterprise of its inhabitants.[86]

It is noteworthy that industry was conspicuous enough to catch the attention of a casual observer. The D&H Canal may have begun as a navigational facility, but in its maturity it took on the characteristics of an irrigation project—encouraging economic growth along its route. Some of these industries exploited native resources: lumber mills, paper mills and tanneries from the still-abundant forests; grist mills and the tanneries using the agricultural wealth of the rich valley; and millstones, flagstones and bluestones from the looming hills. Other industrial activities had little or nothing to do with local resources. The Ellenville glass works and the Ellenville cutlery—the largest employers in town—and the axe factory started by the Southwicks at Napanoch are examples. The blast furnace and associated rolling mill and foundry established at Napanoch initially depended on local iron ore, but continued to operate with imported ore after the local supply proved inadequate. These enterprises owed their existence largely to the cheap, dependable transportation offered by the canal and the capital it generated.

Of the industries that arose to exploit local raw materials the most notable was the natural cement industry of the Rosendale area. Although it can be argued that natural resources have a way of being discovered sooner or later, so that the cement would have been exploited even if the canal had not appeared, the development of the industry is closely associated with the D&H. Rosendale is near enough to the Hudson that it would have been feasible to build a short canal or rail line solely to serve the cement industry even if the D&H Canal had not existed, but the fact remains that the canal and the cement industry were historical partners.

In time it was the industries, more than the canal itself, that contributed to the surging population of towns along the artery. From 1840 to 1850 the population of Wawarsing gained 2500 to reach about 6400, an increase of 64%.[87] By 1860 it had grown to 8300, a jump of another 30%.[88] Ellenville, the largest village in the town, numbered about 1500 people when it became separately incorporated in 1856 and had increased to about 3000 in 1870.[89] In signs of rapid maturation, the first newspaper in town was founded in 1849 and the first bank was organized in 1863. With the cement industry booming, Rosendale grew by 800 people (30%) in a decade to reach a figure of 3625 in 1870. Similar astonishing gains could be seen in Rondout, while Port Ewen, which was developed from virtually nothing by the Pennsylvania Coal Co. in 1851 boasted a population of about 1300 ten years later.[90]

Virtually every canal lock spawned a settlement of some sort, usually featuring a store, the inevitable bar, possibly other shops and craftsmen, and sometimes boat builders. Several, which grew up in previously uninhabited territory, had "port" in their name, inserting a startling nautical atmosphere into the midst of placid farmland. In the town of Wawarsing alone Port Benjamin, Port Hixon and Middleport (Kerhonkson) sprouted from the fields, while Napanoch "grew as if by magic."[91] Port Ben, a hamlet which almost certainly would not have come into

Rondout in the 1890s. Before the coming of the D&H this was a placid, almost deserted "strand." The building prominent on the water's edge is the D&H lower office, from which the unloading of boats was supervised.
CREDIT
D&H Canal Museum.

being without the canal, had three stores in 1843, was an important shipping point for bluestone and forest products and did some boatbuilding.[92] Deerpark is probably representative of the small places along the waterway. When construction of the canal began it was a quiet town of 963 inhabitants, with a total assessed valuation of $136,764. By 1861, one long generation later, the combined population of Deerpark and Port Jervis, which had been separated from it, was 8209 and the valuation had burgeoned to $1,443,314.[93]

The growth of Rondout, attributable almost entirely to the canal, was phenomenal by any standard. In its boisterous youth it was known more for raw energy than elegance. Its inhabitants were primarily "hard laborers and those of foreign birth," living in "clusters of shanties, with here and there a more pretentious but scarcely more lasting building."[94] But the ever-increasing activity of the canal was an engine that pulled Rondout to greater prosperity. By 1843 it reportedly exceeded in tonnage any river port between New York City and Albany.[95] It also surpassed the rest of Kingston in population, so that the older town could no longer contain its lusty offspring. In 1849, when Rondout was separately incorporated, it immediately became the most populous town in Ulster County. An entry in an 1861 gazetteer observed that "Its appearance is much improved . . . . It contains 8 churches, a bank and newspaper office," and a population of nearly 6000.[96] Even in 1847 the waterfront had filled up with bustling stores, shops and hotels, and new construction, more substantial than the earlier shanties, was scaling the adjacent hills.[97] Rondout won the competition to dominate the passenger steamboat service down the Hudson. After the canal was completed a night boat line began running twice a week from the nearby port of Twaalfskill. Five years later this boat line transferred to Rondout. Eventually six-day-a-week service to New York was available.[98]

In addition to contributing to an increase in absolute numbers, the canal helped increase diversity. Irish immigrants, impelled by grim economic necessity, have always been associated with the canal era—and also, unfortunately, with the tradition of excessive reliance on strong drink. Speaking of Sullivan County, Quinlan writes that "After the completion of the Delaware and Hudson canal, Ireland added largely to the population of the valley."[99] Rondout was "at an early period of its growth, a maze of crooked lanes bordered by rude shanties and inhabited by a floating population of Irish laborers. The village still [1861] contains a large proportion of Irish, and has a large and increasing number of German inhabitants."[100] The population of recent immigrants was probably not distributed evenly along the canal, for Child's directory lists only 27 presumably Irish surnames among its 973 individual entries for Wawarsing in 1871.[101]

In Pennsylvania the D&H irrigated the same kind of economic fertility. By 1850 Honesdale, starting from virtually nothing, had attained a population of 2263, and in 1880 reached around 8000, considerably more than its present count. Honesdale took on the attributes of a settled, prosperous place, with a bank, hotels, iron works and numerous stores and other businesses. For reasons not immediately obvious, cigars were manufactured in town. More important, as Leslie points out, was the construction of canal boats; in 1868-69 one yard near Honesdale built 60 boats.[102]

Carbondale ascended, but at a lower trajectory: although in 1850 its population of 4945 was substantially higher than Honesdale's, by 1880 it had been overtaken. On the surface it seemed to have maintained the growth the D&H had boasted of

Asa S. Clyne's store on the canal at Port Ben. The man in the center may be Clyne, who it is said weighed 200 pounds when he joined the Union Army and came home at half that after surviving Confederate captivity at Andersonville.
CREDIT
D&H Canal Museum.

in the early 1830s and fulfilled the expectations of its founders, yet a tone of unmistakable disappointment was visible. As early as 1875 Hollister observed—perceptively, as it turned out—that Carbondale "has probably attained its meridian."[103] What Hollister grasped intuitively, a later historian, Burton W. Folsom II, examined in detail. Seeking to explain why Carbondale had lost its early advantage and been displaced by Scranton as the leading city of the valley, he found that it was overly dependent on the D&H and New York City capital. As a result, it "never developed a strong local elite which could attract or finance new industries to promote diversification."[104] Scranton emerged as the only city in the Lackawanna region capable of self-sustained growth. It overtook Carbondale and drew away many of the older town's most ambitious citizens.

Archbald remained a village dominated by coal. In this early 1860s view, even substantial houses are overshadowed by a coal breaker. Photo by Johnson.
CREDIT
National Canal Museum.

Down the valley, in an example of a process that was repeated many times in the coal district, the opening of mines led to the rise of the village of Archbald at a virtually uninhabited site. In September 1845 developers Daniel Bacon and John P. Farnham advertised lots "handsomely located in the new village of Archbald . . . adjacent to the new mines of the D&H Canal Co."[105] This situation provided material for Charles Silkman's mercilessly satirical pen. Archbald, owing to its founding, was pro-D&H during the controversies of the mid-1840s, and a meeting in favor of the company was held there on March 2, 1846. Silkman was inspired to respond that " 'the village of Archbald' from the best information we can get, has, we believe, *eight* inhabitants (when all at home) that the 'respectable number of the citizens of Lackawanna valley,' held a meeting at this 'village' of one dwelling, one store-house, and one barn, numbered *seventeen*, [Nathan] Smith's traveling Committee included."[106] If Carbondale could not overcome its "company town" origins to attain independent growth, there was less hope for a later settlement like Archbald to become more than a small mining community.

> **MILES L. TRACY, Esq.,**
>
> Paymaster, Canal Department,
>
> *SIR :--I have received from you, per hands of* ....
>
> *Superintendent Foreman,* .... *Dollars and* .... *Cents, in full for* .... *days'*
>
> *labor, rendered the* **DELAWARE & HUDSON CANAL COMPANY,** *on the* .... *Division*
>
> *of their Canal, during the Month of* .... *, 187 , at* .... *Dollars and* .... *Cents*
>
> *per day, and I hereby authorize him to receipt the said amount on your Pay Rolls, and this shall be*
>
> *your sufficient receipt for the same.*
>
> ...., 187 .

CREDIT
D&H Canal Museum.

While other businesses rose, the canal itself continued to provide a stable core of employment. Durfee lists by name large numbers of D&H employees in and around Carbondale, while McAndrew does the same for the PCC at Hawley.[107] This is a rich lode for genealogists, but also testifies to the economic impact of the transportation companies on the community. Work on the D&H was often a lifetime commitment. George A. Whiting spent most of his career as agent of the D&H "in the purchase and management of the horse department, overseeing the teaming, etc.."[108] This was an era of implied contract between companies and supervisory or skilled employees, in which men understood that in return for dedicating their working lives to the company's interest they would enjoy relatively secure and respectable employment.

The canal companies would be expected to be the main employer in towns such as Carbondale, Honesdale, Hawley and Rondout, but their impact was powerful in smaller places along the line. Figures from the 1860 census for the three towns the D&H passed through in Sullivan County---Mamakating, Highland and Lumberland---give striking proof of this:[109]

Mamakating		Highland		Lumberland	
Boatman	103	Boatman	14	Boatman	11
Watchman	7	Watchman	5	Canalman	2
Lock Tender	8	Lock Tender	6	Lock Tender	1
Boat Builder	13	Boat Builder	1	Boat Builder	6
Ship Carpenter	1	Carpenter	1		
Forwarder	1	Laborer	7		
Boat Calker	1	Agent	1		
Boss	1	Overseer	2		

McCausland's Ship Yard, Dry Dock and Saw Mill, Rondout.
CREDIT
National Canal Museum.

A decade later the impact seemed to have diminished in the important canal town of Wawarsing (which includes Ellenville). Of some 973 individual listings for the town in Child's 1871 directory, only 44 were canal-based occupations (including boat builders, keepers of stores along the canal, etc.) There were 14 businesses engaged predominantly in supplying canal needs. The directory, of course, does not attempt to be as thorough as the census. Perhaps surprisingly, 535 persons were still engaged whole or part-time in agriculture, but even here the influence of the canal was strongly felt. As a 1907 history of Ulster County summarizes (referring to the town of Rochester) "The opening of the canal . . . gave an opportunity to place agricultural products in the larger market."[110] Similar developments could be seen in the Lackawanna Valley, although it had relatively less good agricultural land. Durfee called the coming of the D&H a "God-send to the entire valley," for it "opened up a great market for the product of the valley, especially of their flour."[111]

Merchandise traffic remained gratifying, as shown on Tables 1 and 2. Table 2 shows an astonishing variety of goods being shipped from Ellenville in 1843; coal may have been the "bread and butter" but there was certainly an abundance of condiments. In 1869 Jacob Hermance purchased the famous Merchants and Tanners freight line from J. H. Tuthill & Son. Assets included eight canal boats, 14 mules, a freight house and docks at Rondout, and the lease of a dock at the foot of Jay Street in Manhattan.[112] Hermance in turn sold out to Reuben Van Sickler in 1876. A warehouse in Ellenville used by this business survived until 1988.[113]

One of the most revealing, if unintentional, testimonials to the value of the canal is contained in a petition to the state legislature by inhabitants of Marbletown in 1844. These residents of Marbletown (which includes High Falls) appealed for a bridge over Rondout Creek immediately above the falls

for the accommodation of a greater portion of the inhabitants in said town and the town of Olive for the carrying of wood, lumber, grain, and such other articles as they may have occasion to market and have carried by the Delaware and Hudson canal from this place, where there is a very considerable business done, having two large flouring mills in successful operation and a third almost compleated, an extensive iron foundry in operation, a large tannery, and a vast water power unemployed, three houses in the mercantile business, besides a considerable business done in manufacturing of water lime or cement, of which a large quantity abounds at this place, and also the burning and making stone lime in large quantity of the best quality for a building material, and which is being extensively used as a manure . . . [commas added][114]

With the exception of a few illustrious personages like Washington Irving and Philip Hone, it is difficult to contend that the canal itself introduced a more refined human element. Unlike the Erie, the D&H was not a great mover of people. Throngs of fervent New Englanders, conditioned by two centuries of introspection to seek earthly or heavenly salvation, did not migrate over the D&H, so it experienced no equivalent of the "Burned-over District" that bordered the Erie. However, the wealth it created contributed to a vigorous blossoming of all sorts of artistic and educational activities in the port towns, with schools, newspapers, lyceums and cultural societies springing up as if fertilized by the murky waters of the ditch. A private academy was founded in Ellenville in 1853, while Napanoch gave rise to a literary association and a lyceum. Blumin devotes many pages to describing the abundance of social and improvement associations that flourished at Rondout after 1845.[115] Rondout, with a population of at least 6000, was probably enjoying its peak period in the 1860s. The famous historical popularizer Benson J. Lossing, a Poughkeepsie resident, found the mouth of Rondout Creek

continually crowded with vessels engaged in carrying coals and other commodities. Immense piers have been erected in the middle of the stream for the reception and forwarding of coal. Here, and in the vicinity, are manufactories of cement, and also extensive quarries of flagstone——all of which, with the agricultural products of the adjacent country, giving freights to twenty steamboats and many sailing vessels. Lines of steamers run regularly from Rondout to Albany and New York, and intermediate places, and a steam ferry-boat connects the place with the Rhinebeck Station.[116]

Tannery on the canal at Sparrowbush along the Delaware. It was built by Morris Schultz and later owned by Cooper & Swazey. After being closed for a few years, it was re-opened by David Hammond. Under the Norris Leather Corp. and the Crowhurst Leather Co. it lasted into the early 1900s. Tanneries were another means of providing solid local employment from natural resources, but at a cost of stripping hillsides over a wide region.
CREDIT
Photo and information courtesy Norma Schadt, Deerpark Town Historian.

Capital, whatever its excesses, often served the arts, and this was true indirectly of the D&H. Jervis McEntee, son of early D&H engineer James McEntee and named for another famous engineer, was born in the year the canal was completed and grew up to become an important "Hudson River" painter. Beyond his actual artistic output, he helped hold the movement together with his circle of personal contacts. The wealth accumulated by D&H board member Lynde Catlin helped finance his son George's study and paintings of western Americana.[117]

More important than any commodity it carried, the D&H brought the intangible cargo of change. Furthermore, it was a change controlled in New York City, so that the locals who were most affected had little power to influence its direction. This was recognized in an acute and personal way by John W. Johnston, who lived through most of it. He recalled that while the young generation welcomed the novelty, many of the older folk "intently wedded to their unpretentious homes and meager possessions, preferred the sociable, harmonious life, which, though contracted and scanty, long usage and experience had endeared to them."[118] Subsequent events proved that their misgivings were not entirely unfounded, for any alteration in established patterns is bound to have some adverse effects. Some communities were greatly benefited—or created—but others were left to wither on a dying branch. Quinlan writes that Bloomingburg, in Sullivan County, "was a place of considerable business" until the coming of the canal sent it into decline.[119] In Pennsylvania Bethany and Dundaff gave way to Honesdale and Carbondale, much as New England hilltop towns slid downhill when industry and transportation settled in the valleys. Later in the cycle, Hawley entered a rapid decline after the completion of the Erie branch. Homowack in Ulster County, once an important center for teaming to the canal, was largely displaced when the railroad came.[120]

Those who considered that they had been harmed by the D&H had no hesitation about resorting to the courts. Numerous inhabitants of Orange and Sullivan Counties filed a petition in 1834 in which these neighbors of the D&H claimed that "owing to the bad construction of the canal, and the imperfect state of the basins, and the improper construction and location of the waste weirs, and the careless and negligent manner in which the water is occasionally let out of the canal, they are subject to great damage and inconvenience," etc.[121] Although the petition was dismissed on legal grounds, the complaint of the abutters accords with other evidence about the poor condition of the canal in its first years and shows that it was hardly a source of universal joy. Similar controversy arose as a result of the enlargements. Latent hostility toward the D&H, aggravated by sensitivity over property rights, flared up when members of the Cuddeback family threatened a party under engineer Samuel B. Farnum with pistols if they stepped on family land near Pine Woods.[122] Two of the Cuddeback boys were apparently jailed for a time, but later there were moves to calm the dispute by building an extra bridge or making a cash payment—a small contribution to the cost overruns on the third enlargement.[123] In 1852 John Henry Burgy of Port Hixon sued the canal company for $5000 for loss of acreage and other damages. Although Burgy was represented by one of the most powerful citizens of Ulster County, the jury ruled in favor of the canal company and required the plaintiff to pay costs of $137.82.[124] In the following year the owner of a mill on the Rondout sued—also without success—after the D&H raised the level of its dam at Eddyville.[125] On other occasions the D&H was the injured party. In 1841 Russel Lord complained to the owners of a leather factory at Beatysburg that their bark (used in tanning) was clogging the channel. In his letter the engineer observed that the company "would regret very much to be under the nesesaty [sic] of resorting to a legal remedy."[126] The intrusion of a major institution like the canal was bound to have far-reaching, varied and unpredictable effects.

Even during the busiest years of the canal there was room for packet and excursion boats. The new packet *The Fashion*, with a capacity of 100 passengers, created a sensation when it went up the canal for the first time in June 1850. Its passage gave the usually reserved editor of the *Rondout Courier* a chance to revel in the opulence that was gradually replacing the democratic simplicity of the early republic:

> Those who know nothing of the economical adaptation of space, and compact and elegant fitting up of a packet, would be astonished at the capacity and comfort of the Fashion. There is a forward saloon, connected with the dining saloon by a passage through an apartment formed for the storage of beds and bedding during the day. The saloons are richly furnished and carpeted, the forward one in perfect boudoir style.[127]

Later in the history of the canal, after the PCC had eased congestion by removing its traffic, the use of the waterway by pleasure craft arose. In 1872 John Lester Burton of Port Jervis fitted up a packet named the *Dyberry*, with a capacity of 400. It was meant for use by picnic and excursion parties and, unlike the *Fashion*, made no pretense of running a regular passenger schedule. "In these sweltering days when one's thoughts naturally turn to cool groves and shady places, we are reminded that the Dyberry offers to our people a very pleasant manner of reaching many of the delightful groves near our village," enthused the editor.[128] The vessel was a success in 1872, but in the following year, in a significant turn of events, Burton transferred his excursion business to the newly constructed Port Jervis & Monticello RR. Pleasure traffic on the canal continued, however, especially as traditional uses slowed. Private boats were often rented by the multitude of social organizations that flourished in the late nineteenth century for outings and fundraising efforts. One private vessel, the *Iowa* made a memorable and much-photographed cruise in 1891. Recreational use of the waterway, though of minor importance on the old canal, is one of the few elements of continuity with the present day.

They might listen for the noise of hundreds of boatmen, the sounds of whose voices and the music of whose horns echoed from the mountains and hills.

Railroaders at the Tiller

IN 1858, the year John Wurts's tenure as president came to an end, the D&H Canal rested at a symbolic point of balance. It had been in operation for 30 years, and it had 40 years of existence remaining. In its first 30 years the company had experienced phenomenal, if by no means uninterrupted, growth. Over the next 40 years it would increase in size and complexity, but its character would change. As it evolved into a railroad company the canal and gravity railway declined through a long twilight of obsolescence toward extinction. No single factor caused this fundamental change, although it was actively pursued by two strong-willed leaders. It was the outcome of a series of events set in motion by the conflict with the Pennsylvania Coal Co. and accelerated by broad economic and technological trends.

It would be a mistake to assume that the D&H managers were so absorbed with the PCC case that the company stagnated in other respects. The grinding legal struggle consumed the energies of several lawyers and probably weighed on the minds of the managers like a dull ache, but did not bring other activity to a standstill. An important consideration is that the D&H seemed genuinely to believe in the merits of its case and was confident of a favorable outcome. If the PCC suit was like a migraine, at least there was hope for relief.

In the early and mid-1850s the D&H continued to acquire coal lands, gradually creeping southward in the Lackawanna Valley. It also began another round of improvements to the gravity railway. As the earlier stages of remodeling had challenged and ultimately enhanced the reputation of Archbald, this campaign gave Charles Pemberton Wurts his opportunity. Under his supervision the line was largely rebuilt between Carbondale and Waymart, adding to the perplexity of any modern guide who attempts to describe the railway at a given time. The number of ascending planes was increased from five to eight; six of them were double-tracked; and new tracks for the light track were built.[1] As part of this project, the strap rail and hemp rope dating to the early years of the system were replaced with T-rail and wire rope.[2] The durability of the old materials was amazing, but their continued use had given the company a backward image.

Under the original conception the rebuilding was supposed to have been combined with an extension to reach what were called "the Company's lower coal lands in the Lackawanna Valley." At a meeting on February 15, 1856 the board decided to postpone the extension until further information "in regard to the coal formations" could be obtained.[3] Three months later the board appropriated $2000 for William J. Roberts of Philadelphia to make a "topographical and geological survey" of the coal lands.[4] Renewing the company tradition of respecting outside scientific opinion, the board seemed determined to avoid repeating the disastrous

FACING PAGE
Jim Jackson, shoveler at Rondout.
CREDIT
D&H Canal Museum.

Plane No.3, where the light track crossed over the loaded track, between Carbondale and Waymart.
CREDIT
National Canal Museum.

FACING PAGE
Henry D. Rogers's 1857 map of the coal fields and their transportation routes. Iron ore around Danville is indicated, as is the "Beach Woods" through which Henry Drinker had long attempted to thrust a rail line. The DL&W RR in Pennsylvania, completed only a year before, is shown quite accurately, but its New Jersey connection is stylized at best. A relatively straight shot from Dover to the Water Gap did not come into being until the DL&W Cutoff was opened in 1911.

error of ten years earlier in which, relying on the intuition of Archbald and Clarkson, it had dismissed the lucrative coal fields around Scranton. A valuable but perhaps also threatening recent precedent had been provided by Scranton-based interests, which had commissioned Pennsylvania State Geologist Henry D. Rogers to survey their coal lands.[5]

Roberts evidently gave a favorable evaluation, and on February 26, 1858 the board authorized an extension to what was called "Dolph Ridge," now in the town of Olyphant—one of the last municipalities named for a leader in the coal industry. The board also approved the issuance of $250,000 in medium-term bonds to pay for the improvement. The extension, about six miles long, was completed within a year and cost about $300,000 including equipment.[6] Although his personal position toward it is unknown, this was the last major advance undertaken during John Wurts's presidency. He was replaced by George Talbot Olyphant on March 31, 1858.

Despite the progress made in the closing years of Wurts's tenure, there was a cautious, hesitant quality to it, as if the infirmities of the leader extended throughout the company. The state of affairs was not at all satisfactory to the dynamic Olyphant. Writing nearly a decade later, he said of conditions at the time of his accession that "it required no sagacity to discover, very soon, what was in fact . . . a secret only to the members of this Board, that we were close to the point of exhaustion."[7] The situation was described even more starkly a few months later in the report of a special committee, undoubtedly influenced by Olyphant:

> The illness of his predecessor, who for five years had felt himself unfitted for the post and had repeatedly urged the Board to relieve him from its responsibilities had introduced inefficiency in many departments and a want of that harmonious working, so essential to prosperity, while the officers and Managers of the Com-

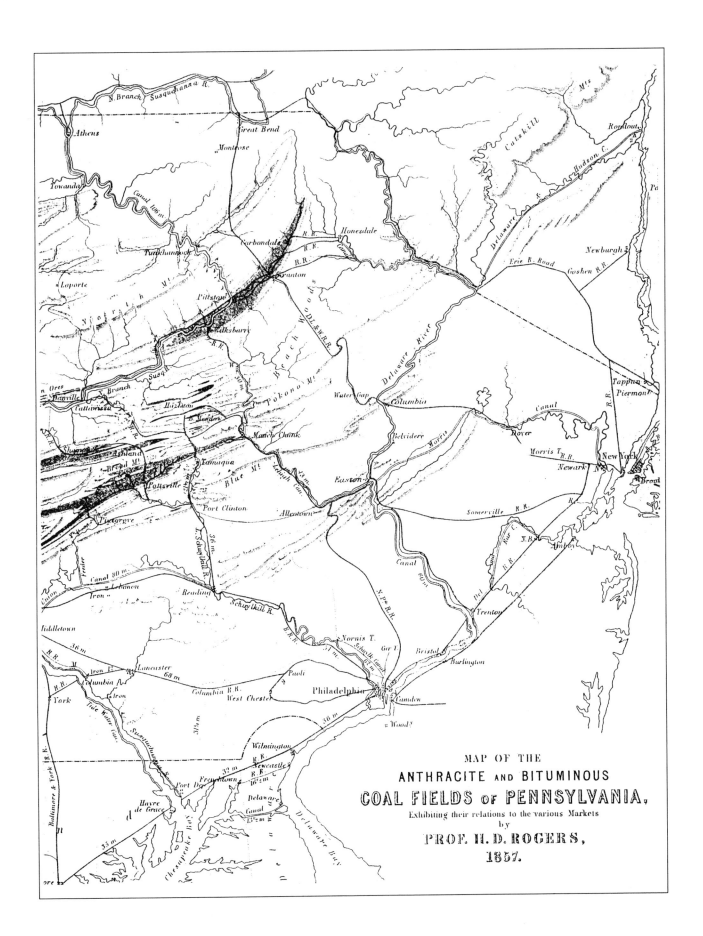

MAP OF THE
ANTHRACITE AND BITUMINOUS
COAL FIELDS OF PENNSYLVANIA,
Exhibiting their relations to the various Markets
by
PROF. H. D. ROGERS,
1857.

pany seemed the only persons ignorant of the facts largely proclaimed by rival companies and dealers in coal stocks that the mines of the Del. & Hud. C. Co. were well nigh exhausted.[8]

Freed of the restraints associated with the ailing Wurts, Olyphant wasted no time driving the stagnating company in the direction he felt it had to go. It is probably safe to assume that the railway extension was approved on his initiative although he was not yet officially in charge. This confident, activist policy was all the more remarkable because it began at a time when the panic of 1857 had created a bleak short-term outlook. As the economy became more centralized and industrialized, it became more interconnected. A decline in commerce meant that fewer steamboats were being built and that existing ones made fewer runs, which had immediate effects on the demand for coal. Olyphant ignored the recession and plunged ahead with his program of enlarging the company's coal resources. On June 3, 1859 the board accepted Olyphant's offer to sell it 2100 acres in Luzerne, Wayne and Susquehanna counties "understood to be valuable coal lands."[9] It is possible that he had purchased these lands as a proxy for the D&H; more likely he and his family already owned them, and this independent wealth accounts in part for the self-assurance he showed in guiding the D&H board. The proposed acquisition was so huge that it exceeded the territory the company was authorized to own. Ever mindful not to arouse dormant hostility, the D&H was careful to obtain a supplement to its Pennsylvania charter allowing it to hold an additional 3000 acres. Having accomplished that formality, it proceeded to purchase a total of 3500 acres (the 2100 owned by Olyphant individually, plus another 1400 in which he was a joint owner).[10]

Next, Olyphant persuaded the board to extend the railway from its terminus in the village named for him to what was called the Van Storch property in Providence. A bond issue of $600,000 was approved for this purpose.[11] The significance of this move lay not in the length of the railroad (only about four and a half miles), but in the fact that it was to be locomotive-powered. Olyphant sensed that the transition to steam railroading would have to be taken in very gradual steps. One of the first two locomotives, built by the closely allied Dickson company, was named C. P. Wurts. Continuity was thus given its due, but Olyphant knew the direction he wanted to go.

The history of these extensions is confusing to unravel because they were done in increments. Another complication results from the fact that the dates for beginning or improving passenger service are easily confused with the dates for completing the line to a particular point. Regular passenger trips were being made to Olyphant from Carbondale in November 1859.[12] At nearly the same time the D&H board gave formal approval for the extension to Providence. Olyphant had begun work on this in July, based on the concurrence of individual members.[13] Wurts almost certainly would not have operated in this irregular way; it is a testimony to Olyphant's self-assurance. In the early months of 1860 the line gradually crept toward Scranton.[14] It was reported in February that passenger cars had begun running to Providence, within two and a half miles of Scranton.[15] This news item, cited by Steers, is puzzling; for while it purrs that "The cars are elegant and comfortable, well cushioned and well warmed," it adds that "they run by gravity on fair locomotive time." This could mean that service initially was provided by gravity equipment and that locomotives did not arrive until later.

As the railroad advanced, the stage lines that had fed it gradually retreated until the need for them disappeared altogether. After the railroad reached Providence,

Valley Junction, where the locomotive line met the gravity railway, was an obscure place, but vital to the expanding D&H. Photo by Johnson,
CREDIT
National Canal Museum.

there was little purpose left for the stages from Carbondale, and the proprietors gave up the run down the valley. The significance of this change was described as an "index" by a local newspaper. In a revealing and somewhat poignant article the writer recognized that the relentless American mania for speed has a cost, but the overriding belief in technological progress and the fear of being left behind seemed to offer no choice but go along—to board the train, as it were:

> The revolution in the mode of travel which has been going on through the country for some years has finally arrived at our doors, and is destined to obliterate the old landmarks. The old stage coach has been so long associated with all our ideas of travelling, that it seems like parting with an old friend. It was, too, an accommodating friend. It took us up at our own doors and there safely left us on our return. It did not whirl us off at the rate of 20 or 30 miles an hour, as if in a hurry to get us away from home, and anxious to get rid of us, but took us easily and gracefully some 4 or 5 miles an hour which used to be thought quite fast enough for steady people to travel. It will not do for this fast age. Other people travel faster, and it will not answer to have them get ahead of us. We must progress until we can keep time with the fastest of them. We must keep up with the age. We must dash through to New York and Philadelphia in the time we used to spend very pleasantly in going to Wilkes-Barre without the least idea that we were loitering, or suspecting that we had spent a day doing what we should have accomplished in an hour. Those old days of quiet action, enjoyment and leisure are gone, and we Rip Van Winkle-like, must wake up . . . . We have to part with old friends. We will gratefully acknowledge past favors, assure them of our best wishes for the future, and take our place resolutely among the wide-awake actors of 1860.[16]

Any remaining uncertainty about the identity of the company had been resolved in Olyphant's mind. It had clearly become a coal company in which canals and railroads were part of the marketing apparatus. Whether or not there was a conscious decision to downgrade the canal, its relative importance diminished as production increased and new markets were developed. Perhaps Olyphant, with his independent resources and unhampered by long ties to the D&H, was free to form a more objective opinion. He was capable of taking a magisterial view of the industry and reading the signs of change.

One portent that almost certainly made a deep impression on him, although it has been overlooked by other writers on the D&H, was the completion of the Delaware, Lackawanna & Western (DL&W) RR. Members of the Scranton family, assisted by individuals hostile to the D&H, had succeeded in obtaining a railroad charter in 1848. It was only after gaining financial backing from New York City, particularly banker Moses Taylor, and West Jersey magnate John I. Blair, that railroad plans for the burgeoning town of Scranton could move forward. Combining new and old charters as the DL&W, a complete line of railroad was driven from Binghamton, New York, on the Erie RR, through Scranton to the Delaware Water Gap. With extraordinary boldness and cunning Blair had formed a connection over the Warren RR in New Jersey to reach the Central RR of New Jersey, which provided access to New York harbor.[17] The portion from Scranton to the Water Gap resembled Henry Drinker's old Susquehanna & Delaware charter so closely that the DL&W thought it advisable to give him a token payment of $1000 to quiet any claim.[18] Unlike many railroad dreamers Henry Drinker lived to see trains steaming along the approximate routes he had envisioned, although the benefits he derived were mainly spiritual.

Completion of the DL&W in 1856 opened the first competing outlet from the Lackawanna Valley. As such it represented a failure of the D&H policy of discouraging rivals by enlarging and opening up its canal. As John Wurts had foreseen, failure to monopolize traffic out of the Lackawanna Valley had led to the creation of a powerful rival. An additional threat lay in the fact that this competitor used a supposedly more efficient form of power. Whatever D&H managers thought privately about this development, they chose not to acknowledge it publicly; the company's annual reports avoid mention of the DL&W.

The threat posed by the DL&W, with its new route to the Jersey side of the Hudson, may have been a factor in encouraging the D&H to construct a huge dock and storage yard at Weehawken, NJ, between 1859 and 1861.[19] Although this site was convenient to railroads, the yard did not necessarily represent a move to diminish the importance of the canal. With the industry expanding so rapidly, the old batch methods of storing coal in small city yards and on boats was clearly inadequate. Perceptive as always, Olyphant understood that he needed to expand storage capacity to keep pace with his projected increases in production and to smooth out seasonal fluctuations.

A request by Carbondale residents in November 1859 for the D&H to extend its railroad through to Scranton to make a connection with the DL&W may be taken as an ominous sign, showing the magnetic attraction that Scranton and its new railroad were beginning to exert.[20] The D&H was not in a strong position to refuse, though it was not until late 1861, by which time the Civil War was raging, that Olyphant was authorized to obtain an estimate for the final extension to Scranton.[21] The line was probably completed during 1862, though it may not have operated at its full capacity until later.[22] This is suggested by the fact that in early 1863 the chief engineer requested $16,600 for 100 new coal cars to equip the extension.[23]

The PCC helped push the D&H toward becoming a railroad, although it was an indirect shove. In itself, the irritation provoked by the PCC did not sour the

D&H managers on their canal. Quite the opposite was true, for the canal as a mechanical entity was functioning with considerable success. Beginning in 1853, the year the enlargement was essentially completed, the canal regularly carried over 900,000 tons of coal yearly. In most years through 1860 the PCC portion exceeded that of its host.[24] With two companies cooperating only to the minimum degree necessary, this was a remarkable achievement. It would have flabbergasted those who had scoffed at visionary predictions that the system would one day carry 100,000 tons or who recalled the weary struggle to attain a capacity of 200,000 tons.

Instead, the PCC influenced the course of the D&H largely by example. A little-known but suggestive episode points out the direction of the PCC's thinking as early as 1853, when the unsatisfactory trend of relations with the D&H was already evident. Never lacking in boldness, President Ewen was investigating the possibility of constructing a gravity railway across New Jersey to the Hudson—some 140 miles! Toward this end he acquired the dormant charter of the New Jersey Hudson & Delaware RR, which had been renewed in 1842.[25] Ewen enlisted the support of Abram S. Hewitt, a youthful New Jersey iron manufacturer and son-in-law of the illustrious Peter Cooper. Hewitt, whose notable career as a political reformer lay far in the future, had built a flimsy animal-powered tram line from his mines at Andover to the Morris Canal at Waterloo, New Jersey. In 1853 he was engaged in converting this to a steam railroad and extending it to the Sussex County seat of Newton. Always ready to welcome railroad connections (as long as his own interests were protected) he spoke in behalf of Ewen's grandiose scheme and allowed his chief engineer to survey a portion of it.[26]

Another fascinating historical sidelight is that this immense project presumably would have been supervised by James Archbald, who was then being paid $3000 a year as chief engineer of the PCC.[27] Archbald was the undisputed master of the gravity railway, and the NJH&D proposal would surely have represented the ultimate expression of that form. Between the Lackawanna and the Hudson, it would have had to surmount the Poconos, the Delaware River, Kittatinny Ridge and assorted highlands and rivers in New Jersey. Possibly this immense plan was intended to alarm the D&H board and make it less determined to pursue its toll collection efforts, but there is no evidence the D&H leaders were aware of it. More likely the proposal was simply beyond the grasp of even someone with the ambition of John Ewen—or he finally concluded that the potential returns would not justify the enormous capitalization. With this latest disappointment, the NJH&D went back into hibernation, not to revive until 1867. At that time, 35 years after the charter had been obtained, the first construction took place. It became absorbed into the Midland RR scheme of 1870 and was later incorporated into the New York, Susquehanna & Western RR.[28] Although even then only a small portion of the original plan was actually built, the ability of these long-dormant charters to remain viable, like seeds excavated from ancient tombs, seems to confirm their fundamental soundness. Few of the original projectors were as fortunate as Henry Drinker and lived to witness the realization of their premature visions.

Ewen's strategy of finding an outlet to make himself independent of the D&H survived his failure to build a 140-mile gravity railway. In 1860 he adopted a more practical, and to the D&H infinitely more dangerous, approach and obtained authority to build a railroad from Hawley to Lackawaxen. Although this railroad was financed by the PCC, it was developed in close alliance with the Erie RR, which it met at Lackawaxen, and conformed to the Erie's broad (six foot) gauge. Immediately upon completion of the 16-mile line in December 1863, it was leased to the

Erie. At that time it was still uncertain whether the United States would ultimately have a railroad system with a single national gauge or a variety of regional or competing systems kept separate by differing gauges. Hawley, where the PCC gravity railway transferred coal to the new locomotive-powered branch, became a busy railroad center; but almost instantly its importance as a canal town ceased. Thereafter the PCC ran only two or three boats down the D&H to serve local customers.[29]

To the D&H this development rang like the proverbial fire bell in the night. It followed by only a few months the disappointing outcome of the suit against the PCC. Now the D&H stood to lose not only the hope of recovering past tolls but the prospect of obtaining any more. Furthermore, the new route, with its capability of year-round and perhaps cheaper operation, presented a direct challenge to the D&H's own coal business. Once again John Ewen, with his almost vengeful malice toward the D&H, had forced the older company into a drastic reevaluation.

To Olyphant's credit he did not panic, but reacted with a sure decisiveness. On November 17, 1863—before the first coal shipments had gone out over the Hawley branch—the D&H board appointed a committee to confer with the president of the Erie RR "to ascertain if a favorable arrangement can be made for the transportation of our coal to the west, in the event of the construction of a connecting road between our works and the road of that Company."[30] After meeting with Erie President Nathaniel Marsh the committee reported that "while no definite result has yet been reached, there is every prospect that a favorable arrangement can be made for a transportation of this Company's coal from Susquehanna westerly."[31] Few would have predicted this outcome 15 years earlier, when the D&H had obtained an injunction to prevent Erie work gangs from bombing canal boats in the Delaware Valley, but it was entirely in character with the times. If Cornelius Vanderbilt could, when convenient, reach a temporary understanding with Daniel Drew, anything else was possible. The D&H-Erie pact foreshadowed not only that arrangement, but also the DL&W's absorption in 1868 of the Morris & Essex, notwithstanding the vicious conflict the two companies had waged in the 1850s. The men who conducted this diplomacy were shrewd and calculating, as hard as the substances they dealt with. As in sports and war, there were elements of a game in their rivalry, in which the combat sometimes seemed to matter almost as much as the outcome, and the competitors felt a closer kinship among themselves than to outsiders. Moreover, as with the diplomatic revolutions of Europe, these realinements occurred only after a significant shift in the balance of power. In the 1850s the DL&W and the Morris & Essex were approximate equals in strength; the M&E might easily have emerged victorious. The DL&W took over its rival only after it no longer presented a serious threat. Subsequently, the DL&W broke its alliance with the Jersey Central when that company seemed to be growing too powerful. Likewise, the D&H approached the Erie only after Ewen's maneuvers had pointed up the vulnerability of the D&H while at the same time strengthening the Erie.

Although the initial contacts between the D&H and the Erie did not produce a formal agreement, the direction of their thinking soon became apparent. On February 16, 1864 the D&H board approved a subscription not to exceed $100,000 in the stock of the Jefferson RR. This company was supposed to construct a line from Carbondale to join the Erie main line at or near Lanesboro, Pennsylvania.[32] The Jefferson charter had originally been granted in 1851. This was after D&H opposition had compelled the Erie to remain in the Delaware Valley, and the Jefferson was apparently an effort to make up for the loss of the main line with a branch over much the same route through interior Pennsylvania. The D&H, ever watchful, was not fooled and stifled the feint as it had the main thrust. Thereafter, interest in the Jefferson charter waned, and it was kept alive largely by one individual, Charles S. Minor of Honesdale.[33]

For reasons that are not clear, though the Civil War was obviously a factor, the project languished even with D&H support. For several years nothing was done beyond surveying. It was only in September 1868 that a contract between the D&H and the Erie provided the mechanism to complete the line. Under this agreement the D&H would pay for construction, and the Erie pledged to complete the branch by June 1, 1870 and thereafter to transport coal for the D&H.[34] The D&H spent about $1.5 million to construct this line, and since it was providing the financial muscle, it determined the route.[35] Whereas the original Jefferson charter provided for joining the Erie at Lanesboro, Pennsylvania, the actual junction point was shifted nearer to Susquehanna. According to one source the contractor adopted an unnecessarily tortuous route.[36] In later years the struggle to climb Ararat Summit on this line became one of the legendary ordeals of eastern railroading.

Because of unanticipated obstacles, perhaps related to the unwise route, construction lagged; and the line was not opened until October 1870. Its completion was part of a major railroad building campaign that transformed the D&H irrevocably into a predominantly railroad enterprise. Anticipating completion of the Jefferson line, the D&H leased the Albany & Susquehanna RR in February 1870. This line, which extended from Binghamton to Albany and opened valuable markets, was snatched from the clutches of Jay Gould and Jim Fisk in perilous combat. Later the D&H built an "easy line" connection between the Jefferson road and the A&S at Nineveh, New York. Interestingly, the D&H board had first discussed building this connection in 1866, at a time when it controlled neither the Jefferson nor the A&S, although it had established a harmonious relationship with the Albany road.[37] Presumably it would have depended on the Erie to transport D&H coal from Lackawaxen over its main line to a point near Lanesboro. Compared to the Jefferson line this detour would have added more than 80 miles and at least one additional transfer of cargo. Acquisition of the A&S opened up some of the territory the youthful company had sought to penetrate with a canal extension in the late 1820s. No one on the D&H board in the 1860s had sat there 40 years earlier, but there was a human connection in the person of Isaac N. Seymour. He had joined the company when it was organized in 1825, rose to secretary in 1841 and treasurer in 1844. He lived until January 19, 1873 and, although the corporate minutes do not explicitly say so, he represented the continuity of living memory.[38]

The D&H was also busy in the opposite direction, as the portion of the Jefferson RR charter between Hawley and Honesdale had been kept alive. Under its dramatically altered policy toward railroads, the D&H now pushed the construction of this nine-mile stretch. D&H managers and prominent local supporters of the company invested heavily in the new project, which was completed in mid-1868.[39] A rail link now extended from Honesdale through Hawley to connect with the Erie main at Lackawaxen. Building the Jefferson line from Carbondale to Susquehanna created an interior rail line between two points on the Erie, although it relied on the unconventional gravity railway for part of the distance. The original Jefferson RR scheme had been realized on a different basis and on a somewhat different route. Except for the gravity line, the route, like the Albany & Susquehanna and the DL&W, was built to the Erie's broad gauge. At that moment the six-foot width had

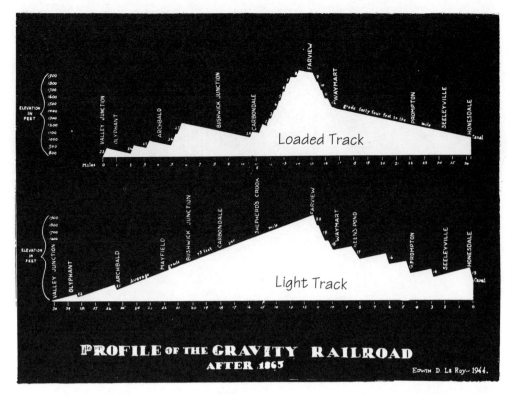

PROFILE OF THE GRAVITY RAILROAD
AFTER 1865

Edwin D. Le Roy ~ 1944.

Profile of the gravity rail-
road after 1865. Drawing by
Ed LeRoy.
CREDIT
National Canal Museum.

fair prospects of becoming the national standard, or at least a powerful regional
entity if no national standard was agreed; and many believe it would have been a
better choice for the industry, though more costly to build. In 1868 the board
appropriated $56,000 to install a third rail on its locomotive road, presumably to
accommodate six-foot rolling stock on the existing 51½ inch trackage.[40]

The gravity railway and the other D&H rail lines in the heart of the Lackawanna
Valley did not escape the vigilant attention of President Olyphant. Between 1866
and 1869 the light track down to Carbondale was rebuilt and three additional planes
were built on the east side of Moosic Mountain. These changes permitted a
continuous descent of 14 miles for trains of empty cars, substantially increasing the
efficiency and capacity of the railway.[41] As part of this alteration a stunning piece
of new trackage was built, shaped like a horseshoe but with an even tighter radius.
Dubbed the Shepherd's Crook, it became a notable attraction. These changes were
virtually the final revisions to the gravity, giving it the appearance it retained for
the remainder of its existence.

Olyphant had still more drastic changes in mind. In the Annual Report for 1867
he warned "It will be necessary, at no very distant day, to make some important
changes in our Railroad, by widening its guage [*sic*] from 4 feet 3½ inches, to make
it conform to the guage of connecting roads, and by the substitution, below
Carbondale, of a locomotive road for our present gravity system." In the following
year he repeated the warning, concluding that replacing the gravity line would be
found "the most effectual, and in the end the most economical" policy. Extension
of the steam railroad from Olyphant to Carbondale was accomplished by his
successor in 1871. Based on Olyphant's projections, it would seem that the gravity
line below Carbondale was discontinued around that time, but company records
are not clear on this point.

One of the paradoxes of the gravity railway is that it was better known in its
decline than in its period of greatest vitality. This is largely due to the fact that in
the spring of 1877 the company responded to long-standing public demand and
began running passenger cars over the original section from Carbondale to Hones-

dale. At Carbondale connections were made with scheduled passenger trains on the Jefferson branch. This was another ironic turn of events, for one of the main criticisms of the D&H during the Silkman frenzy of the mid-1840s was that the company would not be willing or able to offer adequate passenger service. One possibly unforeseen result of the new venture was the need to construct snow sheds where drifting was a problem, since publication of a regular schedule carried with it some obligation to run trains at all times of the year. The D&H over Moosic Mountain came to resemble in this one respect the crossing of the Sierras in California.

Another probably unanticipated consequence was the immediate popularity of the route for excursions. A part of the population had been able to win some leisure time and was developing a greater willingness to use it. Once inaccessible, the coal

ABOVE
Typical of the historical interest and affection the D&H Canal continues to inspire, the Waymart Area Historical Society is dedicated to restoring the only remaining D&H gravity railway depot. It is located on South Street in Waymart, about 150 feet from where it was originally built in 1875.
CREDIT
Waymart Area Historical Soc.

RIGHT
Gravity passenger cars about to leave the station at Honesdale and ascend Plane No. 13 toward Carbondale. The nearest overpass carries the track for loaded cars and the next is a typical highway bridge on the Cherry Ridge Road.
CREDIT
D&H RR Collection, NYS Library.

regions could now be reached by convenient rail service from every direction. The last quarter of the nineteenth century was the great age of picnics, organized outings and other social gatherings. The gravity railway, highlighted by the Shepherd's Crook, offered dramatic scenery, as well as a thrilling ride. Probably the managers were astonished by the enthusiasm for excursions. At the peak of passenger operation, the company needed 36 excursion cars, as well as 12 for regular service.[42] A similar phenomenon occurred on the Pennsylvania Coal Co. gravity railway.

The turn to railroads was part of a systematic policy, outlined in the 1867 Annual Report, of expanding coal sales beyond tidewater. Until then, the D&H, like the other anthracite canals, had emphasized delivering coal to tidewater terminals, from which it could be distributed. Although the D&H had access to New York and Albany, it was at something of a disadvantage because there were no large population centers directly on its route. With the interior of the nation filling rapidly and railroads spreading their network, the policy of concentrating on tidewater deliveries had clearly become inadequate. Once again the D&H managers were farsighted enough to recognize that the comfortable old methods would have to be altered.

In December 1860 the D&H had received a proposal from the Lackawanna & Bloomsburgh RR, which offered to transport coal over its road. The Bloomsburgh, chartered in 1852, had reached its southern terminus of Northumberland, Pennsylvania, earlier in 1860.[43] The prospect of an expanded market down the Susquehanna Valley should have seemed appealing to the D&H, and Olyphant certainly viewed it as such. Despite his recommendation that "a connection such as was contemplated in the proposition, would be very desirable to this Company," the other members present were cool, and nothing came of the idea.[44] Possibly the naysayers were concerned that the "Bloom" was too strongly influenced by the DL&W, which later assumed full control; possibly they were merely lacking initiative.

Olyphant probably resolved not to repeat this disappointment, and in later years a series of similar arrangements were approved. The agreement with the Erie in 1868 was predicated in part on the assumption that the railroad would transport D&H coal to Rochester and Buffalo "on favorable terms" once it reached those places.[45] In the following year the policy was pursued more explicitly when the D&H made a contract with the Northern Central Ry for the transportation of coal from mines in the vicinity of Wilkes-Barre to Baltimore and intermediate points. "This gives a new outlet for our coal, and the market thus opened is being developed much more rapidly than was anticipated," declared the Annual Report for 1869. Similar arguments led to the acquisition of the Albany & Susquehanna, which not only opened new markets but led to further accessions, ultimately bringing D&H trackage into Montreal, as well as portions of western Vermont.

A similar approach led to a conference with the DL&W in January 1871. This could have opened attractive prospects for the D&H, as the DL&W by then provided access to a sizable chunk of upstate New York, as well as the string of New Jersey towns along the Morris & Essex. The M&E paralleled the Morris Canal over much of its route, and it must have been a tempting prospect for the D&H to compete with its old rival on its home territory. Some of the satisfaction would have been dampened by the fact that the Morris Canal was no longer independent, having been taken over by the Lehigh Valley RR. A promising relationship between the D&H and the DL&W was cut short when the D&H counsel expressed a negative opinion about the company's power to enter into such an arrangement.[46]

Probably the most striking manifestation of Olyphant's policy took place after he left the presidency. This concerned the grand "Midland Railroad" scheme, originated by a Lincolnesque businessman of Oswego, New York, Dewitt C. Littlejohn and others, who sought to defy the prevailing terrain by constructing a railroad from Jersey City to Oswego "athwart the rivers and valleys, at right angles to the mountains."[47] In 1890 the successor of this railroad pushed a line into the Lackawanna Valley, making it something of a competitor to the D&H, but initially the D&H saw it as a route to additional markets in upstate New York. (The Midland crossed the D&H-controlled Albany & Susquehanna at Sidney, New York.) Littlejohn and his associates rammed through a piece of legislation in 1866 known as the Town Bonding Act. This law allowed New York municipalities to mortgage themselves far into the next century to pay the cost of bringing a railroad into their community. With towns that were by no means wealthy willing to make such sacrifices, it was difficult for the prosperous D&H to refuse Littlejohn's request for a $50,000 loan in March 1871. In the following year a more substantial loan of $200,000 was approved.[48]

A more urgent request came forward in June 1873, and the D&H responded with another handsome loan of $100,000 to the New York & Oswego Midland "with a view of obtaining relief in their present financial embarrassment."[49] This gesture was not enough to stave off collapse. Disrespect for geography was punished in the court of finance, and in the following month the Midland went bankrupt.[50] In the interim the D&H had guaranteed the Midland's leases of branches to Utica and Rome, New York.[51] As a result the D&H remained involved with these branches for years afterward, even operating them for a time. After a grim twilight struggle in the depressed 1870s the Midland reemerged as the New York, Ontario & Western, a picturesque line that left a legacy of regret and affection when it finally expired in 1957. Unlike many of its other ventures, the D&H investment in the Midland may not have paid off. The record is not clear as to whether the loans were ever repaid. Increased traffic over the Midland might have recovered the principal, but after 1890 the O&W would have preferred to serve its customers with coal from its own Lackawanna Valley sources.

The Canal Flows On

WHAT WAS HAPPENING ON THE CANAL during this momentous period when the company revolutionized its system of distribution and became inescapably involved with railroads? In family terms the canal was like a spinster daughter knitting in the shadows while dynamic young men, full of promise, courted the flashy younger sisters. Both were easy to ignore but still useful. Each year the seasonal ritual of filling the canal and reopening navigation stirred the torpid towns along the route. This annual renewal resembled and was related to the revival of agricultural activity; both depended on weather and water supply. As the season wore on, both were threatened by drought and flood alike.

The canal suffered a major loss with the departure of Russel F. Lord, the man who had been most closely identified with it during its years of hardship and prosperity. Lord has been depicted most fully by John W. Johnston, who knew him well. For all his inclination to be hypercritical, Johnston seems to have been genuinely troubled and fascinated by the potent contradictions in Lord's personality. The Lord he described was an energetic and demanding man, who drove himself and his subordinates unsparingly. As Johnston relates, many of these subordinates adored their boss, creating strong bonds of loyalty that enabled the company, through no cost to itself, to extract extraordinary effort from these men. Like Lord, they wore themselves out patrolling the canal in all kinds of weather.

The combination of Lord's driven personality and constant exposure to foul weather made it almost predictable that he would develop an alcohol problem. By June 1862, when a severe flood struck the Lackawaxen and Delaware valleys, the problem had become acute. This was the same flood that devastated the Lehigh Valley, causing permanent changes in its navigation system. For the first time Lord's decay had progressed to the point where he was unequal to an emergency. As Johnston puts it, he "evinced a marked decline in the judgment and skill which formerly distinguished his management."[52] With glee tempered by sympathy, he relates how Lord, in effect, attempted to pump dry the Lackawaxen.

The evidence that Lord's condition could no longer be ignored created an awkward situation for the company. To its credit, it dealt gently with a man who, although only 60, had broken himself in its service. At the board meeting of June 2, 1862, the president reported "that the health of Mr. R. F. Lord . . . was so impaired as to require relaxation from the cares of business."[53] The board resolved to grant him six months' leave of absence "for a visit to Europe or elsewhere," with salary to be continued. As a face-saving gesture, they further offered $1000 to cover expenses of a European trip on which Lord would "make such observations as may be of use to the Company." At a time when corporations did not have formal retirement systems, this was a generous example of what today would be called a golden parachute. Long afterward, when the canal was being closed, the company granted a lifetime pension to a supervisor who had worked many years on the canal but was not likely to be of further service. This was thought to be the earliest example of a company adopting a formal pension.[54]

Russel F. Lord.
CREDIT
Minisink Valley Historical Soc.

Not yet ready to recognize the inevitable, Lord replied in September 1862 that he "would not be able to avail himself of the offer of a trip to Europe at present."[55] In April 1863, troubled by the prospect of Lord stumbling through another season of navigation, the board renewed its offer.[56] The slipping engineer made it through most of 1863, an exceptionally busy season due to the demands of the Civil War, but tendered his resignation on October 20, 1863, effective January 1, 1864.[57] Not long afterward the board approved a somewhat surprising request from Lord to substitute a trip to Cuba for one to Europe.[58] Lord, once a dynamic figure who inspired admiration and fear along the line of the canal, lived only three—unhappy—years longer.[59]

Departing, Lord left a legacy in the form of a request to double Locks 51-56 at the Neversink, and the aqueduct over the river. Soon after Lord's resignation, the board recommended spending $150,000 for doubling the locks and another $75,000 for the aqueduct. It further appropriated $70,000 to begin work that winter by

D&H office at Rondout and some of the staff.
CREDITS
D&H Canal Museum [above].
Patricia & DeWitt Clinton Collection [right].

acquiring stone and other materials.[60] This might have seemed like a token of respect to the unfortunate engineer, and indeed compassion might have influenced the decision; yet it would not be in character for the company to approve such a large appropriation for reasons of sentiment. It shows that the managers still considered the canal to be a vital element of the system and were concerned with improving its efficiency.

There is no evidence whether President Olyphant was in accord with this way of thinking. If not, he was astute enough to mask his true feelings and avoid precipitating a conflict. More likely, his attitude was revealed in a proposal to investigate constructing a railroad on part of the canal. In June 1866, however, the counsel of the company gave an opinion that it did not have the right to abandon any portion of its canal for that purpose.[61] This temporary setback did not alter Olyphant's strategy. In early 1867 New York State granted the D&H general railroad privileges, allowing the company to construct, own and maintain rail lines.[62] As a canal company it had not previously sought or obtained such rights. This measure gave the D&H authorization to acquire the Albany & Susquehanna and other lines, but one can speculate that Olyphant had further intentions toward the canal in mind.

In discussing the acquisition of the A&S, the Annual Report for 1869 used language that would have chilled anyone concerned with the long-term survival of the canal:

> It had become evident to the managers that, to meet the rapid increase in consumption east and north of the mines, transportation facilities would require to be largely extended, either by the enlargement of the canal—involving a large expenditure—or by the possession or control of a railroad line running nearly parallel therewith. The enlargement of the canal would give increased capacity only, while the possession of the Albany & Susquehanna Railroad gives, in addition, markets that are practically closed to the canal, a much-needed winter communication, and protects us from competition that might . . . have seriously affected the value of our present improvements.

Reminding the canal of its inherent weakness, the Annual Report for the previous year had noted that a main factor in reaching agreement with the Erie RR was its ability to supply coal to the Weehawken dock *during the winter months*.[63]

Olyphant also turned his attention to organizational matters, reflecting the growing complexity of the company's operations. Although the canals, broadly speaking, pioneered in corporate structure, forming a pattern for later railroads, the canal organizations were no more than flimsy frameworks compared to the dense, highly-compartmentalized bureaucracies the mature railroads developed. John Wurts, painfully cost-conscious, made only grudging additions to the company's administrative staff. Unwillingness or inability to delegate responsibility contributed to the overwork that prematurely ruined his health. Olyphant, a generation younger, expressed a more advanced view of corporate operation, gradually drawing what began to resemble a modern organizational chart. At the beginning of 1860 he separated mining and railroad operations and appointed Thomas Dickson to the new office of Superintendent of the Coal Department at an annual salary of $4000.[64]

This marked another vital innovation in the corporate evolution of the D&H. For the first time in its history, and akin to some contemporary practice, a D&H president groomed his successor. John Wurts had not done that, although it would have been a relatively simple matter to extend the Wurts dynasty. In their Philadelphia business the brothers had, in fact, provided for succession by bringing in

Musgrave; but by the time he was introduced into the D&H he was probably too old to be seen as a serious candidate. As has been noted, there was a feeling among the senior Wurts brothers that the younger generation was composed of a less stern alloy. Most of this generation of Wurtses who developed any involvement with the D&H or northeastern Pennsylvania were sons of George. The most prominent of these, Charles P. Wurts, stuck to his engineering specialty and showed no inclination to move into management, although there were ample precedents for such a transition on the D&H. Archbald and Lord participated heavily in management; earlier, Wright and Jervis had moved into full-time managerial roles, though not on the D&H.

None of the men associated with the growth of the D&H came from a patrician background. Even Philip Hone, who made himself into an American aristocrat, was a product of the artisan class. Thomas Dickson, who was born in England of Scottish parents, conformed to this pattern. His father was a mechanic, hired to work in the D&H shops at Carbondale. As a boy Thomas Dickson drove mules for the D&H, though it may have been done for the experience or as a temporary measure, rather than out of necessity.[65] He flourished in an age when the democratic ideal of the United States as a classless society remained an article of faith, and the career of such men seemed to confirm its validity. Whatever he achieved was the result of his ability and force of character.

President Olyphant gave Dickson latitude not only to manage coal production but to take a broad strategic view of the industry and to recommend policy. In 1867 Dickson was elevated to the vice presidency, further increasing his influence. Probably at Olyphant's request, Dickson in October 1867 prepared a report that is equally admirable for its depth of understanding and breadth of vision. After describing the dimensions of the coal field, which by then were well established, he observed that there were seven carrying companies drawing on the resources of the region:

1.	Delaware & Hudson Canal Co., capacity	2,500,000	tons
2.	Delaware, Lackawanna & Western RR	2,500,000	
3.	Penna. Coal Co., via Erie Ry	1,200,000	
4.	Lehigh & Susquehanna RR, via M&E RR	1,000,000	
5.	Lehigh Valley RR	1,500,000	
6.	Lackawanna & Bloomsburgh RR	500,000	
7.	"Wyoming Valley" Canal	1,000,000	
	Total	10,200,000	

By Wyoming Valley Canal, Dickson probably meant the North Branch. Unlike some of his predecessors he was watchful of the DL&W and noted that it had nearly completed double tracking its main line.

After observing that small, privately-owned parcels of coal land were disappearing steadily, Dickson advocated a vigorous course of action to preserve and enhance the company's position. The only section where the D&H could significantly enlarge its holdings lay along the east side of the Susquehanna extending north from Nanticoke to the Pennsylvania Coal Co. property near Wilkes-Barre. Foreseeing the division of the coal region among a few powerful companies, Dickson recommended the acquisition of "every acre possible," particularly around Wilkes-Barre. Confidently he asserted "We can place coal at Tide Water, from lands in the vicinity of Wilkes Barre, as cheaply as any of the present lines."[66]

This report gave Olyphant the ammunition he needed, and he responded by presenting board with a sweeping summary of the company's position, as well as a strategic plan for future growth. Olyphant may have known that his health was failing, and his message reviewed his time as president, beginning with the remark noted earlier that President Wurts had been a "confirmed invalid" for several years before his actual retirement. Looking to posterity, Olyphant sought once and for all to demolish the temptation to stand still as a niche player in an expanding market. He recognized that capitalist imperatives compelled change and demanded risk. Remaining stationary was not a viable option. Recalling how at the time of his accession some members of the board would have been content to maintain an annual production of 500,000 tons, Olyphant argued that "ceasing to grow was in fact beginning to die."

Olyphant perceived that efficiencies of scale would overcome slow gains in the costs of labor and materials and lead to lower unit costs in a larger production. As this happened, it would be difficult to hold the line on retail prices. If the D&H failed to increase its output, it would eventually be priced out of the market. Those who advocated a static policy failed to recognize that the industry would not remain static to accommodate them. Olyphant worked out the calculations and demonstrated that in 1867 the company could not have made a profit on a production of only 500,000 tons. Increased production had lowered the unit cost from the $5.50 per ton that would have prevailed at 500,000 tons to $3.85, so that at an average selling price of $5 the company remained profitable in a competitive environment.[67]

This presentation apparently gave Olyphant the mandate he sought for a vigorous campaign of expansion. In 1866 the D&H had signed a 20-year agreement with the Union Coal Co. to transport coal from that company's holdings in the Pittston–Wilkes-Barre area.[68] The contract was restricted to 500,000 tons a year and

Receipt for a partial load of coal to Saugerties, New York, only 12 miles from Rondout. Olyphant feared that if the company did not expand production it would be priced out of all but this insignificant local market.
CREDIT
D&H Canal Museum.

The end of the D&H rail line at Scranton in the 1860s leaves no question about its reason for being.
CREDIT
Photo by Johnson, courtesy National Canal Museum.

resembled, in broad outline, the agreement with the PCC. In approving this arrangement, the D&H board demonstrated that the disappointing outcome of the PCC contract did not in itself cause the company to reject the canal or thoughts of expanding its traffic.

Unforeseen circumstances gave the D&H an opportunity to carry out Dickson's strategy on a massive scale. The company initially had subscribed to $250,000 of Union Co. mortgage bonds.[69] Subsequently, the D&H loaned the Union Co. $1,300,000 to purchase the property of the Baltimore Coal Co. near Wilkes-Barre. New bonds issued for this purpose were almost entirely taken by D&H stockholders, expanding their interest in the coal region.[70] Despite this assistance, the Union Co. ran into financial trouble. Earlier, Dickson had observed acidly that President Quintard of the Union Co. found "that it was easier to make calculations upon paper, than to produce coal."[71] The D&H thereupon bailed out Quintard and took full control of his company, including the former Baltimore Co. and Howard Coal & Iron Co. properties it had acquired. It was estimated that this expansion would cost a total of $2,650,000, but it made the D&H an enormously more powerful force in the Lackawanna coal district. This enlargement of its anthracite empire was the equivalent of Caesar's addition of Gaul to the Roman Empire. The D&H gained more than 3000 acres of owned coal land, as well as another 1100 acres controlled by lease. Included in the conquest, like captives marching in an imperial triumph, were four breakers, 17 miles of railway connecting at Scranton, four locomotives, 550 coal cars and about 100 canal boats.[72] In absorbing the assets of other companies, the D&H gained a fine railroad bridge over the Susquehanna between Wilkes-Barre and Plymouth.[73]

The complexities of operating this dense tangle of private railways, mines, breakers and housing are often overlooked in the emphasis on main trackage or on total production figures. Furthermore, the task of integrating formerly independent systems was bound to be more difficult than administering a single system that had grown up gradually, and presumably with some logic. Dickson, however, proved equal to whatever challenges were thrown at him. The massive expansion also required another readjustment of the company's financial structure. Between 1857 and 1864 more than $2 million had been spent on capital improvements, of which the major elements were $1,100,000 for the railroad extension to Scranton and rolling stock, and $575,000 on real estate for the Weehawken dock and for coal lands.[74] Much of this had been paid out of retained earnings and, as in the 1840s, it was necessary to correct the imbalance by additional capitalization. In 1864 the stock was increased to $10 million, which brought it approximately in line with the cost of construction.[75] In 1868 the D&H made the largest borrowing in its history, issuing $3.5 million of bonds, almost all of which was devoted to railroad building.[76]

It was this massive expansion that prompted the final remodeling of the gravity railway that began in 1866, including substantial rebuilding to increase capacity at Honesdale. Similarly, interest turned again to enlarging the capacity of the canal. The board assumed that the proposed doubling of locks could double the capacity of the canal to four million tons. Continuing the reasoning of Lord and John Wurts in the 1850s, the board concluded that "there is reason to believe that such an improvement, apart from the mere increase of tonnage, would enable us to effect an economy in the transportation of coal, which would abundantly compensate us for the expenditure it would involve."[77]

In his annual message of 1868 President Olyphant endorsed the project to double the locks.[78] This confirms that, whatever qualms he may have felt about the waterway, he recognized its continuing importance. Statistics reveal that he had little choice. In 1870, despite several years of effort to serve markets directly, nearly half of the company's coal production was still delivered at Rondout. In that year the D&H sold 2,205,356 tons, of which 1,050,963 were delivered at Rondout, 15,640 at Honesdale, 24,252 along the line of the canal, 440,788 at Scranton, 86,086 along the line of the Erie RR, and 247,218 through on the Erie.[79] Furthermore, the tidewater terminals were growing in importance due to changes in shipping. Beginning in the 1870s, the practice of towing coal barges around Cape Cod to Boston and northern New England ports became important. "Economically, coastal towing was very attractive. Several shiploads of coal could be transferred quickly with a small total crew (aboard tugs and barges) including only one pair of licensed navigating officers."[80] The D&H presumably participated in this phenomenon, but it was not exclusively to the benefit of the canal. Most of the tidewater shipments would have been loaded at the Weehawken facility, which could have been stocked as easily by the Erie RR as by boat.

Due to slow increases in efficiency, it was characteristic of canals to achieve their peak tonnage even as railroads brought a relative decline in their importance. The Morris Canal attained its greatest volume in 1866, the Delaware & Raritan in 1871,

LEFT
Coal barges being towed out of Rondout Creek. Although the name of the steamboat in the background is not visible, it is probably the famous *Mary Powell*.
CREDIT
Hudson River Maritime Museum.

RIGHT
The Cornell Steamboat Co. tug *Coe F. Young*, named for a D&H superintendent, pulls three canalboats up the North River just beyond The Battery. A D&H boat is on the far right; the others are returning to the Champlain Canal.
CREDIT
Steven Lang.

the Erie in 1872, and the D&H apparently in the same year.[81] Only two years after this highwater mark on the Erie, its tonnage was exceeded by the New York Central RR.

One justification for continued investment in the canal may have been the expectation that steam power would someday be used as a means of propulsion. Despite changes in leadership, the D&H had retained a corporate interest in science and an openness to innovation. In 1864 Olyphant informed the board that he had spent $1000 to purchase a collection of fossils assembled by former mine superintendent James Clarkson.[82] Several years earlier, in Olyphant's first full year as president, the annual report observed that "The probable introduction of steam as a motive power upon the Erie Canal is an event of sufficient importance to this Company to call for at least a passing notice. The experiments now being made have had a measure of success," which justified the hope that a major increase in the consumption of Lackawanna coal would result.[83] This applause hoped to call forth an encore of the successful campaign to convert steamboats to anthracite. Nor was Olyphant content to supply other canals. In October 1859 he advised the board that it would be necessary to build about 20 new canal boats for the coming season "and asked the opinion of the Board as to the policy of constructing a portion or a whole of them to be propelled by steam."[84]

In 1859 the matter was referred to committee. Toward the end of that boating season a steam-powered sidewheeler, the *Lady Ann*, built by a Mr. Jane at Rochester, New York, journeyed over the canal. Even the Civil War did not interrupt progress, and near the end of the 1862 season a steamboat named *Lady Jane* made a trial run from Honesdale to Rondout.[85] After a dormant period of several years, the project resurfaced in 1866 when Olyphant informed the board that one Baron de Mesnil "proposed to make a trial on our Canal of a new mode of propelling boats." This was not necessarily a reference to steam, since other methods of propulsion such as cable were also being tried. The board approved the experiment but, with customary caution, was "not willing to enter into any negotiation for the purchase of the alleged improvement until its value shall have been determined by actual trial."[86] One suspects that the baron was a colorful character, but nothing further is known about him. He last appears on December 18, 1866 when he was granted an extension to next July 1 to complete his experiments.[87]

In sharp and disappointing contrast to the enormous success of anthracite in river and ocean navigation, the use of steam power on towpath canals never became practical. A variety of factors were probably involved. Whether powered by steam or animal, canal boats were limited to the same slow speed; faster movement risked washing away the canal banks. Steam engines increased the weight of boats and took up space, adding costs that might be difficult to recover. As Alvin F. Harlow wrote, "Time and again this great discovery was announced, but always it came to naught."[88] By 1870, acknowledging that previous attempts had failed, the New York Legislature offered a prize of $50,000 for the invention of a successful steam canal boat.[89] Others experimented with cable or chain, and later electric, propulsion. Even John B. Jervis, near the end of his career still concerned with the canal versus railroad debate, reportedly came forward with a proposal to extend the life of canals. His plan called for laying tracks on the towpath and replacing horse power with some sort of steam engine, in effect combining the two systems.[90] Eventually some steamboats operated on the Erie Canal, but in 1883 they numbered only 92 of 4000 on the canal.[91]

On the D&H, as with other tentative ventures in its history the records do not reveal the outcome. The disposition of Clarkson's fossils is uncertain, and no further mention was made of the distinguished baron. Though they may not have understood it, the failure to introduce steam power was a serious setback to everyone who depended on the canal. Each year railroads increased their speed, capacity and efficiency. The more they advanced, the more backward canals seemed. There was no more chance of making dramatic gains in the performance of canals than there was in the animals that powered them.

The Canal Drains Toward Insignificance

GEORGE T. OLYPHANT was keenly aware of the circumstances under which he had entered the presidency. Concerned about the state of his health, he was determined not to repeat the experience of John Wurts, who had been incapable of carrying out the duties of his office, but had not been allowed to resign. The company could not again float without a firm hand on the tiller for several years, as it had done in the mid-1850s. Olyphant submitted his resignation on April 19, 1869, although he remained on the board. His surmise about the state of his health was probably accurate, for he lived only four more years. To no one's surprise Thomas Dickson was chosen to succeed him. Because of John Wurts's long tenure, this was only the fourth change at the helm of the D&H in its 44-year corporate history. Thanks to Olyphant's careful preparation, it was the most orderly and positive of these transfers.

In Thomas Dickson the canal acquired a confirmed enemy. Olyphant had tolerated it, though aware of its shortcomings, partly out of necessity and partly because he had begun his association with the company when the canal was still indispensable. Although he pursued a sustained policy of reducing its importance, yet he understood the attachment to the canal felt by his older associates. Dickson, who made his career building and operating locomotives and had been instrumental in the great D&H railroad expansion, represented a faster-paced era that had little patience or sympathy with the slow-moving, unreliable canal.

Dickson had been with the company long enough to recognize, if not share, the affection many of his colleagues felt toward the canal. While his intentions were firm, he had to move cautiously. Writing more than ten years later, he made his feelings clear:

> It is known to the majority of the members of the Board that, from my first connection with the Company, I have looked forward to the abandonment of the Canal, and the substitution of a Railway as inevitable. This change I would have advocated long ago had I not been aware, that there was a traditional prejudice among the members of the Board, in favor of Canal Navigation. So strong was this feeling, that at the time I entered the service of the Company, arrangements had been made to increase the capacity of the Canal by doubling of the Locks and the expenditure of over $1,000,000. Indeed, work had begun, and it was reluctantly abandoned after an earnest expression of my views to the then president [Olyphant].[92]

If the new president could not immediately follow his impulse to abandon the canal, he was able to halt further expenditures on it. In the plan for fiscal 1870 no new expenses on the canal were authorized.[93] Before Dickson could carry out more of his program, it was overtaken by the depression, the most severe of the nineteenth century, that began in 1873. Most of the remainder of the decade was spent in a painfully slow recovery. Dividends were suspended for the first time since 1839, leaving Dickson no opportunity to pursue aggressive schemes for reshaping the transportation system.

By failing to make improvements on the canal, Dickson was in practice condemning it to waste away. The further it fell behind the mechanical advances being made by railroads, the stronger his arguments against it became. By 1880 the economy had recovered, and Dickson finally was able to propose the radical changes he had planned from the start. Furthermore, an unusual series of droughts made canal navigation less certain than usual and reinforced Dickson's condemnation of the waterway. The phenomenon is puzzling, since there is no apparent reason why canal operations should have consumed more water than before; probably there was a natural cycle of dry weather. If so, it could not have come at a worse time for backers of the canal.[94]

Dickson attacked on October 27, 1880. Exasperated beyond the limit of his patience, or taking advantage of the situation, he reminded the board that the latest suspension of navigation due to drought was "a forcible reminder of the weakness of that portion of our system." He then added the statement quoted earlier that he had always "looked forward to the abandonment of the Canal." Dickson knew he had to make an overwhelmingly strong case for abandonment, given the "traditional prejudice" in favor of the canal. He spelled out three powerful objections to canals:

> *First.* They are more expensive to maintain, and more liable to damage, and can be used a portion of the year only.
> *Second.* As in the case of our Canal, the question of a water supply is becoming more serious every year.
> *Third.* Under the most favorable conditions, traffic cannot be moved upon them as cheaply as by rail.

He followed with figures showing that maintenance of the canal for the years 1875-79 averaged $2210 per mile per year even though it operated only eight months. By comparison, the figure for the Albany & Susquehanna RR was $1025.

Dickson was not a lawyer, but he climaxed his argument in a style that would have done a prosecutor proud, and demanded the death sentence for a canal he regarded as incorrigible:

> with canals but little if any improvement has been made in appliances since DeWitt Clinton united the waters of Lake Erie with the Hudson, in other words, canals attained the limit of their usefulness years ago, while rail roads are progressive and keep abreast of general progress. These facts being accepted, our remedy is clearly the placing of rails upon the canal banks, or in brief, the abandonment of water, and the substitution of steel. While this proposition may be startling to those who have regarded the canal as the sheet anchor of our prosperity, I propose to show that this can be done not only without injury to our credit, or disturbance of our finances, but on the contrary, will benefit both, and that the savings in transportation will make a handsome return upon the necessary investment.

By his calculation, the average cost of transportation on the canal was $1.04 a ton, while the estimate for rail was 50 cents. On an annual tonnage of 1,500,000 there would be a saving of $750,000—sufficient to recover the estimated $3.3 million cost of laying a single track in less than five years.[95]

In his harsh judgment of the canal Dickson was somewhat unfair in asserting that it was unchanged since the days of DeWitt Clinton. In addition to the great expansion of capacity, mechanical innovations such as the drop-gate lock had improved efficiency. Still, Dickson's impression was formed by the timeless picture of boys leisurely leading animals down the towpath. A scene that might have seemed charming to tourists offended his ingrained belief in progress. It was not even a case of the hare and the tortoise; for the steam hare ran tirelessly around the year, while the tortoise hibernated four months.

The president was moving quickly, not wanting to let the canal faction regroup. On October 28, 1880 he submitted the question of substituting rail for canal to counsel. Meanwhile, he won the board's approval "to make only such expenditures as are necessary to ensure the safety of Navigation."[96] Legal opinion was apparently not as decisive as Dickson would have liked, so as a temporary measure he persuaded the board to study improving the Albany & Susquehanna to handle additional tonnage "with a view of relieving the canal."[97]

Following D&H custom, Dickson wanted to be sure there were no legal objections to the course he was pursuing. This meant a delay of several months while the state legislature gave its blessing. In June 1881 an act emerged from the legislative mill which allowed New York corporations owning canals "to construct and operate railroads alongside or in lieu thereof."[98] This was a remarkable specimen of broadly based legislation, since there was at most one other company in the state that might have been affected.

When Dickson launched his attack on the canal, he may have seen it as part of a bolder strategy. The effort to lay rails on the towpath may have fitted into a larger scheme to build a new railroad on the west shore of the Hudson in competition with the Vanderbilt interests. This idea had apparently originated in 1872, when the D&H board subscribed to $40,000 of stock in a railroad called the New York & Albany. After the depression of 1873 receded, the idea was revived by President Hugh J. Jewett of the Erie RR. A consideration for the D&H and Erie was their mutual animosity toward the New York Central & Hudson River RR, a Vanderbilt-controlled line that followed the "water level route" up the Hudson from New

The canal seemed deceptively timeless.
CREDIT
D&H Canal Museum.

York to Albany and west to Buffalo. In a letter to his board, Dickson wrote that this company was "extremely hostile and directs all the business they control . . . from our lines, and do not give us a passenger or ton of freight, that they can possibly avoid."[99] This was blunt language even in a private communication.

The plan outlined by Jewett called for the use of the Erie from Jersey City, including its terminal facilities, to Montgomery, New York; taking the Wallkill Valley RR to Rondout; and building an extension of the Wallkill Valley to Albany. It was estimated that this venture would cost $4,000,000. In his usual cogent style Dickson set forth the arguments for building the new road:

> It would give us the control and supply during the winter period of the coal required by the inland towns, on the west shore of the Hudson, and would give increased value to our Rondout property. Finally it would bind still more securely, the alliance that now so happily exists between the Erie Company and ourselves, and put us in a position to assert our independence of the N. Y. Central.

The only disadvantage he cited was that it might "still further intensify the hostility of the N. Y. Central," which might retaliate by building a branch to Saratoga and competing there.[100]

The West Shore proposal quickly developed into one of the most convoluted and cynical of the many questionable railroad schemes of the time. Since the story is marginal to the D&H Canal, this is not the place to present the entire nefarious plot. Briefly, two other players had entered the scene. Thomas Cornell, shipowner and Kingston's wealthiest and most powerful citizen, had gained control of the Wallkill Valley RR. According to a recent account, he was in the process of weaning that company from the Erie RR, with which it connected at its southern end.[101] Meanwhile, the old Midland RR had regained a lease on life. Reorganized as the New York, Ontario & Western, it was contemplating a railroad at least part way up the west shore of the Hudson.

It is possible that these newcomers worried the Erie and the D&H as much as the New York Central. In short order, committees of the first two met with Central kingpin William H. Vanderbilt. Shrewdly assessing the risks, Billy Vanderbilt took a more conciliatory approach to the two established companies. Admitting that he could not prevent the Cornell-O&W combination from building a line, he observed pointedly that

> it would be highly advisable, that it should be built and controlled by strong corporations, having harmonious relations with each other . . . rather than it should be under the management of a company having no friendly relations with the three lines . . . and at all events interested as a new competitor in the reduction of traffic rates.[102]

This unmistakable expression of sentiment was followed promptly by an authorization for Dickson "to negotiate a tripartite agreement" among the three for control and use of a new railroad from Albany to New York City.[103]

The West Shore story played out to a grim but consequential conclusion. If the Erie and D&H had been trying to smoke out Vanderbilt (a dubious proposition), Cornell played the same tactic with the West Shore company. Having alarmed it, but leaving unresolved the question of whether he genuinely intended to build a new railroad, he sold out to the other company at a handsome profit.[104] In time the railroad was completed at prohibitive cost. As the New York, West Shore & Buffalo, it engaged in an unequal rate war against the Vanderbilt interests. After the

FACING PAGE
Similar views of Island Dock before and after installation of mechanized loading facilities. One of the new elevators is visible on the river front. With the Dodge Yarding System canal boats were unloaded and coal automatically piled at the rate of 1000 tons a day. When reloading into boats or barges, coal was automatically screened and weighed at the same time.
CREDIT
D&H Canal Museum.

excess capitalization had been wrung out through bankruptcy—ruining many investors in the process—Vanderbilt took over the line at a more realistic price. Almost as an afterthought, the Wallkill Valley fell into his grasp. What elevated this sordid episode to more enduring importance was the intervention of the Morgan banking interest.[105] Appalled by the unnecessary losses to stockholders and coupon clippers, J. P. Morgan decided that the railroad boys could no longer be trusted with their toys and began to impose a new kind of order on the industry.

The two projects—replacing the canal with a railroad and the railroad to Albany—were linked in Dickson's mind. At the board meeting on October 26, 1881 the connection was made explicit. The question of building an extension of the railroad from Albany to meet the NY,WS&B at Coxsackie was raised, and Dickson "called the attention of the Board to the suspension of Canal Navigation from the drouth [sic] and urged some action looking toward the substitution of a rail road for the canal."[106] The suspension was some six weeks ahead of the norm, so the president's irritation was understandable.

Although it was not an outcome to which he was accustomed, Dickson made no progress on either proposal. As has been related, the West Shore RR project slipped into the hands of men associated with the O&W, although who was really in control was a matter of speculation. Having lost its influence on the Wallkill RR, the Erie probably also lost its interest in the West Shore concept, since it would not have had a convenient connection north of Newburgh. All through 1882 the towpath railroad project continued to receive attention. On May 17 Dickson presented estimates of the cost, and further discussion followed. Late in the year the Executive Committee passed a resolution in which it "earnestly recommends to the Board, the construction of a Rail Road along the bank of the Canal, the necessary Legislation having been obtained for that purpose."[107]

Despite all his force of personality and his determination, Dickson was not able to eliminate the canal in his lifetime. In referring to it as an anchor, he may have been more accurate than he realized, and even he had not the strength to haul it up. At a cost of $3 to $4 million, the replacement railroad would have represented a 15-20% increase in capitalization—perhaps too big a morsel to swallow at one bite. Despite nearly 15 years of effort to diversify marketing, in the calendar year 1881, 1,776,590 tons (55%) of the 3,211,496 tons mined and sold by the company were still shipped to tidewater.[108] This total included transport by both rail and canal, so it was not entirely an argument in favor of the canal, but perhaps such statistics strengthened the case of those on the board who were inclined to appeal the canal's sentence. They won a reprieve by an unexpected and tragic means when Thomas Dickson died July 31, 1884. The board spoke truly in its tribute:

> He was furnished with an intellectual strength, a faculty of rapid and accurate judgment, a power to grasp and arrange multifarious details, and an intuitive knowledge of men, which, together with his immense power of will, communicated a unity and a momentum to his endeavors that compelled universal respect.[109]

Yet at his death canal boats still floated down to Rondout.

Dickson was succeeded by Robert M. Olyphant, a younger brother of Dickson's predecessor. This second in the procession of Olyphants did not share Dickson's active determination to close the canal. He seemed content to let it drift quietly into terminal obsolescence. Dickson had in effect slain the canal although, like a wounded animal, it stumbled ahead for a while longer. There was no further talk of improvements, and only a minimal sum for routine maintenance was

appropriated each year. One partial exception was a substantial investment in the early 1890s in mechanized loading facilities at Rondout, with five elevators, each capable of raising 500 tons a day. Looking into these structures, a reporter "found dark looking objects, and close inspection reveals the fact that they are alive and human beings."[110] There were, however, fewer of these human beings than there had been before mechanization, and those remaining earned considerably less.

With the railroad interest predominant in the D&H, it would be a mistake to think of the canal in its last 20 years as attempting to compete with railroads. By then the company could choose among an abundance of railroad outlets. Although the mechanism by which the decision was made is not clear, D&H management had full control of how much coal to send down the canal. Beyond the power of lingering tradition and inertia, it is debatable why the canal was retained. Cost is not likely to have been the reason, since it was by then accepted that rail transport of D&H coal was cheaper, except for consumers directly on the canal. Since the canal passed through a region of small towns, this captive market was not a major factor. One possibility is that the company assigned enough coal to the canal to keep it alive as a reserve. D&H managers may have shared the belief of their counterparts on the New York State system that canals, by their very existence, served as a regulator of railroad rates. This doctrine, which persisted into the 1950s, was responsible in large measure for the massive effort that modernized the nineteenth century towpath canal into its present form as the New York State Barge Canal.

In the final years of the D&H Canal when, in Chester Lloyd Jones' incisive phrase, it became "but of incidental importance in comparison with the larger interests of the company," conditions among the canal folk worsened. In a parallel to present trends, Johnston relates how canal families could earn a livelihood only by putting wives and children to work on the boat, and even then it was a scanty

A family boat, *Little Freddie*, heading east at the Delaware aqueduct. Capt. George Cameron and his wife are the boat crew, with their twin sons handling the mule team.
CREDIT
D&H Canal Museum.

subsistence. Characteristically Johnston, with his local viewpoint and tendency to personalize issues, blamed the decay of the canal lifestyle on one individual—General Manager Coe F. Young, for whom he felt a corrosive jealousy. Johnston failed to comprehend that larger forces had altered accustomed relationships. The prolonged contest between canals and railroads had finally been settled in favor of the railroads. Recognition of this fact placed the remaining canals under tremendous pressure to cut costs. An official like Coe F. Young was well suited to wring expenses out of the canal, whether or not he filled his own pockets in the process, as Johnston asserts.[111]

There are two explanations of Young's rise to prominence. The more favorable asserts that, leaving his home in Sussex County, New Jersey, after an embarrassing incident, he accidentally fell in with Thomas Dickson, then a youth of about the same age. Dickson's family was traveling up the canal so that his father could begin employment at Carbondale. The two boys became fast friends, and when Russel Lord's departure gave Dickson the chance he put Young into the vacant position.[112] Johnston presents a less charitable account, in which Young drifted through a variety of occupations, most of them related only marginally, if at all, to the canal. His break came when he won the affections of Thomas Cornell's younger sister. In a phrase no one can resist quoting, Johnston described the object of Young's attention as a woman "whose flowers of maidenhood, if ever brilliant, had lost their attraction by the attritions of about 30 years."[113] Not being closely acquainted with the Rondout end of the canal, Johnston did not fully understand the extent of Cornell's wealth and power, but recognized him as having sufficient influence to fulfill Young's driving ambition.[114]

There may be some truth to Johnston's placing the blame for the sorry condition of the canalers on Coe Young. The days were long past when the august board of managers convened to determine rates for the coming year. With the overwhelming emphasis on railroads, as well as Young's closeness to the D&H leadership, it may well be true that the general manager had more freedom to set rates and policies than did his predecessors when the canal was in its prime. According to Johnston, Young removed most of the competent, dedicated supervisors who had been hired by Lord and might have seemed dangerously independent. Johnston also claims that regular cleaning of the canal was ignored, although if this negligence was continued for long, the canal dimensions would shrink to the point where navigation would become impossible.

Another accusation leveled by Johnston is that Young followed a deliberate policy of keeping canalers from earning adequate income or paying off their boats. Although entire families boated, the only result was that entire families slid deeper into poverty. A situation that might have struck outsiders as quaint and congenial was the product of harsh necessity. It seems reasonable to conclude that in the years of its obsolescence the D&H Canal attracted people who were deficient in ambition, education and aggressiveness. But by more recent times, when a surge of nostalgic interest in the canal arose, the memory of its bustling, dynamic peak had been lost; and it was the recollection of the slow-paced, era of decline that stamped itself in memory and created the misleading impression that it was typical. Most of the photographs of the canal likewise depict the bucolic period when it had become a backwater in the minds of the D&H managers. The same is true of the gravity railway which, due to the passenger traffic, was more familiar in its senility.

FACING PAGE
Terms of Boating, 1889.
CREDIT
Kenneth A. Shuker.

The Delaware & Hudson Canal Co.

RONDOUT DEPARTMENT.

Rondout, March 19th, 1889.

Mr. *Herman Manthai*

Herewith we give you our terms for carrying Coal for this Company in 1889. You will inform the undersigned at Rondout on or before the 25th inst. whether you intend to run Boat No. *A Y Y* this season on the annexed terms. If so, you will have to repair said Boat at your own expense, by the opening of canal navigation for the transportation of Coal.

Should you fail to comply with either of the above requirements, we shall consider the Boat as above abandoned by you to the Company.

Note.—It is intended to have the Canal open for navigation on the 25th inst., and you are hereby notified to be on your boat with full crew, prepared to navigate the same, on the morning of that date. *Yours Truly,*

S. S. SMITH,
Superintendent Rondout Department.

RATES OF FREIGHT

And Terms for Boating Coal for the Delaware & Hudson Canal Company on their Canal and on the North and East Rivers during the Boating Season of 1889 in Company Boats.

The rates of freight for boats making trips from Rondout to Honesdale and returning to Rondout laden with coal will be Seventy (70) cents per gross ton of 2,240 lbs., on all coal so delivered at Rondout Port Ewen or Rhinebeck from opening of canal until the close of canal navigation. Proportionate rates of freight will be paid on coal delivered on the line of canal between Honesdale and Rondout. All full trips end at Rondout.

The boats to be unloaded by the Company or consignee without charge to the boatmen.

The boatmen to trim the boat, tend guy and move their boats promptly to the place designated for unloading when required so to do.

An installment of Fifteen (15) dollars will be reserved from the freight on each trip toward the payment of the boat.

There will also be reserved $7 and the fraction of a dollar out of the freight of each trip until the close of the season, as per contract.

The river freight from Rondout to New York will be 17 cents per gross ton, reserving therefrom Five (5) dollars per trip towards the payment of the boat; to points between and including Castleton and Troy will be Sixteen (16) dollars per cargo, reserving therefrom Three (3) dollars per trip towards payment of the boat; and to points between and including Coxsackie and places north of Peekskill will be Eight (8) dollars per cargo, reserving therefrom two (2) dollars per trip towards payment of the boat.

Demurrage at the rate of $4 per day will be paid for all absence from Rondout, beyond the control of the boatmen, of over four (4) full working days on river trips to New York and other points where New York rate of freight is paid. Also, to points between Castleton and Troy inclusive. Between Coxsackie and points north of Peekskill, demurrage will be paid for all absence from Rondout beyond the control of the boatmen of over three (3) full working days. In computing the time of absence no part of the day of leaving Rondout will be reckoned, but the day on which the boat returns will be called a full day.

No demurrage will be paid for detention at Honesdale or Rondout, nor in any other case, except on river trips, as above specified.

Towing and wharfage free.

All orders given by parties on line of canal or its vicinity for the payment of freight to insure recognition must be verified by the nearest Canal Superintendent or Collector.

S. S. SMITH,
Superintendent Rondout Department.

Rondout, March 19th, 1889.

N. B. The clause in Contract referring to Caulking and Painting of Boats will be strictly enforced this season. If Boats are not Caulked and Painted above top water line on arrival at Rondout after making the second trip, **THE COMPANY WILL, AT THEIR OPTION, DO THE WORK AND CHARGE CONTRACTOR FOR THE SAME,** *which amount for material and labor will be deducted from freight.*

Many who remembered the canal in more prosperous times expressed regret and sympathy over its visible decline. One newspaper article wrote poignantly but perceptively:

> Years ago boating on the Delaware & Hudson canal was one of the most profitable pursuits that a poor man could engage in . . . . Those were palmy days for the boatmen, many of the most thrifty and intelligent of whom saved enough to purchase comfortable homes, and even to lay aside something for a time of need . . . . Added to the disadvantage in freights are the delays to which the canaller is now subjected while making a trip. His progress is regulated by the company, that sends the coal to market only as fast as wanted. His running hours vary, sometimes embracing both night and day. Generally, however, he is permitted to run only during the day, and there are times when he is detained a great portion of that . . . . On reaching Honesdale, if others are ahead of him, the boatman has to wait until his turn comes before he can get a load. The same is the case at Rondout, where he delivers his cargo. This delay at each end of the canal frequently makes the round trip, that under favorable circumstances is two weeks, as many months, so that his income is barely sufficient to keep body and soul together . . . . So poor was the boating season last year in consequence of the causes mentioned that hundreds left the canal in a condition bordering on absolute want.[115]

With the company paying boatmen a lower rate per ton in the 1870s than in the 1850s and no possibility of compensating by making more runs, the boatmen were caught in a relentless squeeze.[116]

The exploitation of children continued, probably worsened, as penury overtook the boatmen. Local newspapers contain regular accounts of abuse. In one example, a boy who had been taken from a "Catholic Protectory" in New York City asked to be paid for the period while the boat was being unloaded. In response the captain "sprang at him and shamefully beat and kicked the waif." The columnist went on to assert that

> James Dowling is not the only fatherless and homeless boy who has received kicks and blows as compensation for work performed. There are scores of others who are similarly treated. Heartless 'skippers' take them from charitable institutions, promising to give them good care, and then put them on the towpath to follow half-starved mules from morn till night, in rain or snow. The unfortunates get their 'board' and 'clothing,' and when the boating season is ended in the fall they are either returned to the institution from which they came or else turned out upon the world."[117]

While the "canawlers" of the 1870s and later may have been too demoralized and inarticulate to protest, others were not so hesitant. Under the strains of the troubled 1870s editorial hostility toward the D&H erupted again. With its dividends suspended, the D&H disputed the property assessments levied by some of the towns it passed through. Other citizens complained about the company's pricing policies, claiming that coal was 50 cents a ton cheaper in Newburgh than in Port Jervis. To some extent these situations stemmed from the constant pressure on the canal to lower the differential with railroads by raising prices or shaving costs. Residents along the canal line were not inclined to take a macroeconomic view and gave vent to the resentment of power and wealth that always bubbles uneasily beneath the surface. To many at that time the large corporate organization, with its distant, impersonal management and mysterious manipulation of money remained unfamiliar and deeply suspect. Using inflamed language that would have delighted Charles H. Silkman 30 years earlier, a Port Jervis newspaper fulminated:

DELAWARE & HUDSON CANAL COMPANY.

CANAL DEPARTMENT.

TIME OF FOREMEN, MECHANICS, &c.

Month of _May_ 189 _6_

R. S. Smith

Section Foreman.

NAMES.	OCCUPATION.	Days.	Nights.	Total.	RATE.	AMOUNT.
R. S. Smith	Sect Foreman	1 mo			55	55 00
W. C. Rose	Resr Foreman	1 mo			60	60 00
W. C. Rose	Horse	26			75	19 50
J. D. Boyce	Carpt Foreman	26			1 50	39 00
Samuel Wallace	Blk Smith	26			1 65	42 90
C. M. Banks	Carpt	26			1 40	36 40
Wm Sherwood	Foreman	26			1 50	39 00
Wm Sherwood	Horse	26			75	19 50
Edgar Stanton	Foreman	26			1 50	39 00
Edgar Stanton	Horse	26			75	19 50
Jacob Stanton	Ex Foreman	26			1 50	39 00
Wm Jordon	Ex Foreman	13			1 50	19 50
						$428.30

We don't know of anyone in this neighborhood who has tears to shed over the downfall of the Delaware and Hudson, but we know a great many who, if they could, would give its prostrate carcass a heavy kick. Their rapacity had brought ruin upon the corporation, and the verdict of the people is 'served them right.'. . . There is no parallel to be found anywhere to such an unanimous disgust and hatred, as is shown to this company. It really has no friends left, and the once proud concern now goes about almost beggared and none are so poor as to do it reverence.[118]

As the 1890s wore on conditions on the canal became more acute by every measure. According to one report the D&H in 1864 had employed along the canal 549 laborers, 100 mechanics, 53 foremen and assistants and 64 teams. By 1882 the number had fallen to a total of 203 (these figures do not include boatmen, who were not company employees).[119] The number of boats on the canal declined from 1400 in 1870 to only 250 by 1898. In that year the coal tonnage fell to 500,000, a total that would have been respectable in 1850 but had become almost inconsequential. On several occasions the company advanced money to the boatmen to save them from starvation over the winter.[120] Conditions on the docks at Rondout were no better. As a result of mechanized loading facilities, "loafers" and "trimmers" who had previously earned as much as $22 a week were reduced to an average of $10.[121]

No numerical data can capture the human effects of living through a period of rapid decline after decades of fairly steady, confident, growth. Even Johnston, for all his railing against certain aspects of canal management, grew nostalgic when seeing it in its decadence. Trying to imagine what the spirits of former superintendents (or his own youthful self) would find if they returned, he mused:

They might listen for the noise of hundreds of boatmen, the sounds of whose voices and the music of whose horns echoed from the mountains and the hills, might expect to witness the busy stir of boats once constantly agitating the water and employing the machinery of the canal; . . . but instead we see a few boats in motion running at slow, easy rate, managed by a captain aided by his wife and children with their condition indicated by rags and seeming poverty, now knowing and caring little whether they would be permitted to run through the hours of the day, or to complete their trip in 2, 3, 4 or 5 weeks.[122]

Aid to distressed boatmen was only a temporary expedient. The managers revealed their real intentions toward the canal at the beginning of 1893, when they wrote down its book value to $100,000.[123] Prior to that it had been carried on the books at the cumulative cost of construction and improvements, which totaled over $6 million. In New York the managers were beginning to draw the curtains, but along the line of the canal few people probably knew about or understood the significance of this step. As late as 1895 the company spent considerable sums to repair damage caused by a severe flood, but this reflected only an unwillingness to take at that moment the action that was becoming inevitable.

Considering how long it had been talked about, the momentous decision to discontinue the canal seems to have been reached rather hastily. In late 1898, at the close of a dismal season of navigation, the board was advised that the Erie RR "by the acquisition of trackage rights over the Erie & Wyoming Valley RR was now in a position to transport this company's coal direct from the mines to tidewater without its going over the Gravity Road and the canal."[124] More than ten years earlier the Pennsylvania Coal Co. had set another example that the D&H could not afford to ignore. After several years of surveys and indecisive beginnings, the PCC had chartered the Erie & Wyoming Valley RR. It was completed at the close of

1885 with the help of the Erie RR, which agreed to operate it. The new road replaced the PCC gravity railway, which was immediately abandoned.[125]

After formalizing an agreement with the Erie under which that company would transport all of its coal beginning January 1, 1899, the D&H board on December 28, 1898 at last made the irrevocable decision it had hesitated to take for so many years and resolved "to apply to the Legislatures of the States of New York and Pennsylvania for such legislation as counsel may deem necessary to authorize the Company to cease to use and maintain the canal, and to lease, sell or otherwise dispose of the same as may seem judicious."[126]

However many hints the company had dropped over the years that the old system was doomed, many along the line refused to believe that such a vital institution, which had so profoundly shaped their communities, could cease to exist. Probably it was an interview with the general attorney of the D&H, Lewis E. Carr, who happened to be in Port Jervis for a meeting, that finally convinced the populace. Carr relayed the grim reality that shipping coal by the gravity railway and canal cost 50 cents a ton more than it would over the Erie. Added to the extra costs of handling, this meant that the old route caused a loss of $75,000 to $100,000 a year.[127] Around the same time the company ordered all canal tools to be collected at Ellenville and began laying off canal and gravity employees.[128] By whatever means, there must have been a general conviction that the end of an era was at hand, for when the last boat carrying D&H coal passed down the canal on November 5, 1898 it was widely photographed.

Boat No. 1107 being loaded.
CREDIT
Neversink Valley Area Museum.

There was a ceremonial quality about this self-conscious final voyage. It was the late autumn of the year and the last autumn of the canal, and the palpably elegiac mood gave this journey into oblivion the character of a funeral procession. Along with the photographers who recorded it, many others observed this extended parting. This one boat, which received perhaps too much attention, represented the thousands of nameless boats that had passed before it in 70 years and carried the mixed and sometimes contradictory feelings people along the route held for the Delaware and Hudson Canal. From the heights they watched the last boat slip across the marvelous Delaware aqueduct, a structure that seemed to represent the company in its full vigor, its openness to innovation. They saw the boat, which carried the unexceptional number 1107, creep beneath the looming cliffs along the Delaware, where the very existence of the canal symbolized the company's determination to persevere against all obstacles. One by one it floated through the little canal ports of New York, saying farewell. And the lights went out behind it, and the locktenders closed the gates, closed the doors of their houses, and rocked meditatively in the dim glow of lamps at twilight. Then it came to Rondout, the broad Hudson, journey's end.

It was the end of the century, and an institution that characterized and dominated the century was passing too. Ahead lay an uncertain and perhaps frightening future. As John W. Johnston demonstrated, the lifecycle of the canal, which resembled so closely that of a human, could be encompassed within a single human lifetime. It had begun in a world that seemed fresh and full of hope, where the Wurts brothers had walked in clear sunlight through untrodden woods as if at the dawn of creation. All their dreams of wealth and growth had succeeded beyond their wildest imaginings, but now the wealth flowed to an impersonal financial power in New York. The industry they had created against such adversity had imposed a monotonous sooty poverty on a scarred landscape. The lumbermen and raftsmen—coarse and truculent individualists—had retreated almost as completely as the Indians who preceded them. In their place marched troops of regimented laborers, many of them children, eking out a paltry subsistence, hoping to seize a few simple pleasures. The tracks of the D&H and other anthracite railroads, from which women in baggy peasant dresses surreptitiously snatched lumps of coal, linked a succession of shabby towns with their rows of identical faded houses. From each backyard tattered clotheslines of faded laundry fluttered in the dingy sunlight that many of the men seldom saw. Boat Number 1107, Captain Frank Hensberger at the helm, carried many burdens down to tidewater at the close of the canal century, and there was a great weariness at the end of the journey.

DELAWARE & HUDSON RAILWAY.
THOS. DICKSON, Gen. Supt., Honesdale, Pa.
Trains leave Scranton for Providence and Carbondale at 10 20 A. M. and 4 20 P. M. Returning, leave Carbondale for Scranton at 8 20 A. M. and 2 20 P. M.
Distance, 17 miles. Fare, 3¼ cents per mile.
Connects at Scranton with Delaware, Lackawanna & Western, and Lackawanna & Bloomsb'g Railways.

Epilogue

NONE OF THE NUMEROUS ACCOUNTS of travel over the D&H and the PCC gravity railways seem to describe in detail the characteristic sounds of these operations. Many of the sounds would have been the familiar friction of iron wheels rolling over jointed track. Others might have been quite distinctive, but they are lost to our hearing and we will never know for certain. On the canal side, the hollow peremptory blast of the conch shell many boatmen sounded to alert locktenders of their approach no longer echoes down the valley from Rondout to Port Jervis. Nor will the groaning of the gates or the rush of water as the boats were flushed out of the lock into the channel be heard again.

In discarding its canal the D&H abandoned also its large investment in coal handling equipment at Rondout. Since the towpath railroad advocated by Dickson had not been constructed, this meant abandoning not only a canal but an entire distribution system. A historic transportation orientation which had been nourished for three-quarters of a century was discontinued. Not only Rondout, where the D&H office still lorded it from the hill and the streets carried the names of the company's founders, was forsaken, but the entire mid-Hudson region. D&H tracks brought Lackawanna coal directly into Albany, but it served its traditional New York City and lower Hudson markets only over the rails of other companies.

In departing the region it had sustained, the D&H left a deeper void than would an ordinary company. When it was created, the canal passed through country that was largely uninhabited. The settlements and businesses that grew up did so largely in response to the needs and location of the transportation system. While the D&H managers had systematically pushed the canal into decrepitude, most people along the route had refused to heed the abundant warnings; to them the canal remained important, and they refused to imagine their communities without it. (The canal is emphasized here because the gravity railway, with the exception of its late-appearing tourist traffic, did not spawn as many self-sustaining settlements or industries.) Removing the canal might be the equivalent of removing the spinal cord, thereby, many feared, converting the organism to a lower form of life.

The economic importance of the canal in its immediate region persisted into its late years and is confirmed in an out-of-the-way source. In 1885-86 the D&H appealed its assessment in Rosendale, and the case made its way to the New York Supreme Court. In the course of the proceedings, other property owners were called as witnesses. One, James Ferguson, related that in 1883 he had paid the substantial price of $3100 for a house on a quarter-acre lot. Asked why, he replied "This place was on the canal; it is right on the canal and dependent almost solely on the canal." A follow-up inquiry concerned whether there was any other place on the canal he could find for doing business. Ferguson responded "No other located—it happened to be a place where I could catch the boatmen."[1] After the canal was closed the numerous business once built to face it looked out on a stinking, unhealthy ditch that reminded them daily of lost prosperity.

The decline of the canal so closely paralleled the decline of the businesses and industries it had fostered that there was a tendency to blame the fading canal and its managers for the other misfortunes. More likely, the troubles of the local enterprises were due to an independent and much more profound force—the concentration and specialization of economic activity that is continuing today, now on a global scale. It is this remorseless trend that has sapped the independence and vitality of small towns and cities. The best proof of this is that the railroads, which displaced the canals, could not reverse the underlying trend; indeed, they have suffered grievously because of it. When the canal arrived it seemed to channel not only traffic but also human energy and purpose. Although the timing of the canal's failure may have been largely coincidental, it seemed to symbolize the loss of direction in the region it once served.

Population figures, because they are cluttered by various kinds of extraneous "noise," provide only a rough measure, but are nevertheless indicative of decline. Wawarsing, which had grown so rapidly, reached a peak in 1880; by 1920 its population had declined by 19%. Ellenville, however, while no longer increasing, was able to remain stable over many decades, as its industries and tourism sustained it. Marbletown, which includes the once-thriving village of High Falls, endured a prolonged, catastrophic decline, interrupted only by a period of reservoir construction in 1910. From a peak of 4223 in the 1870 census, population dropped by more than half to 2017 in 1920. Rochester, containing several canal villages, showed a similar trend. Rosendale presents the prime case of economic collapse that can be only marginally attributable to the decay of the canal. Once the town "resounded with the drilling of cement rock and whir of cement grinding mills,"[2] but it paid the penalty for overdependence on one industry as portland cement steadily replaced the natural article for a variety of technical and economic reasons. As a result Rosendale's population, which had nearly doubled between 1850 and 1880, fell by 69% between 1900 and 1920 and in 1980 had not recovered to the level of 1900.[3]

As noted, population figures convey only a crude impression of economic change. A more telling statistic may be the assessed valuation of the D&H Canal in the town of Rochester, which fell from $400,000 in 1855 to $25,000 in 1899, after abandonment.[4] Much more detailed work is needed with both census and valuation data to isolate the influence of the canal from external factors such as the relative and absolute decrease of the agricultural population, in order to draw an accurate picture of the canal's economic impact.

The downturn observed at Hawley when the PCC stopped delivering coal to the D&H spread to the remainder of the canal. John W. Johnston grew up with the canal and in his old age witnessed its passing. His depiction of his home locale of Pond Eddy after the last boat had slipped into oblivion could be applied equally to any canal village:

> The abandonment of the canal . . . has inflicted a sad, damaging blow to the industry and prosperity of the place. Now the evident marks of dilapidation, stagnation and decay appear in almost every part, and tend to cast a sense of gloom around the heart of one like myself, so familiar with its residents and its industries in the brighter years.[5]

Looking back on the vanished glories of the canal terminus, Donald Ringwald wrote, "Through the years Rondout Creek has slowly become a quiet waterway. Where once there was so much activity that at times it was difficult for a steamer to navigate the stream, there is now but little traffic."[6]

The D&H Canal, perhaps already abandoned, at Pond Eddy. The Delaware River lies beyond the towpath, and the grade of the Erie RR is visible on the hillside in Pennsylvania.
CREDIT
Minisink Valley Historical Soc.

In a remarkably perceptive article written in 1900, scarcely a year after the last boat came down from Honesdale, one C. V. R. Luddington discerned the cyclical nature of the canal era:

> There was not an incorporated city or village on its whole line when the D.& H. Canal was built except Kingston; Rondout . . . had not been then "discovered." The whole valley was wooded and wild a half mile east and west of the canal . . . . [Now] the valley as far as I have seen, is a desolation, stores closed, dwellings abandoned, churches without congregations and school houses almost without teachers or children. Fires have been so frequent that it is almost impossible to obtain insurance.[7]

The circular trend Luddington detected has become still more evident in the nearly a century that has passed since he made his prescient observation. Traces of the canal's social and economic impact have become less visible than the physical remains, even though many of the structures have been lost or obscured. The numerous "ports" strung along the canal like beads, and which twinkled like festive strands of light in the busy years when the locks worked through the evening hours, have returned to the insignificance or even non-existence that would have been their status had the canal never appeared. Similarly, the larger places that prospered with the canal—Rondout, Rosendale, Ellenville—have declined precipitously or struggled to find new direction. Not only does little remain of the industries that grew up with the canal, but even the pre-existing agriculture, quarrying and lumbering/tanning have largely vanished. The hopeful intellectual flowering wilted with the canal and now, in retrospect, serves as a pathetic reminder of the brave aspirations that small American towns once dared to nurture.

Unfinished Business

FOR 70 YEARS the reawakening of the canal had been a dependable sign of spring, a survival of the ageless seasonal cycle into an industrial age that increasingly insulated itself from the restrictions of the natural world. Human nature being reluctant to accept catastrophic change, there must have remained many in the spring of 1899 who hoped for signs of a renewal of boating despite all evidence to the contrary. Even President Olyphant seemed to have left the curtain open for a ray of hope. In late 1898, after the new contract with the Erie had been announced, he had been quoted as saying that "the use of the canal would cease until there should be a decided recovery in the price of coal."[8]

In early 1899, instead of the customary rituals of reopening, the D&H took a series of steps to make the abandonment of the canal final. In February, while rustics in the backwater ports along the canal clung to their tattered belief in its permanence, the D&H board passed a resolution that represented the death notice for the traditional system:

> Whereas, it has become evident that the Company is able to fulfill its corporate purpose of opening and bringing to market a supply of stone coal . . . more economically by rail over its own or other lines than by its canal; therefore
> Resolved, that the Company cease to operate its canal. . . .[9]

Following its time-tested practice of securing legislative endorsement for major changes in direction, the board obtained the necessary legal authorization to discontinue the canal and at the same time to adopt a new corporate name. The

cumbersome and obsolete title of "The President, Managers and Company of the Delaware and Hudson Canal Company,"[10] which harked back to the formative period of American capitalism, was replaced by the simpler "Delaware and Hudson Company." The new title was not only more accurate, but seemed smoother and faster-paced, in keeping with a more rapid and mechanized age. It represented an intermediate stage on the road to today's contrived acronyms.

The end of the traditional canal and gravity railway system left several important items of unfinished business. These actions were essential, but also in many respects highly revealing and tied up many strands of the company's history. First and most immediate was the issue of disposing of the canal and its related facilities. In this the company showed an unseemly haste, almost like a widower whom gossip condemns as too eager to remarry. The rush is perhaps understandable from the point of view of the managers, to whom the canal represented a festering mass of potential liability. If the canal remained relatively intact in company hands, there was always the prospect of unwelcome pressure to reopen it.

Little time was wasted, and on May 31, 1899—barely a month after obtaining authorization to abandon the canal—the board resolved to make arrangements for selling the waterway. An offer was promptly received from Samuel D. Coykendall (1837-1913), president of the Cornell Steamboat Co. Coykendall, a near equal to Cornell in ambition and ruthlessness, offered $10,000 for the property. At first glance this seems shockingly inadequate, since as recently as 1896 the cost of the canal was shown as more than $6 million. However, the book value had earlier been written down to $100,000, and it was calculated that Coykendall's assumption of taxes and obligations under the 1899 law equalled $90,000. Thus the board was able to rationalize that "the offer was considered the equivalent of about $100,000."[11]

Meanwhile, two board members had been approached by officers of the NYO&W RR who requested an opportunity to bid on the canal. Operating on the reasonable assumption that others might be interested in the property as a railroad route—as the D&H itself had contemplated—Olyphant or board members approached the Erie and the PCC, as well as the O&W.[12] Apparently these companies thought it was shrewder to bluff or play a waiting game than deal directly with the D&H and be drawn into a bidding war. Later they had reason to rue this excess cleverness, but at the time they claimed to be uninterested. Thus, for the seemingly ludicrous sum of $10,000 Samuel Coykendall acquired the historic canal from Honesdale to Rondout, with all its "franchises, rights, privileges, etc." This left the company's substantial tracts of land on the Rondout hanging like an overripe apple at the end of a dead branch, and these too were later sold to Coykendall for $150,000.

From the perspective of the managers they were well rid of the archaic waterway. There was no line on the balance sheet for sentiment, and there is no reason to doubt that the new system was more efficient. Freedom from worry about damage suits over the condition of the canal must have been a great relief. As if dancing on the soggy grave of the old canal, the annual report for 1899 declared that "the enhanced earnings are due to a great extent" to the abandonment.[13] In a similar vein, the annual report for 1900 boasted that "the Honesdale Branch of the Pennsylvania Division has been in full operation for two months, and has proved the wisdom of the change from the old Gravity road to one of standard gauge." (This referred to a steam railroad that had been built along the general route of the gravity railway, although it had been unable to follow the tight curves of the old line precisely.)

The Delaware Valley & Kingston: The Epilogue Railroad

IN THEIR EAGERNESS to rid themselves of the canal the D&H managers may have given little thought to what would become of it. In their relief at having disposed of it, they may not have been concerned with the intentions of the purchaser. Coykendall, following a pattern similar to Coe F. Young but with even more success, had married a daughter of Thomas Cornell. Having demonstrated managerial skill and toughness during his father-in-law's lifetime, he continued without interruption after Cornell's death in 1890. The Cornell-Coykendall family empire embraced mines, railroads, shipping, resorts and banking.[14] According to local lore, which is probably well-founded, Coykendall sought to consolidate the cement properties along the lower portion of the canal. Some owners resisted, adding to the ranks of those who hated and feared Coykendall, but he made considerable progress toward his goal.[15] Control of the former D&H Canal and adjacent real estate fitted perfectly into this plan, but left open the question of what Coykendall proposed to do with the remaining 90% or more of the former route.

A response to this problem emerged so promptly and so neatly that it has the appearance of being prearranged. Shortly after the sale of the canal a new entity known as the Delaware Valley & Kingston RR was formed and by November 1899 was far enough advanced to file a complete set of maps of a route following the old D&H Canal from Lackawaxen to Kingston. Coykendall's connection with this enterprise was uncertain. The filing of maps was handled by his attorney and took place only a day after his acquisition of former D&H landholdings between Kingston and Eddyville.[16] He had sold at least part of the canal route to the new company, and was listed as one of its directors, but was not an officer and seemed not to be prominent in its subsequent affairs.

The identity of the DV&K backers and their purpose created a sensation. Subsequent developments both closed the circle on the historic transportation alinement the D&H had formed and provoked a conflict that proved decisive in the history of the anthracite industry. In an astonishing turn of events, the promoters of the upstart Delaware Valley & Kingston proved to be the historic rival of the D&H, the Pennsylvania Coal Co. Most of the leading directors and officers of the DV&K were PCC men, notably William V. S. Thorne, who was president of the new entity. If the suspicion of a prearranged deal between Coykendall and the PCC is correct, it could explain the coal company's lack of interest in purchasing the D&H property directly.[17]

As predicted at the time, the new railroad would make Kingston "one of the largest distributing points for coal in this part of the country . . . besides making it one of the busiest and most important railway centres in the State."[18] Its effects, however, extended far beyond a fabulous boom for Kingston. Formation of the DV&K represented the PCC's decision to haul its own coal to market and thereby presented a direct affront to the Erie, with which it had enjoyed close relations for decades. President Thorne later explained that the new project "is simply a business proposition, based on its own merits, and is not for the purpose of antagonizing or injuring any of the other railways." After this diplomatic denial, he turned to the heart of the matter, asserting that the PCC and others felt that they had been "unfairly treated on account of the high rates of freight charged on their product."[19]

Thorne invoked the spirit of the departed canal and spoke perceptively of its enduring impact on the region it had shaped:

The Delaware and Hudson Canal has been a transportation route for more than seventy years, and during that period much of the country along its line has been occupied by agricultural and manufacturing interests, and many industries and small towns have been built up. Since the Delaware and Hudson Company discontinued the shipping of coal by the canal these people have suffered severely, and will be greatly benefited by having a modern railway replace the antiquated canal, thereby affording them much needed and ample means for reaching the best markets. . . .[20]

More than solicitousness for the abandoned people along the abandoned canal, however admirable, lay behind the rise of the DV&K. It constituted an open challenge to the anthracite combine being formed by J. P. Morgan and the big money interests he represented. Then and later the powerful banker sought to organize America's mature industries—railroads, steel, coal, shipping—into tightly controlled trusts or combines that could crush any opponents. This cartelization of business, intended to eliminate destructive competition, was accomplished by buying out independent interests, often at extravagant prices. Morgan, it was said, disliked bargaining. Furthermore, in a phrase that soon became bitterly fashionable, it was "other people's money," and Morgan's bank, as underwriter for these transactions, profited in proportion to the size of the deal. Much as Thomas Cornell had once been considered a smaller scale version of the Vanderbilts, Coykendall's alleged intentions in the natural cement industry resembled what Morgan and the enormous fortunes behind him were attempting in coal. In both cases opposition arose from people who cherished their traditional independence.

The true meaning of the DV&K became apparent at a tumultuous meeting on November 22, 1899 at New York's Waldorf-Astoria Hotel. There 68 representatives of the Anthracite Coal Operators' Association gathered to condemn "unfair discrimination in freight rates" by the anthracite railroads. These independent operators claimed to account for a third of the annual anthracite production of 47 million tons. Unwilling to be morganized, they alined themselves wholeheartedly behind the PCC and the DV&K plan.[21]

The bold stance of the independent operators was said to be "the first determined fight ever waged" against a Morgan combine.[22] It was not a challenge that the Morgan consortium could afford to ignore; nor was the banker inexperienced at snuffing out periodic uprisings in his domain. Only a few years before he had brutally crushed a daring but impractical revolt by Archibald McLeod, who tried to build the Reading RR into a competitor. McLeod allegedly had the temerity to remark that he would rather run a peanut stand than submit to Morgan domination.[23] In view of the outcome once he provoked the titan's wrath, one hopes McLeod had secured favorable contracts for peanuts.

The cartel responded at first with a direct heavy-handedness that was not at all alien to its method. Under cover of darkness, Erie RR crews dumped 100 carloads of rock and cinders into the canal from the railroad bridge at Lackawaxen—a curious reversion to the warfare of fifty years before. Apparently they hoped thereby to destroy the canal's usefulness and also possibly to establish a claim to the property under the legislation that allowed the abandoned canal to be replaced by a railroad. Perhaps with tongue lodged in cheek, a Port Jervis newspaper observed that "A great company like the Erie could not deliberately commit an act of vandalism and must, therefore, have some good reason and good law behind their action."[24]

Like an angry moose the combine had marked its territory with dump cars. The young challenger, the DV&K, soon put a stop to this display by obtaining an injunction.[25] After that the trust settled in for a long legal contest, hoping to obtain by endurance what it had not achieved by threat. The first round consisted of hearings by the New York Railroad Commission, which had to grant permission for the DV&K to begin building. During the months of February and March 1900 the commissioners heard testimony at a hotel in New York City. Representatives of the Erie and the NYO&W RRs came out in open opposition to the new railroad, although it is interesting to note that they were operating officials, rather than high ranking corporate officers. They professed to be shocked by the very suggestion that such a thing as the anthracite trust existed. More to the point, they argued that no additional railroads were needed, as the Erie could handle all the traffic that appeared.[26] To counter this claim in the most effective way possible, President Thorne produced contracts with independent coal operators who had agreed to furnish the new road 2,500,000 tons of freight annually. Since almost all of this then went out over the Erie, this testimony must have been chilling to that company's executives. Showing where his main interests lay, Samuel Coykendall noted that annual cement shipments came to 3,500,000 barrels, of which a third moved over the canal.[27]

Meanwhile, three parties of surveyors were said to be at work on the DV&K route. There is some question about whether any construction in Pennsylvania would take place under its charter. According to some accounts the DV&K rights extended only to the state line, but maps filed later show that it ended at Honesdale.[28] Reaching that town would have been of little value to the PCC/DV&K alliance, since it would have meant relying on D&H rail lines. Hawley, fed by the PCC-controlled Erie & Wyoming Valley RR, was the real focus of their interest. However, another problem existed between Hawley and Lackawaxen: although the PCC owned the rail line between those points, it was under lease to the Erie, a contract not due to expire until January 1, 1911. To remain fully independent the PCC would have to build a duplicate rail line down the Lackawaxen Valley, perhaps on the old D&H towpath.

In New York the proposed route followed the canal in a general way, but not precisely. At many points where the canal curved around obstacles the railroad planned a more direct route. In High Falls the survey shows the center line of the DV&K passing through the five locks, which would have created an impossible situation, unless the projectors were thinking of reverting to the antiquated gravity railway concept. In the early 1880s, when the D&H itself was talking about replacing the canal with railroad track, one report had the rail line diverging at High Falls to join the Wallkill Valley RR.[29] That scheme would hardly have worked for the DV&K at a time when the Wallkill Valley was under the control of Vanderbilt-Morgan interests.

Resisting enormous political pressure, the Railroad Commissioners approved the DV&K application. This decision "speaks well for the independence of that body" correctly opined a New York newspaper.[30] The coal combination responded as expected by appealing the commission's action in the New York Supreme Court. At a minimum the cartel was hoping to outlast its rival. "The independent coal operators have declared their intention to carry out their plans at all risks, but it is believed that the long postponement, together with the cost involved, will eventually defeat [them]."[31] In fact the appeal process used up only four months, not enough to discourage the new venture. On September 15, 1900 the Appellate Division of the Supreme Court sustained the railroad commissioners. Except for a minor appeal still lingering in Pennsylvania, this gave the DV&K a clear field, and it was expected that construction could begin by the end of the year.[32]

As the DV&K unfurled its wings, the pressure of time became greater on the anthracite trust. The series of unaccustomed setbacks left the combine no choice but to resort to its ultimate and most persuasive tactic. On December 14, 1900 it was announced that Morgan had secured the controlling interest in the PCC, which carried with it control of the DV&K and the E&WV railroads. The purchase price—$27.6 million—seemed staggering, since the company had a capital of 100,000 shares with a par value of $50, for a total of $5 million. Others reportedly considered this figure of 552% low, since shares had recently traded at 740%. On the other hand, the agreement allowed the PCC to reserve $10 million in treasury assets, equal to a 200% distribution.[33]

To some observers the deal symbolized the contrast between the old-fashioned conservatism of the PCC and the free-wheeling methods of the contemporary financial markets. In a statement that would not have been out of place in yesterday's newspaper, a columnist wrote "Modern finance builds for the present and lets the future care for itself . . . . Distribute the surplus, capitalize the property on a modern basis, and the devil take the hindmost. Such seems the new theory, and on that are built the paper fortunes of some capitalists of the day."[34] By the standards of Morgan and his cohorts, the PCC, trading (on the infrequent occasions when it did) at 700% of par was breathtakingly undercapitalized. One commentator noted that the company had only five presidents in its history, almost never published a financial report, and regularly paid 16% dividends. In a revealing article on the departure of this solid enterprise the columnist reported

> . . . several pathetic instances in the passage of this old company into other hands. They are witnessed when venerable men and aged women enter the office of the company, at No.1 Broadway, with their modest certificates of stock to surrender the same or have them transferred. Some of the original subscription shares issued in 1848 have come to hand, and other certificates represent only one transfer, made necessary by the division of the estates of original holders.
>
> Cheek by jowl with these venerable holders, representing conservative old New York, are the impudent messenger boys from district telegraph companies, hired by modern stock brokers, who fling in their certificates and demand a transfer. It marks a transition from the old to the new in one of the last of the old New York corporations. It must be admitted that the old is much more decorous than the new.[35]

One conspicuous proof of their old-style integrity was the insistence of the PCC directors that all stockholders share equally in the windfall. Thus holders of one or two shares were able to sell out on the same terms as big banks and financiers, even though their meager holdings would not have been needed to secure control.[36]

In January 1901 the Morgan company announced the financial mechanism for carrying out the purchase of the PCC. It was proposed to issue $32 million new Erie RR 4% bonds and 50,000 shares additional preferred stock in return for transferring all stock of the E&WV and DV&K and at least a majority of PCC to the Erie. In a fairly unusual measure the Erie directors explained their action in a public letter, stating that "For some time past your officers have believed that it would be to the great advantage of the Erie Railroad Company to make permanent arrangements for continuing the connection and the business" of the PCC and the E&WV. The letter added the significant confession "especially in view of the fact that recently the connection and the relations of the [Erie] with these properties have been seriously threatened."[37] Rumors circulated that Morgan would also buy the D&H and the O&W, but greater direct ownership was not really necessary to secure his objectives.[38] Before long a new policy was announced under which the sale of D&H coal at all points reached by the Erie RR was to be turned over to Erie agents.[39]

The further piling of debt on an already heavily burdened Erie, while in keeping with Morgan methods, was disturbing to some Erie investors. One, a man with the intriguing name of Richard Pine-Coffin, brought suit against J. P. Morgan and the Erie, claiming that the purchase would be detrimental to Erie stockholders. He also objected to the profit made by the Morgan bank. Morgan responded that the $2.3 million it cleared on the transaction represented less than 9%, "which was only fair and just."[40] Another long legal duel ensued; while its outcome is uncertain it had no effect on the PCC acquisition.

Except for a few who made the mistake of selling out prematurely, PCC stockholders came out all right. So also did E. L. Fuller, owner of the Mt. Pleasant Coal Co. and a leader of the revolt of the independent operators, who reportedly "disposed of his personal coal interests to advantage."[41] Other independent owners who had bet their fortunes on the rebellion may not have been so fortunate, and it is probably no accident that on the same day the Morgan purchase of the PCC was announced another story told that a syndicate was trying to buy up all the individual mines between Wilkes-Barre and Carbondale.[42] At first the United Mine Workers greeted the consolidation as a positive development, on the theory that it was "best to deal with some centralized power."[43] It may be that by expanding its control the combine was clearing the decks for a decisive showdown with the union, and in 1902 the most severe strike to date descended on the anthracite region. These events at the turn of the twentieth century shaped the remaining history of the anthracite industry. Morganism created financial stability, with dependable payment of interest and dividends, but also seemed to foster a certain stagnation, a reluctance to innovate. In the 1820s the Wurts brothers were present at the beginning, and the company they created indirectly set off the crisis that gave the industry its mature form.

During the Summer noisome sections of the abandoned canal may have threatened the health and certainly offended the sensibilities of neighbors. At other times of the year, as had been true when the canal was functioning, it offered delightful recreation, as evident in this 1908 scene on the East Basin at Port Jervis.
CREDIT
Minisink Valley Historical Soc.

The Canal Trickles Away

THE D&H had ended its involvement in the canal with a clean cut. Thereafter, the canal's descent into final disuse was like a wasting illness. Distinct from the effort to convert the canal to a railroad right-of-way, there were numerous attempts to keep at least portions of the waterway in service. Many imaginative proposals to use the canal arose, some with a surprisingly modern ring. In 1899, for example, someone suggested using the towpath as a bicycle trail, the "wheel" craze then being in full bloom.[44] Measures to revive the canal in its accustomed role were introduced into the legislature as late as 1912 but went nowhere.[45] As is seen frequently today with abandoned rail lines, people are understandably reluctant, for both economic and sentimental reasons, to accept the loss of familiar transportation routes.

In November 1899, a time of the year when the operators would normally be thinking about closing for the winter, the eastern end of the canal was reopened. It was said to be for the transportation of bluestone, but others suspected that it may have been to deliver material for the DV&K RR.[46] This explanation, though appealing, seems unlikely. Speaking about the future of the canal in June 1899, Coykendall had informed the region that he would keep it open to Ellenville if tolls covered his expenses. True to his promise, Coykendall kept the canal open to Ellenville through 1901. During this period it hauled materials for the state reformatory at Napanoch, still a brooding presence in the landscape.

Coykendall had apparently sold to the DV&K the portion of the former D&H route reaching only as far east as Huguenot. The Erie RR inherited this when it assumed control of the DV&K property. Meanwhile, the NYO&W RR, having been sufficiently alarmed, decided not to let another opportunity slip and purchased the canal route from Summitville eastward. In 1902 the O&W completed an extension of its branch from Ellenville to Kingston, following roughly the line of what had been termed the "Kingston route" during the early disputes over laying out the D&H Canal.[47] The blast of locomotive whistles probably dispelled much of the gloom caused by the loss of the canal as a transportation outlet east of Ellenville and explains why the canal was not reopened after 1901. A gap of about 17 miles was left between Huguenot and Summitville, and this was sold to the Erie RR—a tactical maneuver that later bought the Erie considerable abuse over sanitary problems caused by the festering ditch. As early as 1901 two railroad bridges over the canal along the Delaware had been filled in, and four highway bridges between Honesdale and Hawley had been removed. A Scranton junk dealer purchased the iron in locks from Honesdale to Mongaup.[48]

Physically, it might have been possible to revive the canal alongside the new railroad, but economically there was little justification, despite the occasional harmless political gesture of fanning the embers in the legislature. Yet a portion of the old canal through the cement district from High Falls to Eddyville maintained a faint existence for some years longer. This shadowy period, when the D&H Canal was no longer operated by the D&H, was depicted by old-timers in the 1960s and may have contributed to misleading impressions about typical activity on the waterway when it was in its prime.

When Samuel Coykendall was disposing of the former canal properties, he sold the High Falls to Eddyville section to the Consolidated Rosendale Cement Co. on March 26, 1902. The cement company kept separate accounts of the canal, as well as of the Hickorybush & Eddyville RR, a cement-hauling shortline it owned. The canal actually showed a profit in some years—over $4000 in 1906. After 1909, however, receipts dropped to insignificant levels, probably due to the closing of the A. J. Snyder cement plant. Records of the Consolidated company show that the canal remained in service through at least 1911.[49] This corresponds approximately to the recollection of Earl Mack, who remembered seeing a boat bringing coal to LeFever's in 1913 but admitted that he might have been off by a year.[50] Portions of the canal may have remained in use even longer—it is virtually impossible to be sure when the last boat floated on the last piece of the canal. An occasional small boat could have used the canal even if it was not maintained to its full width and depth, but after a while failure to maintain the locks would have extinguished these last sparks of activity. If the passage of Boat No. 1107 in 1898 had been sunset, the gradual fading of the canal in later years was a slow twilight leading to darkness.

A stranded canal boat decorated the landscape at Mongaup, probably near the former boatyard. The scene predates 1912, as it appears in a postcard mailed in April of that year. In the inscription John Steinman, who may appear in the photo with his wife Elizabeth, wrote to his mother in nearby Pike County, "I thought that I would send you a picture of our canal boat. [T]his picture is just across the canal from our house." The small building in the background is an old school house.
CREDIT
Minisink Valley Historical Soc.

Table 1

Articles other than coal shipped on D&H Canal
(Tons, except as noted)

	1836	1846	1856	1866
Merchandise	6,856	10,083	14,330	20,824
Leather and hides	769	2,188	6,538	7,817
Plaster	757	752	715	30
Cement	4,000	7,840	29,996	74,816
Tanner's Bark	493	168	2,177	2,433
Stones, Brick and Lime	685	2,038	7,440	11,970
Mill Stones		230	184	265
Staves, Hoop poles, Lath	1,092	1,245	1,195	693
Manufactures of Wood	1,246	1,763	1,125	1,483
Sundries, Posts, Rails,				
Pig Iron &c		480	2,878	4,372
Window glass	174	771	1,409	2,190
Lead Ore	30			
Charcoal		730	1,647	
Bituminous coal, up canal			353	607
Cords of wood	8,836	2,971	4,501	12,508
Shingles	455,600	293,000	194,000	273,100
Ship timber (cu. ft.)	34,104	48,375	51,140	51,105
Square timber (cu. ft.)	59,364			
Hard lumber (ft.)	2,768,868	3,170,223	3,031,596	5,510,189
Hemlock lumber (ft.)	3,789,989	6,774,724	12,785,073	12,986,214
Pine lumber (ft.)	11,395,053	729,465	520,658	620,632

Table 2

Statement of articles cleared on D&H
Canal at the office of the D&H Canal Co.
at Ellenville, during the season of 1843.

	Lbs.
Merchandise	2,889
Liquors	4,740
Flour, Meal and Grain	83,620
Provisions	10,070
Gypsum	14,238
Cement	3,750
Unground tanner's bark	200
Leather	988,387
Iron castings	1,671
Edge tools	2,790
Brick, stone, clay	53,400
Hoop poles	1,625
Staves and headings	146,990
Lath, fence posts and rails	9,120
Manufactured wood	621,315
Glassware	704,005
Lead and lead ore	735
Sundries	78,870
Fruit	9,795
Stoneware	7,659
Firewood (cords)	799
Shingles, Northern hemlock	32,000
Unenumerated	78,105
Ship lath (cu. ft.)	597
Pine timber (cu. ft.)	919

Lumber	(board measure)
Pine lumber	7,142
Plain maple	12,587
Hemlock	639,149
Cherry and white wood	8,206
Curled and speckled maple	1,200
Ash and oak	48,433

Notes

Abbreviations for Manuscript Collections

DM   Delaware & Hudson Co. corporate minutes; microfilm, New York State Library.

HD   Diary of Philip Hone; microfilm, New-York Historical Soc.

HM   Hugh Moore Canal Park and Museum Archives, National Canal Museum, Easton, PA.

RL   Russel F. Lord Papers, Minisink Valley Hist. Soc., Port Jervis, NY.

WH   Wurts Family Papers, Hagley Museum.

WP   Wurts Family Papers, Pennsylvania Hist. Soc., Philadelphia.

Wurtses Wandering in the Anthracite Wilderness
Pages 5-23

1. Stephen D. Blackmer, "Fossils, Fuel and the Forest: The Effect of Coal on New England's Use of Wood Fuel in the 19th Century" (ms Yale Univ. School of Forestry and Environmental Studies, 1982).
2. Malcolm A. Booth, "The Delaware & Hudson Canal, with Special Emphasis on Deerpark, N.Y." (M.A. thesis, SUNY, Oneonta: Cooperstown Graduate Program, 1965), 6.
3. Vernon Leslie, *Honesdale and the Stourbridge Lion* (Honesdale, PA: Stourbridge Lion Sesquicentennial Corp., 1979), 14.
4. Wurts, Charles Pemberton, comp., *A Genealogical Record of the Wurts Family* (privately printed, 1889); Leach, Frank Willing, "One of a Series of Sketches for the Philadelphia North American, 1907-1913. Based on the Manuscript of John Sparhawk Wurts, compiled 1902" (Philadelphia, Historical Publication Soc., 1932). Another descendant, John W. Wurts (1910-1972) prepared a genealogical chart of the family, which may be seen at the D&H Museum, High Falls, NY.
5. *History of Morris County* (New York: W. W. Munsell, 1882). The writers of this volume seemed to have no inkling that a fairly prominent family had originated in the county.
6. Nicholas B. Wainwright, *The Philadelphia National Bank* (Philadelphia: Philadelphia National Bank, 1953). Later this bank invested heavily in transportation stocks, but apparently not in the D&H (116).
7. H. Benjamin Powell, *Philadelphia's First Fuel Crisis: Jacob Cist and the Developing Market for Pennsylvania Anthracite* (University Park, PA: Penn State Univ. Press, 1978).
8. Delaware & Hudson Co., *A Century of Progress: History of the Delaware and Hudson Company 1823-1923* (Albany: J. B. Lyon, 1925), 14.
9. C. P. Wurts, *Wurts Family*, 57.
10. Horace Hollister, *Contributions to the History of the Lackawanna Valley* (New York: W. H. Tinson, 1857), 246.
11. The map accompanying Cist's sketch book does not use the name Carbondale (see note 13).
12. Hollister, *Lackawanna Valley*, 287.
13. Jacob Cist, "Sketch Book of Coal Mines Luzerne" in Academy of Natural Sciences, Philadelphia.
14. Hollister, *Lackawanna Valley*, 288.
15. Another historian of the region, Durfee, states that the "Log Tavern" was built in 1824. This seems unlikely, for it leaves the question of where the miners would have lived prior to that (J. R. Durfee, *Reminiscences of Carbondale, Dundaff and Providence*. Philadelphia: Miller's Bible Publishing House, 1875), 6.
16. Horace Hollister, "History of the Delaware and Hudson Canal Company" (unpublished manuscript, 1880, in Hagley Museum), 16.
17. John T. Schlebecker, *Whereby We Thrive: A History of American Farming* (Ames, IA: Iowa State Univ. Press, 1975), 90.
18. John Wurts to Maurice Wurts, Feb. 24, 1823; WH.
19. Slackwater navigation used long pools formed by damming the river at intervals, thus controlling the current without building a separate channel. Canal boats passed over the dams through locks, while rafts were supposed to float over a portion of the dam.
20. John to Maurice, Feb. 24, 1823; WH.
21. Managers of the Delaware and Hudson Canal Company, "Charter of the Delaware and Hudson Canal Company, with the Severall Acts Supplementary to the Same" (New York: Elliott & Palmer, 1832).
22. William Wurts to Maurice, Dec. 19, 1828; WH. William soon remarried; he had six children by his first wife and eight by his second.
23. This was noted by John Wurts in a letter to Maurice, Apr. 30, no year, but probably 1823; WH.
24. John to Maurice, Feb. 28, 1823; WH.
25. William to Maurice, Mar. 19, 1823; WH.
26. John to Maurice, Mar. 10, 1823; WH.
27. John to Maurice, Mar. 14, 1823; WH.
28. William to Maurice, Mar. 19; Mar. 26, 1823; WH.
29. John to Maurice, Feb. 24, 1823; WH.
30. William to Maurice, Apr. 8, 1825; WH.
31. John to Maurice; WH.
32. WH.
33. William to Maurice; WH.
34. Powell, *Philadelphia's First Fuel Crisis*, 42.
35. Hollister, "Delaware and Hudson," 19-21, 29.
36. The confusion is deepened by the fact that Hollister's description of a map (p.15) actually corresponds to the map drawn in 1823 and included in the Wright/Sullivan report of the following year.
37. Powell, *Philadelphia's First Fuel Crisis*, 144. The purchase was made from Jacob Cist's father-in-law; furthermore, according to Hollister ("Delaware and Hudson," 16) some coal lands initially purchased by the Wurtses but then abandoned were acquired from an individual with the same name (Hollenback). There were connections within connections.
38. *National Cyclopedia of American Biography*, vol.IX.
39. *Memoir of DeWitt Clinton* (New York, 1829).
40. WH. Two coal companies had been chartered in New York in 1814, during the worst of the wartime coal shortage. One, the North American Coal Co., had a capital of $750,000; the other, given only as "Coal Company" was authorized a capital of $700,000 (A. T.

Goodrich, *The Picture of New-York and Stranger's Guide* [New York: 1818], 162.) Whether William was referring to one or both of these is unknown.

41. *Appleton's Cyclopedia of American Biography*, 1888.
42. Barbara N. Kalata, *A Hundred Years, A Hundred Miles* (Morristown, NJ: Morris County Historical Soc., 1983), 55, 117.
43. Ronald E. Shaw, *Canals for a Nation* (Lexington, KY: Kentucky Univ. Press, 1990), 42.
44. Ruggles to Clinton, Apr. 9, 1824; WH.
45. 21.
46. John to Maurice; note added to letter Charles H. Ruggles to John Wurts, Nov. 28, 1824; WH. According to one account the D&H worked more actively to undermine the Morris Canal. Probably based on the Newark (NJ) *Sentinel of Freedom*, Jan. 17, 1825, H. Jerome Cranmer reported an accusation that agents of the D&H generated "a powerful opposition" to the New Jersey canal "out of doors." (Cranmer, "Improvements without Public Funds: The New Jersey Canals," in Carter Goodrich, *Canals and American Economic Development* [Port Washington, NY: Kennikat Press, 1972]), 145.
47. Printed broadside; WH.
48. Bethany, PA, *Republican Advocate*, Apr. 30, 1824; from the Sullivan Whig.
49. The Seneca Lock Navigation Co., incorporated 1813, was entitled to a capital of only $50,000 (later increased, with state aid). Its directors also formed the Seneca and Susquehannah Lock Navigation Co. in 1815. This proposal was authorized $300,000 capitalization, but the directors evidently were so occupied with the smaller project that nothing was done on the larger one, which was meant to build a canal down Seneca Lake to the Chemung River (Noble E. Whitford, *History of the Canal System of the State of New York*, vol.I [Albany: Brandow Printing Co., 1906]), 762.
50. "Charter of the Delaware and Hudson . . ."
51. WH.
52. Dorothy H. Sanderson, *Carrying Coals to Rondout* (Ellenville, NY: Rondout Valley Publishing, 2nd ed., 1974), 10. The original source is Samuel W. Eager, *Outline History of Orange County* (Newburgh, NY: S. T. Callahan, 1846-47), 391.
53. Josiah White "Pocket Journal" cited in Norris Hansell, *Josiah White, Quaker Entrepreneur* (Easton, PA: Canal History and Technology Press, 1992).
54. "Report of Messrs. Benj. Wright and J. L. Sullivan, Engineers, Engaged in the Survey of the Route of the Proposed Canal, from the Hudson to the Head Waters of the Lackawaxen River, etc." (Philadelphia: John Young, 1824). A map accompanying this report contains information identical to that presented by Hollister ("Delaware and Hudson," 15-16), renewing the question of whether there was an earlier map, now lost.
55. Joseph Dow, *The Dearborns of Hampton, N.H.* (Salem, MA: Salem Press, 1893); *Appleton's Cyclopedia of American Biography*, 1888; catalog, Boston Athenaeum.
56. The map, the full title of which is "MAP of the Route of the Proposed and Enacted Hudson and Delaware Canal, with the River Lackawaxen, and Its Head Waters, Shewing the relative situation of the Coal Mines,"

seems to be different from that described by Hollister. It is reproduced in Sanderson, *Carrying Coals*, 13.
57. New York Legislature, 47th Session, Chap.174, 192.
58. 17.
59. DM, Dec. 21, 1825.
60. Daniel H. Calhoun, *The American Civil Engineer* (Cambridge, MA: MIT, 1960), 62, 99-105. In his Preface (ix) Calhoun refers to Sullivan as a "stray" engineer, implying that he was an individual more than a representative type.
61. John to Maurice, Aug. 1, 1825; WH. Earlier Sullivan had offered to be present in New York during the election of the D&H Board of Managers, but it is not known whether he was in fact present (Sullivan to Maurice Wurts, Feb. 22, 1825; WH).
62. Wright to John Wurts; WH.
63. John to Maurice, Aug. 1, 1825; WH.
64. *Century of Progress*, 19.
65. The company advertised that the materials were also on display at "Sykes's Hotel," where a "Committee of the Lackawaxen Company" had established itself. This may be a reference to a coffee house opened by William Sykes in July 1822. Located in William Street fronting Beaver, it was only a short stroll from the Tontine (I. N. Phelps Stokes, *The Iconography of Manhattan Island* [New York: 1916-28; reprinted Arno Press, 1967], vol.5, 1623.)
66. DM, Mar. 9, 1825.

Plotting a Course
Pages 25-45

1. There is no indication in their extant correspondence that they did.
2. "Charter of the Delaware and Hudson . . ."
3. DM, Apr. 1, 1826.
4. Neal FitzSimons, *The Reminiscences of John B. Jervis* (Syracuse: Syracuse Univ. Press, 1971), 65.
5. Ibid., 67.
6. Ibid., 68.
7. Ibid. Of course "that day" was only slightly more than a year earlier.
8. Ibid., 69. According to Jervis, Sullivan had proposed this system for three-fifths of the distance between the rivers.
9. *Century of Progress*, 27; DM, Mar. 8, 1826.
10. Maurice Wurts [?] to John B. Mills, n.d.; WH.
11. Thomas Young to Maurice Wurts, July 31, 1825; WH.
12. Maurice Wurts to A. Bruyn Hasbrouck, Feb. 12, 1825; WH.
13. DM, Apr. 13, 1825.
14. DM.
15. Maurice Wurts to Hasbrouck, Feb. 12, 1825; WH.
16. John to Maurice; WH.
17. Hasbrouck to Maurice Wurts, May 4, 1825; WH.
18. L. Elmendorf to Maurice Wurts, Mar. 9, 1825; WH.
19. Hasbrouck to Maurice Wurts, Feb. 3, 1825; WH.
20. John to Maurice, Mar. 17, 1825; WH.
21. D&H lists of stockholders, May 1826, May 1827.
22. Apr. 13, 1825; DM.
23. John to Maurice, May 2, 1825; WH.
24. *Century of Progress*, 28.

25. HD.
26. Nathaniel Parker Willis, a well-known nineteenth-century writer, is said to be responsible for the change of name (Arthur G. Adams, ed. *The Hudson River in Literature.* New York: Fordham Univ. Press, 1988, 233).
27. Hasbrouck to Maurice Wurts, Feb. 21, 1825; WH.
28. Elmendorf to Maurice Wurts, Mar. 9 [1825]; WH.
29. Nov. 7, 1825; DM.
30. Hasbrouck to Maurice Wurts, Feb. 21, 1825; WH.
31. Ronald E. Shaw, *Erie Water West* (Lexington, KY: Univ. of Kentucky Press), Chap.8.
32. Michele A. McFee, *Limestone Locks and Overgrowth* (Fleischmanns, NY: Purple Mountain Press, 1993), 52.
33. John Wurts to Nathan Smith, Feb. 17, 1825; WH.
34. Ibid.
35. William to Maurice, Apr. 7, 1825; WH.
36. Meredith to William Jessup, Dec. 21, 1824, cited in H. F. Bartle, "The Coal Canal," 2nd instalment, *Pike-Wayne* (PA) *Eagle*, June 18, 1959.
37. Powell, *Philadelphia's First Fuel Crisis*, 125.
38. Hollister, "Delaware and Hudson," 135.
39. John to Maurice; WH.
40. John to Maurice, Apr. 4, 1825; WH.
41. John to Maurice, Apr. 5, 1825; WH. This testifies to John's defensiveness about the act, since it was not within Pennsylvania's power to regulate tolls in New York.
42. Ibid.
43. DM, June 15, 1825.
44. Ibid.
45. Undated, unsigned document No.5½; WH.
46. John to Maurice; WH. The election had taken place March 8.
47. John to Maurice, May 9, 1825; WH.
48. William to Maurice, Apr. 12, 1825; WH.
49. A later calculation, the purpose of which is not entirely clear, indicates either that the four Wurts brothers collectively owned about 40% of the Lackawaxen Co. or stood to receive that proportion of the deferred stock—which should have amounted to the same thing (C. S. Wurts to Maurice, Nov. 7, 1825; WH).
50. William to Maurice, Mar. 26, 1825; WH.
51. Charles S. to Maurice, Apr. 1, 1825; WH.
52. John to Maurice, May 2, 1825; WH.
53. John to Maurice, Apr. 14, 1825; WH. The resolution was approved April 13.
54. John to Maurice, June 11, 1825; WH.
55. Ibid.
56. DM.
57. *Century of Progress* (30), by failing to note that the stock was deferred, glosses over the complexity of the situation, with its innate conflict of interest.
58. DM, July 2, 1825.
59. DM, Aug. 9, 1825.
60. Ibid.
61. John to Maurice, July 21, 1825; WH.
62. DM.
63. HD, Feb. 21, 1833. A tone of resentment is visible on this occasion, when Hone complains that he gave up a family dinner to perform this duty.
64. Company filings show that Ellmaker owned 268 shares in 1827. Other than Maurice Wurts, he was the only

substantial Philadelphia holder of D&H stock (Joseph White owned eight shares). (List of D&H stockholders, May 1827.)
65. John to Maurice, June 15, 1827; WH.
66. Ibid.
67. DM, Feb. 25, 1826.
68. Smith to Maurice Wurts, Jan. 2, 1827, with endorsement by William Wurts, Jan. 4, 1827; WH.
69. Smith to Maurice Wurts, Feb. 4, 1827, transmitting copy of letter Smith to Bolton, Feb. 2, 1827; WH.
70. Smith to Maurice Wurts, Jan. 2, 1827; WH.
71. John to Maurice, Aug. 1, 1827; WH.
72. Ibid.
73. Ibid.
74. Ibid.
75. John to Maurice, Sep. 7, 1827; WH.
76. Ibid.
77. Calhoun, *American Civil Engineer*, 102-103.
78. Charles S. to Maurice, May __, 1825; WH.
79. John to Maurice, June 11, 1825, with addition by Charles S.; WH. The "Hauto" stock was probably a share in the receipts of George Hauto, a former partner of White and Hazard in the Lehigh enterprise. Hauto was a charming scoundrel, and in 1820 White and Hazard bought him off with a toll on every bushel of stone coal brought down the Lehigh, on the theory that it would be cheaper in the long run to be rid of him. (See Eleanor Morton, *Josiah White, Prince of Pioneers* [New York: Stephen Daye, 1946], 128-130, and Josiah White's *History*, originally written 1832; printed by Lehigh Coal & Navigation Co., 1909, 41-45.)
80. John to Maurice, July 21, 1825; WH.
81. John to Maurice, June 29, 1825; WH.
82. John to Maurice, Aug. 26, 1825; WH.
83. Charles S. to Maurice, Nov. 17, 1825; WH. The lists of stockholders filed by the D&H indicate that no member of the family owned stock in May 1826. Only in the following year did Maurice appear as owner of 378 shares.
84. Ibid.
85. John to Maurice, Nov. 20, 1825; WH.
86. William to Maurice, Dec. 31, 1825; WH.
87. Ibid.

Linking the Delaware and the Hudson
Pages 47-87

1. Shaw, *Erie Water West*, 93.
2. Vincent Edward Powers, "Invisible Immigrants: The Pre-Famine Irish Community in Worcester, Mass." (Ph.D. dissertation, Clark Univ., 1976; cited in Shaw, *Canals for a Nation*).
3. Catherine Tobin, "Irish Labor on American Canals," Center for Canal History and Technology *Proceedings*, vol.IX, 1990, 164.
4. Shaw, *Canals for a Nation*, 38.
5. Powers, "Invisible Immigrants."
6. McFee, *Limestone Locks*, 95.
7. Edward J. O'Day, "Constructing the Western Railroad: The Irish Dimension," *Historical Journal of Massachusetts*, vol.XI, No.1, Jan. 1983.

8. A list of "Balances due from Contractors on the Delaware and Hudson Canal . . . Sept. 19, 1827" lists 63 contractors, surely a large proportion of the total, of whom only one or two names are probably Irish (WH). Another list of contractors is presented in James McEntee's Memoirs (1874), reproduced in Sanderson, *Carrying Coals*, 17.
9. John W. Johnston, *Reminiscences* (Highland, NY: Town of Highland Cultural Resources Commission, 1987), 27.
10. DM, Sep. 7, 1825.
11. *Niles Register*, vol.30, Apr. 22, 1826.
12. Johnston, *Reminiscences*, 26-27.
13. Ibid., 28.
14. Peter Way, "Shovel and Shamrock: Irish Workers and Labor Violence in the Digging of the Chesapeake and Ohio Canal," *Labor History*, vol.30, No.4, Fall 1989, 516.
15. Ibid., 497.
16. *Niles Register*, vol.29, Oct. 1, 1825.
17. *Ulster Sentinel*, July 12, July 19, 1826 (emphasis in original).
18. James S. McEntee, "Story of the Canal," *Olde Ulster*, vol.VI, No.10, Oct. 1910. (The account was written in 1874.)
19. HD, undated entry. The line "dark unfathomed caves" is from Thomas Gray's "Elegy Written in a Country Churchyard," which would have been familiar to all cultured readers.
20. FitzSimons, *Reminiscences of John B. Jervis*, 73.
21. Jervis to Maurice Wurts, Nov. 25, 1825; WH.
22. *Niles Register*, vol.29, Oct. 1, 1825.
23. DM, Mar. 8, 1826.
24. D&H List of Stockholders, 1827.
25. This individual was almost certainly the son of patriot hero Gen. Philip Schuyler. The General had a son of this name, born around 1773 (Don R. Gerlach, *Proud Patriot*: Syracuse Univ. Press, 1987). He would have been in his early fifties during the D&H construction and was old enough to have assisted his father in the arduous work on the Western Inland Lock Navigation in the 1790s.
26. DM. The board approved the contract on June 23.
27. DM, Nov. 7, 1825.
28. Alvin F. Harlow, *Steelways of New England* (New York: Creative Age Press, 1946), 186-188.
29. DM, Nov. 16, 1825.
30. DM, Aug. 7, Aug. 14, 1826.
31. *Niles Register*, vol.30, June 3, 1826.
32. Harvey Segal "Cycles of Canal Construction" in Carter Goodrich ed., *Canals and American Economic Development*; Christopher T. Baer, "Canals and Railroads of the Mid-Atlantic States, 1800-1860" (Eleutherian Mills-Hagley Foundation, 1981).
33. Paul Jones, comp., "Two Masonic Ceremonies in Connection with the Building of the Delaware and Hudson Canal," 1965 (ms at D&H Museum, High Falls, NY).
34. DM, Aug. 7, 1826.
35. Jervis to Maurice Wurts, WH.
36. Paul Jones, "Two Masonic Ceremonies".
37. Ibid., from *Ulster Sentinel*, Nov. 29, 1826.
38. DM, Nov. 8, 1826.
39. Thomas C. Proctor, "The Middlesex Canal," Center for Canal History and Technology *Proceedings*, vol.VII, 1988.
40. Shaw, *Canals for a Nation*, 53.
41. McFee, *Limestone Locks*, Chap.3.
42. DM, Mar. 8, 1826.
43. McEntee, "Story of the Canal," 291.
44. DM, Mar. 8, 1826.
45. DM.
46. Dwight Porter, "Reports on the Water-Power of the Region Tributary to Lake Ontario, and of the New York State Canals," in *Reports of the Water-Power of the United States*, 60-64 (Washington: GPO, 1885) cited in Michael S. Raber and Patrick M. Malone, "The Significance of the New York State Canals: An Overview" (South Glastonbury, CT: Raber Associates, 1993).
47. DM, Aug. 29, 1838.
48. DM.
49. DM.
50. *Ulster Sentinel*, Sep. 16, 1826 (from Sullivan Whig, Sep. 13).
51. DM.
52. DM.
53. *Niles Register*, Feb. 21, 1829.
54. In a later summary the D&H board admitted that "the stock had become depressed, so that the company could not relieve itself by the creation of new shares of stock" (DM, Nov. 19, 1844).
55. Reported in the *Ulster Sentinel*, Jan. 10, 1827.
56. *Century of Progress*, 36.
57. DM.
58. Carter Goodrich, *Government Promotion of American Canals and Railroads, 1800-1890* (New York: Columbia Univ. Press, 1961), 271. Government participation in mixed projects brings the total to 70%.
59. Segal, "Cycles of Canal Construction," 187.
60. Chester Lloyd Jones, *The Economic History of the Anthracite-Tidewater Canals* (Philadelphia: Univ. of Pennsylvania, 1908), 77. The speech was made Nov. 16, 1875.
61. *Century of Progress*, 43. Jervis's salary was $4000, more than Bolton's.
62. *Ulster Sentinel*, June 6, 1827.
63. Maurice Wurts to Samuel Flewelling, Sep. 18, 1827; WH.
64. E. D. LeRoy, *The Delaware & Hudson Canal and Its Gravity Railroads* (Honesdale, PA: Wayne County Historical Soc., 1980, 6th ed., 1985), 16.
65. FitzSimons, *Reminiscences of John B. Jervis*, 76.
66. Unidentified Kingston newspaper, WH. An undated, untitled draft of what appears to be Maurice Wurts's address on the occasion is included in the papers.
67. *Niles Register*, July 14, 1827; *Ulster Sentinel*, Aug. 1, 1827. The Rondout aqueduct had been built so tightly that President Bolton and U. S. Senator Nathan Sanford "stood under it without being discommoded by any leak."
68. *Ulster Sentinel*, Aug. 1, 1827.
69. D&H annual report, 1828.
70. *Ulster Sentinel*, Apr. 23, 1828.
71. A notice appeared in the *Ulster Sentinel*, Aug. 29, 1827. The boats, like the first lot, were to be 70 feet long and eight feet, eight inches wide. A request for 20 more boats was advertised on Oct. 10, 1827. This notice speci-

fied the kind and dimensions of the timber to be used and was careful to specify that the timber and plank were to be well seasoned.

72. DM.
73. John to Maurice, Nov. 5, 1827; WH.
74. Rev. David Torrey, ed., *Memoir of Maj. Jason Torrey* (Scranton: James S. Horton, 1885). David Torrey was Jason's son.
75. Kingston newspaper; WH.
76. Also, the Minutes for May 2, 1827 record that the managers "accepted the proposition by Mr. Torrey for his land at forks of Dyberry."
77. David Torrey, *Memoir of Jason Torrey*, 104; Frederick Bailey to Maurice Wurts, July 31, 1827, WH; Vernon Leslie, *Honesdale: The Early Years* (Honesdale: Honesdale 150 Committee, 1981), 14.
78. WH.
79. DM (in which the name is spelled Kimbal).
80. John to Maurice, Aug. 1, 1825; WH.
81. Leslie, *Honesdale: Early Years*, 9. Leslie adds that on October 15 Wurts sold this land to the company for $4000. D&H Minutes do not directly support this assertion, but company real estate maps show the tract as "Conveyed by Maurice Wurts to the D. & H. Co. Oct. 15, 1827."
82. DM, Jan. 19, 1828.
83. Leslie, *Honesdale: Early Years*, 9.
84. Jason Torrey to John Bolton, Feb. 4, 1828; HM.
85. Unsigned note apparently in John Wurts's handwriting, dated June __, 1825 and enclosed in a letter to Maurice dated June 29; WH.
86. David Torrey, *Memoir of Jason Torrey*, 103.
87. DM, June 6, 1829. This agreement may contribute to the persistent belief that Torrey donated half of his land for the canal basin. David Torrey wrote that the boundary between the two properties ran "precisely between the legs of the bronze statue of the soldiers monument."
88. DM. This suggests that the 1829 agreement (see preceding note) had not been put into effect, or did not cover the whole boundary.
89. John Wurts to Russel F. Lord, Apr. 16, 1840; RL.
90. Leslie, *Honesdale: Early Years*, 7. Surprisingly, David Torrey does not claim credit for his father, saying only that "The quick-grown village early received the name of Honesdale" (*Memoir*, 105).
91. William to Maurice, Nov. 28, 1825; WH.
92. 38. The action was taken August 2.
93. DM.
94. HD, Oct. 10, 1828.
95. 38.
96. HD, Oct. 26, 1828.
97. HD, June 23, 1830.
98. HD, Oct. 26-30, 1828.
99. The Erie Canal, already completed, was 363 miles in length; later the Wabash & Erie system in Indiana and Ohio attained a total of 397.5 miles. (Richard G. Waugh, Jr., "Canal Development in Early America, Part I," *The Best from American Canals*, No.I. York, PA: The American Canal and Transportation Center, 1983.)
100. Ibid.
101. The total consists of 106 lift locks, two guard locks (to restrain the Delaware River at the crossing) and two weigh locks. The figure of 108 is commonly seen, derived by excluding one of the smaller categories. By coincidence this equals the mileage, deceiving some into assuming there is an automatic relationship of one lock per mile.
102. This does not mean that the highest point on the D&H was 1073 feet, since there were several ascents and descents. A crucial indication of efficiency of operation is feet of lockage per mile. The D&H, with a figure of about 10, was similar to the Chenango Canal, considered quite rugged. By comparison the nearly ideal Erie Canal worked out to 1.86 feet and the Champlain Canal 2.72 (*1877 Annual Report of the* [New York] *State Engineer and Surveyor on the Canals of the State,* 98).
103. Report of Wright and Sullivan, 1824.
104. Robert Patterson Robins, "A Short Account of the First Permanent Tramway in America," reprinted from Proceedings of the Engineers' Club of Philadelphia, vol.5, no.5 (Philadelphia, 1886).
105. Ibid.
106. John Ashhurst Leiper, *Thomas Leiper, Scottish Patriot of the American Revolution* (Wallingford, PA: Historic Delaware County, Inc., 1976).
107. FitzSimons, *Reminiscences of John B. Jervis*, 70.
108. *Century of Progress*, 28; F. Daniel Larkin, *John B. Jervis* (Ames, IA: Univ. of Iowa Press, 1990), 20-21.
109. William to Maurice, Dec. 31, 1825; WH.
110. DM, Mar. 8, 1826.
111. John to Maurice, Nov. 20, 1825; WH.
112. William to Maurice, Dec. 31, 1825; WH.
113. DM.
114. Larkin, *John B. Jervis*, 20.
115. Granite Railway Company, *The First Railroad in America* (Boston, 1926); H. Hobart Holly, "The Granite Railway," *Quincy History*, No.26, Fall 1991. Philip Hone made a visit to Quincy for similar purposes on Sept. 11, 1828.
116. *Century of Progress*, 43-47.
117. DM, Nov. 7, 1827; FitzSimons, *Reminiscences of John B. Jervis*, 79. Jervis letters cited by Larkin show that, contrary to Jervis's statements many years later, he had found the error and advised the company before it received Renwick's report (*John B. Jervis*, 27).
118. Maurice Wurts to Samuel Flewelling, Sep. 18, 1827; WH.
119. Details of the construction and mechanical operation of the railway have been described in LeRoy *Delaware and Hudson* and several other publications.
120. Report of Canal Committee to Board of Managers, Nov. 7, 1827, transmitted to Maurice Wurts; WH.
121. John to Maurice, Nov. 5, 1827; WH.
122. DM.
123. DM, Jan. 16, 1828.
124. DM, Nov. 5, 1828.
125. DM. The significance of the end points of the turnpike lies in the fact that they were on the Delaware and Susquehanna rivers.
126. Frederick Bailey, Treasurer and agent, Milford & Owego Turnpike Co., to Maurice Wurts, July 31, 1827; WH.

127. Maurice Wurts to Samuel Flewelling; WH.
128. Bolton to Maurice Wurts; WH.
129. DM.
130. Maurice Wurts to Flewelling, Dec. 10, 1829; WH.
131. DM, Dec. 19, 1829.
132. *Ellenville Journal*, Aug. 6, 1901, presenting information attributed to Isaac Alliger, then 84.
133. DM, Feb. 13, 1828. Ringwald gives the name of the vessel as *Rondout*, 71 1/2 feet long, built by Paul K. Darrow at Poughkeepsie (Donald C. Ringwald, *Steamboats for Rondout*, Providence, RI: Steamship Historical Soc. of America, 1981), 11.
134. Ringwald, *Steamboats for Rondout*, 13.
135. DM, Dec. 24, 1828.
136. "Substance of Mr. Bradish's Remarks in the Committee of the Whole House upon the Bill, Entitled 'An Act to Loan the Credit of the State to the President, Managers and Company of the Delaware and Hudson Canal Company'" (Albany: Crowell and Van Benthuysen, 1829). Unfortunately, the actual date of the speech is not given.
137. HD, Mar. 10, 1829.
138. DM, May 4, 1829.
139. HD, May 27, May 28, 1829.
140. HD.
141. DM, June 21, 1828.
142. A letter from Jervis to Bolton indicates that a short trial run of the locomotive was made August 6. Larkin, *John B. Jervis*, 30.
143. DM, Aug. 13, 1829.
144. FitzSimons, *Reminiscences of John B. Jervis*, 86-91.
145. Ibid., 88.
146. P.61; Leslie, *Honesdale and the Stourbridge Lion*, 92.
147. Ibid.; Leslie, *Honesdale: The Early Years*; Smith Hempstone Oliver, *The First Quarter-Century of Steam Locomotives in North America* (Washington: Smithsonian, 1956), 14-21.
148. HD, Aug. 16, 1829. The drop in price was realistic since, as Hone recorded after being notified of the failure by Flewelling, "the alteration necessary in the road to obviate the consequences . . . will be expensive and occasion so much delay, that the quantity of Coal to be brought down this season will fall far short of our former calculations."
149. DM.
150. Manville B. Wakefield, "The Delaware & Susquehanna Canal," *The Best of American Canals*, No.1, 1980.
151. Whitford, *Canal System*, vol.I, 740.
152. The company was incorporated Apr. 20, 1825 with a capital of $500,000 (Whitford, ibid.).
153. DM. Whitford asserts that the D&H influence had been responsible for the Delaware & Susquehannah charter.
154. DM, Dec. 19, 1827.
155. DM, Dec. 23, 1828. The minutes for May 7, 1828 record that a proposition by Richard Page was rejected. No details were provided about the proposal, so it cannot be determined whether it related to the extension.
156. DM, Feb. 3, 1830.
157. Wurts to Flewelling, Sep. 18, 1827; WH. The letter was sent from "Dyberry Forks."
158. DM.
159. Maurice Wurts to Flewelling; WH.
160. DM, Sep. 26, 1827.
161. DM, May 22, 1830.
162. H. Jerome Cranmer, "New Jersey Canals" in Goodrich, *Canals and American Economic Development*.
163. Richard F. Veit, *The Old Canals of New Jersey* (Little Falls, NJ: New Jersey Geographical Press, 1963) cites the state's two canals, the Morris and the Delaware & Raritan as prime examples of developmental and exploitative canals respectively.
164. *Ulster Sentinel*, May 30, 1827.
165. Ibid., June 10, Sep. 10, 1828.
166. Ibid., July 9, 1828.
167. Ibid., Jan. 22, 1828.
168. Ibid., Aug. 15, 1827.

Coming of Age
Pages 89-131

1. HD, Oct. 14, 15, 1829.
2. Maurice Wurts to Flewelling, Dec. 1, 1829; WH.
3. Ibid.
4. Larkin, *John B. Jervis*, 32.
5. Flewelling to Maurice Wurts, Dec. 11, 1829; WH.
6. DM, Jan. 6, Feb. 6, 1830. Blackwell and McFarlane were prominent ironmakers in Dover, NJ, where the two main commercial streets preserve their names.
7. Dec. 9, 1830 (emphasis in original).
8. Hansell, *Josiah White*, 78.
9. The possibility that Jervis felt disappointed is conjectural, as there seems to be no direct confirmation in his writings. He continued with the D&H as a consulting engineer into early 1831.
10. FitzSimons, *Reminiscences of John B. Jervis*, 81.
11. Maurice Wurts to Flewelling; WH. It is not certain whether the reference is to Wurts's brother-in-law Thomas Young.
12. Mark Richards[?] to John Wurts, Apr. 27, 1824; WH.
13. The managers approved a resolution to this effect Feb. 10, 1830; DM.
14. Hansell, *Josiah White*, 77-78.
15. Ibid., 61.
16. John to Maurice, Sep. 24, 1825; WH. John had noted earlier that the Lehigh company had put a set of locks in one of their dams "and this they call commencing the slack water navigation within the provisions [of their charter]." They also watched the Delaware & Raritan and considered buying stock when the subscription books opened (John to Maurice, May 2, May 6, 1825; WH).
17. John to Maurice, Aug. 26, 1825; WH.
18. Ibid.
19. DM, Jan. 14, 1826.
20. N. Smith to Bolton, Feb. 4, 1827; WH.
21. John to Maurice, Nov. 5, 1827; WH. This was the same letter in which John advised against locomotive power and opined that "canalling is better than merchandizing." Rejoicing over the completion of the canal had brought on a rare lapse into joviality and optimism.
22. *Laws of Pennsylvania*, Chap.LXXVII, Apr. 1, 1825. The provisions of this act extended only to the Lackawaxen and any one of its branches, as specified in the charter.
23. DM, Feb. 14, 1829.

24. Report of a public meeting held at the house of John Lord, Buckingham, PA, Feb. 8, 1830; HM.
25. DM, Apr. 11, 1829. *The National Intelligencer* (Philadelphia), vol.99, Apr. 18, 1829, reported that in the previous week raftsmen, after holding a meeting, blew away about 80 feet of the dam.
26. DM, Dec. 19, 1829.
27. John Wurts to Russel Lord, May 14, 1846; RL.
28. *Bethany Enquirer*, Feb. 10, 1830.
29. DM, Feb. 10, Feb. 13, 1830.
30. HD, Feb. 10, 1830.
31. *Bethany Enquirer*, Jan. 27, Feb. 10, Feb. 17, 1830 (emphasis in original).
32. HD, Feb. 14, 1830.
33. HD, Feb. 15, 1830.
34. HD, Feb. 16, 1830.
35. DM, Feb. 20, 1830. On this date the board approved propositions made by Jervis February 1.
36. DM, June 30, 1830. If, in this agreement, the D&H was gambling that the state would never undertake the challenging northward extension of the Delaware Canal beyond Easton, they were proven correct by events.
37. Mar. 17, 1830.
38. Edward Steers, "The Delaware & Hudson Canal Company's Gravity Railroad," Center for Canal History and Technology *Proceedings*, vol.II, 1983.
39. HM.
40. Hansell, *Josiah White*, 86.
41. Henry V. Poor, *History of the Railroads and Canals of the United States of America* (New York: John H. Schultz & Co., 1860; reprint Augustus M, Kelley, 1970); Booth, "Delaware and Hudson Canal."
42. *American Rail-Road Journal*, vol.I, 1831, p.19.
43. Walter Arndt Lucas, *The History of the New York, Susquehanna and Western RR* (New York: Railroadians of America, 1939; 2nd ed., 1980), 10.
44. Quoted in *Wayne* [PA] *Inquirer*, Mar. 23, 1832.
45. Kalata, *A Hundred Years*, 168-72.
46. John Langdon Sullivan, "A Report, descriptive of a Route for a Rail Road from the Hudson through Paterson to the Delaware River, thence to the Susquehanna and the South Western Counties of New-York" (New York: Clayton & Van Norden, 1831). Sullivan's titles were nothing if not explicit; his 1828 report had an even longer one.
47. Lucas, *NYS&W*, 10; Kalata, *A Hundred Years*, 187. The agricultural county of Sussex would hardly have had the capital to attempt such a project on its own.
48. The fact that Sullivan's report did not refer to the Hudson & Delaware by name is not significant, since the company was organized only after his surveys had proved it feasible.
49. Sullivan, 1831 report, 9.
50. Hollister, *Lackawanna Valley*, 314.
51. Ibid., 325.
52. Torrey, *Memoir of Jason Torrey*, 56.
53. Robert J. Casey and W. A. S. Douglas, *The Lackawanna Story* (New York: McGraw-Hill, 1951), 26-27.
54. Powell, *Philadelphia's First Fuel Crisis*, Chap.8.
55. *Newton* [NJ] *Herald* in *Wayne*, [PA] *Inquirer*, Mar. 23, 1832.
56. *Wayne Inquirer*, Feb. 3, 1832.
57. Sullivan, 1831 report.
58. Calhoun, *American Civil Engineer*, 67; Kalata, *A Hundred Miles*, 36-37.
59. *American Railroad Journal*, vol.II, No.32, Aug. 10, 1833.
60. Sullivan, 1831 report. Another consideration is that Sullivan may still have had rights to Lackawaxen stock, which would have had little value until converted to D&H.
61. *Wayne Inquirer*, Oct. 28, 1831, Feb. 3, 1832.
62. DM.
63. Richard G. Waugh, Jr., "Canal Development in Early America, Part 2," *The Best from American Canals*, No.I.(York, PA: The American Canal and Transportation Center, 1980).
64. P.70.
65. *Mitchell's Compendium of the Internal Improvements of the United States* (Philadelphia: Mitchell & Hinman, 1835; reprint American Canal Center, Glen Echo, MD, n.d.).
66. *American Railroad Journal*, vol.5, No.39, Oct. 1, 1836.
67. WH. The typescript version of this letter gives the middle initial as T, perhaps a misreading of B, which seems to be correct.
68. Apr. 20, 1830; WH. Unfortunately, the addressee is not indicated. It seems to be someone involved in operations, possibly Jervis; although the engineer's austere personality makes him a unlikely participant in conspiracy. The reasons for the "disgust" are not explained, but may be related to Bolton's efforts to name the community after himself.
69. N. T. E. to Maurice Wurts, Jan. 9, 1830; WH.
70. HD, Apr. 9, 1831; DM, Apr. 13, 1831.
71. Prominent individuals in the community, notably ex-congressman Abraham Hasbrouck, also objected to the name and refused to use it (Bob Steuding, *Rondout, A Hudson River Port*, Fleischmanns, NY: Purple Mountain Press, 1995, 58). The name Rondout was agreed by all concerned, although the details of its adoption are not known (Stuart M. Blumin, *The Urban Threshold*, [Chicago: Univ. of Chicago, 1976], 77).
72. Hollister, "Delaware & Hudson," 46.
73. Johnston, *Reminiscences*, 40.
74. DM, Mar. 4, 1845.
75. Dec. 19, 1828; WH.
76. Jan. 16, 1829; WH.
77. Dec. 2, 1829; WH.
78. Dec. 1, 1829; WH.
79. New York City Common Council *Minutes*, Mar. 7, 1831 (vol.XIX, p.537).
80. *Niles Register*, vol.37, Oct. 24, 1829.
81. *Wayne Inquirer*, May 27, 1831.
82. DM.
83. Ringwald, *Steamboats for Rondout*, 20.
84. DM.
85. Leslie, *Honesdale and the Stourbridge Lion*, 110.
86. Oliver, "First Quarter Century," 47.
87. DM.
88. Wright to President of Chesapeake & Ohio Canal Co., Oct. 31, 1831, in House of Representatives Document No.101, 22nd Congress, 1832.
89. Jervis to Russel F. Lord, July 17, 1832; Neversink Area Hist. Soc.
90. DM. The deed was executed Dec. 14, 1832.

91. DM, Jan. 8, 1842.
92. John to Maurice, Jan. 16, 1829; WH.
93. *Ulster Republican*, Aug. 29, 1838. Blumin explains the political imperatives underlying the brief campaign (*Urban Threshold*, 202).
94. *Political Reformer* (Kingston), Aug. 14, 1839, emphasis in original..
95. *Ulster Republican*, May 1, 1839.
96. C. P. Wurts, *Wurts Family*.
97. George Wurts to Maurice, Mar. 17, 1828; WH.
98. Charles to Maurice, June 11, 1832; WP.
99. "Up-country" directors was a term later employed on the New Haven RR because of the requirement that a majority of its board had to be residents of Connecticut. It is not known to have been used on the D&H but seems descriptive of men like Wickham and Hasbrouck. Bolton actually remained on the board until the election of March 1832 but was not an original manager.
100. DM. An earlier proposal to request $900,000 had been tabled on Feb. 17, 1830.
101. *Albany Argus*, quoted in HD, Dec. 10, 1828.
102. HD, Mar. 10, 1829.
103. New York City Common Council *Minutes*, Feb. 14, 1831 (vol.XIX, 486). The terms of the sale were not described.
104. DM, Sep. 4, 1830.
105. DM, Jan. 6, 1832.
106. DM, Feb. 7, 1832; Apr. 3, 1833.
107. DM, Oct. 8, 1832.
108. The *James Kent* was purchased from Edward Dunscomb for $3500 (DM, Feb. 13, 1832). The date the *Delaware* was acquired is uncertain.
109. DM, June 23, 1830. There is some uncertainty as to when the company purchased the *Lackawanna*. According to Ringwald it was "enrolled" June 1831 (*Steamboats for Rondout*, 17).
110. Edwin L. Dunbaugh, *Night Boat to New England, 1815-1900* (Westport, CT: Greenwood Press, 1992), 21.
111. Ringwald, *Steamboats for Rondout*, 21.
112. DM.
113. John Wurts to William Worrell, June 21, 1831; WP.
114. DM, Sep. 12, 1832.
115. HD, Dec. 13, 1831. Hone noted this somewhat defensively, for the company was being criticized for raising the price at the expense of the poor.
116. John to Maurice, Feb. 20, 1833; WP.
117. DM, June 20, 1831.
118. For the rapid displacement of charcoal by anthracite in steam generation see Frederick Moore Binder, *Coal Age Empire* (Harrisburg: Pennsylvania Historical and Museum Commission, 1974), Chap.3.
119. John Wurts to William Worrell, June 21, 1831; WP.
120. Ibid.
121. DM, Feb. 20, 1830.
122. John Wurts to Worrell, June 21, 1831; WP.
123. *Century of Progress*, 70.
124. DM, Nov. 8, 1837.
125. Binder, *Coal Age Empire*, Chap.4.
126. Ibid, 92.
127. Codman Hislop, *Eliphalet Nott* (Middletown, CT: Wesleyan Univ. Press, 1971), 351. The D&H annual report for 1831 adds that one ferry was still making successful use of anthracite.
128. DM, May 12, 1831.
129. John Wurts to Worrell, June 21, 1831; WP.
130. DM, Feb. 13, 1832.
131. HD, Jan. 14, 1834.
132. Described in Ringwald, *Steamboats for Rondout*, 17.
133. Hislop, *Eliphalet Nott*, 354, 361.
134. HD, Jan. 5, 1835.
135. *Annual Report, 1834* (the D&H fiscal year ended March 1) quoting the *Journal of Commerce*, Mar. 18, 1835. The Journal described the *Essex* as 126 feet long on deck, with 24-foot beam and nine foot hold. The engine had a 34-inch cylinder, with a six-foot stroke, and produced 60 horsepower. There were two boilers, each seven feet long.
136. DM. In another clause, the company agreed to take payment in Nott's patented boilers at a 20% discount. This would have enabled them to resell at a profit, or possibly even develop their own steamboat line.
137. DM, May 6, 1835; *Annual Report, 1835*. Hislop's biography of Nott presents a more complicated account of the inventor's financial arrangements with the company.
138. A substantial discrepancy. Hone provides the longer figure in his diary; the faster number was given by a correspondent to the *Philadelphia Enquirer*, quoted in Hislop, *Eliphalet Nott*, 369. The return trip on June 25 took ten hours (HD, June 27, 1836).
139. HD, June 23, 1836.
140. Ibid.
141. *Annual Report, 1840*. This was the same triumphant report that declared "The making of iron with anthracite coal is also no longer regarded as an experiment, even in this country."
142. HD, Apr. 20, 1840. The Astor House, by all accounts New York's most luxurious, had been completed in 1836.
143. The North Battery, not to be confused with Castle Clinton in Battery Park, was a similar discontinued fortification at the foot of Hubert Street, about a mile north on the Hudson shore (New York City Common Council *Minutes*, Apr. 11, 1831 [vol.XIX, 627]).
144. Advertisement provided by Bill McKelvey.
145. DM, Jan. 6, Feb. 9, 1832.
146. DM, Dec. 3, 1830.
147. DM, Jan. 18, 1831.
148. *Ulster Sentinel*, Apr. 18, 1827.
149. DM.
150. *Reminiscences*, 41.
151. Document from Russel Lord papers in Sanderson, *Carrying Coals*, 96.
152. *Reminiscences*, 42.
153. DM, Feb. 13, 1832.
154. Franz Anton von Gerstner, *Die Innern Communicatione der Vereinigten Staaten von Nord Amerika* (Vienna: L. Vorsters artistische Anstalt, 1842), vol.I, 78-83.
155. HD, June 26, 1833.
156. HD, Aug. 17, Aug. 20, Aug. 21, 1831.
157. HD, June 22, 1833.
158. DM, Oct. 7, 1835.
159. DM, Oct. 19, 1835.

160. HD, June 18, June 22, 1833.
161. HD, Feb. 18, 1830.
162. HD, Aug. 21, 1831 (at Honesdale).
163. HD, June 14, 1831; Feb. 23, 1832. The New York & Harlem RR, chartered Dec. 22, 1831, went on to enjoy immense success despite Hone's misgivings.
164. HD, Jan. 10, 1835.
165. HD, Feb. 13, 1835.
166. HD, June 24, 1830.
167. HD, June 19, June 20, 1833.
168. *Ulster Palladium*, Mar. 14, 1832; *New-York American*, Mar. 20, 1832.
169. Letter dated Mar. 17 in *New-York American*, Mar. 20, 1832.
170. Steuding, *Rondout*, 68.
171. *American Railroad Journal*, vol.I, June 2, 1832, from *Ulster Plebian*.
172. *Bethany Enquirer*, July 7, 1830.
173. *Century of Progress* (96), gives the 1831 figure as 54,000, but weekly summaries published in the Bethany Enquirer show that the total reached the larger amount. Hone (Diary, Jan. 17, 1833) states that in 1832 the railway carried 89,548 tons; the difference may represent coal that was sold at Honesdale and did not move over the canal.
174. *Wayne Enquirer*, June 8, 1832, from *New York American Advocate*.
175. *Century of Progress*, 98.
176. *American Railroad Journal*, vol.VI, Jan. 14, 1837.
177. HD, Jan. 26, 1831; *Century of Progress*, 96.
178. HD, Jan. 3, 1834.
179. HD, Mar. 19, 1835.
180. *American Railroad Journal*, Feb. 25, 1837.
181. HD, May 10, 1837.
182. DM.
183. John Wurts to Russel Lord, Mar. 9, 1838; RL.
184. Lord to John Wurts, May 7, 1838; RL.
185. John Wurts to Lord, June 5, 1839; RL.
186. DM, Jan. 24, 1838.
187. HD, Nov. 28, 1839.
188. Shaw, *Erie Water West*, 232.
189. May 12, 1830 (emphasis in original).
190. *Wayne [PA] Patriot*, Sep. 28, 1832.
191. *Honesdale: Early Years*, Chap.VII.
192. John Wurts to Lord, Jan. 4, 1841; Kingsbury to Lord, Feb. 1, 1841; RL.
193. Donald H. McTernan, "The Esopus—Minisink Way," M.A. thesis, SUNY, Oneonta, 1969.
194. Herbert C. Kraft, *The Dutch, the Indians, and the Quest for Copper: Pahaquarry and the Old Mine Road* (South Orange, NJ: Seton Hall Museum, 1996).
195. Charles Gilbert Hine, *History and Legend, Fact, Fancy and Romance of the Old Mine Road, Kingston, N.Y., to the Mine Holes of Pahaquarry*, 1909 (reprint Rutgers Univ. Press, 1963).
196. In this context a comparison with mining ventures elsewhere in the northern colonies may be instructive. In the mid-1640s John Winthrop the Younger opened a graphite mine in present-day Sturbridge, MA. Although somewhat more accessible than the alleged mines at Pahaquarry, it proved unsuccessful after consuming a considerable investment. The small iron manufacturing operations that sprang up at various points during this period relied on bog iron, extracted by a process which did not really constitute mining and did not require extended transportation (see E. N. Hartley, *Ironworks on the Saugus*: Univ. of Oklahoma Press, 1957).
197. James Eldridge Quinlan, *History of Sullivan County* (Liberty, NY: G. M. Beebe and W. T. Morgans, 1873; republished 1965), 391; Lewis Historical Publishing Co., *Southeastern New York*, 3 vols. (1946), vol.I, 71.
198. Petition to the Court of Ulster County, Apr. 28, 1743, in McTernan "Esopus—Minisink Way."
199. Another consideration is that the Esopus-Minisink road or trail did not continue along the New Jersey side of the Delaware as did the alleged mine road. As McTernan and Kraft observe, there is probably justification for the existence of a mine road to lead mines at Napanoch which were opened around 1730.
200. McEntee, "Story of the Canal."
201. Sanderson notes, HM.
202. LeRoy, *Delaware & Hudson*, 22.
203. Von Gerstner, *Die Innern Communicatione*, vol.I. This compares with 25% on the Schuylkill Navigation (Jones, *Anthracite-Tidewater Canals*, 150.
204. Marius Schoonmaker, "The History of Kingston," 1888, in Blumin, *Urban Threshold*, 13.
205. *American Railroad Journal*, June 2, 1832, vol.I, 357.
206. Ringwald, *Steamboats for Rondout*, 17.
207. *Ulster Republican* in Blumin, *Urban Threshold*, 52.
208. *History of Ulster County* (Philadelphia: Everts & Peck, 1880), 151.

Thunder Along the Delaware, I: The Erie Railroad Pages 133-159

1. HD.
2. Irving to Mrs. Van Wart, Aug. 1, 1841. Pierre M. Irving, *The Life and Letters of Washington Irving* (New York: G. P. Putnam, 1863; reprinted Gale Research, Detroit: 1967), vol.III, 168-70.
3. Irving to Mrs. Sarah Storrow; Honesdale, July 31, 1841. Stanley T. Williams, *The Life of Washington Irving* (New York: Oxford Univ. Press, 1935), vol.II, 97.
4. Wurts to Lord, Feb. 27, 1840; RL.
5. Wurts to Lord, Mar. 5, 1840; RL.
6. Wurts to Lord, Jan. 12, 1843; RL.
7. Edward Hungerford, *Men of Erie* (New York: Random House, 1946), 32.
8. Calhoun, *American Civil Engineer*, 117.
9. Hungerford, *Men of Erie*, 32.
10. HD, Jan. 23, 1837.
11. RL.
12. Hudson Coal Co., *The Story of Anthracite* (New York: Hudson Coal Co., 1932), 99.
13. DM, Jan. 6, 1841.
14. Wurts to Lord, Jan. 8, 1841; RL.
15. DM, Feb. 10, 1841.
16. Wurts to Lord, Mar. 8, 1841; RL.
17. Wurts to Lord, June 4, 1841; RL.
18. DM, June 23, 1841.
19. Jan. 18, 1841; WP.

20. *House of Representatives Document* No.101, 22nd Congress, 1832.
21. Spiro G. Patton, "Charles Ellet, Jr., and the Canal Versus Railroad Controversy." Center for Canal History and Technology *Proceedings*, vol.II, 1983.
22. John T. Schlebecker, *Whereby We Thrive* (Ames, IA: Iowa State Univ. Press, 1975), 93. The issue was re-opened in the 1890s during the debate about the future of the New York State canals, and the same conclusions about relative costs were reached (Noble E. Whitford, *History of the Barge Canal of New York State*, Albany: J. B. Lyon, 1922, 47).
23. Wurts to Lord, Dec. 1, 1840; RL.
24. Wurts to Lord, Jan. 4, 1841; RL. It is uncertain whether the report is correct; it would seem an odd time of year to put a force of that size to work.
25. Morris Canal & Banking Co. Minutes, Dec. 31, 1840, cited in Kalata, *A Hundred Years*, 343.
26. Wurts to Lord, Dec. 1, 1840; RL.
27. Wurts to Lord, Jan. 4, 1841; RL.
28. Albright Zimmerman, "Problems of a State-Owned Delaware Division Canal," Center for Canal History and Technology *Proceedings*, vol.X, 1991, 119-121. White had inventive and engineering capabilities that the Wurtses in general lacked and was fortunate to live at a time when it was possible for a talented individual to lead the various technologies his enterprise required.
29. Wurts to Lord, Dec. 1, 1840; RL.
30. Wurts to Lord, Jan. 4, 1841; RL.
31. Kalata, *A Hundred Years*, 345.
32. Wurts to Lord, Jan. 15, 1841; RL.
33. Wurts to Lord, Jan. 23, 1841; RL.
34. Wurts to Lord, Jan. 15, 1841; RL.
35. Ibid.
36. Ibid.
37. Wurts to Lord, Jan. 23, 1841; RL.
38. Wurts to Lord, Feb. 25, 1841; RL.
39. Ibid.
40. Ibid. The Feb. 25 letter seems not to have reached Lord promptly. On Mar. 7 Wurts wrote again, restating his concerns and his strategy, but by then the outlook was even grimmer: "there is increased probability of the bill passing, unless active means are taken to prevent it," he wrote.
41. Wurts to Lord, Mar. 17, 1843; RL (emphasis in original).
42. Zimmerman, "Problems of a State-Owned Delaware Division Canal," 125-27.
43. Wurts to Lord, Jan. 12, 1843; RL.
44. Figures in this and preceding paragraph from Jones, *Anthracite-Tidewater Canals*. Nor was the D&H market in New England any longer secure. "In 1822, Boston had received only four coal cargoes from Philadelphia; by 1835 that had risen to 2,631" (Robert G. Albion, et. al., *New England and the Sea* [Middletown, CT: Wesleyan Univ. Press, 1972], 127.)
45. *Century of Progress*, 125.
46. DM, Mar. 4, 1845.
47. Wurts to Lord, Mar. 8, 1841; RL.
48. DM, Mar. 24, 1841.
49. Wurts to Lord; RL.
50. DM, May 24, 1841.
51. Wurts to Lord, June 4, 1841; RL.
52. Moses Y. Beach, ed., *The Wealth and Biography of the Wealthy Citizens of the City of New York*, 10th ed. (New York: 1846). According to Beach's estimate the city's largest fortune was John Jacob Astor's $25 million. This comprised nearly 10% of the total value of the city's real and personal estate. Put another way, Astor's worth nearly equalled the city's total bank capital, which Beach listed as $27,908,980. A modern and far more systematic scholar has condemned Beach's data as "riddled with errors and inconsistencies" (Edward Pessen, *Riches, Class, and Power before the Civil War*. Lexington, MA: Heath, 1973, 10). Pessen's criticism is undoubtedly merited, but for purposes of this study Beach's coarse comparisons are adequate.
53. LeRoy, *Delaware & Hudson*, 38, without citing a source.
54. Testimony of Frederick R. Marshall, Nov. 2, 1860; D&H Canal Co. vs. Pennsylvania Coal Co. (New York: W. C. Bryant, 1858), vol.VI, 3713.
55. DM, Mar. 4, 1845. *Century of Progress*, 128, provides different figures: $108,439 for the cost of enlargement, yielding a saving of $163,429. Possibly these figures refer only to the canal.
56. DM, Mar. 4, 1845.
57. Ibid.
58. One can see an obvious parallel to contemporary companies trying to immunize themselves against a hostile takeover.
59. DM, Nov. 19, 1844.
60. DM, Dec. 1, 1846.
61. DM, Mar. 4, 1845.
62. Ibid.
63. "Notice to Boatmen," draft, Feb. 20, 1841; RL.
64. Maurice Wurts to Lord, July 3, 1843; RL.
65. Maurice Wurts to Lord, Oct. 31, 1845; RL.
66. In 1845, looking ahead to 1846, Maurice based his estimates on averages of 12 trips with 50 tons or 13 with 47 tons, for a total of 600 tons per boat per season (Maurice Wurts to Lord, Oct. 31, 1845; RL).
67. Maurice Wurts to Lord, Oct. 21, 1846; RL.
68. Maurice Wurts to Lord, June 11, 1846; RL.
69. Maurice Wurts to Lord, Oct. 21, 1846; RL.
70. Maurice Wurts to Lord, July 29, 1846; RL.
71. John to Maurice, Feb. 20, 1833; WP.
72. Steers, "D & H Gravity RR," 160; Gerald M. Best, "The Gravity Railroad of The Delaware & Hudson Canal Company," Railroad & Locomotive Historical Soc. *Bulletin* No.82, Apr. 1951, 11.
73. DM, June 20, 1840.
74. Steers, "D&H Gravity RR;" Best, "Gravity RR;" *Century of Progress*. The two latter accounts rely heavily on a paper written by John Torrey of Honesdale in 1892. Steers relies more on a report from Archbald to John Wurts dated Feb. 5, 1847, in general a more reliable source.
75. DM, Dec. 23, 1846.
76. Steers, "D&H Gravity RR," 164.
77. DM, Nov. 17, 1847.
78. DM, Oct. 14, 1844.
79. DM, various dates.
80. A new "insular dock" for deposit of coal at Rondout cost an additional $44,783 according to the *Annual Report for 1847*.

81. Hollister, "D&H," 60. Even the usually hyper-critical John W. Johnston has only positive things to say about Archbald, perhaps in part to set up an unfavorable comparison with Lord and others responsible for the canal, with whom he had closer contact.

82. Lord to John Wurts, Jan. 16, 1843; RL.

83. Peter Osborne, III, "The Delaware and Hudson Canal Company's Enlargement and the Roebling Connection," Center for Canal History and Technology *Proceedings*, vol.III, 1984, 122-23.

84. DM, Feb. 13, 1846.

85. Wurts to Lord, May 14, 1846; RL (emphasis in original).

86. Osborne, "Roebling Connection,"125.

87. Wurts to Lord, Dec. 17, 1846; RL.

88. DM.

89. Wurts to Lord, Dec. 29, 1846; RL.

90. DM, Jan. 6, 1847.

91. Osborne, "Roebling Connection," 126.

92. Ibid.; Robert M. Vogel, "Roebling's Delaware & Hudson Canal Aqueducts" (Washington: Smithsonian, 1971).

93. Osborne, "Roebling Connection," 128.

94. Ibid., 124-25.

95. DM, May 24, 1841.

96. Osborne, "Roebling Connection," 128. A letter from John A. Roebling was published in *American Railroad Journal*, vol.XXII, Jan. 13, 1849. At that time he wrote that the Delaware and Lackawaxen aqueducts "are now completed and ready for the opening of navigation next spring."

97. John to William and Charles S.; WP.

98. Maurice to William, Oct. 24, 1845, quoting a letter from D&H Vice President Isaac L. Platt; WP.

99. Wurts to Lord, Sep. 4, 1846; RL.

100. Ibid.

101. Wurts to Lord, Dec. 16, 1846; RL.

102. DM, Dec. 28, 1846.

103. Ibid.

104. Manville B. Wakefield, *Coal Boats to Tidewater* (Fleischmanns, NY: Purple Mountain Press, 1992), 106-07.

105. Lord to Wurts, Jan. 6, 1849, in D&H vs. PCC, vol.I, xxx.

106. DM.

New Territory, New Trouble
Pages 161-183

1. 119.

2. 120.

3. Hollister, "D&H," 140.

4. Ibid., 69.

5. Ibid., 68.

6. The Wurts papers at the Hagley Museum end around 1830, with a few exceptions, while the collection at the Pennsylvania Historical Society begins in 1845.

7. Maurice to William, Aug. 19, 1845; WP.

8. John to Charles, Feb. 11, 1845; WP.

9. Charles to unknown addressee, probably John Wurts, May 1, 1845; WP (emphasis in original).

10. William to John, July 28, 1845; WP.

11. Ibid.

12. Maurice to Charles and William, Oct. 24, 1845, with copy of James Archbald report to John Wurts; WP.

13. Maurice to William, Oct. 24, 1845; WP.

14. Maurice to William, Oct. 22, 1845; WP.

15. Isaac Platt to John Wurts, n.d., included in Maurice to William, Oct. 24, 1845; WP.

16. Maurice to William, Oct. 22, 1845; WP.

17. Maurice to William, Oct. 24, 1845; WP.

18. DM, Nov. 11, 1845.

19. DM, Nov. 28, 1845.

20. Ibid.

21. John to Charles, Dec. 1, 1845; WP.

22. Hollister, "D&H," 70.

23. Ibid., 75.

24. *Wilkes-Barre Republican Farmer*, Mar. 1846, quoted in Hollister, "D&H," 93.

25. Hollister, *Lackawanna Valley*, 277.

26. Hollister, "D&H," 111.

27. Ibid.

28. Thomas Young to William Wurts, Jan. 12, 1846; WP.

29. Maurice to William, Jan. 12, 1846; WP.

30. William Wurts to John J. Phelps, Feb. 12, 1846; WP.

31. William Silkman to William Wurts, Mar. 13, 1846; WP.

32. Charles Silkman to Nathan Smith, Feb. 19, 1846; WP.

33. Hollister, "D&H," 80-85.

34. John to Charles, Nov. 15, 1845; WP.

35. Hollister, "D&H," 95.

36. Maurice to Charles, Mar. 24, 1846; WP.

37. Durfee, *Reminiscences*, 102.

38. Hollister, "D&H," 131.

39. John to Charles; WP.

40. William to Charles, Feb. 13, 1846; WP.

41. Isaac Platt to James Archbald, July 17, 29, 1846; WH.

42. DM, July 23, 1846.

43. Hollister, "D&H," 140.

44. Ibid., 149.

45. John to Maurice, Jan. 28, 1847; WP; DM, Oct. 3, 1846.

46. DM, Jan. 6, 1847.

47. Maurice to William, Feb. 13, 1846; WP.

48. DM, Oct. 3, 1846.

49. John to Maurice, Jan. 28, 1847; WP.

50. DM, Dec. 23, 1846.

51. Ibid.

52. DM, Jan. 6, 1847.

53. Maurice to Charles, Feb. 16, 1847; WP.

54. John to Maurice, Jan. 28, 1847.

55. Irad Hawley to William and Charles Wurts; WP.

56. Maurice to Charles, Mar. 9, 1847; WP. According to this letter, Charles (with or without William) owned 1800 acres of land at Cobbs Gap.

57. Irad Hawley and A[quilla] G. Stout to William and Charles Wurts, Apr. 20, 1847; WP.

58. Edward K. Spann, *The New Metropolis* (New York: Columbia Univ. Press, 1981), 7. Moses Y. Beach's listings in his *Wealthy Citizens of New York* testify to the number of affluent New Yorkers with New England origins. In his classic *The Rise of the New York Port* (New York: Scribner's, 1970), Robert G. Albion devotes considerable attention to the importance of New England men in New York commerce. Connecticut natives in particular are cited, but unfortunately the Hawleys are not mentioned by name.

59. Elias S. Hawley, *The Hawley Record* (Buffalo: E. H. Hutchinson, 1890), 417, 570.

60. Beach, *Wealthy Citizens of New York* (1846). Beach was the publisher of the *New York Sun*, which Edward Pessen (*Riches, Class, and Power*), 11, describes as a "scandal-mongering newspaper." He incorporated many gossipy tidbits in his directory, but it is noteworthy that he had no such entries for Irad or Judson Hawley, except that Judson (Irad's brother, three years older) was "a bachelor, of the firm of Hopkins & Hawley, large grocers." If the Hawleys are mysterious to the modern student, it is some consolation that they seemed elusive even to a contemporary gossip.

61. Irad Hawley to Charles Wurts, June 22, 1847; WP.

62. List of Subscribers to Washington Coal Co., Sep. 18, 1847; HM. The bulk of the Philadelphia reserve, $32,000, was subscribed by longtime Wurts associates William and John Worrell (Irad Hawley to Charles Wurts, Aug. 5, 1847; WP).

63. Irad Hawley to Charles Wurts, Aug. 3, Aug. 9, 1847; WP.

64. Hollister, *Lackawanna Valley*, 299.

65. The D&H had relied a good deal on Dimmick in its efforts to fend off the Erie RR, but became disenchanted with him. John Wurts wrote of him, "I begin to think that Smith has read his character truly when he called him 'an ass,' though I don't think he is a 'knave'" (John to Charles, Apr. 8, 1845; WP).

66. Durfee, *Reminiscences*, 102.

67. Report of the Annual Meeting of the Managers of the Wyoming Coal Association, June 12, 1848; Steers Collection, HM.

68. Steers, "D&H Gravity RR," 159-61; Steers Collection, HM.

69. Irad Hawley to Charles Wurts, June 30, July 9, 1847; WP; DM, July 15, 1847.

70. Irad Hawley to Charles Wurts, July 2, 1847; WP.

71. Irad Hawley to Charles Wurts, July 9, 1847; WP.

72. DM, Aug. 2, 1847.

73. DM, June 16, 1847.

74. D&H vs. PCC, vol.VI, 3416.

75. DM, Nov. 7, 1850.

76. DM, Oct. 27, 1848.

77. DM.

78. *Rondout Courier*, Jan. 19, 1849.

79. *Rondout Courier*, Apr. 5, 1850.

80. Testimony of Lorenzo A. Sykes, May 4, 1858; PCC vs. D&H, vol.II, 914.

81. DM, Nov. 7, 1850.

82. Ibid.

83. *Reminiscences*, 47.

84. DM, Nov. 26, 1847.

85. The operation and personnel of the PCC railway is described by Edward Steers, "The Pennsylvania Coal Company's Gravity Railroad," Center for Canal History and Technology *Proceedings*, vol.I, 1982.

86. DM, Oct. 11, 1848. On May 10, 1849 the amount was increased to $12,000.

87. DM, June 1, 1848.

88. WP.

89. J. H. Battle, ed. *History of Columbia and Montour Counties* (Chicago: Warner, 1887).

90. Hollister, "D&H," 100-104. The meeting was held Sep. 30, 1846.

91. William Henry to George Wurts, July 19, Aug. 1, 1845; WP. The addressee is probably the son of Dr. George Wurts, the older brother of the D&H Wurtses, who had died in 1835.

92. Maurice to William, Aug. 29, 1845; WP (emphasis in original). John Wurts was quoting a Mr. Patterson of Baltimore.

93. Isaac Platt to James Archbald, Oct. 28, 1845; WH.

94. Alexander Wurts to Charles Wurts, Mar. 5, 1846; WP. The letter is addressed "Dear Brother," although, if this is the correct Alexander and the addressee is Charles Stewart Wurts, Alexander was actually his nephew. Charles Stewart did not have a brother named Alexander.

95. William Henry to William Wurtz (sic), Apr. 28, 1847; WP.

96. John to William and Charles, May 10, 1847; WP.

97. Lucas, *NYS&W*, 11.

98. Maurice to Charles, Nov. 4, 1848; WP.

99. William Wurts to Irad Hawley, Aug. 1, 1849; WP. The request also covered shares held by Charles S. Wurts.

100. John to Charles, Oct. 25, 1849; WP.

101. Charles to Maurice, Jan. 3, 1850; WP.

102. DM, Apr. 12, 1844.

103. DM, May 16, May 22, 1848.

104. DM, June 2, 1849.

105. DM, June 20, 1849.

106. John to Charles, Oct. 1, 1849; WP (emphasis in original).

107. John to Charles, Oct. 25, 1849; WP.

108. John to Charles, Nov. 12, 1849; WP.

109. Maurice to Charles, Oct. 15, 1849; WP.

110. John to Charles, Oct. 5, 1849; WP.

The First Skirmishes
Pages 185-223

1. DM, Oct. 4, 1850.

2. DM, June 13, 1850.

3. Letter from President George T. Olyphant, Dec. 4, 1867; DM, Dec. 5.

4. Maurice to Charles, Oct. 15, 1849; WP.

5. DM, Oct. 4, 1850. Wurts added "It will probably be some time before Mr. Archbald will be able to give personal attention to business and perhaps he never can, and I certainly think he never should attempt to labor as he has done."

6. DM, Dec. 29, 1851.

7. DM, Nov. 29, 1849. According to later testimony of Russel Lord the D&H let boats and received PCC coal at Rondout. The D&H paid freight charges, and the coal went into the common D&H stock (D&H vs. PCC, vol.I, 188; testimony Dec. 31, 1857).

8. DM, June 13, 1850.

9. Indenture, Wyoming Coal Association/Pennsylvania Coal Co., May 30, 1851; Steers Collection, HM.

10. DM, July 29, 1851.

11. DM, Apr. 26, 1852.

12. DM, May 11, 1852.

13. DM, May 8, 1852.

14. DM, July 28, 1852.
15. DM, Aug. 4, 1853.
16. DM, June 17, 1856.
17. List of Stockholders, Wyoming Coal Association, May 30, 1851; Steers Collection, HM.
18. DM, June 2, 1849.
19. DM, May 29, 1851. The resolution was passed April 3.
20. Hollister, "D&H," 83.
21. *Annual Report for 1853.*
22. Hollister, "D&H," 137-38.
23. DM, June 5, 1852.
24. Ibid.
25. *Rondout Courier*, cited in C. P. Wurts, *Wurts Family*, 55.
26. DM, Apr. 20, 1857.
27. DM, Mar. 15, 1858.
28. DM, Apr. 10, 1858.
29. DM, May 18, 1858.
30. C. P. Wurts, *Wurts Family*, 93.
31. *Century of Progress*, 156.
32. John Wurts to Lorenzo A. Sykes, May 12, 1857; WH.
33. Ibid., May 8, 1857.
34. Ibid., May 12, 1857.
35. Ibid., May 8, 1857.
36. Binder, *Coal Age Empire*, 58.
37. John Wurts to Lorenzo A. Sykes, Oct. 3, 1857; WH.
38. Isabella Bird, *The Englishwoman in America* (London: 1854).
39. Federal Writers' Project, *Boston Looks Seaward* (Boston: Northeastern Univ. Press, reprint 1985; originally 1941), 112.
40. Feb. 20, 1847. As a comparison the *Journal* gave the total capitalization of the great textile center of Lowell, MA, as $10,550,000. The largest company, Merrimack Manufacturing, had a capital of $2,000,000.
41. Spiro G. Patton "Delaware & Hudson Company vs. Pennsylvania Coal Company during the 1850s," Center for Canal History and Technology *Proceedings*, vol.XI, 1992, 7.
42. D&H vs. PCC, vol.I, Exhibit A.
43. PCC witness William J. McAlpine calculated that the cost per ton on small boats was 17.11 to 20.62 cents lower than on 125-ton and 120-ton boats, respectively (D&H vs. PCC, vol.VI, 3402).
44. D&H vs. PCC, vol.III, 1567.
45. Ibid. II, 1029, 1096, 1116, 1331; III, 1573.
46. William A. French of Homowack (formerly Red Bridge); D&H vs. PCC, vol.II, 1239. Another boatman, James McCue of Mamakating, testified "I made [earned] my home on a small boat" (ibid., 1937).
47. D&H vs. PCC, vol.I, 82-89.
48. Shaw, *Erie Water West*, 295.
49. Shaw, *Canals for a Nation*, 46.
50. D&H vs. PCC, vol.VI, 3363-64 (May 18, 1860).
51. Ibid., 3370.
52. Ibid. III, 1930 (testimony of James McCue).
53. Patton, "D&H vs. PCC," 20.
54. D&H vs. PCC, vol.VI, 3958.
55. DM, Jan. 28, 1857.
56. Steuding notes that as early as 1851 Morris Canal recruiters had been trying to lure D&H boatmen to New Jersey (*Rondout*, 84).
57. D&H vs. PCC, vol.VI, 3434.
58. Ibid., 3584.
59. Patton, "D&H vs. PCC," 22.
60. 179.
61. "Decisions in Litigation between D&H and the Pennsylvania Coal Co.," Ulster County Court of Appeals, 1872; New York Public Library.
62. Ibid.
63. DM, Apr. 22, June 25, 1874.
64. D&H vs. PCC, vol.I, 475 (Feb. 23, 1858).
65. Testimony of James McCue, Mar. 17, 1859; ibid. III, 1935.
66. Testimony of William Van Wagenen, Feb. 27, 1858; ibid. I, 524. Van Wagenen ran a store in Eddyville.
67. Testimony of Frederick R. Marshall, Nov. 20, 1860; ibid. VI, 3271. Marshall was foreman of the Lackawaxen section.
68. Testimony of George F. Von Beck, Apr. 6, 1858; ibid. II, 777.
69. Ibid., 954. Sykes may have been trying to account for the frequent labor unrest of the early 1850s.
70. Testimony of Jacob B. Fitch, Nov. 30, 1860; ibid. VI, 3810.
71. Testimony of Lorenzo A. Sykes, May 7, 1858; ibid. II, 956.
72. Testimony of Alpheus Galloway, July 13, 1858; ibid., 1078. Galloway testified that his wife often steered; presumably she belonged to the "naturally ingenious" category.
73. Donald Ross, "The Very Last Days of the D&H Canal," *Canal Days*, vol.II, No.I, Feb. 1968.
74. Johnston, *Reminiscences*, 46.
75. *Harpers New York and Erie Rail-Road Guide Book* (New York: Harper & Bros., 1851), 68.
76. *Tri-States Union*, June 30, 1859.
77. Port Jervis *Evening Gazette*, July 19, 1870; *Tri-States Union*, Aug. 4, 1870.
78. DM, Oct. 27, 1836.
79. Port Jervis *Evening Gazette*, May 15, 1873.
80. Thomas F. Gordon, *Gazetteer of the State of New York* (Philadelphia: T. K. & F. G. Collins, 1836).
81. *Ellenville Press*, Aug. 3, 1905, in Sanderson, *Carrying Coals*, 179.
82. Roy Ghear, "The Last Days of the Canal in High Falls," and Earl Mack "Recollections," D&H Canal Soc. *Bulletin*, vol.II, No.1, Feb. 1968.
83. Figures on saloons from Lewis Historical Publishing Co., *Southeastern New York*. In several instances the number of saloons approximated the number of general stores, but in Eddyville this relationship did not prevail.
84. *Kingston Journal*, Jan. 15, 1873.
85. Shaw, *Canals for a Nation*, 193.
86. "L. W." in *Ulster Republican*, Sep. 24, 1856; Sanderson notes. HM.
87. Katherine T. Terwilliger, *Wawarsing: Where the Streams Wind* (Ellenville: Rondout Publishing, 1977), 61.
88. Hamilton Child, *Gazetteer and Business Directory of Ulster County*, 1872.
89. Terwilliger, *Wawarsing*, 61.
90. *French's Gazetteer, 1861*, in Sanderson, *Carrying Coals*, 138.

91. Terwilliger, "Napanoch," Delaware & Hudson Historical Soc. *Canal Days*, vol.I, No.4, Dec. 1967.
92. Terwilliger, "Port Benjamin," *Canal Days*, vol.II, No.2, Apr. 1968. The place was named for the legendary Benjamin Depuy.
93. Booth, "Delaware & Hudson Canal."
94. *Rondout Courier*, Feb. 26, 1858.
95. Kingston *Democratic Journal*, Dec. 10, 1843.
96. *French's Gazetteer*, in Sanderson, *Carrying Coals*, 138. Kingston's population was then less than 4000.
97. Kingston *Democratic Journal*, May 13, 1847.
98. Donald C. Ringwald, "When the Steamboats Reigned," *Kingston's Hudson-Champlain Souvenir Booklet* (Kingston Anniversary Booklet Committee, 1959).
99. Quinlan, *Sullivan County*, 429.
100. *French's Gazetteer* in Sanderson, *Carrying Coals*, 138. In 1855 half of Kingston's population was foreign-born, a large proportion consisting of unskilled or semi-skilled laborers (Blumin, *Urban Threshold*, 80-86).
101. This figure is derived from impressionistic analysis of the names and is subject to the usual uncertainties in distinguishing Irish from Scotch-Irish. Also, the number of entries relative to the number of inhabitants suggests that not every resident was listed, and in directories of this kind the lower-income and more transient elements of the population are most likely to be omitted. The presence of Roman Catholic churches in Ellenville at that time indicates that there may have been a more substantial Irish presence.
102. Leslie, *Honesdale: Early Years*, 42.
103. Hollister, *Lackawanna Valley*, 247.
104. Burton W. Folsom, II, *Urban Capitalists: Entrepreneurs and City Growth in Pennsylvania's Lackawanna and Lehigh Regions, 1800-1920* (Baltimore: Johns Hopkins Univ., 1981), 21. His PhD. dissertation "Urban Networks: The Economic and Social Order of the Lackawanna and Lehigh Valleys during Early Industrialization, 1850-1880" (Univ. of Pittsburgh, 1976) presents additional reasons why towns dependent on extractive industry and inhabited largely by low-income miners were not suited for rapid growth and diversification (13-20).
105. Durfee, *Reminiscences*, 109.
106. Hollister, "D&H," 84 (emphasis in original).
107. Durfee, *Reminiscences*, esp. 17-22; M. J. McAndrew, *History of Hawley, Pennsylvania* (Hawley: 1927).
108. Durfee, *Reminiscences*, 78.
109. Compilation of 1860 census returns for Sullivan County in Ellenville Library & Museum local history collection.
110. Alphonso T. Clearwater, ed. *History of Ulster County* (Kingston: W. J. Van Deusen, 1907), 351.
111. Durfee, *Reminiscences*, 50.
112. *Rondout Courier*, Apr. 16, 1869.
113. Patricia Clinton, "The Delaware & Hudson Canal in Ellenville," text for a talk delivered to the D&H Canal Soc., Oct. 28, 1990.
114. Found in papers of Allen E. Goetcheus, who died 1953 at the age of 77; D&H Canal Museum, High Falls.
115. Blumin, *Urban Threshold*, 151, et.seq.
116. Benson J. Lossing, *The Hudson, from the Wilderness to the Sea* (New York: Virtue & Yorston, 1866), 184.

117. Beach, *Wealthy Citizens of New York*.
118. Johnston, *Reminiscences*, 21.
119. Quinlan, *Sullivan County*, 438.
120. Nathaniel Bartlett Sylvester, *History of Ulster County* (Philadelphia: Everts & Peck, 1880).
121. New York State Senate No.77, Feb. 26, 1834 (copy in Ellenville Public Library, local history collection). Portions of the petition have a surprisingly modern ring of ecological concern. Describing the effects of large expanses of stagnant water caused by the poor canal construction and management, the citizens claim that it "has a tendency not only to injure the property of the petitioners, but also to jeopardize their health and the health of their families."
122. Farnum to Lord, Aug. 8, 1849; RL. Pine Woods was the name of a lock about two miles east of Port Jervis.
123. Farnum to Lord, Oct. 30, Nov. 27, 1849; RL.
124. Katherine T. Terwilliger, "Port Hixon," from an article by Herbert Small, *Ellenville Journal*, Jan. 21, 1971.
125. Bruce v. President &c. of Delaware and Hudson Canal Co., 1853 (courtesy Bill McKelvey).
126. Lord to Messrs. Young & Schults, Aug. 18, 1841; RL.
127. June 7, 1850.
128. *Tri-States Union*, June 21, 1872.

Railroaders at the Tiller
Pages 225-261

1. Steers, "D&H Gravity RR," 177. Steers presents considerable contemporary reporting on the construction of the railway.
2. Best, "Gravity RR," 17.
3. DM, Feb. 15, 1856.
4. DM, May 15, 1856.
5. Published as "Report on the geology and mining resources of that part of the Lackawanna coal basin which includes the lands of the Delaware, Lackawanna & Western railroad company, and those of the Lackawanna iron and coal company" (Boston: 1854).
6. *Annual Report for 1859*. The line actually terminated at a point called Valley Junction.
7. Olyphant letter to the Board; DM, Dec. 5, 1867.
8. DM, Mar. 6, 1868.
9. DM, June 3, 1859.
10. DM, June 3, June 22, 1859.
11. DM, Dec. 3, 1859; Feb. 8, 1860.
12. Steers, "D&H Gravity RR," 179, citing the *Carbondale Advance*, Nov. 19, 1859.
13. DM, Dec. 3, 1859.
14. The best evidence for the date of completion is provided in the D&H *Annual Report* for fiscal 1860, which states that the line would be ready for use on May 1, 1860.
15. Steers, "D&H Gravity RR," 182, citing the *Carbondale Advance*, Feb. 18, 1860.
16. Ibid., 181, citing the *Carbondale Advance*, Jan. 28, 1860.
17. Larry Lowenthal and William T. Greenberg, Jr., *The Lackawanna Railroad in Northwest New Jersey* (Morristown, NJ: Tri-State Rwy Historical Soc., 1987).
18. Casey & Douglas, *Lackawanna Story*, 72.
19. D&H *Annual Reports* for 1859, 1861.
20. DM, Nov. 29, 1859.
21. DM, Nov. 19, 1861.

22. Steers, "D&H Gravity RR," 183.
23. DM, Mar. 17, 1863.
24. Poor, *History of Railroads and Canals*, 355.
25. Lucas, *NYS&W*, 11. The charter was transferred Dec. 30, 1853.
26. Lowenthal & Greenberg, *Lackawanna RR in Northwest NJ*, 140.
27. WH, Box 3.
28. Lucas, *NYS&W*, 12.
29. Edward Steers, "A Historical Survey of the Erie and Wyoming Valley Railroad," Center for Canal History and Technology *Proceedings*, vol.III, 1964, 174.
30. DM, Nov. 17, 1863.
31. DM, Dec. 15, 1863.
32. DM.
33. McAndrew, *Hawley*, 42. This individual was not the same and apparently not related to the Charles Miner of Wilkes-Barre who had been an important promoter of canals in the 1820s.
34. *Annual Report for 1868.*
35. *Annual Report for 1869.*
36. Railroadians of America, *The Next Station Will Be*, vol.VII (Livingston, NJ: Railroadians of America, 1982), n.p.
37. DM, May 12, 1866.
38. DM, Feb. 5, 1873. Proof of the company's regard for its venerable employee is shown by the naming of its fifth locomotive Isaac N. Seymour.
39. McAndrew, *Hawley*, 42.
40. DM, Apr. 23, 1868.
41. Best, "Gravity RR," 19-20.
42. Steers, "D&H Gravity RR," 175.
43. Thomas T. Taber, *The Delaware, Lackawanna & Western RR in the Nineteenth Century* (Muncy, PA: Thomas T. Taber, III, 1977), 193-96.
44. DM, Dec. 28, 1860.
45. *Annual Report for 1868.*
46. DM, Jan. 30, 1867.
47. Alvin F. Harlow, *The Road of the Century* (New York: Creative Age Press, 1947), 319.
48. DM, Mar. 11, 1871; Jan. 15, 1872.
49. DM, June 4, 1873.
50. William F. Helmer, *O&W* (Berkeley, CA: Howell-North, 1959).
51. DM, Nov. 26, 1872.
52. Johnston, *Reminiscences*, 63.
53. DM.
54. *Century of Progress*, 317.
55. DM, Sep. 23, 1862.
56. DM, Apr. 21, 1863.
57. DM, Oct. 20, 1863.
58. DM, Feb. 16, 1864.
59. Johnston, *Reminiscences*, 65.
60. DM, Nov. 17, 1863.
61. DM, June 19, 1866.
62. DM, May 9, 1867.
63. *Annual Report for 1868* (author's emphasis).
64. DM, Dec. 3, 1859.
65. Burton W. Folsom, II, "Urban Networks: The Economic and Social Order of the Lackawanna and Lehigh Valleys during Early Industrialization," Ph.D. dissertation, Univ. of Pittsburgh, 1976, 71.
66. DM, Oct. 15, 1867.
67. DM, Dec. 4, 1867.
68. DM, June 28, 1866.
69. DM, Aug. 21, 1866.
70. *Annual Report for 1867.*
71. DM, Oct. 15, 1867.
72. *Annual Report for 1867*; DM, Jan. 3, 1868.
73. Jim Shaughnessy, *Delaware & Hudson* (Berkeley, CA: Howell-North, 1967), 60.
74. DM, Feb. 17, 1864.
75. DM, Jan. 30, 1864.
76. *Annual Report for 1869.*
77. *Annual Report for 1867.*
78. DM, May 13, 1868.
79. DM, Mar. 11, 1871. The totals do not tally, perhaps because the D&H included sales of coal from previous stocks.
80. W. H. Bunting, *Portrait of a Port: Boston, 1852-1914* (Cambridge, MA: Harvard Univ. Press, 1971), 324.
81. Veit, *Old Canals of New Jersey*, 53, 80.
82. DM, Apr. 19, 1864.
83. *Annual Report for 1859.*
84. DM, Oct. 31, 1859.
85. Herman R. Lytell, "Story of the Delaware and Hudson Canal," unpublished manuscript, Minisink Valley Hist. Soc., 229-33. The similarity of names suggests that both vessels were built by the same person.
86. DM, Sep. 18, 1866.
87. DM, Dec. 18, 1866. In this record the name was spelled Misnel.
88. Alvin F. Harlow, *Old Towpaths* (New York: D. Appleton, 1926), 324.
89. Lytell, "Story of the D&H Canal," 232.
90. *Tri-States Union* (Port Jervis), Apr. 3, 1878.
91. Harlow, *Old Towpaths*, 325.
92. Dickson letter to the Board, DM, Oct. 27, 1880.
93. DM, Mar. 26, 1870.
94. Another possibility is that other demands for water were increasing, but there is no obvious reason why that would be the case.
95. DM, Oct. 27, 1880.
96. DM, Oct. 28, 1880.
97. DM, Dec. 14, 1880.
98. DM, June 22, 1881.
99. DM, Sep. 22, 1880.
100. Ibid.
101. Carleton Mabee, *Listen to the Whistle: An Anecdotal History of the Wallkill Valley Railroad* (Fleischmanns, NY: Purple Mountain Press, 1995), 37.
102. DM, Dec. 29, 1880.
103. DM, Mar 4, 1881.
104. Mabee, *Listen to the Whistle*, 38-40.
105. Harlow, *Road of the Century*, Chap.14.
106. DM.
107. DM, Dec. 5, 1882.
108. DM, 1882.
109. DM, Aug. 2, 1884.
110. *Albany Telegram*, Aug. 1, 1891.
111. *Reminiscences*, 95 et. seq.
112. Port Jervis *Evening Leader*, Dec. 12, 1898.
113. *Reminiscences*, 85.

114. Johnston (p. 95) maintains that the more flattering account was dictated by Young himself, as was indeed common in local histories of the period. However, Dickson and others portrayed would have had to accept the version he presented.

115. *Wayne County Herald*, July 18, 1878, reprinted from the *New York Sun* (and presumably showing the influence of former canal boy Amos J. Cummings).

116. Rates per ton fluctuated around a dollar in the 1850s. Lytell ("Story of the D&H Canal," 88) states that they fell to 90 cents by 1870 and to 70 cents in 1877. These figures are confirmed by published "Terms of Boating."

117. *Albany Telegram*, Aug. 1, 1891.

118. *Tri-States Union* (Port Jervis), Feb. 8, 1878.

119. *Wayne Independent*, Jan. 17, 1884, cited in Sanderson, *Carrying Coals*, 249.

120. Lytell, "Story of the D&H Canal," 303-04.

121. *Albany Telegram*, Aug. 1, 1891.

122. Johnston, *Reminiscences*, 122.

123. DM, Jan. 25, 1893.

124. DM, Oct. 17, 1898.

125. Steers, "Erie & Wyoming Valley RR."

126. DM, Dec. 28, 1898.

127. *Port Jervis Gazette*, Nov. __, 1898.

128. *Honesdale Independent*, Nov. 8, 1898.

Epilogue
Pages 263-276

1. New York State Supreme Court "On the relation of the President, Managers and Company of the D&H Canal Company against Assessors of the town of Rosendale, defendants, 1885-1886, 322. Thanks to Gayle Grunwald and Dietrich Werner for providing this document.

2. Lewis, *Southeastern New York*, 53.

3. Barbara Shupe, *New York State Population, 1790-1980*, in New York State Library.

4. *Ellenville Press*, Aug. 17, 1899.

5. Johnston, *Reminiscences*, 165.

6. Ringwald, "When the Steamboats Reigned."

7. *Ellenville Press*, Mar. 1, 1900, in Sanderson, *Carrying Coals*, 251.

8. *New York Tribune*, Oct. 30, 1898.

9. DM, Feb. 23, 1899.

10. *Laws of New York State*, 122nd Session, Chap.469, passed Apr. 28, 1899.

11. DM, June 6, 1899.

12. DM, June 13, 1899.

13. *Century of Progress*, 317.

14. Coykendall's biography and character are described in Steuding, *Rondout*, Chap.15.

15. Ross, "The Very Last Days." Earl Mack, the source of these recollections, stated that Coykendall was "one of the most hated men in the canal communities from Rosendale to Eddyville."

16. *New York Tribune*, Nov. 11, 1899.

17. Ibid.

18. Ibid., Nov. 27, 1899.

19. Ibid.

20. *New York Times*, Nov. 23, 1899.

21. Ibid.

22. John L. Weller, *The New Haven Railroad* (New York: Hastings House, 1969), 41-42.

23. Port Jervis ?, Nov. 23, 1899; New York Times, Nov. 23, 1899.

24. *New York Tribune*, Nov. 27, 1899.

25. *New York Times*, Mar. 23, 1900.

26. *New York Times*, Mar. 24, 1900.

27. *New York Tribune*, Nov. 27, 1899; Erie RR valuation maps, June 30, 1918. An article in the *New York Herald*, Dec. 17, 1900, stated that Coykendall had only purchased the canal in New York State.

28. *Tri-States Union*, May 20, 1881.

29. *New York Herald*, Dec. 17, 1900.

30. *New York Times*, May 11, 1900.

31. *New York Times*, Sep. 16, 1900.

32. *New York Times*, Dec. 14, 1900.

33. *New York Herald*, Dec. 17, 1900.

34. Ibid.

35. *New York Times*, Dec. 14, 1900.

36. *New York Times*, Jan. 19, 1901.

37. *New York Times*, Jan. 10, 1901. To set the matter straight, Morgan declared "It's nobody's business but my own if I buy a property."

38. *New York Times*, Aug. 17, 1902.

39. *New York Times*, Feb. 13, 1901.

40. *New York Herald*, Dec. 17, 1900.

41. *New York Times*, Dec. 14, 1900.

42. *New York Herald*, Dec. 17, 1900.

43. Patricia Clinton, "The Delaware & Hudson Canal in Ellenville," text for a talk delivered to the D&H Canal Soc., Oct. 28, 1990.

44. Wakefield, *Coal Boats to Tidewater*, 201-202.

45. Port Jervis ?, Nov. 20, 1899.

46. *Ellenville Journal*, June 30, 1899.

47. The O&W probably did not acquire the canal right-of-way east of High Falls, since its rail line deviated in that vicinity, and the lower end of the canal remained in operation. Research in county deed records would clarify these points.

48. *Port Jervis Gazette*, Aug. 1, 1901.

49. Consolidated Rosendale Cement Co. records. Thanks to Dietrich Werner for making this information available.

50. Mack, "Recollections."

Bibliography of Secondary Sources Cited in Notes

Beach, Moses Y. *The Wealth and Biography of the Wealthy Citizens of the City of New York*, 10th ed. New York: Pub. by the author, 1846.

Best, Gerald M. "The Gravity Railroad of the Delaware & Hudson Canal Company." Railroad & Locomotive Historical Soc. *Bulletin*, No.82, April 1951.

Binder, Frederick Moore. *Coal Age Empire*. Harrisburg,: Pennsylvania Historical and Museum Commission, 1974.

Blackmer, Stephen D. "Fossils, Fuel and the Forest: The Effect of Coal on New England's Use of Wood Fuel in the 19th Century." Unpub. paper, Yale Univ. School of Forestry and Environmental Studies, 1982.

Blumin, Stuart. *The Urban Threshold*. Chicago: Univ. of Chicago, 1976.

Booth, Malcolm A. "The Delaware & Hudson Canal, with Special Emphasis on Deerpark, N.Y." M.A. thesis, SUNY, Oneonta, 1965.

Calhoun, Daniel H. *The American Civil Engineer*. Cambridge, MA: MIT, 1960.

Casey, Robert J. and W. A. S. Douglas. *The Lackawanna Story*. New York: McGraw-Hill, 1951.

Cranmer, H. Jerome. "New Jersey Canals" in Carter Goodrich, ed., *Canals and American Economic Development*.

Delaware & Hudson Co. *A Century of Progress: History of the Delaware and Hudson Company 1823-1923*. Albany: J. B. Lyon, 1925.

Durfee, J. R. *Reminiscences of Carbondale, Dundaff and Providence*. Philadelphia: Miller's Bible Publishing House, 1875.

FitzSimons, Neal. *The Reminiscences of John B. Jervis*. Syracuse: Syracuse Univ., 1971.

Ghear, Roy. "The Last Days of the Canal in High Falls." D&H Canal Soc. *Bulletin*, vol.I, No.1, Feb. 1968.

Goodrich, Carter, ed. *Canals and American Economic Development*. Port Washington, NY: Kennikat Press, 1972.

Hansell, Norris. *Josiah White, Quaker Entrepreneur*. Easton, PA: Canal History & Technology Press, 1992.

Harlow, Alvin F. *Old Towpaths*. New York: D. Appleton, 1926.

----*The Road of the Century*. New York: Creative Age Press, 1947.

----*Steelways of New England*. New York: Creative Age Press, 1946.

Helmer, William F. *O & W: The Long Life and Slow Death of the New York, Ontario & Western Railway*. Berkeley, CA: Howell-North, 1959.

Hislop, Codman. *Eliphalet Nott*. Middletown, CT: Wesleyan Univ., 1971.

Hollister, Horace. "History of the Delaware and Hudson Canal Company." Unpublished ms, 1880, in Hagley Museum.

----*Contributions to the History of the Lackawanna Valley*. New York: W. H. Tinson, 1857.

Hudson Coal Co. *The Story of Anthracite*. New York: Hudson Coal Co., 1932.

Hungerford, Edward. *Men of Erie*. New York: Random House, 1946.

Johnston, John W. *Reminiscences*. Highland, NY: Town of Highland Cultural Resources Commission, 1987.

Jones, Chester Lloyd. *The Economic History of the Anthracite-Tidewater Canals*. Philadelphia: Univ. of Pennsylvania, 1908.

Kalata, Barbara N. *A Hundred Years, A Hundred Miles*. Morristown, NJ: Morris County Historical Soc., 1983.

Larkin, F. Daniel. *John B. Jervis*. Ames, IA: Iowa State Univ., 1990.

LeRoy, E. D. *The Delaware & Hudson Canal and Its Gravity Railroads*. Honesdale, PA: Wayne County Historical Soc., 6th Printing 1980.

Leslie, Vernon. *Honesdale: The Early Years*. Honesdale, PA: Honesdale 150 Committee, 1981.

----*Honesdale and the Stourbridge Lion*. Honesdale, PA: Stourbridge Lion Sesquicentennial Corp., 1979.

Lewis Historical Publishing Co. *Southeastern New York*, 1946.

Lowenthal, Larry, and William T. Greenberg, Jr. *The Lackawanna Railroad in Northwest New Jersey*. Morristown, NJ: Tri-State Railway Historical Soc., 1987.

Lucas, Walter A. *The History of the New York, Susquehanna & Western RR*. New York: Railroadians of America, 1939; 2nd ed., 1980.

McEntee, James S. "Story of the Canal," *Olde Ulster*, Vol.VI, No.10, Oct. 1910.

McFee, Michele A. *Limestone Locks and Overgrowth*. Fleischmanns, NY: Purple Mountain Press, 1993.

McTernan, Donald H. "The Esopus-Minisink Way." M.A. thesis, SUNY, Oneonta, 1969.

Osborne, Peter III. "The Delaware and Hudson Canal Company's Enlargement and the Roebling Connection." Center for Canal History and Technology *Proceedings*, vol.III, 1984.

Patton, Spiro G. "Delaware & Hudson Company vs. Pennsylvania Coal Company during the 1850s." Center for Canal History and Technology *Proceedings*, vol.XI, 1992.

Poor, Henry V. *History of the Railroads and Canals of the United States of America*. New York: 1860; reprint Augustus M. Kelley, 1970.

Powell, H. Benjamin. *Philadelphia's First Fuel Crisis: Jacob Cist and the Developing Market for Pennsylvania Anthracite*. University Park, PA: Penn State Univ., 1978.

Proctor, Thomas C. "The Middlesex Canal." Center for Canal History and Technology *Proceedings*, vol.VIII, 1988.

Quinlan, James E. *History of Sullivan County*. Liberty, NY: G. M. Beebe and W. T. Morgans, 1873; republished 1965.

Ringwald, Donald C. *Steamboats for Rondout*. Providence: Steamship Historical Soc. of America, 1981.

----"When the Steamboats Reigned," *Kingston's Hudson-Champlain Souvenir Booklet*. Kingston Anniversary Booklet Committee, 1959.

Ross, Donald. "The Very Last Days of the D&H Canal." *Canal Days*, vol.II, No.1, February 1968.

Sanderson, Dorothy H. *Carrying Coals to Rondout*, 2nd ed. Ellenville, NY: Rondout Valley, 1974.

Segal, Harvey. "Cycles of Canal Construction" in Carter Goodrich, ed., *Canals and American Economic Development*.

Shaughnessy, Jim. *Delaware & Hudson*. Berkeley, CA: Howell-North, 1967.

Shaw, Ronald E. *Canals for a Nation*. Lexington, KY: Univ. of Kentucky, 1990.

----*Erie Water West*. Lexington, KY: Univ.of Kentucky, 1966.

Steers, Edward. "The Delaware & Hudson Canal Company's Gravity Railroad." Center for Canal History and Technology *Proceedings*, vol.II, 1983.

----"A Historical Survey of the Erie and Wyoming Valley Railroad." Center for Canal History and Technology *Proceedings*, vol.III, 1984.

----"The Pennsylvania Coal Company's Gravity Railroad." Center for Canal History and Technology *Proceedings*, vol.I, 1982.

Steuding, Bob. *Rondout, A Hudson River Port*. Fleischmanns, NY: Purple Mountain Press, 1995.

Sylvester, Nathaniel B. *History of Ulster County*. Philadelphia: Everts & Peck, 1880.

Taber, Thomas T. *The Delaware, Lackawanna & Western RR in the Nineteenth Century*. Muncy, PA: Thomas T. Taber III, 1977.

Terwilliger, Katherine T. "Napanoch." Delaware & Hudson Historical Soc. *Canal Days*, vol.I, No.4, 1967.

----"Port Benjamin." *Canal Days*, vol.II, No.2, 1968.

----"Port Hixon." *Ellenville Journal*, Jan. 21, 1971.

----*Wawarsing: Where the Streams Wind*. Ellenville: Rondout, 1977.

Torrey, Rev. David, ed. *Memoir of Maj. Jason Torrey*. Scranton: James S. Horton, 1885.

Veit, Richard F. *The Old Canals of New Jersey*. Little Falls, NJ: New Jersey Geographical Press, 1963.

Vogel, Robert M. *Roebling's D&H Aqueducts*. Washington: Smithsonian, 1971.

Von Gerstner, Franz Anton. *Die Innern Communicatione der Vereinigten Staaten von Nord Amerika*. Vienna: L. Vorsters artistische Anstalt, 1842.

Wakefield, Manville B. *Coal Boats to Tidewater*. Fleischmanns, NY: Purple Mountain Press, 1992.

Waugh, Richard G., Jr. "Canal Development in Early America, Part 1" in *The Best from American Canals*, No.1. York, PA: The American Canal and Transportation Center, 1983.

Weller, John L. *The New Haven Railroad*. New York: Hastings House, 1969.

Whitford, Noble E. *History of the Barge Canal of New York State*. Albany: J. B. Lyon, 1922.

----*History of the Canal System of the State of New York*. Albany: Brandow Printing, 1906.

Wurts, Charles Pemberton, comp. *A Genealogical Record of the Wurts Family*. Privately printed, 1889.

Index

176, 225-226, 228, 235, 245, 254, 269
Groundbreaking, 49-51, 130
Headquarters, 25, 107
Lackawanna Valley coal lands, 161-174, 225-228, 242-245
Loans, bonds, 61-62, 77, 102-103, 115, 144-145, 177, 226, 228, 238, 244-245
Locks (canal), locktenders, 53, 59-60, 65, 125, 143, 155, 176
Merger with Wurts Bros., 36-37, 40-43, 93, 104-107, 109, 170
New York legislation, 13-16, 60-61, 249, 269
Organization, 22-23, 26
Pennsylvania legislation, 35-36, 40-41, 42, 66, 73, 93-94, 127, 141, 145, 152, 154, 167, 189-190, 228
Pennsylvania Coal Co., dispute with, 185-188, 194-201, 225, 233, 244
Railroads, 228, 231-238, 241, 244, 247-253, 269, 272
Regional development, 87, 94, 106, 121-122, 125-127, 130-131, 213-223, 263-267
Stock, 20, 22, 25, 32, 40, 59, 61, 81, 111, 122, 124, 145-146, 162, 177, 245
Surveys, 18-20, 27-34, 73, 80-81, 225
Tolls, 35-36, 58, 82, 96, 117, 118, 186, 189
Delaware & Raritan Canal, 44, 84, 92, 101, 139, 142, 245
Delaware & Susquehannah Navigation Co., 81
Delaware Division Canal, 84, 92, 95, 139-140
Delaware, Lackawanna & Western RR, 231, 233, 237, 242
Delaware Valley & Kingston RR, 270-275
Delaware Water Gap, 30, 32, 97, 100, 101, 102, 127, 180, 231
Deposit, NY, 61, 80, 111, 136
Depuy, Simeon, 58
Dickson, Thomas, 62, 192, 241-244, 247-252, 254, 263
Dickson Locomotive Co., 192, 228
Dimmick, William H., 172
Dover, NJ, 180
Drinker, Henry W., 30, 100, 102, 163, 180, 231
DuBois, Jacob, 195
Duer, John, 36, 136
Dundaff, PA, 96, 222
Dyberry canal, 82, 104

Easton, PA, 33
Eckford, Henry, 14-15

Eddyville, NY, 33, 55, 57, 58, 65, 77, 112, 123, 131, 175, 211, 222, 270, 275
Eldred, Nathaniel B., 35, 101, 102, 105
Eldridge, N. T., 111, 113
Elizabeth & Somerville RR, 101
Ellenville, NY, 130, 213, 220, 221, 259, 264, 275
Ellet, Charles, Jr., 138, 142
Ellmaker, Levi, 37, 41
Elmendorf, Lucas, 31, 34
Endicott, ___, 111
Engineering profession, 21, 26, 34, 43, 59, 64
Erie Canal, 10, 14-15, 18-19, 26, 34, 47, 48, 49, 52, 55, 58, 71, 83, 84, 91, 96, 101, 117, 127, 142, 147, 197-199, 210, 211, 221, 246
Erie (NY & Erie, etc.) RR, 135-138, 140, 143-144, 151, 156-158, 162-165, 167-168, 174, 189, 231-237, 241, 242, 245, 249-252, 258-259, 267, 270-275
Erie & Wyoming Valley RR, 258-259, 272-273
Esopus Creek, 33-34
Ewen, John, 181, 188, 195, 201, 232-233
Farmington Canal, 18, 57, 62
Farnham, George, 80
Farnum, Samuel B., 222
Fell, Jesse, 5-7
Ferguson, James, 263
Flanders, NJ, 7
Flewelling, Samuel, 66, 89, 103, 105
Foster, Rastrick, 77-80, 106
Fuller, E. L., 274
Fulton, Robert, 112, 114

Gallatin, Albert, 83
Gore, Daniel and Obadiah, 5-7
Goshen, NY, 22, 30-31, 87, 136
Griffith, Calvin, 210

Hall, Ransome D., 116-117, 130
Hamilton, Alexander, 97
Hasbrouck, Abraham, 31, 34, 41, 52
Hauto, George, 12, 44
Hawley, Irad, 144, 146, 164, 171-174, 180, 181-182, 185-188
Background, character, 171-172
Hawley (Paupack Eddy), PA, 63, 69, 177, 217, 232-234, 266, 272, 275
Hazard, Erskine, 12
Henry, William, 179-180
Hensberger, Frank, 260
Hermance, Jacob, 220
Hewitt, Abram S., 232
Hickorybush & Eddyville RR, 275

High Falls, NY, 55, 58, 175-176, 220, 264, 272
Highland, NY, 217
Holbert, Benjamin, 154
Homowack, NY, 222
Hone, Philip, 14, 16, 23, 41, 52, 61, 69, 73, 77, 94-95, 102-105, 109, 111, 113, 115-116, 118, 124, 136, 144, 170, 171, 190, 221, 242
At D&H Groundbreaking, 32, 49-52, 59, 87, 130
Character, 16, 103-104, 121-122, 133, 136, 144, 190
Tours D&H, 70-71, 89, 121-123, 133
Honesdale (Forks of Dyberry) PA, 28, 30, 65-70, 72-75, 78-79, 106, 112, 117, 121, 124-127, 133-134, 141, 146, 147, 162, 190, 193, 210, 215, 217, 222, 234-235, 245, 246, 269, 272, 275
Hoosac Tunnel, 31
Hornell, NY, 82
Hosack, David, 13-14
Howard Coal & Iron Co., 244
Hudson, NY, 113
Hudson & Delaware RR, 97, 100, 101-102
Hudson River Association, 115
Huguenot, NY, 275
Hyde Park, PA, 166

Irish laborers, 47-49, 63, 175, 215
Iron industry, 7-8, 113-114, 179
Irving, Washington, 67, 133-134, 221
Ithaca, NY, 100

Janeway, George, 22
Jefferson RR, 233-234, 236
Jervis, John Bloomfield, 21, 26, 52, 55, 57, 60, 69, 106-107, 113, 138, 150-151, 199, 242, 246
D&H Chief engineer, 62-64, 93-94, 106
Gravity Ry 72-76, 78-79, 89-91
Surveys D&H route, 27-30, 32-33, 40, 65
Jewett, Hugh J., 249-251
Johnston, John W., 47-49, 117-118, 130, 176, 222, 238-239, 254, 258, 260, 266
Jones, William G., 116
Judson, L. C., 64

Keen's Pond, 30, 71
Kimble, Samuel,, 67
Kingsbury, E., 127, 141
Kingston, NY, 18, 22, 27, 30-34, 55, 87, 108, 127-128, 130, 214, 267, 270, 275
Kittatinny Ridge, 32, 128

D&H SUPPLEMENT

Since publication of the original volume, continuing research has uncovered further information. In most cases the additions expand on or reinforce the original book; however, since I would have included this material if I had it at the time, it seems important enough to present now. The page references relate to the first edition. In addition, an article by Michael Knies based on the newly available James Archibald collection of correspondence is included. —Larry Lowenthal

Page 9: Origins

A retrospective letter from Wurts brother-in-law Thomas Young in 1845 refers to "that coal which I found in 1817, near the road which you & [sic] David Noble built. . . ." Based on context, this was probably in the vicinity of Cobbs Gap, and the road may have been part of the system by which William Wurts hauled some coal overland and eventually to Philadelphia. This statement confirms that the Wurtses were active by that time but does nothing to resolve the fundamental question of why they were involved in the anthracite region at all.[1]

Another passage in the same letter mentions land that William and Maurice owned in Venango and Warren Counties.[2] This may be the location of the tract mentioned on page 8. It had nothing to do with the coal business, and, in fact, Young suggested exchanging it for lands in the anthracite district.

Page 35: Thomas Meredith

The animosity between Thomas Meredith and the Wurtses, which appears again on pages 95-96, goes back to the earliest days of the D&H. On February 11, 1825, Charles wrote to John in Harrisburg "I am pleased to learn that you have come to a better understanding with Meredith." Obviously, that hope was not justified by events. Meredith presented his opposition in terms of fear of monopoly. This became common rhetoric of the Jacksonians a few years later and often served as sort of a code to express the emerging class conflict that the Jacksonians either recognized or exploited. Charles argued that if the canal charged the lowest possible tolls it would allow everyone in what was otherwise a "wilderness" to become rich. However, as Charles admitted, he did not know whether that would become company policy, and assuming that Meredith was open at all to logical persuasion, this argument did not sway him.

Page 35: Merger

In a recent book, economic historian Robert E. Wright asserts that "coal companies did suffer from a fundamental error in business judgment. They erroneously believed that to be successful they had to be highly vertically integrated, owning every step of production and distribution. . . ."[3] While most of the anthracite industry pursued vertical integration from the beginning, one field, the Schuylkill, had a different, and not entirely successful, model. Due to restrictions placed upon the Schuylkill Canal Company by an anticorporate republican ideology and vested interests, the canal company was unable to purchase coal property to accompany its transportation artery. Consequently, dozens of small independent coal companies sprang up to provide coal (often subcontracting with boatmen to deliver their coal to market). The Schuylkill territory provided more than 60 percent of the coal supplied to market for much of the nineteenth century, but the lack of a company-controlled anthracite supply complicated Schuylkill Canal operations and prospects, and eventually the canal lost substantial market share to the Reading Railroad. The Reading was also limited in its ability to own anthracite lands, but by the early 1870s, its President Franklin Gowen was able to get legislation passed enabling the Reading to pursue vertical integration.

Although the nonintegrated model was tried in the Schuylkill area, it was certainly not a tempting one for anthracite entrepreneurs. The small-company attitude that prevailed in the Schuylkill region was primarily an irritant to the vertically integrated anthracite corporations in other areas, in that they had to regularly fend off charges of monopoly. Since the Schuylkill model was not chosen by the Schuylkill Canal entrepreneurs, but rather thrust upon them by the state, it is understandable that entrepreneurs in other regions were not interested in pursuing that model, but rather did what they could to avoid it. Nonetheless, the early development of the D&H and its limitations in direct ownership of coal lands, was a result of the same anti-monopoly feelings that created the non-vertical model in the early Schuylkill anthracite industry. For the D&H, these restrictions on coal land ownership led to the unsatisfactory attempt to create a friendly rival in the form of the Pennsylvania Coal Company, which would own coal lands but work cooperatively with the D&H, rather than antagonistically as John Wurts feared an unknown company would. Later, it is noteworthy that, even after decades of operating experience, the anthracite railroads preferred to control their own coal sources until government regulation prevented that.

Through most of its history, the D&H was a highly vertically integrated company, though not perhaps to the ultimate degree, which would have included control of retail deliveries. The time when a different course would have seemed possible was during the mid-1820s, when two distinct enterprises were actually being combined. Perhaps with the Lehigh and Schuylkill examples in mind, it does not seem that an alternate structure was considered. In theory, ownership of the mines, coal production, and transportation at various stages could have been conducted by separate companies, but that possibility seems never to have occurred to any of the principals. The need to operate in two states, the undeveloped character of the coal region, the difficulty in raising capital, and the long lag time before returns could begin all argued in favor of integration. In fact, the company extended integration even further, by operating a bank, both for convenience and as an immediate source of profit. As shown on page 105, there was some discussion of detaching the Pennsylvania portion of the canal, but that seems to have been contemplated more for political reasons than as an economic measure.

Page 62: $1 Million Corporation

This is one of those boasts that serious historians welcome about as much as a tick, because it substitutes a random, but memorable, scrap of information for meaningful understanding. The D&H may have been a $1 million corporation, but it nearly

became a failed one. Moreover, capitalization is only one way of measuring an enterprise's success or importance. A dissertation by H. Benjamin Powell asserts that the distinction of being the first million-dollar corporation belongs to the Schuylkill Navigation Co.[4]

Page 91: Coal Quality

Defective coal was a self-inflicted injury that almost proved fatal to the D&H. The organ affected was the company's reputation, and recovery was slow. Wurts correspondence indicates that they prepared and distributed a pamphlet defending the quality of their coal. (No copies of this pamphlet have been found.) Later, John Wurts spoke of producing a new edition to make the argument that their coal was superior to the Lehigh in manufacturing iron.[5] Despite the Wurtses' energetic publicity efforts, it took a long time for D&H coal to melt the distrust that had made a strong impression early in the company's existence. In 1833, in a generally upbeat letter, John wrote that "our great effort must be to remove the prejudice against the coal by extending its consumption. . . ."[6]

Page 102-103: The Crisis

The financial and managerial crisis of 1831 was a period of intense emotion. Bolton refused to serve on the board with Maurice. Hone agreed that the board needed to be shaken up, but, innately cautious, he was reluctant to force Bolton to resign because of the effect on public opinion. John Wurts thought that Maurice could be elected, but even he hesitated to press for that outcome and warned Charles that if Bolton were pushed out "we must stand ready to get investments from Philad.a [sic]." John recommended Philadelphian William Worrell for a seat on the board and told Charles unequivocally "you must at all events get his consent to serve," since his presence alone would reassure Philadelphia and boost the stock price by one or two percent. John urged Hone, with his enormous prestige and granite integrity to assume the presidency, but he "peremptorily declined," probably recognizing that the position would consume his life, as it eventually did to John Wurts. After Hone's rejection, John proposed Judge Wright, but Hone responded that he was afraid to try it at that time.[7]

A surprising revelation that emerges from the pressured correspondence of this period is how little acquainted the Wurtses were with the D&H board, even after supposedly cooperating with them on a project of exceptional magnitude. John described a conversation with Hone in which he discovered him to be "a high minded, honorable fellow, open, candid and undisguised in all his thoughts and actions," as if he were speaking of a near-stranger. John added, however, that he was "surprised to find how little [Hone] knew of the subject."[8] Elsewhere, John described the board as "miserably weak" and "surprisingly ignorant"— blunt language that stressed the urgency of the changes that soon occurred.[9]

Page 108: Charles Stewart Wurts

Charles S. Wurts may have been more involved with the D&H than implied, but it was from the perspective of family interest, rather than corporate. He was not involved in D&H management, but while remaining in Philadelphia to run the family business, he functioned as a counselor and confidant to brother John and handled the Philadelphia investors who were important in the early years, especially since their original shares were paid by installment.

Page 124: Recovery

Having survived the severe trials of 1831, John Wurts was uncharacteristically euphoric under the improved conditions of 1833. He told Charles "I am convinced that with proper efforts, a foundation may be laid that will to a great extent exclude our competitors." The "Schuylkill people" seemed less threatening. William Wurts had apparently decided to "come on here," presumably meaning to join the D&H, and John thought it was the right course, as "there is a wide field of operation here."[10]

Despite the favorable outlook, which proved to be overly optimistic, John was already complaining of the strain. Writing to Charles, he declared that he was "constantly on the rack." More frequent contact had altered his opinion of Hone, whom he described as "a man of pleasure"—that is, not suited to the heavy work of leading the board.[11]

Page 124: Panic of 1837

Wurts letters add details on the effects of the 1837 financial crisis. As early as June, John reported that "we have already begun to creep into our shell," as the inability to procure short-term money was impeding operations.[12] As the troubled year ground on, John contemplated quitting, and apparently expressed that intention to some members of the board, but they replied that "the work cannot go on if I quit." His salary, if it had ever been higher, had been restored to $3000. Since the company was in no position to pay a dividend, he feared that "although I work as hard as man can, six days in the week, I am nevertheless growing poorer every day. . . ."[13] Again in early 1838 John offered his resignation, but this was probably more an exercise in self-pity than a real prospect. "When a man is chained to a vast machine, which he must keep in motion, or be content to let it stop and bury himself and many others in its ruin, he can't very well break the chain and fly from it, even if he were selfish enough to attempt it. . . ."[14]

Page 130: Other Cargo

Wurts letters expand on commodities other than coal that the D&H hauled in its first decade. Based on a letter from Maurice, John wrote that "The lumber of Wayne and Luzerne is beginning to engage the attention of the North river dealers." He reported that the number of private boats was increasing along the canal, particularly at Ellenville, "where it will require at least four boats to do the business of the Leather factories in that vicinity." This business seemed to be extending into Sullivan County.[15]

Pages 138, 143: Reading Railroad

Considering his propensity to worry, John Wurts was surprisingly unconcerned about the emergence of the Reading Railroad. In two letters in 1842, he seemed relatively untroubled by the new competitor, although he recognized that the railroad would drive coal prices lower and acknowledged that short selling by Philadelphia speculators, who were impressed by the Reading, was depressing D&H stock. A tour of the Schuylkill region in October "resolved many misgivings that I had in relation to our ability to meet the competition which the Reading Rail Road has created in the coal trade."[16]

Pages 144, 146: Enlargements

John Wurts was cagey about the enlargements, as with most things. In May 1844, he informed Charles "We are busy at work to double our delivery as soon as possible. But we do it as quietly as possible—don't want it known."[17] John regretted that the company, influenced by the difficult years that preceded, had made premature contracts that locked it into unnecessarily low rates and committed their full capacity. "We have turned away since we stop'd [sic] selling, applicants for more than 50,000 tons."[18]

Page 162: Coal Lands

Another Wurts nephew, George, and family member Thomas Young, were actively scouting coal lands in 1844-45.[19] The Wurts Papers leave no doubt that family members owned and acquired coal lands. Documentation is scattered in many files, and a sustained investigation might be able to assemble a more complete picture of these activities.

Page 169: Practical Geology

After several years of experience, Charles Wurts concluded that "[Nathan] Smith has unquestionably so far proved himself a better judge of the coal formation of the valley than Archbald & Clarkson." He added that "They have adopted opinions which in many cases, opening into the coal have proved to be erroneous, and it is curious to perceive how ingenious they are in endeavoring to make the facts fit into their theory. Clarkson, though if they [sic] constrained to give up, will do it very tardily and reluctantly. Archbald will I think be willing to find himself wrong."[20]

Page 170: The Anthracite Rivals, cont.

The Wurtses were constantly reassessing the threat presented by their inveterate competitors. Writing from Wilkes-Barre, an informed correspondent advised William Wurts in 1851 "I am not surprised at, particularly the hostility of the Schuylkill Region. The Lehigh I hope will not interfere; they have always been considered a highly honourable Co. [sic] . . . . Phila [sic] has never done any thing for us in the north. Why now put there[sic] nose in our dish. . . . Our Northern Counties will most assured-ly rise as they shd [sic] do to a man & repel this invasion into their life blood interests."[21]

Later, Maurice wrote of the "swindling course of the Reading Rail Road Co.," which had "disorganized and prostrated" the coal trade.[22] Somewhat surprisingly, considering his tendency to fret, John Wurts did not seem disturbed by the birth of a railroad that became the Delaware, Lackawanna & Western. Writing from Rome on March 1, 1851, he observed that "the projected road from Legget's Gap through Cobb's to the Water Gap to Jersey City must if made enhance very much the value of the lands owned by yourself and William in Luzerne County. . . ."[23]

A letter from Charles Dupuy, Jr., a D&H official in Rondout and also a stockholder, to Maurice Wurts in 1851 is quite revealing. Based on an assumption that the company would produce 825,000 tons of coal in that year, he estimated that 205,000 tons would remain unsold at the end of the year and would have to be stored in yards or on boats, thereby depressing next year's price. He then took the liberty to ask "are we straining every nerve" to increase the company's market and replied in the negative. "The Philadelphians," he observed, "are crowding into the New York market their coal as they did last fall, and when the season winds up, they will laugh at us, as they did then, for giving them the market—while we were contented to put our coal in in [sic] pile." He suggested that the company make a more determined effort to expand its retail sales and also push more forcefully into the "Eastern" (New England) market by putting a permanent agent in Boston.

On the subject of coal handling, Dupuy reported that they were "yarding" 600 tons per day "by labor" and about 400 tons "by crane." However, confirming the growing reliance on machinery, he expected to double the quantity handled by crane "in a few days."[24]

Pages 182, 191: The PCC and John Wurts's health

It was John Wurts's nature to internalize the rising conflict with the PCC. Maurice wrote that "he blames himself for not guarding more carefully the interests of the D & Hudson."[25] Whether justified or not, John considered himself utterly unable to cope with the demands of his position. A statement to that effect in October 1849 has been noted. Several months of additional stress did not improve his outlook, and in May 1850 he confided to Charles, "I never felt so little confidence and courage in facing what is before me, because I feel myself so incompetent to the effort."[26] Characteristically, the course of events deepened John's customary gloom. Responding to a temporary decline in the stock price, he referred to "a growing distrust in the minds of many that the prosperity of the company had reached its climax."[27]

The D&H core group found the behavior of the PCC totally incomprehensible, and as the split between the companies widened, the D&H leaders developed a bitter resentment toward their former partners. Maurice Wurts described the PCC as "perverse, crooked, selfish and hostile."[28] Later in the year, Wurts ally William Musgrave complained that the PCC was luring boatmen and other D&H employees despite an agreement to avoid doing that. Referring to the PCC, he declared "Truly they have not the first idea of what ought to constitute the course of gentlemen and men of business."[29]

Maurice, who saw John more frequently, was sensitive to the effects of endless stress on John's health and mental state. In this concern he was prompted by John's wife Martha, who felt that his labors for the D&H were killing her husband.[30] Maurice blamed the situation largely on the conflict with the PCC, calling the disputed contract "a source of vexation and mortification which will continue, I fear, as long as the same persons retain controul [sic] of that concern."[31] A few months later he added that "John continues to be annoyed by the perverse conduct of the Penn[a] Coal Co." Maurice recommended that the Wurtses and their associates sell their stock in PCC, which he considered to be in a "wild and unregulated state."[32] If nothing else, this is interesting as evidence that they still held stock even as the controversy deepened. Maurice was confident that the D&H position was strong and that the company would prevail, but "the labour & care it causes to Brother John is a great evil growing out of it."[33] Finally, Maurice said flatly that John must retire soon "or his life will become a sacrafice [sic] to our interests." Maurice hoped to purchase the company house in Rondout, where he

lived, so that John and Martha could occupy it, but this does not seem to have occurred.[34]

Meanwhile, Maurice himself was in declining health, and only two years remained to his life. William was also in poor health. If the PCC and other worries were not sufficient, the Wurts Brothers were also vexed by squatters who occupied and cut timber on land they owned in the Pittston area. A letter from William Silkman described "serious depredations."[35] Despite justified indignation, it seemed that little could be done to stop the encroachment. By 1855, with Maurice already dead, the once bold saga of the Wurts Brothers ebbs away in frustration and despair, as William grieves "Your uncle and myself are now so old and in such feeble health that we can do but little for ourselves."[36]

It is risky and perhaps presumptuous to attempt to diagnose historical persons, yet it is difficult to avoid thinking that John Wurts displayed many symptoms of clinical depression. Certainly there was much in his life experience to reinforce his sour view of human nature, but by most measures he was a success and many men would have envied him. From the company point of view, John's self-sacrificing dedication was an unexpected and perhaps undeserved benefit. His family urged him to retire, and he seemed to want to, but he felt that he could not retire without selling his D&H stock. That, he believed, would be unfair to other holders; so, unless that was merely a rationalization, he hung on until he finished wearing himself out.[37]

Page 185: William Musgrave

John Wurts favored Musgrave for the board but admitted that it was "a difficult and delicate" matter because "no one on the Board knows Mr. Musgrave but Maurice and myself." John had again offered to resign, but the board insisted he stay on and offered to find someone "to take the labor off [his] hands." Money, to John's way of thinking, was "a stumbling block." One member proposed that a $3-4000 annual salary would suffice to induce someone like Musgrave to take up part of John's workload, but at the same time John's salary would be cut to $3000 per year.[38]

Page 193: Coal Breakers

A John Wurts letter in 1844 confirms that the D&H was well aware of coal breakers: "I cannot answer Mr. Richardson's inquiry as to the kind of breaker we shall use—as yet we have used none, for we have had ample call for lump coal. But we are perfecting one against the time when it will be necessary to use it—as yet however our plan is not finally settled."[39]

Page 232: PCC Railroad

An 1856 map shows the route of the proposed PCC railroad as beginning at Hoboken, New Jersey, passing through Acquackanock (present Passaic and Clifton), Paterson, Bloomingdale, and Lafayette, crossing the Delaware River near the mouth of Flat Kill, and thence direct to Pittston.[40]

Page 232: Reservoirs

For 39 days in fall 1854, a scarcity of water impeded operation of the canal. The only expedient was to lighten boats so they could pass through. This was surely dismaying to the managers, since it defeated the purpose of the enlargements, and makes one wonder whether the water issue had been taken into account adequately in planning the enlargements. During the crisis of 1854, Russel Lord enlarged the Lords Pond reservoir and proposed adding a new source on the Shell Drake (Sheldrake) branch of the Neversink north of Monticello.[41]

A later report indicates that Lord carried out his plan and also provides a valuable list of the reservoirs used by the D&H to supplement the natural flow of rivers:[42]

—*Beaver Dam Reservoir*: five miles to the canal via the Bushkill and the Neversink; 22-foot head and flows 250 acres.
—*Martins Pond Reservoir*: four miles to the canal at the Wurtsboro feeder; 18-foot head and flows 150 acres. This was a natural pond with the outlet dug out and enlarged.
—*Yankes Pond Reservoir*: four miles to the canal at Wurtsboro summit level; 23-foot head and flows 600 acres. This was a natural pond, raised and the outlet excavated.
—*Wolf Pond Reservoir*: six miles to the Neversink and comes in at the feeder dam; 24-foot head and flows 500 acres. This was a natural pond.

—*Lords Pond Reservoir*: five miles to the canal via the Neversink feeder; 24-foot head and flows 450 acres. This was a natural pond with an outlet cut.
—*Shell Drake Reservoir*: 1-1/2 miles to the Neversink, then 15 miles down the river; 32-foot head and flows from 350 up to 1000 acres. This pond was entirely artificial.

Pages 181-206: The D&H/ PCC Conflict

After the first edition was published, the papers of James Archbald became available. Michael Knies, Special Collections Librarian/Associate Professor Weinberg Memorial Library University of Scranton, worked extensively with them and gave several presentations and published articles based on them. The following article presents his summary of his findings, as they relate to the conflict between the companies, in which Archbald was a central figure.

Notes

1 Thomas Young, Blakeley, PA, to William Wurts, May 8, 1845. Wurts Papers; business papers, Historical Soc of Penna., (Acc. 1988A,) Box 2, Folder 3. Hereafter WP (as in first edition).
2 Charles Wurts to John Wurts, Feb. 11, 1825, WP, Box 1, Folder 1.
3 Robert E. Wright, *The First Wall Street* (Chicago: Univ. of Chicago Press, 2005), 175.
4 "Coal, Philadelphia, and the Schuylkill," PhD dissertation, Lehigh Univ., 1968, page 118.
5 John Wurts to Charles Wurts, Jan. 30, 1831, Feb. 1, 1831, WP, Box 1, Folder 3.
6 To Charles Wurts, Feb. 20, 1833, WP, Box 1, Folder 6.
7 John Wurts to Charles Wurts, Feb. 4, 1831, WP, Box 1, Folder 3.
8 John Wurts to Charles Wurts, Jan. 30, 1831, WP, ibid.
9 John to Charles, ibid.
10 John Wurts to Charles Wurts, Feb. 20, 1833, WP, Box 1, Folder 6.
11 John Wurts to Charles Wurts, Apr. 12, 1833, Ibid.
12 John Wurts to Charles Wurts, June 14, 1837, WP, Box 1, Folder 9.
13 John Wurts to Charles Wurts, Nov. 23, Dec. 2, 1837, WP, Box 1, Folder 11.
14 John Wurts to Charles Wurts, Feb. 2, 1838, WP, Box 1, Folder 12.

15 John Wurts to Charles Wurts, Apr. 12, 1833, WP, Box 1, Folder 6.

16 John Wurts to Charles Wurts, Jan. 8, 1842, WP, Box 1, Folder 18; Box 1, Folder 19.

17 WP, Box 1, Folder 21.

18 To William and Charles Wurts, June 3, 1844, Ibid., Folder 22.

19 Thomas Young to William Wurts, May 8, 1845, WP, Box 2, Folder 3.

20 Charles Wurts to "Dear Brother," May 30, 1848, WP, Box 4, Folder 35.

21 M. (probably Hollenbach or Hollenbeck, an early and prominent family in the area), to William Wurts, Aug. 25, 1851, WP, Box 6, Folder 7.

22 Maurice Wurts to "Dear Brother" (not John, from context), Feb. 12, 1852, WP, Box 6, Folder 12.

23 Probably to Maurice Wurts, WP, Box 7, Folder 23.

24 To Maurice Wurts, July 19, 1851, WP, Box 1, Folder 2. This letter testifies to the lack of initiative and sense of demoralization that seemed to afflict the company due to John Wurts's chronic infirmity (page 185) and also relates to the penetration of Schuylkill coal into the New York market (page 142).

25 To "Dear Brother," Feb. 26, 1852. WP, Box 6, Folder 12.

26 May 20, 1850, WP, Box 5, Folder 26.

27 John Wurts to "Dear Brother," March 1, 1851, WP Box 7, Folder 23.

28 To "Dear Brother," Feb. 12, 1852, WP, Box 6, Folder 12.

29 To "My dear Wurts," July 23, 1852, WP Box 6, Folder 16.

30 Maurice Wurts to "Dear Brother," Feb. 12, 1852, WP, Box 6, Folder 12.

31 To "Dear Brother," Feb. 26, 1852, ibid.

32 Maurice Wurts to Charles Wurts, June 16, 1852, WP, Box 6, Folder 15.

33 Maurice to ?, July 13, 1852, WP, Box 6, Folder 16.

34 Maurice Wurts to "Dear Brother," Aug. 14, 1852, WP, Box 6, Folder 17.

35 To William Wurts (younger), Sep. 30, 1852, WP, Box 6, Folder 18.

36 To William (younger), June 7, 1855, WP, Box 6, Folder 34.

37 Maurice Wurts to "Dear Brother," Feb. 26, 1852, WP, Box 6, Folder 12.

38 John Wurts to Charles Wurts, May 23, 1850, WP.

39 John Wurts to Charles Wurts, June 20, 1844, WP, Box 1, Folder 22.

40 W. Lorenz, "Map of the canals and railroads for transporting anthracite coal from the several coal fields to the city of New York, 1856," (Hunckel & Son, Baltimore), Library of Congress Map Division.

41 Lord to William Musgrave, Jan. 23, 1855.

42 W. C. Rose, Cuddebackville, NY, to R. F. Lord, Jan. 3, 1857. The letter refers to maps, but these have not been located.

Going to War:
The Delaware & Hudson versus the Pennsylvania Coal Company, 1848-1853, New Perspectives from the James Archbald Papers
by Michael Knies

This article is based on James Archbald's collection of correspondence, which is located at the Lackawanna Historical Society in Scranton, Pennsylvania. The collection has only recently been processed and made available to the public. Consequently, the Archbald papers provide a new perspective on the anthracite industry in northeastern Pennsylvania. The material complements other collections such as those at the Pennsylvania Historical Society, the Hagley Museum, the Minisink Valley Historical Society, and the National Canal Museum.

Most of the correspondence that Archbald received came from upper level management in the Delaware & Hudson Canal Company and the Pennsylvania Coal Co. (PCC). There is very little material actually written by Archbald in the collection, so his views on the topics discussed can only rarely be ascertained. The bulk of the most interesting correspondence reflects the concerns of upper management: labor relations, finances, land acquisition, legal problems, conditions within the coal industry, and, in the present case, the deterioration in relations between the D&H and the PCC.

James Archbald was born in Scotland in 1793 and immigrated at age fourteen to America with his parents. He worked for John Jervis as a contractor on the Erie Canal and again for Jervis on the Delaware & Hudson. He remained with the D&H and eventually became superintendent of gravity railroad and coal mining operations. When the Pennsylvania Coal Company began designing its gravity railroad during the second half of the 1840s, Archbald supervised its construction in 1849 and 1850. From this point until his resignation from both the D&H and the PCC at the end of 1853, he worked for both companies.

The venture that eventually became known as the Pennsylvania Coal Company was initially formed for two reasons. The D&H needed more coal and wanted to prevent a competitor, New York & Erie Railroad, from entering the area. The company was expanding its canal during the late 1840s to carry up to one million tons of coal. It was, however, bringing only about 500,000 tons to market. Its charter limited the amount of coal land the company could own, and due to political opposition, it was unlikely the charter could be changed. The PCC, which had been created as a separate company in the late 1830s but had a number of D&H officials and sympathetic individuals as part of its board of directors and management, including Archbald, was allowed by its charter to own coal lands near Pittston. The D&H management initially viewed the PCC as a collaborator in its efforts to consolidate its hold on the anthracite territory of northern Luzerne County. This cooperative relationship quickly deteriorated. By the time James Archbald left the employment of both companies in 1853, the PCC was at war with the D&H. In 1857, the two companies entered into a protracted lawsuit whose primary causes occurred during the period discussed in this paper.[1]

At first, D&H president John Wurts seemed to have achieved his goal. The PCC was closely identified with the D&H. James Archbald served as chief engineer for both companies. The companies shared board members and, at first, common goals. In late 1846 John Wurts had expressed his concern that the D&H needed to control additional coal lands to prevent "an inconvenient and perhaps dangerous rival [from entering] into the market over whom we will have no control and from whom we can expect nothing but keen competition." In 1851, it looked like the D&H had consolidated control over the Lackawanna Valley. Within a year, the PCC would become the "dangerous rival" that Wurts feared.[2]

So what went wrong?

There are at least four reasons that can be teased out of the Archbald correspondence.

1. There was a lack of respect by the D&H for the leadership of the PCC. Both Irad Hawley and John Ewen, the first two PCC presidents in the new, independent, incarnation, had been executives for the D&H, but John Wurts referred to Hawley as "entirely unfit." In a somewhat less explicit note Wurts wrote to Archbald concerned about the PCC coal delivery estimates "I am not sure however that I can rely on them. . . . They are very sanguine and may easily be mistaken." John Ewen at least looked good on paper. Born in 1810, he studied civil engineering and surveyed and laid out the Williamsburg part of Brooklyn. He served as resident engineer of the Newcastle and Frenchtown Railroad and served as chief engineer of the New York and Harlem Railroad. In 1836, he became street commissioner of New York, and in 1845, he was appointed comptroller of the currency. In 1848 he became D&H vice president.[3]

From reading the Archbald correspondence, it seems unlikely that he was relaying inside information from the D&H president to the PCC executives and back again, but it also seems unlikely that Hawley and Ewen were unaware of Wurts's opinion of their abilities.

2. Early PCC delivery problems. Perhaps John Wurts was at least partially correct in his opinion of the PCC leadership. The PCC planned to begin delivering coal to market in the spring of 1850 using the town of Hawley as its shipping point (the D&H used Honesdale). For a year or two the D&H would be transporting and marketing PCC coal and consequently planned its delivery strategy based on PCC estimates. Both companies hired canal boatmen as subcontractors, with the D&H apparently acting as boatman recruiter for both companies. If coal was not delivered to the canal on time, the boatmen, who were paid by the trip, could very well decide to leave and work on another canal, thereby disrupting delivery for the rest of the season. The PCC was considerably late in delivering coal to market and also significantly undershot their delivery estimate. In order to keep the PCC boatmen from leaving, the D&H would have to allow the PCC boats to carry D&H coal to market. John Wurts's brother Maurice, another D&H executive, wrote: "It will therefore be necessary for us, in order to keep the Penna Co. boatmen, to let them start with our coal, and provide loading for them at Honesdale which will very much increase the quantity of coal to be loaded there, and may cause so much detention to boats at that point as to greatly discourage the large number of new boatmen. We have had great difficulty in procuring them, and it will be ruinous to our business this year to lose them. The question is, what can be done to provide for so large an addition to the loadings at Honesdale."[4]

The D&H was also concerned that such an accommodation for the PCC might cause a coal shortage for the D&H by the end of the season. Consequently the D&H proposed that after the PCC got its act together and if the D&H experienced a coal shortage, the PCC would be required to let its boats stand idle while the D&H loaded PCC coal in order to replace the quantity the D&H had given to the PCC earlier in the season. Irad Hawley actually thought that the PCC was doing the D&H a favor by delivering its coal to market early in the season and considered the D&H proposal to be "unjust and not in the spirit of our agreement." (At the same time, Archbald wanted to resign from the D&H and put all of his efforts behind the construction of the PCC works. The PCC leadership was opposed to Archbald's resignation from the D&H because it might aggravate the "present jealous feeling existing and might cause quite a hostile feeling toward the Pennsylvania company" and that such a move might cause a "serious rupture" between the two companies because "there is nothing concerned with the business of the D&H of which they are so jealous as of your services." Consequently, Archbald continued working for both companies.)[5]

Delivery problems continued through the season, and John Wurts grew more aggravated at the PCC management. "It is most unfortunate and will I fear prove a most disastrous business, that we (I mean the Delaware & Hudson Canal Co.) have not been accurately informed as to what the Penna Co.

could do and when it would be ready to deliver coal. As the agent of both companies, we have acted on the information given to us by the officers of the Pennsylvania Co., supposing they knew their own affairs, and that we might rely on the assurances given to us by them." "In a word we are in a serious scrape, which might have been avoided had the Penna Co. known its true position and knowing it had been frank in communicating it to us." Of course, Archbald knew, as well as anyone, when the PCC would be able to deliver coal, but he left it up to the main office to tell the D&H. But, as can be seen in a 26 November 1849 letter to Archbald, John Wurts knew that Archbald, being in charge of mining and gravity operations, would have known when deliveries would start. Perhaps Wurts was, in a discreet way, blaming Archbald for the crisis. Eventually the two companies came to an agreement and the crisis abated, but some damage had been done to the relationship.[6]

3. Coal quality problems. Not all anthracite is created equal. Early in its existence, the D&H had been plagued by poor quality coal which had seriously damaged the company's reputation. Consequently, John Wurts was very concerned about coal quality, particularly because the D&H was transporting and selling PCC coal and would be affected by any bad image the PCC coal might get in the market. The PCC was also quite concerned.

There was a considerable quality difference in coal mined by the PCC at its two primary sites, Pittston and Dunmore. Pittston coal was a generally very high-quality, while Dunmore coal was plagued by slate and other contaminants. The PCC was attempting to break into the steamship market and had agreements with the Collins line, but Collins would only take the high-quality Pittston coal. Collins was taking so much Pittston coal that the company did not have enough to send to market. The PCC tried mixing Pittston and Dunmore coal in order to make the Dunmore more marketable. Part of the problem was simply appearance. Consumers wanted clean-looking coal, and rusty coal might be rejected even if it burned well. John Ewen wrote: "The rusty coal from Dunmore, however good in quality, and however small the quantity put in to a boat, has a tendency to condemn the cargo in the view of those purchasing. We think well therefore of your proposition to discontinue the mining of rusty coal at Dunmore. Ought none of it to be sent to market. The coal is judged of greatly from its appearance by those who purchase and even in some cases by those who burn it, where their prejudices overpower their judgment."[7]

The PCC Dunmore coal was so bad that the D&H was alarmed that its reputation would be damaged by PCC coal appearing in New York at the D&H docks and being sold by the D&H. The D&H wanted PCC coal unloaded at Rondout. Ewen noted, somewhat sarcastically, "Our friends of the Delaware & Hudson however fell into such a panic a few days since in consequence of the appearance of slate in three cargos of slide dock [size coal] and regarded it as so seriously affecting the reputation of their coal, that they consulted us on the expediency of preventing our coal from coming to the city and landing it at Rondout." Ewen claims to have calmed their fears by arguing "that there really was no great cause of apprehension, the appearance of slate in that size coal being nothing new. . . ." He added that if William Musgrave would look in the D&H's own files from the year during which Ewen was an officer for the D&H, he would find applications for relief from purchasers of their slide dock coal because of the large quantity of slate included. But Musgrave of the D&H was not calmed. He wrote Archbald stating that after investigating several cases of bad coal complaints, "In every instance we have ascertained that the coal came from Hawley & where we have investigated personally we have found complaints well founded. I have been absolutely alarmed at the frequency of the cases." Eventually, Ewen accepted the D&H concerns. When he commented that "not only the reputation of our coal, but that of the Delaware and Hudson Company may be injured, of which they seem to express some fears." Ewen wrote that he was attempting to impress upon members of the board how critical the coal-quality situation was. He was "fearful" that the reputation of their coal would damage future sales. "It is of the utmost importance that we should avoid such a result and make the best use of the time left us, during the present season, to establish a highly favorable reputation for

our coal, which I was in hopes we were doing. According to the accounts from the Del.Co. it seems we are not." And again, "The checquered coal is very objectionable. We ought not to send any coal but the very best so as to avoid every possible objection. A single boat load of inferior coal is certain condemnation of the customer who receives it."[8]

Ewen was also skeptical about the quality complaints and suspicious about the D&H. But he still wanted more high-quality Pittston coal mined. "It is necessary also that the quantity from Pittston should be increased, if only to improve the quality of the coal now sold through the Del. & Hud. Co. to whom occasional complaints are made of impurities which they say turn out to be in our coal. . . . I am, however, satisfied from my own observations when last on the works that proper care is taken with the coal in this particular [impurities or slate], and that the average was as good as the coal of the Del. & Hud. But as we are situated just now it ought to be a good deal better so as to attract attention from customers on account of its superior quality that there may be no hesitation on their part in purchasing from us another year when we shall sell our own coal." Ewen's mind was not at rest concerning coal quality. Another series of complaints forwarded by the D&H got him concerned again. "I do not know what we can do to rectify this evil. The daily business would be too large to find what we consider effective. The only way is to improve it at the mines by picking up the dull heavy pieces, composed of coal and slate, and the pieces of short fracture coal which appears to burn badly and makes a poor fire."[9]

Ewen told William Musgrave of the D&H that he felt it was "impossible that any considerable portion of our coal could be so bad, as our coal was observed to be of particularly good quality when I was last at Hawley." He grew suspicious of the D&H again: "I've written to Mr. Hathaway, our agent at Rondout, to examine the coal referred to and to take note of the coal hereafter arriving in the boats of both companies for I fear they are laying an anchor to windward in case they should not succeed in selling the coal to throw it on our hands as unmerchantable. They are I am told piling our coal separately in the yards in this city. Now when I speak of the Del. Co. I do not mean the president and the directors, but a power wielded in spite of them by one who still assumes to control, and does in fact control, the affairs of the company." Ewen did not name the mysterious power. Perhaps it was John and Maurice's brother William Wurts, who no longer held an official position with the D&H but remained involved in coal and iron investing. On the other hand, Maurice Wurts lived in Rondout but he did hold positions in the D&H.[10]

Once again, the crisis slowly abated but more damage to the cordial relationship had been done.

4. Canal Toll Agreement. As mentioned, one of the reasons for the creation of the PCC was to provide more coal for the expanded D&H Canal. The PCC, of course, would have to pay toll for coal shipments on the D&H Canal. And the two companies (composed of interlocking directorships) created a formula that would turn out to be a disaster.

PCC tolls were based not on the amount of coal transported by the new company, but on the amount of coal sold by the D&H. "If in any year the quantity of lump sold by the D&H prior to May 1 shall be less than half of the estimated sales for such year, the tolls of the Penna Co. shall be regulated by the average ratio of sales of lump coal by the D&H for such year." Musgrave and the D&H took this to mean the estimated production for the entire season; for 1852, this was 540,000 tons of all types of coal and 358,000 tons of lump. Unfortunately D&H sales amounted to only 16,000 tons of lump by May 1, thereby starting an acrimonious exchange of letters, embittering relations between the companies and ultimately paving the way to a multi-year lawsuit. It is difficult to understand why the companies agreed to base their toll structure on the assumption that fifty percent of the D&H lump coal would be sold by the beginning of May, relatively early in the season. But this assumption, made in 1847 and agreed to by the management of the proto-PCC, which included Irad Hawley, would irreparably damage relations between the companies in 1852.[11]

Musgrave stated that the toll, based on the agreed ratio formula, but in a spirit of conciliation, would be 55 cents a ton. The "average ratio of sales of lump coal by the company up to this date is three dollars & sixty-one cents & fractions of a cent per ton: & if it could be assumed with absolute certainty that there would be no variations from this average rate during the year caused by subsequent sales & there was no other consideration connected with the question of rate of coal, it might now perhaps be fixed definitively for the season." Musgrave went on to state that it was possible that the present average ratio of sales might be affected by future sales. But in addition to this the D&H had reserved the right "to add to the toll that would otherwise be payable one-half the saving or reduction made by the enlargement of the canal." The PCC was already disputing that the enlargement, begun in 1848, but not completed until 1853, had resulted in any savings, and the two companies had established a committee to try to settle the disagreement. The question of whether the enlargement resulted in any savings would be the major issue of the lawsuit.[12]

The D&H "in a spirit of conciliation proposes to commence the season by the collection of tolls at the rate of fifty five cents per ton to which it is entitled. . .by the present average ratio of sales of lump coal, irrespective of other considerations." However, the D&H reserved the right to adjust the coal payment: "The above proposed rate of toll must necessarily be regarded as a proximate estimate, & payments under it will be received as payments on account & the rate per ton of such payments on account must be subject to such variations from time to time as may be produced by changes in the prices at which sales of lump coal shall be made. In so doing, however, this company does not intend thereby to weaken or abandon in any degree its claim to an immediate increase of toll equal to one-half the reduction on freight caused by the enlargement of the canal. On the contrary, it formally adheres to such claims, and does now expressly reiterate it. . . ."[13]

Ewen responded, in a letter filled with quotes from Musgrave's letter, that while he agreed that some payment needed to be made to the D&H for PCC use of its canal, basing that payment on only five percent of the expected sales of lump coal was "a very slight and unreliable ground." But the PCC, "in a spirit of conciliation" and "without waiving any of its legal rights" had come up with a counter proposal. Ewen stated that if the average price of lump coal remained the same throughout the season the toll would come to fifty cents, not fifty-five as Musgrave proposed that the PCC pay on account. Ewen stated that it was unusual for someone to pay a higher rate in advance simply because the D&H thought that they might get higher prices later in the season. He also noted, "I think you have fallen into some confusion between contracts for future sales, and actual sales, according to which the tolls are to be settled after the sales have been completed." One can practically see the steam coming out of Ewen's ears as he wrote. "To make advances on the toll, on coal transported, not at the rate at which deliveries of such coal were actually made, but at a higher rate, at which five percent of the whole quantity may have been contracted to be sold before deliveries were commenced, or at a higher rate at which future deliveries are expected to be made, would be absurd."[14]

Ewen countered that a more reasonable toll would be based on the current deliveries, which would be fifty cents per ton. But even that would probably be too high, since there was a very good chance that the actual price for the remainder of the coal would be lower than the initial contracts. "It is well-known in the experience of your company that the prices are sometimes reduced, not only as respects future contracts but also as respects existing contracts, so far as deliveries under them have not been made. . . ." Ewen contended that this was common practice so that people who made contracts early in the season would not be hurt if prices dropped. One assumes that this common practice was in place to encourage customers to contract early in the season and give the companies some income, rather than wait farther into the year to see how overall coal supplies affected the market price before committing to a contract. Ewen went so far as to point out that in 1851 the D&H had initially priced lump coal as high as $3.50 but by May had reduced the price to $3.15 and made those prices retroactive. Based on the price last year, the toll would be only 32 cents. Ewen then argued that the prices upon which the toll should be fixed would certainly be lower than prices at the opening of the season.[15]

Using the D&H circular for May and June, Ewen noted that their price for lump coal was $3.50 and the toll would be 50 cents. Ewen further argued that in their analysis the market would not bear more than $3.40 per ton of lump coal, at which price the toll would be 45 cents. However, Ewen factored in the types of discounts and deductions the D&H had made in the past and would likely make again. Based on those calculations, Ewen offered 40 cents per ton with the understanding that once the average price for actual coal sales was obtained and the real amount of toll calculated, the PCC would pay any increase and the D&H would refund any overpayments. "It is believed that this role will give as much as can be prudently advanced, in conformity to the principles which ordinarily govern the transactions of individuals in amicable relations. . . ."[16]

But Ewen was being undermined. Musgrave wrote to Ewen noting that there had been an informal meeting between officials of the PCC and the D&H where they came to an agreement that the PCC would pay fifty cents toll. In return, the D&H would accede to the PCC's request that they could pay the tolls once a week in New York rather than at Hawley on each cargo, which was what the contract specified.[17]

Ewen was not amused. "I'm not myself aware of such willingness on the part of the Penna Coal Co., nor do I think it ought to consent to any such arrangement. Fifty cents per ton is the maximum of toll which could under any circumstances be charged on the coal deliverable in May and June. . . . Your proposition to receive such payments on account is also coupled with conditions that are objectionable. I cannot as an officer of the Penna Coal Co. consistently with my views of duty, consent to such arrangement: and if the same be acceded to, it must be by a vote of the board."[18]

Musgrave was not amused either. In speaking for the D&H board he stated: "I am directed by them to inform you that as their efforts to effect an arrangement between the two companies on the basis of mutual convenience, without prejudice to the rights of either in relation to the payment of tolls by the Penna. Coal Co. have proved unavailing, no alternative is left to the Delaware & Hudson Canal Company but to collect the tolls at the legal & customary place. Instructions will therefore be given to our collector at Hawley to collect tolls on the coal cargoes of the Penna Coal Co. at the rate of fifty cents per ton while we are delivering lump coal at

Rondout the rate of three dollars & fifty cents per ton, subject to such change, however, in the rate of toll as may be called for from time to time. . . . On and after the 17th inst., no boat of the Penna Coal Co. loaded with coal will be permitted to pass down the Canal unless toll thereon be first paid at the collector's office at Hawley as above specified."[19]

The PCC responded with a group of resolutions passed by the board in response to the D&H ultimatum in the hopes that the "extreme measure intimated in your letter of the 11th inst. will not be deemed expedient and thereby seriously involve the relations and interests of both companies." The resolutions argued that since both companies agreed that the toll could not be ascertained in accordance with the contract until close of the season, short-term coal payments needed to be fixed "by the voluntary assent of both parties." Furthermore, the PCC was willing to overlook their "strict legal rights" in order to find a solution that would "best promote [the] true interests [of both parties] in the intimate and permanent relations established between them. . . ." Nonetheless, the PCC still held that they should not be required to make overpayments during the course of the season and then be at the mercy of the D&H to refund any overpayments, "especially as the accounts by which the true rate is to be settled are kept by the other party and this company may, by reason of its disadvantage in this respect, be subject to great inconvenience unless it should be the interest of the other party promptly to render and adjust those accounts." Consequently, the PCC resolved "as a matter of conciliation" to pay the D&H once a week at its New York office "at the rate of 45 cents per ton while the Delaware & Hudson Canal Company shall be making its actual deliveries of lump coal at Rondout at $3.50 per ton, subject to such change, however, in the rate of toll as may be called for from time to time. . . ."[20]

The D&H would not budge. William Musgrave responded, "Resolved that it is inexpedient for this company to depart from the terms in relation to payment of tolls communicated to the Penna Coal Co. on the 11th inst."[21] At the end of June, the D&H board minutes stated that the board was postponing consideration of "the expediency of instituting

suit in Pennsylvania against the Pennsylvania Coal Co. for tolls due." There is nothing additional in the PCC minutes concerning the controversy, except for a brief note stating that the PCC was sending the D&H a letter "in relation to a payment of $158,000 on account of toll for the season. . . ." It appears, however, that the PCC had started legal proceedings and had got an injunction preventing the D&H from collecting the toll. The D&H board minutes noted in October that Judge Edwards had ended the injunction and that the PCC "shall be required to pay on account of tolls on their coal, at the rate of 64 cents per ton, until a change shall occur in the price at which this Company shall be delivering its coal at Rondout. . . ."[22]

This insistence by the D&H on charging the PCC fifty cents per ton for lump coal, regardless of any future reductions in the price of coal, is likely the most important reason why John Ewen declared war on the D&H, which resulted in a four-year lawsuit started by the D&H in 1857. But the proto PCC had accepted this agreement in 1847 and Ewen had an opportunity to alter it in 1851 when it became binding on the new PCC. While Ewen thought the toll charges too high and likely considered the D&H to be high-handed or arrogant in its treatment of its junior partner, there is no reason to believe that the D&H would not have honestly settled accounts at the end of the year and refunded collected tolls if the average price for the year declined from the May price. The PCC had a cash crunch and Ewen certainly didn't want to have his money collecting interest in D&H accounts, but his confrontational attitude made it less likely that the D&H management would compromise.

The 1857 lawsuit did not concern the specific details of figuring out the yearly toll, which the PCC apparently conceded was legally binding as spelled out in the contract. The lawsuit would concern whether the D&H could increase tolls based on savings in transportation costs created by enlarging the canal. The PCC would claim that the canal enlargement did not create any savings and therefore should not be used to raise tolls. While there had been previous tensions between the companies on other issues, the 1852 toll confrontation destroyed any amicable feelings between them. Certainly, as will be seen in 1853, Ewen's attitude toward the D&H grew more hostile. One could speculate that had the D&H acceded to Ewen's demands for a lower toll in 1852, Ewen would not have declared war on the D&H. But one can just as easily argue that if the D&H had capitulated to the upstart, Ewen would have taken that as a sign of weakness and would have continued his intransigent stand that the canal enlargement had not created any transportation savings and consequently the PCC should not have to pay increased tolls to help pay for the enlargement.

ARCHBALD'S RESIGNATION

The deterioration between the two companies put Archbald in a curious position. He was working for both companies and corresponding with both presidents. Ewen regularly complained about the D&H, Wurts only rarely mentioned the growing problem, but there was far less Wurts correspondence by this time. Nonetheless, Archbald was aware of the growing tensions. Letters written to Archbald give no indication that Archbald was sharing privileged information with executives from the other company. However, his role was in mining and railroads, not in canal transportation, which became the focus of the lawsuit. Still, it would be revealing to see how Archbald responded—or avoided responding—about the growing rift between the companies. As it turned out, Archbald played only a minimal role in the lawsuit, which consumed four years and created more than 2,000 pages of testimony.

There are very few letters by James Archbald in his collection and practically none from the Pennsylvania Canal Company years. However, he did occasionally leave behind a draft of a letter. One such draft, dated 4 October 1853, is of a letter to John Ewen in which Archbald discussed his plans for leaving the Delaware & Hudson and Pennsylvania Coal companies. "Mr. John Wurts (President) was with us at Carbondale all last week. I have come to an understanding with him by which I can withdraw my services from the Del. & Hud. when the present year closes. I am therefore anxious to make similar conditions with the Penna. Coal Company so that I can be at Liberty either to withdraw for a time from the fatigue of business or turn my attention to the Construction rather than the working supervision of public improvements believing

the former the most agreeable of the two. I make these remarks now that you may have my views and wishes in regard to these matters so that when I come to the city last of the week we can talk understandingly in regard to them."[23]

Ewen did not directly reply, or at least the letter has not survived, but he did begin plans for replacing Archbald and, perhaps, other managers in the mining and gravity-railroad division. After rejecting one candidate because of his "connection with the Pittston Coal Company," Ewen wondered: "Is it necessary in your judgment that the superintendent of the mines, if a person of good business habits, should be a miner? Might not such a person with the aid of such as we might get to drive the work underground, and make the measurements, conduct the general mining businesses as well, having for assistants several miners of the caliber of the man superintending at Dunmore? I presume a practical miner having the other requisite qualifications would be the best at the head of the mine department, but I should like to have your views on this point."[24]

While Ewen apparently resigned himself to Archbald's resignation, John Wurts did not. A Mr. Wentz had some allegations against the D&H and was planning to go to Harrisburg with his complaints. Wurts had no clue what the problem was and wrote to Archbald seeking information. The letter reveals how much John Wurts depended on James Archbald, particularly considering that Archbald had wanted to resign from the D&H a couple of years before in order to devote his energies completely to the PCC. Wurts was concerned that Archbald's resignation, along with that of a mining supervisor, James Clarkson, at approximately the same time, had sent a signal that both were dissatisfied with the company and that there was something deeply wrong with the D&H. "This we know to be untrue, but the public does not, and your resignation with that of Clarkson will be used by Wentz and his coadjutors to advance their schemes whatever they may be. Now I am not aware that anything has been done in the Carbondale department of our business that it is at variance with your judgment and feelings. You are at the head of it, and we have regarded it as in all respects subject to your direction and control, and have looked to you as the responsible party in it. In fact so unqualified is our confidence in you, that we have never made it our business to inquire into and look after matters in your department as we do in most others, and hence it is to you we must look for information and explanation in regard to any matters that may be made a subject of legislative inquiry or complaint. Under the circumstances, it seems to me that your withdrawal from the Company at this time, would in all probability be highly prejudicial to its interest: and I trust that you will take the subject into serious consideration, and come to the conclusion that it is an inexpedient measure. I do not wish to press you unreasonably or pertinaciously to remain. But it seems to me, that the circumstances I have named are sufficient ground for me to urge upon you the importance of continuing, at least until a more favorable moment for quitting shall occur."[25]

This letter was followed by a relatively brief one from Wurts detailing how they had missed meeting each other, which Wurts exceedingly regretted. Wurts was probably desperate for a meeting in order to make one more attempt at getting Archbald to stay. "Now it is often times difficult to write and treat a subject by letter as it can be done by word-of-mouth. For that reason I would much prefer to see you, rather than confer by letter, and if you can come to the city for that purpose I shall be much obliged."[26] But Archbald's mind would not be changed by his entreaties and the last letter in the collection from John Wurts, Archbald's boss for more than 25 years, was a simple request to find someone a job in the west. From this point onward the only company president writing to Archbald would be John Jervis, president of the Southern Michigan and Northern Indiana Railroad, for whom Archbald would serve as a vice president and build a stretch of road from Toledo to Indianapolis during 1854 and 1855.[27]

In 1856, Archbald became general agent and chief engineer of the Delaware, Lackawanna and Western Railroad (DL&W), where he supervised the construction of the Lackawanna and Bloomsburg branch. He remained with the DL&W the rest of his life and died on August 26, 1870, at the age of 77.

The *Carbondale Transcript and Lackawanna Journal* of 18 November 1853 had an account of a spontaneous parade that occurred after a city council meeting. The torchlight parade featured a brass band, which went through town and visited Archbald's home (unfortunately he was not home at the time) as well as that of James Clarkson, who was home and expressed his appreciation. The parade was in recognition of the service the two men had given to the company and to the town over the years, also to acclaim the greatness of their employer, the Delaware & Hudson Canal Company. A letter to Archbald commented upon the event: "The proceedings and resolutions adopted at the public meeting held on the occasion breathe the spirit of goodwill, of confidence, and a deep regret, on account of the final separation: and moreover give signal evidence of the high regard which the citizens generally entertain for your integrity, talents, and public service as a mechanic and civil engineer: and above all the good feelings which the resolution and proceedings breathe in relation to your kind, benevolent, and generous bearing as a good citizen."[28]

Notes

All the correspondence cited, except that cited as from PCC or D&H Board of Managers (BOM) minutes, is located in the James Archbald Collection at the Lackawanna Historical Society in Scranton Pennsylvania. The Pennsylvania Coal Company Board of Managers' minutes are from Manuscript Group 282 in the Pennsylvania State Archives, Harrisburg. The Delaware and Hudson Board of Managers' microfilmed minutes are at the National Canal Museum's library/archives. A more detailed exploration of this topic by this author can be found in two similarly titled articles published in the *Proceedings of the Canal History and Technology Symposium* volumes XXII and XXIII (2003 and 2004) "The Pennsylvania Coal Company: New Insights from the James Archbald Papers, 1850-1851" and "The Pennsylvania Coal Company: New Insights from the James Archbald Papers, 1852-1853 'We Are Now at War.'"

1. Edward Steers, "The Pennsylvania Coal Company's Gravity Railroad," *Proceedings of the Canal History and Technology Symposium* Vol. I (Easton, PA:

Center for Canal History and Technology, 1982), 155–162; Larry Lowenthal, *From the Coalfields to the Hudson: A History of the Delaware & Hudson Canal* (Fleischmanns, NY: Purple Mountain Press, 1997), 170.

2. D&H Board of Managers Minutes, 31 Dec. 1846; Steers, "Gravity Railroad," 160–161; Lowenthal, *Coalfields to the Hudson*, 170.

3. John Wurts to James Archbald, 27 Nov. 1849, "John Ewen," *The National Cyclopedia of American Biography*, Volume XVI (New York, NY: James T. White & Company, 1937), 297.

4. Maurice Wurts to Archbald, 9 April 1850.

5. Irad Hawley to Archbald, 16 April 1850; Hawley to Archbald, 13 May 1850.

6. John Wurts to Archbald, 27 May 1850.

7. Hawley to Archbald, 14 May, 16 May, 20 May 1851; John Ewen to Archbald, 15 May 1851.

8. Ewen to Archbald, 26 May 1851; William Musgrave to Archbald, 26 May 1851, Ewen to Archbald, 29 July 1851.

9. Ewen to Archbald, 20 Aug 1851, first letter, Ewen to Archbald, 29 Aug. 1851.

10. Ewen to Archbald, 29 Aug. 1851.

11. Musgrave to Ewen, 3 May 1852; PCC BOM Minutes, 4 May 1852; D&H BOM Minutes, 2 Aug 1847. The original agreement between the D&H and the Wyoming Coal Association made the "ratio" a little clearer. "On the first day of May in each and every calendar year the quantity of lump coal of the said Delaware and Hudson Canal Company which shall at that time have been sold, to be delivered at Rondout and to arrive by the said canal, during the said calendar year, shall be ascertained and the average price at which such sales have been contracted, shall also be ascertained, and from the average price thus ascertained, Two dollars and fifty cents shall be subtracted, and one-half of the remainder shall be the toll per ton during such calendar year, except that if any discount or deduction, contingent or otherwise shall be agreed upon or contemplated in the contracts for such sales, the said toll shall be reduced correspondingly to such discount or deduction as shall be actually made.

"But provided nevertheless, that if on the first day of May in any calendar year the quantity of lump coal of the said Delaware and Hudson Canal Company which shall at that time have been sold as aforesaid, shall be less than one-half of the estimated sales for such year, the toll during such year shall be calculated in the manner hereinbefore provided on the average price at which the sales of lump coal for such year shall be actually made. And if in any calendar year no sales of the coal of the said Delaware and Hudson Canal Company shall be made, then in that case the toll during such year shall be calculated on the sales for such year of the lump coal by the said The Wyoming Coal Association for the time being or its assigns in the matter hereinbefore provided for calculating the toll on the sales of the said Delaware and Hudson Canal Company."

This 1847 agreement between the D&H and the Wyoming Coal Association became binding on the PCC when it absorbed the Wyoming Coal Association. The agreement between the D&H and PCC was concluded at a 29 July 1851 D&H board meeting.

12. Musgrave to Ewen, 3 May 1852; PCC BOM Minutes, 4 May 1852; Spiro Patton, "Delaware & Hudson vs. Pennsylvania Coal Company during the 1850s, *Canal History and Technology Proceedings*, Vol. XI (Easton, PA: Canal History and Technology Press, 1992)."

13. Musgrave to Ewen, 3 May 1852; PCC BOM Minutes, 4 May 1852.

14. Ewen to Musgrave, 5 May 1852; PCC BOM Minutes, 4 May 1852.

15. Ewen to Musgrave, 5 May 1852; PCC BOM Minutes, 4 May 1852.

16. Ewen to Musgrave, 5 May 1852; PCC BOM Minutes, 4 May 1852.

17. Musgrave to Ewen, 8 May 1852; PCC BOM Minutes, 14 May 1852.

18. Ewen to Musgrave, 10 May 1852; PCC BOM Minutes, 14 May 1852.

19. Musgrave to Ewen, 11 May 1852; PCC BOM Minutes, 14 May 1852.

20. Ewen to Musgrave, 14 May 1852; PCC BOM Minutes, 14 May 1852; D&H BOM Minutes, 15 May 1852.

21. Musgrave to Ewen, 15 May 1852; PCC BOM Minutes, 28 June 1852.

22. D&H BOM Minutes, 28 June 1852; PCC BOM Minutes, 9 Oct 1852; D&H BOM Minutes, 1 Oct. 1852.

23. Archbald to Ewen, 4 Oct. 1853.

24. Ewen to Archbald, 21 Oct. 1853.

25. John Wurts to Archbald, Nov. 1853.

26. John Wurts to Archbald, 3 Dec. 1853.

27. John Wurts to Archbald, 13 Dec. 1853.

28. Howland Fish to Archbald, 8 Dec. 1853.